~~5 95~~
3 57

Race and Authority in Urban Politics

Race and Authority in Urban Politics

Community Participation and the War on Poverty

J. DAVID GREENSTONE and PAUL E. PETERSON

The University of Chicago Press
Chicago and London

PUBLICATIONS OF RUSSELL SAGE FOUNDATION

Russell Sage Foundation was established in 1907 by Mrs. Russell Sage for the improvement of social and living conditions in the United States. In carrying out its purpose the Foundation conducts research under the direction of members of the staff or in close collaboration with other institutions, and supports programs designed to develop and demonstrate productive working relations between social scientists and other professional groups. As an integral part of its operation, the Foundation from time to time publishes books or pamphlets resulting from these activities. Publication under the imprint of the Foundation does not necessarily imply agreement by the Foundation, its Trustees, or its staff with the interpretations or conclusions of the authors.

The University of Chicago Press, Chicago 60637
The University of Chicago Press, Ltd., London

© 1973, 1976 by Russell Sage Foundation. All rights reserved
Originally published by Russell Sage Foundation 1973. Phoenix Edition 1976
Printed in the United States of America

International Standard Book Number: 0-226-30713-1
Library of Congress Catalog Card Number: 76-4148

To Joan and Carol

CONTENTS

PREFACE TO THE PHOENIX EDITION

Of the many political conflicts which distinguish the 1960s from the quieter 1970s, the struggle over citizen participation in the Community Action Program (CAP) of the war on poverty illustrates particularly well the repeated intersection of racial and political authority issues.[1] So entangled was this conflict, its discussion in the work that follows is necessarily complex. To discern its significance, our analysis considers such diverse topics as race and class relations, urban political ideologies, forms of political representation, collective goods and selective inducements, arenas of policy formation, and, not least, the contention that citizens share a "regime interest" in protecting and enhancing the authority structures of their political regime. To help guide readers through the paperback edition, this preface will attempt to state as starkly as possible our three separable though interconnected arguments.

1. An empirical argument (primarily in Parts III and IV) which accounts for the variation of community participation in CAP in the five largest cities of the United States; variation from the high levels in New York and Detroit where independent community groups achieved considerable influence, through much more moderate levels in Los Angeles and Philadelphia, to the low level in Chicago, where officials excluded autonomous citizen involvement.
2. A methodological argument (primarily in Parts I and II) which to make our empirical argument feasible addresses certain problems in comparative analysis through the examination of latent class, race, and regime interests.

---

1. Assistance in the preparation of the manuscript for this Preface was generously provided by the National Opinion Research Center, University of Chicago, where J. David Greenstone currently serves as a Senior Study Director.

3. A broader interpretive argument about race and authority relationships as important components of American politics, which builds on the first two arguments and appears throughout the text.

This interpretation argues, as do certain neo-Marxian scholars, that social structures contain contradictions that can be the source of their own transformation. But in our view these contradictions are plural, rooted not only in class but also in race and authority relations. It is from this perspective that we defend (in Chapter 10) the widely condemned experiments in community participation. In this preface, we shall expand this interpretation somewhat by considering the way in which these race and authority structures shaped both CAP's origins and the impact CAP in turn has had on the structure of the American political regime.

THE EMPIRICAL ARGUMENT: VARIATIONS IN PARTICIPATION

The different levels of participation in the five community action programs most immediately reflected the political settlements or broad policy decisions about CAP taken in the five cities. These decisions were indicated by the very different selection mechanisms each city used to provide representation in CAP for low-income and minority citizens. In New York and Detroit, neighborhood and civil rights groups won an agreement from city officials allowing them to select and thus substantially influence the representatives; by contrast, Chicago city officials successfully insisted that they themselves appoint and thus obtain a controlling influence over poverty councils; and a compromise in Los Angeles and Philadelphia provided that representatives would be selected in local elections, reducing but by no means eliminating official influence over representatives of the poor. The level of overall participation in CAP corresponded closely to these representation arrangements with New York and Detroit most participatory, Chicago least participatory, and Los Angeles and Philadelphia the intermediate cases.

By themselves, these political settlements and their accompanying representation arrangements still did not entirely account for all the variation in participation in the five cities. The settlements were virtually identical in New York and Detroit, yet participation was greater in New York when measured by the extent of neighborhood group influence over the utilization of poverty program resources. Again, the settlements were similar in Philadelphia and Los Angeles, but of the two the level of participation was lower in Philadelphia. Chapter 7 accounts for these specific differences by examining the cities' administrative structures. Where bureaucracies were relatively autonomous (in the two reformed cities of Detroit and Los Angeles), the CAP agencies had greater opportunity to pursue two rather contradictory impulses. On the one hand, they were better able to rationalize their own activities, which in this case meant following ordinary bureaucratic procedures and thus reducing participation. On the other hand, they could also more freely pursue their distinctive organizational mission: encouraging citizen participation in welfare politics, an objective no other administrative entity in this political arena shared. Given the conflict between these two organizational propensities, the community action agencies in the two reform cities used their bureaucratic independence from the dominant political coalition to moderate their very different political settlements. In other words, variations among program outcomes were less in cities where organizations were more autonomous. Specifically, the outcomes in Detroit and Los Angeles were more similar to each other than were the outcomes in New York and Philadelphia, even though the differences between the political settlements in these two pairs of cities were essentially the same.

Since bureaucratic autonomy only modified—it did not reverse—the basic pattern laid down by the five political settlements, a comprehensive explanation must place them within the context of more enduring features of the five cities' political life. As Chapter 8 demonstrates, the settlements were shaped by the resources and relative influence of four political groups: Black Power advocates, Liberal Pragmatists, Community Conservationists, and Progressive Conservatives. Even as the CAP bureaucracies had different roles in machine and reformed cities, so did these political groups. In Detroit and Los Angeles, past reform triumphs made machine politics unfeasible, thereby precluding conflict between machine politicians and their reform opponents. As a result, the settlements varied according to the strength of Black Power advocates. In Detroit, where blacks were numerous and politically well-organized, their leaders became very influential within CAP. In Los Angeles, where blacks were relatively less numerous, internally divided, and unable to build a stable alliance with Mexican Americans, the political settlement was less participatory. By contrast, in the three machine cities, the outcome varied not according to the political strength of Black Power advocates but according to political relationships between competing sets of white politicians. On one side, Liberal Pragmatists, who defended machine politics, vigorously opposed a participatory CAP because it might encourage politically independent neighborhood groups. On the other side, two reform groups, Community Conservationists and Progressive Conservatives, favored extending participatory structures. Liberal Pragmatist dominance in Chicago, therefore, insured an anti-participatory settlement; significant Progressive Conservative influence in Philadelphia somewhat moderated the outcome imposed by the generally dominant Liberal Pragmatists; and in New York, with its powerful liberal Community Conservationist faction, community participation reached its highest levels.

Although the political settlement thus *correlated* with the resources of the black community in our reformed cities and with the relative strength of the reformers in New York, Philadelphia, and Chicago, the *processes* by which these settlements were reached differentiated the cities along yet another line. Not only was group influence connected to policy outcomes by two contrasting types of processes—consensual and conflictual—but instances of *each* such process could be found in both cities with participatory and non-participatory outcomes. There was no relationship, in other words, between type of political settlement and type of process by which it was reached. In resolving this apparent difficulty, Chapter 9 further illustrates the variations in the political position of urban black communities.

On one side, activist groups provoked conflictual policy-making processes in Chicago, Los Angeles, and New York under Mayor Robert Wagner by challenging the mayor's policy preferences. In these cases, groups sought to exercise influence not just through electing sympathetic mayors but directly in the cities' decision-making processes. By contrast, in the three consensual cases—Philadelphia, Detroit and New York, during the administration of Mayor John Lindsay,—all the significant participants accepted mayoral policy preferences as a primary determinant of the political settlement. Here political groups shaped policy only *indirectly* by mobilizing their resources to elect mayors with congenial preferences. In Detroit and New York, where the consensual outcome was *participatory,* the black community had begun to establish itself as an institutionalized actor in the city's politics—one whose interests had to be regularly consulted. In Philadelphia, however, the consensual but non-participatory outcome indicated the extent to which blacks remained so weak politically that their interests were not even vigorously asserted in the process of policy deliberation.

As this empirical argument is expanded in the text, these variables are placed in a larger sociopolitical context in which still additional factors are considered. But it is clear even from this synopsis that political structures influence policy only through complex, diverse, and interdependent political channels of the type stressed in pluralist views of American politics. At certain key points, however, the analysis in the text differs sharply from pluralist doctrines about political motivation. As Chapter 5 stresses, we found political leaders as much or more motivated by ideology as by electoral or organizational considerations, often *not* interested in compromising with opponents to promote consensus, and not necessarily responsive to demands of active minorities with intensely felt preferences. These empirical differences with pluralist studies of American politics point to an underlying disagreement central to our methodological argument.

THE METHODOLOGICAL ARGUMENT: LATENT INTEREST ANALYSIS AND THE COMPARATIVE STUDY OF POLICY FORMATION

As Chapter 1 shows, it is quite possible to offer persuasive accounts of particular political settlements in terms of each city's most prominent characteristics. Chicago's powerful machine opposed participation; Philadelphia's traditional, gentlemanly political culture encouraged a moderately conservative outcome; the fragmented politics of Los Angeles so subdivided its program that even though some opportunities for participation emerged, all sustained demands for community influence were dissipated; due to the prior role of liberal unions in Detroit, its black leaders were especially effective; and New York's vigorous interest-group politics spawned in CAP still more autonomous political formations, this time in the city's minority neighborhoods. Yet these ad hoc explanations, however compelling in each individual case, simply could not be generalized. Evidently, a genuinely comparative analysis must focus not on the unique characteristics of any one city, but on those important in all five cases.

In order to find just such comparable features, some scholars, employing the utilitarian perspective common to those working within the group-theory, pluralist, and political-economy traditions, have rooted their explanations in individual attitudes and preferences. Applying this methodology, we might have identified those favoring and opposed to participation in each of the cities. After then assessing the political strength of the two competing coalitions, we could have predicted the variations in community participation in the five cities. Although these findings would almost certainly have been correct, in our opinion, they would have contributed little to empirical analysis. To determine that participation was greatest where pro-participatory forces were the strongest is almost, though not quite, tautological.

A more empirically interesting set of findings could be developed by attributing certain interests (and therefore political objectives) to particular social and economic groups in the five cities. One could then predict variations in outcomes according to variations in the conflicting groups' political resources. For example, if community participation is assumed to be in the interests of blacks and the poor, then one might predict greater participation where these groups are politically strongest. Indeed a good deal of quantitative comparative research proceeds in this manner. In our case, however, such procedures only yielded very low correlations when applied to all five cities. This finding brings us to the heart of our methodological argument: the correlations were low because these groups do not recognize and thus act on these interests in the same way and to the same extent. It is this difference, among others, which complicates attempts to generalize about such interests across political boundaries, even when the cultural similarity is as great as it is among large American cities.

To connect the activity of such stable social and economic groups to political processes and conflicts in a comparative urban study, one must focus on the different degrees to which such interests are recognized or ignored—that is in latent interest role analysis. Explored more fully in Chapter 2, this approach does attribute to certain social roles a set of interests based on the roles' relationship to the larger sociopolitical structures of the society. Crucially, however, this approach then argues that only under appropriate conditions are interests likely to become manifest to (recognized by) individuals who occupy or play the roles. As these interests become manifest, they can potentially become the bases for ideologies that shape group political practice. In short, identifying the latent interests of social roles provides the grounds for hypothesizing a contingent relationship—which will emerge if the relevant conditions obtain—between the *enduring* contours of the social and political order and *fluctuating* attitudes toward policies and issues.

As shown in Chapters 3 and 4, three sets of role relationships—class, race, and citizen—were potentially significant for the CAP conflict. Insofar as community participation seemed likely to redistribute political resources from an economically dominant entrepreneurial class to economically subordinate workers, the former could be expected to oppose, the latter to support community participation. Groups we label Orthodox Conservative and Orthodox Liberal, which generally articulate the interests of these two classes, opposed and supported participation as one would expect. On the whole, however, since CAP seemed likely to have only a marginal impact on class interests, participants committed to these ideologies were only minor actors on the community action scene. In other words, class interests remained largely latent.

Since the program was more clearly designed to increase the political resources of black and other minority groups in the local polity, racial groups might be expected to take active positions on the participation issue. But even though Black Power and White Power ideologues, articulating the interests of these groups, did debate the merits of the issue, white groups during CAP's very early days were not nearly as organized and active as were Black Power advocates. Instead, Black Power demands generated the involvement of white political leaders concerned with protecting widely shared interests in preserving and extending existing structures of authority in the American regime. These manifest regime interests were themselves rooted in four specific structures of authority discussed in Chapter 4, which govern the relationships between American citizens and their rulers: constitutionalism, participation, rationalization, and pluralist bargaining. Although we shall emphasize that the four structures are not perfectly integrated with each other—it is far from easy to maximize the extension of all simultaneously—each one controls important aspects of the ways in which rulers are selected and can formulate and implement governmental policies. Accordingly, we assume that all citizens, in their role as citizen, share a latent regime interest in the preservation, and indeed extension, of these structures.

Three politically significant ideologies in big city politics are manifest expressions of citizen interests in protecting one or more, but not simultaneously all four, of these authority structures. Liberal Pragmatists, committed to pluralist bargaining processes, opposed community participation on the grounds that by so strongly fostering hitherto excluded black interests, it would upset, weaken, and restrict traditional patterns of bargaining and disturb accommodations important to existing vested interests. Community Conservationists, primarily committed to extending opportunities for democratic participation (but also interested in rationalization), allied themselves with Black Power advocates in favor of this new participatory endeavor. Progressive Conservatives, mainly concerned with rationalization, equivocated, mildly favoring participation on the grounds that it might also help reform urban government, but fearing its potential for disturbing the interests of urban businessmen. By and large, they favored or opposed community participation according to calculations of other electoral or organizational interests.

Given latent interests potentially affected by CAP, this conflict over community participation could have significantly disturbed class as well as race and authority relations. But the actual pattern of ideological conflicts reveals that at the local level the CAP issue centered on race and authority relations, a conclusion which is central to our interpretive argument.

THE INTERPRETIVE ARGUMENT: RACE AND AUTHORITY

The war on poverty has been judged by most observers to be a major public policy disaster. Many commentators—both journalistic and academic—have agreed that this public policy did not restructure the socioeconomic relationships between rich and poor, did not significantly shrink the nation's pockets of poverty, and did not even establish a powerful ongoing bureaucratic structure whose specific low-income clientele received important new benefits. Some observers claim the program attempted too much; others say that it did too little. Some say it needlessly fanned the flames of discontent; others say it co-opted and diffused one of the few social movements that might have redressed the structural inequalities pervading American capitalism. In our view, these judgments, though not entirely incorrect, all fail to appreciate sufficiently the peculiarly political quality of the community action issue. Although apparently addressed to the economic problems of the nation's poor, community action, the heart of the war on poverty was in its content, origins, and consequences a political response to a political problem. Its content addressed the political relationship of black Americans to the American regime, not the economic relationships of poor people to the marketplace; its origins were rooted in a civil rights movement that focused on altering the country's political, not its socioeconomic relationships; and its long-range impact has related to the political conditions of black Americans, not their economic state. To judge the war on poverty as an economic failure is to misinterpret its character. A more relevant political perspective yields a more ambiguous conclusion.

Political Content of Community Action

The content of the community action controversy involved a critical issue of political authority: namely, which interests should participate in and be deferred to in the course of framing public policy. Most importantly, organized black neighborhood and civil rights groups, in calling for maximum feasible participation, insisted that their interests be included among those which elected leaders and agency executives regularly consulted. In effect they thus demanded a change in the structure of pluralist bargaining, a change in the patterns of accommodation and compromise among vested interests that helped legitimate authority in American politics. These black organizations won the sympathy of certain reform-minded white politicians and groups also concerned about authority relations. Specifically, these whites sought to extend democratic participation in political life, a concern that had been especially aroused by civil rights protests against legal disabilities suffered by southern blacks. For these reformers, the legitimating principle of participation took precedence over the competing principle of pluralist bargaining that cautioned against drastic political innovations. They now recognized the legitimacy of demands by blacks in the North, who were less formally but almost as surely excluded from active, influential participation in governmental policy-making structures.

If black organizations and their white allies focused on changes in the structure of authority, this very challenge to political relations was what disturbed many white politicians, and especially Liberal Pragmatists, the most. Just as southerners, concerned about the rapid changes forced on them by civil rights groups, the courts, and federal agencies, resisted these pressures by appeals to the pluralist norms of federalism and states rights, so northern politicians, facing similar demands, also sought to moderate the rate of change by preserving other pre-existing structures of pluralist bargaining. Although these authority issues were most clearly posed in the machine cities, even in Detroit and Los Angeles, reform cities where racial factors were both more explicit and more decisive—mayoral responses to CAP turned on questions of authority. Los Angeles Mayor Samuel Yorty vigorously resisted participation in CAP only after he discovered the challenge to authority the issue posed. Mayor Jerome Cavanagh's responsiveness to the concerns of black leaders in Detroit reflected his Community Conservationist commitment to combining citizen participation with rationalized administrative operations.

The community action controversy so focused on questions of political authority and citizen participation that the economic concerns of the program seemed an altogether secondary question for local politicians. Although a few trade unionists lent sporadic, largely indirect, support to black interests, in no case did an organized group, speaking on behalf of the poor (as distinct from a mainly low-income racial or ethnic minority), debate the economic thrust of the program. On the other side, even though Mayor

Yorty at times acted as if he hardly cared whether the program was ever implemented, no major urban politician disputed the desirability of an economic, as distinct from a political, attack on poverty.

Political Origins of Community Action

That community action should have raised essentially political issues involving the relation of a racial group to the political regime is, on the face of it, not very plausible. After all, the program originated as the keystone of President Lyndon Johnson's war against *poverty*. When announced, this program ostensibly addressed social and economic problems, not political ones. Congress enacted a law entitled The *Economic* Opportunity Act of 1964 whose stated purpose was "to eliminate the paradox of poverty in the midst of plenty . . . by opening to everyone the opportunity for education and training, . . . work, and . . . to live in decency and dignity." Indeed, "maximum feasible participation," although mentioned in the enacting legislation was so little discussed and so ambiguous in its meaning that Daniel Patrick Moynihan has insisted that the original intent was simply to provide employment opportunities for residents of areas served within routinized administrative structures.[2] In his opinion, it was consequently a colossal "misunderstanding" of the purpose of the program that caused big city conflicts over participation.

This view has much to recommend it. Information about explicit goals and objectives during the drafting stages of the legislation simply does not support those who believe community action was carefully crafted to diffuse black protest. To be sure, the program was designed with the needs of black Americans foremost in mind, but for the majority of policy-makers the needs in question were better opportunities for education, training, and employment. Even those administrators and legislators with the broadest vision of the program's purpose focused on structural economic problems, the pockets of economic poverty that had been unresponsive to government monetary and fiscal policies. Along with other Great Society programs, community action was to extend New Deal-style economic programs to racial minorities who had only accidentally and haphazardly been beneficiaries of prior programs.

The conditions of the 1960s were nonetheless very different from the Depression decade within which the New Deal was spawned. As a result of this difference in context, the very meaning of the words used to characterize the issues began to change in subtle ways not clearly understood even by the actors themselves. What was problematic about the war on poverty was the very meaning of the concept of poverty itself.

---

2. Daniel P. Moynihan, *Maximum Feasible Misunderstanding: Community Action in the War on Poverty* (New York: Free Press, 1969).

This point can best be appreciated by beginning with the long-standing debate over the proper definition of poverty that has engaged bureaucrats, politicians, and scholars alike. For some, those properly labeled "the poor" are individuals or families with incomes less than some absolute minimum level. For others, poverty is a relative concept, a condition suffered by those Americans with incomes less than, say, half the median figure for the entire population. For still others, a blurred, highly technical middle position, such as three times the cost of an adequately nutritious and tasty diet, is the appropriate standard for determining poverty levels. Finally, the matter is further complicated by the question of specific in-cash and in-kind transfer payments and services to those of low income in such specific areas as medicine and education.

This debate could continue indefinitely, however, because all parties treat "poverty" as if it were a label for some specific, clearly delineated economic condition. A better approach, we believe, is to interpret poverty not as a picture which attributes some specific social condition, e.g., income level, to the poor, but as an activity, a tool, or more specifically, an exhortation which calls for adoption of a particular attitude or behavior. Depending on the context and the views of the speakers, to call certain individuals poor is to claim that they deserve either pity, help, charity, scorn, punishment, justice, or a new political order. Of course, not every such claim has equal force; the concept of poverty is not uniformly meaningful or useful in all social analyses or political actions. Such usefulness depends in part on the appropriateness of the concept for the particular context in which it is employed.[3]

Consistent with this observation, it was the context of the 1960s which gave the concept of poverty both racial and political meaning. In the first place, civil rights protest had focused on black deprivations. Differentials in the conditions and opportunities of blacks as compared to whites had become so widely publicized that blacks became the most readily identifiable poverty group. Even strictly economic interpretations of the war on poverty's origins concede that when Johnson proposed a poverty war, most Americans, and certainly most policy-makers, understood that "poor meant black."[4] But this very focus on blacks, some of whom were not in any way economically poor, also politicized the concept. Since the civil rights campaign had, as the name suggests, focused on denials of certain rights of citizenship, their political exclusion as well as their economically deprived state were both seen as integral parts of black poverty. It therefore became necessary for a program attacking poverty to treat both the political and economic aspects of the disease.

---

3. Ludwig Wittgenstein, *Philosophical Investigations,* trans. G. E. M. Anscombe (New York: Macmillan, 1968).
4. S. M. Miller and Martin Rein, "Participation, Poverty and Administration," *Public Administration Review,* vol. 29 (1969), p. 15.

The processes by which the program developed this political orientation are familiar to students of group and organizational behavior. Minority-based neighborhood groups, civil rights organizations, and groups of black social-welfare professionals, acutely aware of past political exclusions, insisted that they be involved in the development and administration of community action programs. The Office of Economic Opportunity (OEO) and its local Community Action Agency (CAA) affiliates, new agencies needing distinctive missions and supportive constituencies, frequently responded positively. They interpreted "maximum feasible participation" to mean formation of alliances with activist elements in the minority community. Of course, the political, if not the racial, coloration of these activists varied with local conditions, but even in Chicago, where autonomous group involvement was held to a minimum, black machine politicians found patronage opportunities greatly extended. In general, organizational need for external political support together with pressure group demands combined to implement participation in terms of concessions to blacks not foreseen by policy-makers such as Moynihan.

This group and organizational activity could only occur, however, within the new social context that gave poverty both racial and political dimensions. Prior to the protests of the 1960s, a New Deal-style economic program neither would nor could have taken minority organizations as its primary constituents. As it was, the Johnson Administration and congressional leaders disowned the most militant, change-oriented activities community action spawned. That less radical, though still significant, forms of "maximum feasible participation" became constituent components of CAP, that the war on poverty could nonetheless become primarily a war against political exclusion of black Americans, was hardly due to a bureaucratic "misunderstanding" of the proper role of concerned interest groups. On the contrary, this agency-group interplay was conditioned by a social context so changed by civil rights controversies that the very meaning of poverty had been altered to include political deprivation. In brief, the political orientation of the war on poverty was rooted in the context of 1960s' protest politics which had made minority exclusion from policy formation a central issue.

Political Consequences of Community Action

If these political considerations were the source of community action's participatory thrust, it is the program's political consequences that deserve great weight in any overall assessment of this Great Society undertaking. In our concluding chapter we argue that the many carefully argued critiques of the program failed adequately to appreciate its concern with a racial group, a primordial, ascriptively defined category not easily translated within the theoretical structures of modern social science. Events since the publication of *Race and Authority in Urban Politics* make all the more clear that the program's impact was too significant to warrant the simple label of "failure."

Of course, the effect on the nation's socioeconomic structure was marginal at best. Economic deprivation, particularly among blacks and other racial minorities, continues long after OEO's innovations have either disappeared or become the routinized activities of one or another self-contained, self-perpetuating bureaucratic agency. But the alteration in the political status of black Americans since CAP's inception has been substantial. Not only have blacks been included within the pluralist bargaining structures of many of the nation's largest cities, but they have been largely integrated into the structures of the national political system as well.

These changes have been both quantitative and qualitative. At the local level, black officeholding has increased markedly in the North, dramatically in the South. Instead of the miscellaneous few holding office in 1964, one decade later more than 100 black mayors alone were counted.[5] Local governments, moreover, employed in 1970 a higher percentage of blacks, especially in professional and managerial positions, than did other sectors of the economy.[6] Although almost all industries are formally required by law to be equal opportunity employers, it is the government, both federal and local, which, even during a Republican era, has acted most expeditiously. Moreover, black community and professional groups have ready access to school systems, welfare agencies, and housing offices in ways that are qualitatively different from a mere decade ago. Nationally, the increased number of black representatives in Congress has led to the formation of an organized entity, the Congressional Black Caucus, a group sizable and disciplined enough that it is regularly consulted by leading Democratic policy-makers. Concurrently, the quality of these representatives has changed from the extremes of largely symbolic posturing and narrow patronage preoccupations (typified by former Representatives Adam Clayton Powell and Richard Dawson) to aggressive but pragmatic pursuit of race objectives. Even in somewhat unexpected settings, black faces appear. Not only did black representatives visibly participate in the Watergate denouement but even Gerald Ford's conservative Republican administration found it appropriate to include a black man in its cabinet. That black political interests have become a vested part of the bargaining process was nowhere more evident than in the quiet extension in 1975 of the Voting Rights Act passed only after a great controversy a decade ago.

The political incorporation of black Americans into the political life of the country validates, in our opinion, the favorable endorsement of participatory community action with which we concluded this study. Community action, for

5. "Telescope," *Focus* II, July 1974, p. 6.

6. Paul E. Peterson and J. David Greenstone, "Citizen Participation and Racial Change: The Mobilization of Low-Income Communities Through Community Action," in Robert Haveman (Ed.), *A Ten-Year Retrospective on the War on Poverty* (New York: Academic Press, forthcoming), provides information on this point.

all of its failures in the economic sectors, successfully facilitated political changes earnestly and justifiably demanded by minority groups. We must emphasize, of course, that the qualitative and quantitative increase in black participation rates cannot be attributed solely or largely to CAP activities. Even though the numbers of black politicians who entered the electoral arena via poverty-related activities is remarkably high, CAP was only one of numerous Great Society programs that similarly contributed to these political changes. More importantly, the political orientation of all these programs was, as we argued earlier, a clear response to prior years of civil rights protest. Nonetheless, community participation did provide one important channel through which new social currents could pass, helping the political order as a whole accommodate them when more traditional agencies and institutions were damming and clogging their thrust.

Such government responsiveness to the specifically political needs of a deprived group is characteristic of the American regime. It has always been easier for groups with low social standing to win political concessions than to revamp the socioeconomic order with its great inequalities. One should expect that in this case blacks, too, will find how little effect political influence can have in promoting rapid social and economic progress. To be sure, employment opportunities for middle-class blacks have increased, and opinion surveys report that racial prejudice apparently has markedly declined. Yet it will be difficult to frame additional measures in these areas, and not simply because racially based issues have disappeared from the national political agenda. Given the American regime's liberal respect for private behavior, it is difficult to frame still new legal remedies against persisting social discrimination and racial prejudice. Even though economic redistribution can be achieved without so sharply invading the private sector, economic policies that effectively single out a racial group as their main beneficiary not only violate the constitutional principle of "equal protection," but insofar as they ignore such non-racial factors as American corporate capitalism may also prove to be only marginally productive.

For those concerned with continuing inequalities, any final assessment of CAP must thus be ambiguous. On the pessimistic side, black incorporation into American political life seems to have moderated the potential and pressure for broad-scale social change that once seemed so powerful. Street politics of protest have given way to electoral campaigns, legislative log-rolling, and bureaucratic bargaining. Although this is a more dignified, satisfying, and immediately more effective form of political participation for black elites, ensuing policy changes through such channels are likely to be only incremental. More optimistically, black incorporation could facilitate attention to broader questions of inequality and redistribution in American society. With racial distinctions of declining significance within the strictly political sphere, a time may come when a broader, more effective interracial coalition can be formed to address not just the problems of the poor but more general issues of income inequality and consumer protection. Black political incorporation, however, could hardly have been delayed until such hopes became realities. One need not condone continuing economic inequalities to endorse that transformation of the black American's place in our political regime to which community participation in the war on poverty so clearly contributed.

ACKNOWLEDGMENTS

The debts incurred in the course of this research have steadily increased over the years. Although we hesitate to mention any names for fear of overlooking important assistance, we cannot ignore the substantial help that some may have given us.

Russell Sage Foundation initiated the study, provided the great bulk of the funding for the field research, and patiently encouraged us in our many revisions. The Woodrow Wilson Foundation provided additional assistance at an important early phase of the research. In addition to this institutional assistance, we wish to thank Orville G. Brim, Jr., president of Russell Sage Foundation during the time of our field research, and Morris Janowitz of The University of Chicago, for first envisioning a multicity comparative study of the war on poverty, and for enthusiastically encouraging us to begin it.

A large number of individuals helped us both in collecting the data and subsequently analyzing it, including Isaac Balbus, Marguerite Barnett, Thomas Blau, Rennie Davis, Clarence Gilpatrick, Jeffrey Goodman, Robert Hawkinson, Dewitt John, Ronald Kahn, Marshall Langberg, Eric Levine, Gary Orfield, Allan Rosenbaum, Mark Solomon, and Jerry Webman. Various parts of the manuscript have been read, in one of its many drafts, by David Easton, Richard Flathman, Elizabeth Howe, Ira Katznelson, Michael Lipsky, Theodore J. Lowi, Eileen Sullivan, and George Von der Muhl. We are especially grateful to Eugene C. Lee, David J. Olson, and two anonymous reviewers for Russell Sage Foundation who, together with our project director, Eleanor Sheldon, have read the entire manuscript and bear a heavy responsibility for any readability the present version may have. We also wish to thank Jean C. Yoder, Editor, at Russell Sage Foundation. Many secretaries have typed various versions of the manuscript, but there is one, Mrs. Lorraine Dwelle, without whose care and faithfulness this work would certainly have been lost in some University of Chicago trashbin.

We cannot name the hundreds of individuals who willingly talked with us about their experiences with, and perspectives on, the poverty program, for to do so would violate the anonymity we pledged at the time of our interviews. We hope that we have repaid their cooperation by reporting and interpreting accurately the significance of their activities. We also benefited from the many students at The University of Chicago who suffered through our annual misnamed seminar on the "Politics of Welfare," where we explored so many false steps that the reader is blissfully spared.

No debt could be greater, however, than the one we owe to Joan Greenstone and Carol Peterson, who must have feared, far more frequently than they ever indicated, that they were Dorotheas to two twentieth-century Casaubons.

Though we acknowledge these and many other debts to scholars and friends, unfortunately we cannot attribute to them any of the deficiencies in the volume that follows.

SPECIAL ABBREVIATIONS
Used in this Book

CAA — Community Action Agency, the agency established in every local area that was charged with the responsibility of coordinating the local Community Action Program.

CAP — Community Action Program, a locally administered program to alleviate poverty, funded under the Economic Opportunity Act of 1964.

CPC — City Poverty Council, the committee charged with determining policy for local Community Action Programs. The official title varied from city to city.

NPC — Neighborhood Poverty Council, the neighborhood council selected to represent neighborhood opinion in the formulation and implementation of Community Action Programs in that neighborhood. The official title varied from city to city.

NSC — Neighborhood Service Center, the agency established to administer Community Action Programs and, in some cities, to coordinate other city services in a given neighborhood. The official title varied from city to city.

OEO — Office of Economic Opportunity, the national agency located in the Office of the President, which was charged with administering the Economic Opportunity Act of 1964.

Race and Authority in Urban Politics

INTRODUCTION: PARTICIPATION IN THE WAR ON POVERTY

Quietly, perhaps unintentionally, Lyndon Johnson's presidency inaugurated at least two fundamental changes in American politics. In one change, Johnson's bitterly divisive Vietnam ventures provoked the first sustained, widespread challenge to the assumptions of American military and foreign policy which had prevailed since the 1940s. This book focuses on one episode of a second change, a rejection of certain guiding assumptions in domestic politics that first emerged in the 1930s. In time, this second assault on accepted political formulas would raise questions of political conscience, civil liberties, executive prerogative, racial comity, and technological and corporate impact on the natural environment.

As in the case of the president's Vietnam War policies, this significant domestic innovation was far from immediately apparent. Johnson's 1964 landslide election meant that liberals now controlled the presidency and both houses of Congress for the first time since 1938. This new majority extended New Deal-type welfare programs both to the aged (through Medicare) and to school children (through elementary and secondary education aid). Through the first genuinely effective voting rights bill, it all but completed in 1965 the federal government's legislative attack on racial discrimination which liberals first supported in the 1940s. While many of these programs had been previously advocated by John Kennedy, Johnson's own initiatives built on and added to those of his Democratic predecessor. Not only did he lead the fight for Medicare, education and civil rights, but even before his reelection, he initiated a "war on poverty" which sought to provide for the very poor the welfare-state benefits won by industrial workers in the 1930s.

We will show in this study that of the five largest American cities (New York, Chicago, Los Angeles, Philadelphia, and Detroit) the new antipoverty program, although apparently cast in the tradition of the New

Deal, in fact set off local political struggles which crystallized and dramatized changing alignments in American politics. Race rather than class had become the source of most intense domestic conflicts; the structure of political authority had itself become a political issue; and in many cases, these issues produced decidedly ideological controversies.

ECONOMIC AND POLITICAL APPROACHES TO POVERTY PROBLEMS

Many of the poverty warriors themselves did not readily perceive the new patterns that were to emerge. Initially, the program evoked support from the social groups and political leaders reminiscent of the New Deal coalition. Labor, minority groups, big-city politicians, intellectuals, and southern moderates joined together to push the program through Congress. The enthusiasm associated with the program also had a New Deal flavor. Here once again were wrongs to be righted, suffering to be ended, equality to be pursued and (perhaps most appealing to the American intelligentsia) problems to be solved. Like a miniature New Deal the Office of Economic Opportunity (OEO), which directed the program, created an alphabet soup of bureaus and agencies. The largest and most complex component, the Community Action Program (CAP) emulated New Deal flexibility by allowing local Community Action Agencies (CAAs) to design almost any plausible program that might alleviate poverty (except for the educational instruction of children between six and sixteen who were excluded to avoid a church-state controversy in Congress).*

---

* To facilitate the inter-city comparisons undertaken throughout the text, particular institutions and programs in each city will be identified by a general term rather than by their proper names. In this discussion, we shall refer to the community action agency as the "CAA" rather than by the distinct name given to it in each city (which in several cases changed within a year or so). The neighborhood institutions designed to coordinate city services and to better inform residents of their availability will be called Neighborhood Service Centers (NSCs); the city-wide policy-making board, which included representatives of the mayor, city bureaucracies, private interest groups and the poor, will be identified as the City Poverty Council (CPC); the equivalent neighborhood boards associated with the Neighborhood Service Centers shall be called the Neighborhood Poverty Councils (NPCs); and the predecessor programs funded by the President's Committee on Juvenile Delinquency and Youth Crime, which frequently influenced the early development of the community action program in cities as well as at the national level, shall simply be called the juvenile delinquency program. The use of identical names is meant to suggest only a general *similarity of intended structure and function* in the five cities, i.e., a comparable position as recipient and distributor of federal and local funds under the same or similar laws. It should not be assumed that CAP activities were identical; indeed, the point of our analysis is to stress their variation in the five cities studied here.

In financial terms, the bulk of CAP's efforts conformed to this stress on expanding the scope of the welfare state's economic and social benefits. The CAP's very different goals developed most directly out of the ideas and experiences of the President's Committee on Juvenile Delinquency and Youth Crime established by the Kennedy administration in 1961. As compared to the casework tradition in social work, the President's Committee had accepted a more sociological, less psychoanalytic orientation to the youth and welfare problems of low-income families. According to this perspective, which had been gaining currency among some social workers in the late fifties, youth crime was not so much a product of the psychological problems of the poor as a predictable social outcome of the tension between a desire to "get ahead" and a lack of opportunity to do so.[1] If the Horatio Alger story could be transformed from myth to reality, delinquency could be reduced. This stress on individual mobility provided the rationale for two CAP approaches to the problems of poverty that were consistent with the New Deal tradition.

One approach sought to improve directly the prospect of stable employment by providing new educational and training opportunities. Nationally, OEO established the Neighborhood Youth Corps and Job Corps to supplement the Labor Department's Manpower Development and Training Act. At the local level, many CAPs also emphasized education and employment training for young adults as well as a widely heralded Head Start program for preschoolers. Even the Summer Recreation Programs, OEO's rather naïve response to the demand that it should "do something" to forestall rioting among its clients, were said to provide training and employment opportunities for the program's staff.

The second approach sought better coordination among existing governmental agencies serving a low-income clientele, such as the school system, state employment service, and local departments of welfare, housing, youth, and health, together with private social welfare agencies. In addition, it sought to improve agency communication with clients. These changes, it was believed, would rationalize existing governmental services, thereby making them more readily available to the poor. Accordingly, CAP called for the establishment of broadly representative coordinating committees or poverty councils, both to determine policy for local CAAs and to interrelate the activities of local agencies. In many cities (including the five investigated here) neighborhood service centers (NSCs) were established to coordinate the activities of governmental and (at times) private agencies serving specific neighborhoods. Community representatives were hired by NSCs to provide information to neighborhood residents about the entire range of available services.

These two approaches shared the New Deal's emphasis on reducing the *economic poverty* of individual clients. Yet in contrast to the social security programs of the 1930s, which substantially stabilized the lot of American workers, these economic approaches were likely to have only a marginal effect on the welfare of the poor, certainly much less than even a minimal cash-transfer program along the lines of guaranteed-annual-income or negative-tax proposals. Moreover, the Johnson administration, constrained by escalating Vietnam War costs, never spent more than $2 billion annually for the entire poverty program. From the beginning its scale steadily diminished as a proportion of the total Gross National Product. No serious observer continued to see it as a *war* on economic poverty; by the late 1960s few doubted that the initial rhetoric had aroused expectations which, given President Johnson's preoccupation with Southeast Asia, were wholly unrealistic.

This evaluation, however, does not apply to the third approach of OEO's CAP, the provision for community participation. Though it also followed from the new theory of juvenile delinquency, it was this focus on participation which broke so completely with the older socioeconomic emphasis that its full significance cannot be determined by an ordinary cost-benefit analysis. Drawing on its new sociological orientation, the President's Committee had begun to experiment with community organization and group action in order to restore a "sense of community" to anomic, rootless delinquents.[2] In modifying the rhetoric to OEO's somewhat different goals, certain key poverty officials argued that the poor must acquire power as well as money. The poor, it was argued, lacked such political resources as stable financing, social prestige, and easy access to decision-makers.* Generally, they were known for low voter turnout where parties were weak and for the relative ease with which their vote could be "controlled" by strong party organizations.[3] Most important, the poor had few autonomous organizations which could articulate their collective demands and maximize their electoral influence, requisites for becoming more than a "potential group" in urban politics.[4] In sum, poverty had a *political* as well as an economic dimension. Low-income citizens required not only improved services for individual clients; it was also necessary to mobilize community groups and to develop new political elites that could effectively articulate group interests.

The legal basis for this political approach was the Economic Opportunity Act's celebrated requirement that CAPs "be developed and ad-

---

* The following passage and various other passages throughout the monograph have been reprinted in revised form from our article entitled "Machines, Reformers, and the War on Poverty," in James Q. Wilson (Ed.), *City Politics and Public Policy* (New York: John Wiley & Sons, 1968), pp. 267–292. Copyright 1968 by John Wiley & Sons). Reprinted in revised form with permission.

ministered with the maximum feasible participation of the members of the groups and residents of the area served."[5] The phrase can easily be read as the standard rhetorical obeisance of American politics to grass roots democracy, and in 1964 most key figures in the executive branch and relevant congressional committees failed to consider the phrase seriously.[6] In administering the act, some high officials in the OEO consistently interpreted it simply to mean the substantial employment of low-income individuals in the programs being financed under community action. But others, particularly those with close connections to the civil rights movement, saw larger, more directly political implications. Indeed, the OEO guidelines required that representatives of the poor, chosen "whenever feasible" in accord with "traditional democratic approaches and techniques," comprise approximately one-third of the policy-making body for local CAAs at both the neighborhood and city levels.[7] Interpretation of "democratic approaches and techniques" varied significantly from city to city. But however they were implemented, representation on CAA committees could hardly eliminate, by itself, all the political problems of the poor. OEO's *Community Action* Workbook accordingly recommended to local CAAs that a "promising method was to assist the poor in developing autonomous and self-managed organizations which are competent to exert political influence on behalf of their own self-interest."[8] Only such steps could make political resources available to poor and minority groups.

At the most apparent level, OEO was hardly more successful in attacking political poverty than it was in alleviating economic poverty. To be sure, in two of our five cities some power redistribution occurred as low-income and minority groups gained representation on city and neighborhood poverty councils and managed to influence the operations of various governmental bureaucracies. Yet in most places OEO had to settle for little more than formal representation of the poor on local boards and agencies. In the decentralized American political system, the impact of federal policy can be blunted by established local elites, political, economic, and bureaucratic, unless the latter are themselves committed to its program. OEO's own grass roots rhetoric of community action only provided these elites with a federal mandate for shaping the program to their own needs (which were not necessarily the same as those of the poor). Consequently, the formal representation of the poor that OEO guidelines required only on occasion succeeded in redistributing a significant amount of power.

OEO's attack on political poverty was nonetheless sustained by a basic insight which gave the CAP its greatest importance. The authoritative, *federally legislated* call for participation by the poor in local political and administrative processes sanctioned and thus helped to make manifest new political aspirations among inner city residents. As a result, some political leaders perceived community participation as a direct challenge not only to their base of political power, but to the city's very structure of political authority.

For some others, especially in Washington, the political significance of this break with the New Deal tradition was obscured by its ostensible and more familiar focus on the plight of an undifferentiated population of poor people. This politically shrewd, rhetorical emphasis broadened OEO's clientele to include low-income members of all ethnic backgrounds, including poor white Protestants from Appalachia. In fact, however, key CAP administrators were rather self-consciously responding to the awakening political consciousness of the black community and, to a lesser extent, to that of the Puerto Ricans and Mexican-Americans living in New York and the Southwest, and wherever else they resided in significant numbers. Crucially, important local leaders shared this recognition of CAP's implications for racial politics. Mayors and other politicians, who knew perfectly well that black Americans were the most significant new political force in large American cities, quickly recognized their central place in CAPs. "Maximum feasible participation" announced in the midst of great civil rights agitation meant for some mayors the possibility of building new political coalitions; for others, it meant angry confrontations; but for all it meant a potential increase in black political activity.

At the same time, many black leaders were beginning to recognize publicly that their racial group was large enough so that they could insist on inclusion in the major decisions of urban institutions. When OEO announced its interest in fostering minority group participation in local politics, emerging leaders in the black neighborhoods perceived "maximum feasible participation" as a potentially valuable tool. They anticipated new material resources that could help make black citizens a major factor in both the selection of the political authorities and the shaping of public policies.

COMMUNITY PARTICIPATION AND THE STUDY OF URBAN POLITICS

The implications which the political approach to the "war on poverty" had for urban race relations prompted us to focus particularly on local implementation of the federal participation requirement in its formative early years. Our primary research technique was intensive field study common in the urban studies literature, in which we concentrated on identifying the precise sequence of events which led to the crucial decisions on the community participation issue. This field research was conducted between June 1965 and August 1968, primarily during the first year and a half of that period. Semistructured interviews with over three hundred political participants in the five cities and Washington, D.C. were held during the course of the research. Respondents included representatives of the poor, public officials, heads of public and private welfare agencies, civil rights leaders, and newspaper reporters. In addition, the research involved detailed inspection of newspaper coverage, review of minutes of CAA committee meetings, attendance at neighborhood and city-wide poverty meetings, and examination of public and private documents. Statements in the text are thus based on the authors' close familiarity with the development of community participation in the CAP that was achieved through the extensive consultation of a wide variety of information sources. In all cases, reports of the behavior of the participants is based either on written evidence or on oral evidence obtained from several actors speaking from various perspectives.

Although both we and those involved in CAP policy-formation rather euphemistically refer to community "participation," the fundamental political objective was generally understood to be the organization and consequent institutionalization of black (and other minority group) interests as a constituent component of the urban political regime. We thus have taken as our empirical task the description and explanation of the degree to which each of the five CAPs realized this goal. At another level, our purpose has been to use the findings from this analysis of one program to interpret the character of urban politics in the United States more generally. For the most part, these broader interpretive concerns focus on the most theoretically significant body of work in the contemporary study of urban politics, i.e. that which is commonly known as the pluralist literature.

Pluralist theory was itself a response to an interpretation of the distribution of political power in American cities (developed by Floyd Hunter and others) which argued that a small elite, primarily leading businessmen and their agents, controlled local community policies to protect their own class interests.[9] This interpretation of a single-class cleavage clearly oversimplified a complex urban political process which was marked by a multiplicity of participants and fluctuating power relationships that varied from issue to issue. And the pluralists, while attacking this elitist theory, developed their own interpretation of urban politics which was plainly superior to the power-elite analyses.

Specifically, the pluralists, particularly those influenced by a model of the political process based on economic analysis,[10] argued that opportunities to participate in politics were open to nearly all members of the community; that political activists were broadly, though not perfectly, representative of the community as a whole; that groups or individuals who felt intensely about an issue could find mechanisms to make their views known; that they would be able to obtain some satisfactory response from those in authority; that power varied from issue to issue because different groups and individuals felt different matters were most important; that for any one issue the unwillingness of many individuals to utilize political resources at their disposal created "system slack," producing highly variable patterns of participation and consequent policy outcomes; that politicians eagerly seeking reelection are less motivated by their own ideological preferences than by a desire to implement policies desired by a majority of the electorate; that such officials therefore seek compromises acceptable to most, if not all, participants; that policy change is therefore incremental, making only slight adjustments on the margins; and that as a result most groups, most of the time, secure at least some governmental policies about which they are intensely concerned.

No single pluralist writer has advanced all these propositions, nor do we wish to suggest that this list exhausts the ideas of pluralist writers. In particular, there is one school of pluralists far more concerned with the importance of political institutions than this list of assertions would indicate.[11] But we do think there is an inner consistency among the pluralist propositions just cited that justifies linking them together as part of a more general interpretive framework which, like the earlier elitist view, can be substantially criticized. On the other hand, we do not intend to reject this framework in its entirety, nor even to single out individual propositions as entirely erroneous. Rather, at those points where they become relevant to the presentation of our data, we do intend to show that some pluralist contentions must be significantly qualified. And taken together, these qualifications will provide a substantially different picture of the character of American urban politics.

In Part I, for example, we examine a critical pluralist assumption that the only interests relevant for interpreting urban politics are those which individuals themselves recognize. Pluralists generally reject all discussion of "false consciousness," "manipulation of mass preferences" and "failure to recognize one's true interests" as ideological rhetoric unworthy of value-free social science. By contrast, our case studies of the five cities (see Chapter 1) suggest that both valid and interesting political comparisons either across cities or across time are not feasible if the analyst accepts as his only point of departure the currently observable distribution of political preferences among the citizens. Rather than to concentrate exclusively on conscious attitudes, the analyst needs to discuss the role interests in the community which may give rise to certain preferences after specifiable conditions are fulfilled. Comparative analysis, in other words, requires some concept of latent (unrecognized) role interests. Indeed, Chapter 2 suggests that some pluralist writers make at least implicit use of the concept when it suits their purposes.

The second major pluralist tenet considered here argues that recognized preferences tend to be the discrete demands of individuals and specific groups rather than broad, diffuse ideologies. On the contrary, we assert the crucial impact that important ideologies, which articulate widely shared role interests, have in urban politics. Pluralists often argue that politicians are concerned solely with their electoral or organizational interests, or both, and that in decision-making these considerations take precedence over considerations related to the interests of more widely shared and enduring social roles. This argument plays a central role in pluralist theory; by arguing that politicians are concerned with electoral matters to the exclusion of any ideological commitments, the pluralists are able to support their theory that decision-makers are responsive to voter demands. In fact, however, we shall argue that in the case of community participation, electoral and organizational interests, while not irrelevant to urban decision-making, are sometimes less important than ideologies based on widely shared role interests.

In making this argument, we shall not be limited to the division between workers and employers which concerns elitists such as Hunter. Rather, we shall maintain that race relations between blacks and whites in American society has constituted a societal "contradiction," i.e., a basic opposition of two social roles, which when their role interests are recognized, can produce intense political conflict. Indeed, conflict did emerge on the community participation issue in precisely the way scholars in the Marxian tradition expect conflict to emerge from a social class contradiction.

Our role-interest analysis, moreover, is not limited just to contradictions of this sort. Interestingly enough, still another widely shared role whose interests, when recognized, can lead to widespread conflict, is that of citizen in the American regime. While we agree with the pluralists that the conflict between urban reformers and machine politicians, which has been so widely studied in the urban politics literature, is by no means simply a class conflict, we reject any interpretation of it as being simply a struggle for immediate political advantage. Rather, the struggle involved differing ideological conceptions of proper authority relationships. Indeed, these differing conceptions significantly affected the response of white politicians to black demands for community participation in the

1960s. In several ways then, ideology plays a far greater role in our study than in most pluralist research.

Finally, we reject a common pluralist assumption that if there are widely and intensely held policy concerns, they will be mobilized for political action, and thus rather regularly influence the outcome of the policy-formation process. For one thing, such widely dispersed opinions may not be accurately transmitted to the authorities by the relevant representative institutions, as is shown in Chapter 6 in the case of CAP. Again, the bureaucratic implementation of the policies which are formed may deviate from the goals of those who did dominate the overt policy conflict.* Even more important, we show in Chapter 8 that even widely held preferences in the political sphere may not be translated into policy-relevant demands unless certain mechanisms are available for organizing these preferences into politically effective groups. In the second place, the impact of any given set of preferences depends on the different ways in which policy disputes based on sharply different political demands are resolved. In any particular urban polity, some matters are compromised; but other issues, often those affecting groups hitherto excluded from the process of political bargaining, raise such fundamental ideological questions that compromise is not possible, and the side with the most political power imposes its preferences on the opposition.

Our analysis is nonetheless a modification and not a refutation of pluralist theory. It recognizes not only the independent influence of the structure of political institutions in a given city, but the plurality of forces that bear upon policy questions such as community participation. Indeed, we stress that the composition of such forces varies from one place to another so that no uniform elite makes decisions in America's five largest cities. Moreover, our analysis recognizes that, at times, politicians are primarily concerned with their electoral interests and that they try to fashion compromises which are acceptable to all influential participants.

It did become clear to us that these pluralist observations only partially captured the reality of the community participation controversy. The racial conflict in American society ran too deep, and the diverse commitments to different authority structures were too pervasive, to be interpreted solely within the pluralist perspective. But as becomes clear in Chapter 10, where we argue the case for community control of neighbor-

* On this particular issue, it must be conceded, there is some division among the pluralists themselves. In this discussion, we have focused on the political economy model which has influenced many but not all pluralist writers. For those such as Sayre and Kaufman and Banfield and Wilson, these findings about the independent importance of urban institutions would not be very surprising.

hood institutions in the racial minority areas of large cities, the answer lies not in rejecting the pluralist perspective out of hand. Rather, we must substantially modify this perspective, where necessary, to first take into account the attitudes on both race and authority relations that persisted into the 1970s.

RACE, AUTHORITY, AND COMMUNITY PARTICIPATION: AN ANALYTIC OVERVIEW

These contentions do not exhaust the propositions developed in the ensuing pages, nor is the analysis devoted simply to developing each of these points in its turn. Rather, the book is organized in such a way as to consider the various factors that affected community participation in the five cities. In Part I, a case-study analysis points up the differences among the cities and sets forth the analytic framework. Part II identifies and accounts for the "stakes" and the goals of each major participant in the policy-making process. Part III discusses the most proximate variables accounting for differential participation among the cities. And Part IV discusses the way in which the structures of power and the policy-making processes determined the outcome of the participation controversy. To clarify for the reader the precise way in which our rather complex argument will proceed, it may be useful to conclude this introduction with an analytical outline which specifies these points in somewhat more detail.

Part I describes the variations in the CAPs in the five cities and considers certain problems of comparative analysis posed by the inter-city study of community participation. Chapter 1 interprets in case-study fashion the development of the CAP in each city. The cities are discussed in order of increasing participation, with Chicago first, then Philadelphia and Los Angeles, and finally Detroit and New York. In each case, certain well-known characteristics of that city (e.g., Chicago's machine, Los Angeles' political fragmentation) seem to have influenced the direction that participation in the CAP took. But these characteristics, when applied generally to all cities, could not account in any systematic way for the variation among them. Chapter 2 discusses the problem in comparative analysis of accounting for cultural differences that precluded successful generalization from the case studies. It then offers a role-interest approach to comparisons of social group behavior both across cities and over time. This approach differs from that of the pluralist or political economy approaches, since it takes observable social roles, not preferences, utilities, or demands as its analytical point of departure. On the other hand, it differs from the approach of social stratificationists, since it assumes a variable rather than a determinate relationship between the individual's social role and his policy preferences. It is this variation which accounts for important changes in policy preferences over time, or substantial differences between cities and among individuals, all of whom have the same social role. The reader interested solely in the CAP for its own sake and not for what it can tell us about urban politics or political analysis more generally, can pass this chapter by.

Part II discusses the specific role interests and associated ideologies of the groups involved in the politics of community action, offering a systematic explanation for the perspective they brought to bear on the issue. In other words, we define here the "stake" each group had in community participation. Specifically, participation affected relationships between workers and employers, blacks and whites, citizens and authorities, giving the members of each of these roles a particular and distinct interest in the program's outcome. In their relationships with employers, we argue in Chapter 3 that workers have an interest not only in alleviating the adverse socioeconomic and political consequences of their subordinate role, but also in eliminating the norms that give employers the authority to direct worker activities. Since community participation had a generally egalitarian thrust, but was primarily concerned with race rather than class relationships, the program had clear if somewhat marginal implications for the interests of workers and employers. At the same time, in their relationships with whites, American blacks have an interest not only in reducing the adverse socioeconomic and political consequences of *their* subordinate social role, but also in eliminating the imputation of Negro inferiority that has patterned race relations in the United States. Consequently, it was this position of American blacks that made community participation so immediately important in the politics of large cities. In effect, the CAP issue triggered the blacks' recognition of their role interests in a new sphere of public policy, accounting for the rapid divisions that this policy evoked.

But if racial interests were relevant to the participation controversy, so was the structure of authority in the United States. The call for participation was a call for a significant change in the relationships between authorities and citizens. Thus, every citizen, whether he realized it or not, had a stake in the outcome of the controversy, for the issue had the potential of changing at least some elements of his relationship to public authorities. This relationship between American rulers and citizens, we shall argue in Chapter 4, has been patterned by four orientations that require *participation, pluralist bargaining, rationalization,* and adherence to the requirements of *constitutionalism.* Participation requires that rulers shall be selected by citizens who participate in free, uncontrolled, democratic elections. Pluralist bargaining requires that rulers make no more than incremental changes in the pattern of public policy and then only after consulting the interests that have a legitimate stake in the matter. Policies must be rationalized in the sense that only universalistic or achievement categories are used to distinguish among citizens. And the fundamental requirement of constitutionalism is that policies do not injure basic freedoms of speech, religion, privacy, and assembly. Significantly, these authority criteria at times are in tension with one another, so that citizens do not always agree on their relative importance—producing, paradoxically, potential for conflict about authority relations.

These categories will enable us to interpret in Chapter 4 one of the most puzzling aspects of the community participation controversy. The major opposition to black efforts came not from businessmen antagonistic to changes in class relationships nor from white groups resisting racial equality. In the large cities, businessmen were largely uninvolved in the antipoverty program. And even though white groups in the late 1960s would attack programs for urban housing and school integration, these groups were poorly organized and only marginally involved in the community participation issue during its formative period in the middle of the decade. Thus, the chief opponents to black demands were Democratic politicians who had often relied on black electoral support and encouraged specific black advances within their cities, including the economic orientation in the war on poverty itself. Moreover, the reformers who supported blacks on the community action issue were upper middle-class groups who had hardly been faithful allies of blacks and other minority groups in previous political conflicts.

The conflict took this form because it rapidly made relevant for many whites their citizen-role interest, this time in the context of race relations. In fact, the debate over authority relationships in big cities had for nearly a century divided the political machine from the reform movement. Machine politicians thus rejected black demands for extensive change through community participation, because they had long regarded the principle of pluralist bargaining as overriding. In other words, they believed that only by deferring to the variety of institutionalized interests in the city could conflict be managed and the social order maintained. By contrast, the reform ideology emphasized for many decades rationalized policy-making and widespread citizen participation in urban political processes, leading many reformers to support demands for community participation in the face of opposition from machine mayors.

This interpretation of the conflict stresses the importance of the expressed regime interests and ideologies of the machine and reform politicians. Chapter 5 considers an alternative explanation based on the machine politicians' and reformers' more narrow electoral and organizational interests, i.e., the need to get elected and to maintain the organizations with which they were identified. This interpretation does account for some of the actions that are taken in the course of the controversy, but it leaves unexplained some of the most interesting cases. Accordingly, we offer a framework that considers both narrow political interest and broad regime ideologies as motives for political action.

Having identified and interpreted the stakes of classes, races, and authorities in the participation controversy, we turn in Part III to a detailed analysis of the *most proximate* causal factors that explained the variation in participation among the five cities. Chapter 6 describes the way in which representatives of the poor were selected and the social types that were chosen; it then argues that the formal manner of representing the poor had important effects on the substantive character of their representation. Specifically, we argue that democratic elections and social representativeness reduced the effectiveness with which black interests were represented in CAP. The manner of selecting the poor explained much of, but not all of the variation in participation among the cities. The remainder of this variation, discussed in Chapter 7, was due to the effect of the relatively autonomous bureaucracies in the reform cities of Detroit and Los Angeles, as compared to the other cities where party patronage systems are still active. Where bureaucracies are autonomous, they both pursue their mission more faithfully and adhere more strictly to rationalized bureaucratic procedures. When the mission was participation, the results were complex, for the agency's bureaucratic routines undermined its participatory objective. Thus, OEO's attempt to maximize bureaucratic efficiency and citizen participation was a naïve effort to realize two mutually exclusive goals.

Part IV turns from the immediate processes affecting the community action program to the more remote but basic structures of power and processes of policy-making that produced variations in participation policies. Chapter 8 further develops the distinction between machine and reformed cities that Chapter 7 applied to bureaucratic behavior. We argue that the structures of power affecting participation policy in the machine cities were different from those in the reform cities. In the machine cities participation was a function of the power relationship between the political machine and the reform movement. In the reform cities it was a function of the political strength of the minority group communities. The findings are explained by applying models developed in the political economy literature. In brief, it is argued that political resources of relevant groups varied according to (1) the size of the group's potential constituency; (2) the resources available for securing constituent contributions to the political organization; and (3) the availability of strong political leadership. These factors differed in reformed and machine cities because the entire pattern of organizational incentives was affected by the presence of patronage-oriented political parties.

Chapter 9 turns to the policy-making processes themselves to explicate the precise way in which the varying power relationships in the five cities affected the CAP. We distinguish between consensual and conflictual policy-making processes. When politics are consensual, the most important way in which the group affected policy was through the group's capability of electing as mayor a man whose ideological perspective was friendly to group interests. When policy-making processes were conflictual, the resources used in the policy-making process itself also had an impact on the degree of community participation. We then consider the conditions under which conflictual as opposed to consensual policy-making processes occur, arguing that when a significant interest group, such as blacks, is denied a legitimate position in the pluralist bargaining process, conflictual politics is provoked by its demands.

In Chapter 10, we examine participation as a public policy. Four major literatures—mass society, social stratificationist, pluralist, and liberal progressive—all object to participation as practiced in the CAP but for quite contradictory reasons. The objections of each perspective are considered in developing an argument that participation is a viable strategy for overcoming the racially inegalitarian features of American society. Let us begin, however, with the case history of the CAP in each of the five largest American cities.

PART I

A Comparative Approach to the Politics of Community Action

CHAPTER 1: COMMUNITY ACTION POLITICS IN FIVE CITIES: THE LIMITS OF CASE-STUDY ANALYSIS

Community participation varied among the five cities. Chicago had the least participation, Philadelphia and Los Angeles had significantly more, but Detroit and particularly New York were the cities whose Community Action Program (CAP) could be properly labeled a participatory program. In each city the character of the program reflected many characteristics of that city's politics which have been identified by others in previous research. Within the framework of a case-study analysis, each city's program seems to be fairly easily explained and interpreted. Yet when the factors identified as critical in the case studies are applied generally to all cities, they fail to provide a comprehensive explanation of the various levels of participation within the cities. This was the puzzle confronting us upon completion of our otherwise quite convincing case studies of the CAP.

CHICAGO: MINIMUM FEASIBLE PARTICIPATION

Consistent with its image as a machine city in both popular and scholarly literature, we found that Chicago provided for the least participation in its CAP. Most machine politicians build their organizations by distributing patronage and favors to individuals, ethnic groups, neighborhoods, and other narrow, particularistic interests. Accordingly, such politicians intensely dislike conflict over broad issues of public policy which might activate large numbers of unreliable voters or divide the party organization's diverse supporters.

Chicago stood out among our five cities in the capacity of its mayor, Richard J. Daley, who also headed the local Democratic party, to impose this preference for nonconflictual politics on a wide range of organizations and interest groups. For example, the Democratic machine so penetrated the structure of the National Association for the Advancement of Colored People (NAACP) that it was one of the least militant of the large urban chapters.[1] As late as 1965, Chicago's issue-oriented reform organization, the Independent Voters of Illinois, remained isolated in a few upper middle-class areas along Lake Michigan.[2] Even the relatively militant, issue-oriented industrial unions found it necessary to negotiate quietly with the party organization[3]; and Chicago's newspapers, despite their Republican leanings, criticized the mayor cautiously if at all.[4]

Mayor Daley therefore had little enthusiasm for a CAP which used government money to sponsor political activities that might include picketing and demonstrating against city agencies. An early statement by Chicago's Community Action Agency (CAA) made this view explicit:

> Chicago realizes that many depressed urban citizens are ready for subleadership roles. But Chicago believes their energies would be utilized best in salaried subprofessional roles rather than in mere advisory roles on action committees that lead also to nonproductive protest activities.
>
> Thus, the Chicago approach to urban programming is to develop the human and economic energies of the community so that they merge with the forward thrust of the city instead of diverging from that thrust in protest. . . .
>
> In this manner, Chicago proposes to energize rather than organize depressed communities. Organization has a tendency to fragment and wall off enthusiasm.[5]

Consistent with this orientation, the mayor initially appointed to Chicago's City Poverty Council (CPC) public officials who almost uniformly were dependent upon the Democratic organization, and business and community leaders bound to the city administration by a complex web of formal and informal relationships.* As Table 1–1 reveals, the poor were not represented in any manner whatsoever until 1966.

OEO officials tried to pressure the CAA into revising the composition of its poverty council. Robert Shackford, temporary head of the Midwest regional office, observed publicly in February 1965 that:

> If I were setting up the ideal program, the first thing I would do would be to identify all the community groups that have emerged in the past decade and invite them to nominate members for the planning committee.

* The name of Chicago's CPC was the Chicago Committee on Urban Opportunity; the Community Action Agency (CAA) was known by the same name. Neighborhood service centers (NSCs) were known as Urban Progress Centers, and their Neighborhood Poverty Councils (NPCs) were called Urban Progress Center advisory committees, an appropriate label since they had little formal authority or informal power. Chicago's juvenile delinquency program was called the Joint Youth Development Committee.

TABLE 1–1. Composition of the Chicago Committee on Urban Opportunity[a]

Type of representative	Date					
	11/64		*3/65*		*1/66*	
	%	*No.*	%	*No.*	%	*No.*
Chicago public officials[b]	42.9	21	39.5	22	29.5	23
Other public officials[c]	20.4	10	21.4	12	12.8	10
Community leaders[d]	28.6	14	25.0	14	35.9	28
Professional agency representatives[e]	8.2	4	14.3	8	14.1	11
Representatives of the poor	0.0	0	0.0	0	7.7	6
TOTAL	100.1%	49	100.2%	56	100.0%	78

[a] The data presented in this table were derived from Seymour Z. Mann: *Chicago's War on Poverty* (Chicago: Center for Research in Urban Government, Loyola University, 1966), p. 22, Table X.

[b] This includes elected and appointed public officials as well as those nonprofessionals that hold a policy-making position within the Daley administration, such as members of the Chicago Board of Education.

[c] An elected or appointed official of a non-Chicago jurisdiction. As Mann notes, "In some cases such an official has been closely related by formal or informal relationships to the City administration." The Democratic organization, in other words, has influence beyond the formal governing structure for Chicago.

[d] Unfortunately, Mann does not distinguish here among business, labor, black, and education leaders. While all types are included, most of these individuals were businessmen.

[e] These are, by and large, professional heads of various private welfare agencies.

> And I'd ask the civil rights organizations, too. I wouldn't be afraid of them . . .
>
> And I don't see why we shouldn't have a mother on aid to dependent children in the group . . .
>
> Then I would put real authority into their hands in devising programs. I wouldn't try to impose anybody's ideas or plans on them.[6]

On another occasion, at a February 1965 meeting of church and community groups on Chicago's West Side, one speaker shouted, "If the war on poverty is to really succeed in Chicago, we must quickly find ways of involving the poor in helping the poor." In the presence of Chicago's CAP director, Shackford responded, "I got the message. If there were any doubts in my mind when I left Washington, there is no doubt in my mind now."[7] At the same time, Shackford privately applied more direct pressure. As one federal official reported back in Washington: "In late January (1965) Mr. Robert Shackford . . . informed [the Chicago CAA executive director] that the CPC was not in compliance with the requirements for the Community Action Program. Mr. Shackford is emphasizing 'participation of the poor' in all aspects of the program in all his contacts with the community. He has indicated that approval of more funds for Chicago will be conditional upon complete reorganization."

OEO, however, had not considered the political power of the Chicago Democrats. Not only was Daley a power in presidential politics, but in 1965 the nine Chicago Democrats in the House of Representatives could be depended upon to act cohesively whenever the mayor so desired.[8] These resources gave Daley great leverage in bargaining with governmental agencies. In 1967, the politically naïve bureaucrats who headed the Office of Education boldly withheld elementary and secondary education funds from the Chicago schools until they made some effort to end segregation; responding to local pressures, the White House overruled this decision. Some months later Francis Keppel, the Commissioner of Education, left the Johnson administration under a cloud that had clearly formed at the time of the Chicago debacle.[9] In a similar effort to please the Daley administration, Washington removed Shackford from any further jurisdiction over Chicago's antipoverty program. After less dramatic but still considerable conflict with Chicago's CAA, his two successors were replaced as well. Harmonious relations began to develop only after OEO appointed a regional director who had worked closely with the pro-Daley faction in the local NAACP.

In the end, Chicago did make some concessions to OEO demands. Although the NSCs were originally to have no NPCs, by the fall of 1964 Chicago's CAA recognized that some kind of an NPC was necessary to show compliance with OEO guidelines. But even when NPCs were established, council members were appointed by the center directors who were themselves appointed by the Daley-selected executive director of the overall CAA. Moreover, the center director, not the council members, appointed the council chairman who also served as the neighborhood's representative to the CPC. All in all, these "democratic" procedures exemplified the care with which the Democratic machine in Chicago coordinated and controlled local political activities.

These policies followed the pattern Daley established with the war on poverty's predecessor, the juvenile delinquency program. During 1963 and 1964 Daley had become concerned that this earlier program had allied itself with the civil rights movement, attacking the city's schools and even the mayor himself. Shortly thereafter, Daley ousted these rebellious city employees and imposed a new program that minimized community organization and subsequent agitation. Although it cost the city several million dollars in federal assistance, Daley insisted on this non-militant approach. After this experience, he made it clear that the CAA staff must avoid the "mistakes" of its predecessor. Despite the unhappiness of the welfare agencies, civil rights groups, reformers, and neighborhood organizations, Daley either suppressed or ignored demands for participation in CAP in order to preclude overt expression of discontent in the city.

As a result, the Chicago CAA established a program consistent with Daley's reputation for speed and efficiency. During the first two years of the program Chicago received an average of $236 per year for every poor family in the city (as reckoned by the 1960 census), a sum that compared favorably with the $108 per family in New York and $102 per family in Philadelphia. OEO's director, Sargent Shriver, at one point called the Chicago program the model CAP in the country. Charges of malfeasance and mismanagement of poverty funds, which plagued the program in the other four cities, were very seldom leveled against programs operated by Chicago's CAA. Chicago opened its neighborhood service centers more quickly than did the other four cities; the first center opened in March of 1965, a remarkable achievement considering that the initial funds were not released from Washington until November of the previous year. Even charges of patronage were notably few in Chicago, though this may have been due to the general acceptance of patronage politics within the individualistic culture of the city.[10] It is unlikely that any analysis could determine whether Chicago utilized its funds in a more efficient manner than did the other cities. Certainly, our research was concerned with other matters. But Chicago's CAA seemed capable of acting faster, obtaining more financial support, impressing certain key political figures, and acting in a bureaucratically more responsible fashion than many CAPs.

Perhaps all this apparent success in mounting a widely recognized attack on economic poverty was more easily accomplished without significant participation of the poor. Certainly, the Chicago CAA officials paid little, if any, attention to community organizations. Chicago's NPCs were advisory councils that had no authority over the operations of the NSC. They could not select personnel, nor did they determine the center's programs. It is true that they could refuse to operate any proposed programs, but this negative power was scarcely useful. Since few CAPs were visibly harmful to poor people, there was little reason to refuse a project which would only shortchange the neighborhood's opportunity to share in the program's largess. CAA officials also claimed that NPCs had positive authority over "a special fund" of "approximately $50,000," which could be used by each NPC to develop programs for the community.[11] However, this fund in fact amounted to only $25,000 and the NPC's decision first required the approval of the CPC. The funds, moreover, could not be used for programs operated by community groups but only for NSC operations.

As a result, the NSC staff could so manipulate the appropriation of these funds that the council had no significant influence. For example, the staff of a North Side center decided to use the funds for a summer recreational program and negotiated a coordinated effort with a number of public and private agencies. After these negotiations and two days before the program was to go into effect, the NPC, called into an "emergency session," approved the program without change. Through devices such as these, the center staff ensured that the NPC did not even use those few formal powers it possessed.

Given the antagonism of the Daley administration to participation in the program, the CAA staff had no desire to encourage the formation of community groups critical of governmental agencies. Individuals at all levels within the bureaucracy reaffirmed their commitment to the provision of services rather than to group mobilization. Asked if community representatives from the NSC were going to organize block clubs, an NSC director typically responded that we "are not in these communities to organize. We . . . want to get people services that they are entitled to." But the NSC's caution may have precluded the attainment of even this goal. Community representatives were encouraged to go door-to-door to explain the functions of NSC and discover the residents' problems. Inevitably, they came into contact with problems that welfare recipients had with the Department of Public Aid. To protect the Department of Public Aid from community pressures, representatives were instructed to turn over the problem immediately to the public aid official housed in the local NSC. The indigenous community representatives were given the names of all welfare recipients in the neighborhood—not in order to see if they needed assistance but so that the representative might know which apartments to avoid when contacting people on his daily rounds. Apparently, the Department of Public Aid did not want community representatives to generate new problems.

In sum, however efficiently the NSC was operated, among the purposes which it studiously avoided fulfilling was the political activation of low-income groups. The Daley administration was uninterested in spawning political competitors, and it had the political resources and bureaucratic apparatus sufficient to prevent CAP encouragement of such developments. A certain semblance of participation was a necessary concession to OEO, but the clear preference and actual accomplishment of Chicago's CAA was to keep it at the minimum feasible level.

PHILADELPHIA: COOPERATION AND CO-OPTION

If any of the great cities of the North can be said to have a bit of the traditional southern manner and style, Philadelphia, only miles from the Mason-Dixon line, would have to be so designated.* It adhered to traditional Republicanism until 1951, longer than any of the other great urban centers. Even the Great Depression could not shake lower-income Philadelphians from their allegiance to a Republican party which had long catered to the interests of the city's businessmen. During the thirties, while New York elected reformer Fiorello La Guardia and Chicago threw out "Big Bill" Thompson, its most colorful Republican, Philadelphia voters continued their traditional ways. When the Republicans began to lose local elections in the late forties, the cause was not union agitation or New Deal policies but the disaffection of the business community with the Republican machine.

Unlike Los Angeles, Chicago, and Detroit, Philadelphia was a city old enough to have an almost truly established social elite. In contrast to New York, Philadelphia was small enough so that its elite formed a single, if complex, grouping rather than a multitude of separate circles. Moreover, this elite was not as nationally oriented as was New York's, but formed instead a more provincial leadership concerned with local matters in much the same way as were traditional leaders in southern cities.[12]

A traditionally established elite subtly affects the behavior of other groups and individuals. Perhaps Philadelphia's elite accounts for its business community's unusual civic-mindedness seldom matched outside the South by cities even approaching its size.[13] It was the business community, disgusted with the worn-out, corrupt, conservative character of the Republican organization, which formed the Greater Philadelphia Movement, a reform organization determined to provide dynamic leadership to counteract the continuing deterioration of the city's inner core. Distinguishing itself from the chamber of commerce by its small but elite character, as well as by its more progressive ideas, the Greater Philadelphia Movement sparked the reform of city government, the physi-

* Elazar has argued that the South developed a "traditional" political culture in contrast to the "moralistic" culture of New England and the "individualistic" or "marketplace" culture of the Middle Atlantic states. Although "traditional" and "marketplace" cultures, according to Elazar, have blended together rather well in many areas, the "traditional" culture is marked by unusual quiescence on the part of the poor and minorities and a sense of responsibility on the part of the community elite. Philadelphia, more than any of the other five northern cities, partook of such a culture. Daniel Elazar: *Cities of the Prairie* (New York: Basic Books, 1970), Chapter IV.

cal renewal of the center city and dock area, and the opening up of fairer employment opportunities to blacks. In order to oust corrupt Republicans from local office, many of its key members supported the political ambitions of two leading members of socially prominent Philadelphia families, Democrats Richardson Dilworth and Joseph Clark, believing that their indisputably correct social backgrounds were more important than their somewhat dubious political connections.[14]

This cautious but still progressive reform movement reached its zenith in the 1950s. By the early 1960s its strength had weakened. Ex-Mayor Clark had become a senator and his successor Dilworth had forsaken the mayoralty in a futile effort to become governor. In 1962 Dilworth was succeeded as mayor by an Irish Catholic of humble origins, James H. J. Tate, who had been council president when Dilworth resigned. Tate's roots were solidly placed in the patronage politics of the immigrant Democratic party, and he was incapable of adapting to the styles of the businessmen reformers. Relations between the civic and political leadership thus became increasingly estranged. Yet even with their differences both Tate and the reformers were more concerned with attacking the economic problems of the poor than in heightening their political participation.

This common perspective was well illustrated by the history of Philadelphia's juvenile delinquency program. From its birth the program bore the stamp of the Philadelphia elite's civic consciousness. The program did not rely as heavily on public monies as did its Chicago and New York counterparts. Rather, the businessmen of Philadelphia demonstrated their initiative by securing from the Ford Foundation several million dollars to foster "human renewal" in much the same way as had the Greater Philadelphia Movement in previous years fostered "urban renewal."[15] In this they were aided by the fact that the head of Ford's "gray areas" program was Paul Ylivsaker, previously an aide of Mayor Joseph Clark. Mayor Dilworth gave the businessmen's undertaking his warmest support.

Although the juvenile delinquency program was established as a nonprofit corporation not directly under city control, the attitude of the mayor inevitably affected its development.* When Dilworth resigned

* Philadelphia's juvenile delinquency program was called the Philadelphia Council for Community Advancement. The CAA was originally the Mayor's Program for the Elimination of Poverty, then the Mayors' Task Force against Poverty, and finally (when private welfare groups objected to the reference to the mayor) the Philadelphia Anti-poverty Action Committee. The CPC also had a variety of names but finally was also called the Philadelphia Anti-poverty Action Committee.

The twelve NPCs were known as Community Action Councils and the twelve of-in 1962, the program, which was only barely under way, suffered from Tate's lesser interest. Sensing this decline in support, jealous competitors in the welfare field began to attack the new rival. Significantly, the program even managed to antagonize the black community which it had sought to help. One reason for this was that its director was white and the board almost entirely so. Secondly, the program consistently emphasized an *economic* rather than political approach to the problems of the gray areas. In stating its larger objectives, the program stressed coordinating services to the black community at the neighborhood level, though little actual coordination was ever begun. More concretely, it did fund a few experimental child-care centers which later were hailed as proving grounds for the Head Start program and, most importantly, it supported a manpower training program organized by Rev. Leon Sullivan, the black minister who had won a national reputation through his consumer-boycott campaign.

As the major forerunner in the welfare field, the juvenile delinquency program significantly affected community action politics. At one level, criticism of the juvenile delinquency program's white leadership ensured that the mayor would appoint a black as head of the CAA. But at a deeper level, the program indicated that no significant political force in the city, and certainly not the businessmen reformers, eagerly sought a participatory program in welfare politics. The mayor and other participants could expect that whatever other difficulties might occur, militant political activities were unlikely to be a concomitant of community action. As a result, although the inauguration of the CAP provoked intense bargaining, the conflict remained moderate in its essentials—a quarrel among competing individuals, interest groups, and narrow political factions rather than a bitter confrontation between the black community and political authorities.

Initially, in the summer of 1964 the mayor assigned responsibility for the CAP to the juvenile delinquency agency. There was little risk in this rather surprising step, because the juvenile delinquency program was no more ready to sponsor participation than any other influential organization in the city. The decision, however, did antagonize the city's welfare department and the Health and Welfare Council, who would later force the juvenile delinquency program out of the field of welfare altogether.[16]

fices and staffs of some ten or twelve individuals each, which were "supervised" by these councils, served as the NSCs in Philadelphia. Whereas Chicago had a few large centers housing large numbers of agencies and a sizable professional staff, Philadelphia contained no other city agencies within its centers, had no professional staff at this level, and had several small centers rather than a few large ones. These centers were simply known as Community Action Council offices.

The mayor sought to keep the program under his own official control, establishing a city task force to direct it. But this structure suffered great criticism on the grounds that it would be a source of patronage and that it provided for no representation of the poor. Not only was opposition voiced by neighborhood and civil rights groups but, more importantly, by OEO, local private welfare agencies, and reform groups as well.

At this point Mayor Tate displayed his recognition of the power of the city's elite. He asked the president of the Health and Welfare Council (who was also president of the Federal Reserve Bank in Philadelphia) to chair a committee that would devise a CAP policy-making structure. This committee included five representatives from the private welfare community, two representatives from civil rights groups (Urban League and NAACP), and only three city officials. Significantly, the mayor allowed a committee dominated by private interest groups to shape the program for which his own administration had political responsibility. This committee proposed a CPC structure that included several city officials, strong representation for a variety of interest groups, especially private welfare and civil rights organizations, and an undetermined number of representatives of the poor. Later, a similar committee decided to include twelve representatives of the poor (40 percent of the CPC) chosen in a democratic election. In this case, too, the mayor accepted a decision made outside his official family.

In accepting the election process, Tate and the civic elite implicitly relied on the political quiescence of Philadelphia's black community. Accordingly, the Philadelphia CAP developed along lines that, unlike Chicago, allowed the representatives of the poor some scope for independent action, but never encouraged independent political activities that could significantly affect traditional power relationships in Philadelphia politics. Elected representatives of the poor did not perceive the program as a mechanism for building powerful organizations in low-income communities and initiating protests against the activities of other urban bureaucracies. At the city-wide level, the most distinctive contribution of the representatives of the poor was a well-coordinated lobbying effort designed to pressure the Republican-controlled state legislature to provide more funds for the state's welfare program. But this move was encouraged, not fought, by the Democratic city administration for obvious partisan reasons. In the neighborhoods we investigated, the only important example of participatory behavior involved resistance to an urban renewal proposal. Otherwise, efforts to organize blacks and other minority groups were minor and scattered at best. Representatives of the poor instead concentrated on securing payment for themselves and positions of employment for their family and friends. The CAA eagerly sought to cooperate with these requests, for it focused the energies of the representatives of the poor on patronage concerns rather than policy questions, which consequently came under the firm direction of the CAA staff.

That representatives were more concerned about patronage than policy was hardly unusual in Philadelphia politics. In the City of Brotherly Love, citizens had never battled intensely over broad political issues. Many of Philadelphia's unemployed workers continued to vote Republican throughout the depression. Labor was never a radical or even an aggressive force; reformers were mainly conservative businessmen; blacks had been unusually moderate; and politicians were more concerned with the pork barrel than broad policies. To be sure, the Philadelphia political machine was not as powerful as Chicago's. Organization Democrats did not establish themselves as the local representatives of the New Deal but came into power only much later on the coattails of the reformers, and they never had the abundance of local patronage that was available in Chicago. Yet the reformers had only subverted the organizational structures of the Republican machine, but not the city's traditional political culture that nourished it. As a result, a consensual political style shaped the poverty program, as it did so much of Philadelphia politics, in such a way as to moderate conflict, direct attention to particularistic concerns, and limit black insurgency.

LOS ANGELES: PARTICIPATION IN A POLITICALLY FRAGMENTED METROPOLIS

The pervasive fragmentation of southern California's civic life, fundamental to every interpretation of Los Angeles politics, prevented minority groups from amassing sufficient political resources to achieve significant levels of participation.[17] Yet this same fragmentation also prevented Los Angeles' Mayor Samuel Yorty and others opposed to participation from totally squelching community organization efforts. On balance, CAP policies were clearly antiparticipatory; the program did not materially strengthen the organizational power or political influence of the black and Mexican-American communities. Yet Los Angeles' CAP did promote some voting registration and encouraged community organizations in several scattered areas. Although it was limited, participation in Los Angeles was clearly greater than in either Chicago or Philadelphia.

Both the extent and limitations of this participation reflect the high cost of forming a political coalition in a city as geographically dispersed and socially mobile as Los Angeles. In contrast to the older cities of the East and Midwest, which grew compactly along waterways and later along railroad and trolley tracks, Los Angeles' great population spurt took place when the automobile gave immigrants a greater flexibility in choosing their place of residence. This meant dispersal of industry and commerce, wide roads and later a mammoth freeway network, an almost endless array of single-family dwellings, and comparatively weak, scattered, and poorly sustained cultural institutions. These factors, together with the high rate of in-migration and the absence of European ethnic enclaves, have accentuated the restlessness, social isolation, indeed, anomie and alienation that so many writers have found peculiarly Californian—and southern Californian in particular.[18]

Whatever the accuracy of such social-psychological assertions, this social mobility and dispersion has undeniably handicapped political activists. For one thing, the sheer amount of leg work per voter in an election campaign inevitably discourages campaign volunteers. These problems are substantially aggravated by the structure of the California political system. Political parties were systematically weakened, indeed, almost destroyed by the legislative achievements of the Progressive movement. Local elections are entirely nonpartisan; patronage, the very staple of politics in Chicago and Philadelphia, is almost entirely unknown in southern California. For many years candidates could compete in both party primaries simultaneously, destroying the notion that primaries are a mechanism by which party loyalists select their leaders.

The structure of government itself accentuated this fragmentation. Los Angeles' weak-mayor government gave to the city council veto power over appointments and policies that in New York and Philadelphia are exclusively the prerogative of the mayor. As a result, Los Angeles bureaucracies were much more independent of mayoral control. The school system, as an extreme example, had its own elective board and controlled its own finances. Paradoxically, however, power was so dispersed that the mayor was still the single most powerful individual in a system of enfeebled participants. Opponents of the mayor found it difficult to build the coalitions necessary to implement significant policy changes.

As in the other cities, Los Angeles' CAP was influenced by the juvenile delinquency program, which itself had been shaped by the area's governmental fragmentation.* Unlike the programs in Chicago and Phila-

* The juvenile delinquency program was called the Youth Opportunities Board, which consisted of the five Joint Powers mentioned later in the text. When this Board, which became the CAA, was modified to include a broader array of groups and individuals, including the representatives of the poor, it was called the Economic and Youth Opportunities Agency, and the CPC serving as its board of directors was known by the same name. Los Angeles had no NPCs, but it did have a number of "outposts" as part of its Neighborhood Adult Participation Project, which, though fairly small, served as Los Angeles' NSCs.

delphia, no single participant or institution could control the juvenile delinquency program in Los Angeles. Instead, an agreement was reached under the provisions of California law that joined the state, the city, the county, and the county and city school boards as sponsors of a single agency. Each "power" to this Joint Powers agreement, as it was called, had a representative on the juvenile delinquency agency's board.

Together with his executive assistant, who dominated the deliberations of the board, Mayor Yorty sought to increase his influence over Los Angeles youth services by using the agency to develop a comprehensive system of information on needs and available resources. But the other powers prevented any significant coordination or innovation through the juvenile delinquency program. The program's deputy director, a city school official, limited educational programs to "discrete and remedial services with little emphasis on classroom or curriculum revisions."[19] The state's representative, who worked for the state employment service, sabotaged a proposed training program which would in effect have extended employment services to the very poor.[20] A representative from the county probation department saw little value in the preventive approach to juvenile delinquency that animated the entire program.[21]

Increasingly uneasy at this conservative pattern, a group of black professionals discussed the reform of Los Angeles' welfare system in a series of meetings at 1122 Manchester Street, the home of a leading black social worker, Mrs. Opal Jones. After the Johnson administration had announced its war on poverty, this "1122 Group" decided to concentrate on preventing the Joint Powers board from controlling this new program. In a city with little coordinated political activity, even a small informal organization can have a measurable impact. Accordingly, the 1122 Group, which had less than ten members, successfully encouraged a group of welfare agencies to form an Economic Opportunity Federation (EOF) in order to compete with the juvenile delinquency agency for federal antipoverty funds. Along with a majority of private agency representatives, the EOF board included a number of minority-group politicians. Los Angeles thus became the only one of our five cities in which power was so dispersed that a group of *private* agencies not only claimed preeminence over the local government in receiving federal antipoverty funds but actually obtained tacit support from the state government in the conflict which followed.

This conflict, which was undoubtedly more complicated than similar struggles in the other four cities, went through a number of stages, some of which we shall examine in later chapters.[22] Each stage strikingly revealed Los Angeles' characteristic dispersion of political power. EOF, for example, was strong enough to challenge the Joint Powers bid for control, but Yorty successfully insisted that they accept a merger in which the governmental representatives maintained a majority on the CPC. Yet the results of even Yorty's intervention were paradoxical and sometimes, it seemed, self-defeating. Since he could not control the program in any direct manner, Yorty apparently hoped that the controversy surrounding his demand for a governmental majority would raise the visibility of community action, thus enabling him to supervise the program's general orientation. But the objections to a nongovernmental majority on the CPC only led to the exclusion (as voting members) of representatives from the Los Angeles Chamber of Commerce, the League of California Cities, and the United Way (Los Angeles' community fund)—organizations that would have been expected to join him in opposition to a participatory CAP. And once the composition of the board became an issue of high visibility, OEO, the State of California (whose anti-Yorty governor, Edmund G. "Pat" Brown, had formal veto power over community action proposals), local minority group organizations, and liberal reformers insisted on representation of the poor. Yorty's first tactic was to establish local screening boards which were to choose the representatives of the poor to CPC, hoping to manipulate and control them. Meetings were then held in three communities and, much to the dismay of the civil rights activists, Yorty's allies won control of the first meeting. But the mayor's resources were so limited that he lost in the next two. As Levine states: "Not only was organization ultimately useless for Yorty . . . but it was potentially dangerous—the first neighborhood boards became battlegrounds . . . . Getting and maintaining control . . . required resources which he didn't command, while incurring maintenance costs which could not be supported."[23] In the end, Yorty agreed to the election of representatives by the poverty residents. Political decentralization meant that the mayor, when using his maximum resources, had to compromise even with a rather weak opposition.

Significantly, the whole controversy continued until August 1965 after the Watts riot had focused national attention on Los Angeles and brought in presidential mediator Leroy Collins. The terms of the resulting Collins agreement did not materially differ from earlier proposals, but the federal intervention speeded the resolution of the conflict. With so many autonomous participants, the cumbersome process of reaching a decision had delayed submission of acceptable proposals to OEO, costing Los Angeles much of its federal CAP money for the 1964–1965 fiscal year.*

These same decentralizing forces also limited the mayor's overall

---

* Los Angeles received $25 for each poor family, compared with the $211 received by Chicago families.

influence over program operations. In the first place, the CAA director, Joseph Maldanado, a Mexican-American who had headed the juvenile delinquency program, had at times publicly resisted the mayor over the issue of the CPC's composition, an independent stance which no other director had taken, not even in New York. Maldanado, moreover, appointed to his staff several members of the same 1122 Group that had initiated participatory demands, including Mrs. Opal Jones, who became director of the NSC program, the CAP component most concerned with residents' participation. Jones, in turn, proved to be a thorn in Maldanado's side. In the early days of the program, confronted with the discontent of her proparticipatory staff, she tried to arrange a meeting for them with Mayor Yorty. Maldanado, her ostensible superior, angry at not first being consulted and evidently concerned about Yorty's reaction, fired Jones for insubordination. Jones, however, received the support of Los Angeles black congressman Rep. Augustus Hawkins, who proposed that CAP be decentralized rather than controlled by a single county-wide council. In a compromise, Maldanado rehired Jones but turned over the NSC program to the federation of settlement houses, so that he would not be responsible for her activities. Clearly, it was impossible to set up a system of control that would enable either the mayor or the CAA head to control all CAP activities.

Mayor Yorty also lacked the resources to co-opt the elected representatives of the poor, a strategy that had worked well in Philadelphia. Not only did the representatives continually press for hiring more low-income residents, but they openly opposed the attack on Jones. Yet the representatives' overall record demonstrates the generally nonparticipatory character of the Los Angeles CAP. On less dramatic issues than the firing of a black social worker, they proved ineffective. Confused about the issues on the agenda, including complex budgetary allocations and organizational proposals, their criticisms were usually limited to one essentially procedural, if nonetheless vital, point: the CAA staff had not provided sufficient information, training, and support to enable them to criticize substantive policies effectively. Without the organizational affiliation enjoyed by the spokesman for public and private agencies, the representatives of the poor had no sanction other than their negative vote in the full CPC. The one exception proved the rule. An articulate and persistent Mexican-American, Ursala Gutierrez, obtained substantial poverty resources for her Community Service Organization.

A similar pattern of observable, but sharply limited, participatory activity characterized the CAA's staff. To be sure, the staff had sufficient autonomy from the mayor's office so that in 1966 they claimed to have registered eight thousand black and Mexican-American voters.

But community organization work itself varied considerably from neighborhood to neighborhood, as the NSCs, typically enough, operated rather independently of both Jones and Maldanado. Indeed each NSC directly reflected the personality of its own director. One predominantly Mexican-American NSC established a buyer's club program; in Watts, center aides helped organize a tenants' union, numerous block clubs, and two buyers' clubs; in another area, the NSC director worked closely with the Welfare Rights Organization, participating in demonstrations against the Bureau of Public Assistance; and, in a fourth community, the program assisted a variety of existing community organizations, such as buyers' clubs, a credit union, and several block clubs.

Yet the decentralization which bred autonomy and therefore these scattered instances of participation also prevented any more sustained efforts to reinforce one another or to develop any broad impact on the political life of their particular areas, let alone all of Los Angeles. Moreover, as directors changed, the NSC programs became less participatory. The scattered instances of community organization evident in the beginning had almost totally disappeared a year later. Responding to CAA's own organizational imperatives, pressure by established agencies, and mayoral concern, NSCs concentrated more on manpower development. Indeed, in 1967 the entire operation was transferred to the Department of Labor's manpower development program, entirely ending its participatory focus.

In the end, power dispersion worked to the advantage of entrenched institutions. The coalitions that had challenged Yorty avoided total defeat, but they were never strong enough to capture the program and gradually declined in influence. The CAA staff, responsible to government officials unenthusiastic about widespread minority group participation, was itself too divided internally to defend participation in the face of a long-term national trend away from an attack on political poverty.

DETROIT: CLASS POLITICS AND BLACK PARTICIPATION

Of the five cities, Detroit ranked second only to New York in its level of participation. The Detroit CAA's clearly proparticipatory policy seemed the almost certain, if somewhat indirect, consequence of the United Automobile Workers' (UAW) socially progressive influence on Detroit politics. On the other hand, the limits on participation can also be traced to the entrenched, impersonal, impermeable administrative apparatus that had been created by urban reformers a generation earlier.

Detroit is indeed a union town. Its dominant union had from its founding an abiding commitment to pursue its goals politically as well as through collective bargaining. But the UAW's political influence was not only due to the central importance of the automobile industry to the welfare of the city but also to the nonpartisan, patronage-free character of local politics. The absence of a powerful party machine enabled the union to penetrate the Democratic party in state and national politics and build a formally nonpartisan, liberal coalition in local politics.[24] As the Sarasohns have reported, though these efforts were spectacularly successful in the partisan world of state and national contests, appreciable if uneven gains were made locally as well.[25] And as James Q. Wilson has observed, this alliance, because it depended so heavily on black votes, contributed more or less directly to the emergence of a black community with unusual sophistication and organizational resources.[26] For example, the UAW trained its black members in the techniques of political organization and precinct work in order to strengthen Democratic and prolabor support in black areas, and it systematically cooperated with the liberal members of the black middle class.

Equally important, the many blacks among the union's rank and file were profoundly if less overtly affected by their union's unusually militant tradition.[27] The 1930s' depression-generated battle between labor and management in the automobile industry left a legacy of class identification and awareness in Detroit and Michigan politics almost comparable to class consciousness in western European countries. Certainly, it is unmatched in any large metropolitan area in the United States. Leggett, for example, has shown that in Detroit class sentiments are actively recognized and shared by ordinary workers to a degree without parallel in national samples of workers' attitudes.[28] Originally, black unionists adhered strictly to this class orientation on economic issues when the union supported liberal whites in state and national elections. But later they adopted an actively independent stand on racial issues. By the 1960s black leaders inside and outside the union began to criticize the unions' dominant Reuther faction for ignoring black interests. In the 1961 mayoral election they broke most dramatically from the rest of the UAW to support Jerome P. Cavanagh, who had attacked a police "crackdown" in black neighborhoods. Indeed, they used the black campaign workers trained by the UAW to help Cavanagh win overwhelming support in black precincts.

Cavanagh also had been helped by more general voter discontent over Detroit's heavy unemployment in the 1960–1961 recession. But he recognized his obvious debt to the black community which supported him at a time when business and labor leaders had closed their ranks against him. Since the city had failed to obtain juvenile delinquency funds,

Cavanagh was particularly anxious that Detroit's poverty program be funded early and heavily. Cavanagh established a CPC in June 1964 before OEO's participatory emphasis became clear (indeed, before Congress had passed the Economic Opportunity Act). Even then he appointed, as did no other mayor in the five cities, a number of black leaders to the policy-making body, including the executive director of the Urban League, a NAACP board member, and a black Baptist minister, all of whom had been relatively outspoken on civil rights.*

A number of black leaders were still unsatisfied, however, and a group of them asked the mayor for a private meeting to discuss the CAA. At that meeting Cavanagh agreed that black officials would direct the program and promised to ensure substantial black representation on the CPC. Without further agitation, the CAA developed a plan for six NSCs, whose neighborhood councils would be chosen at meetings attended by representatives of each neighborhood's community organizations. Each neighborhood council, in turn, would elect two representatives to the CPC. Later, it became clear that financial constraints would permit the establishment of NSCs in only four poverty areas, which meant only eight representatives of the poor would be chosen to sit on the thirty-one-seat CPC. But at the request of one of these eight representatives, the four neighborhood councils were each allowed to choose four representatives, thereby doubling their representation. The mayor's quick response to these requests for black influence on policy-making bodies can be attributed in part to the close working relationship Cavanagh had established with his black allies. Cavanagh also knew that the black community had both a relatively large number of able administrators who could be brought into the program as well as the organizational resources for effective protest if he resisted their demands.

Consistent with Cavanagh's decision, the CAA recruited for its staff many leaders from important, even militant black groups in the city. These officials included members, officers, and staff of the Urban League, NAACP, Congress on Racial Equality (CORE), the Student Nonviolent Co-ordinating Committee (SNCC), the West Central Organization organized by Saul Alinsky, and black union officials who had supported Cavanagh in 1961. A CPC member and later chairman of the important subcommittee on participation was none other than Richard T. Austin, who in 1969 became the first black mayoral candidate to win a place in

---

* Detroit's CAA was called the Mayor's Committee for Total Action Against Poverty. After March 3, 1967 the name was changed to the Mayor's Committee for Human Resources Development. The CPC was known as the Policy Advisory Committee. The NSCs were called Community Development Centers, and their NPCs were identified as Area Advisory Committees.

the two-person run-off election. Civil rights organizations were so involved that a critical sociologist could only observe that "the major civil rights groups in Detroit have well established channels of influence over the CAA—so well established, in fact, that the CAA may also have certain subtle informal authority over the civil rights groups."[29]

Not only did the CAA recruit a proparticipatory staff, but the neighborhood poverty councils exercised considerable influence on program development. The agency hired six area residents as Target Area Consultants, who reacted to and criticized project proposals from a client's perspective, and who also provided the NPCs with an alternative to the information it received from the CAA staff. With the consultants' help, the NPCs were able to rewrite proposals to provide, among other things, for more community aide and counselor aide positions that offered employment for local residents. NPC pressure also made it easier for low-income residents with limited formal education to obtain these jobs. Indeed, the NPCs became sufficiently important so that several of their members developed a new political role, that of "professional representative of the poor." Lena Bivens and Julian Witherspoon, both prominent NPC officers and representatives to the CPC, became familiar public figures. They complained to both the press and city officials about certain aspects of the Detroit CAP and more generally articulated black interests with increasing skill and effectiveness, something almost unknown in the Chicago, Philadelphia, and Los Angeles programs.

The Detroit CAA also followed a participatory policy in its often substantial support for various community organizations. For example, Goodman reported in 1966 that in one community "the Virginia Park Citizens' Service Corporation has been dickering with the DHC (Detroit Housing Commission) for more than a year and a half over just what powers the corporation—which is fairly representative of residents in the neighborhood—is to have in surveying and planning for the area's rehabilitation. . . . [The CAA] has provided a fair amount of staff assistance to this group, which is led by a [poverty council member]. . . ."[30] In another area of the city, CAA organizers intervened on behalf of tenants demanding enforcement of the city's building code, even though these activities were known to arouse the ire of health department personnel. In other instances the NSCs helped community organizations to demand improved government services, registered voters, developed low-cost housing projects, and improved their members' buying practices.[31] And the CAA was also "instrumental in . . . recruiting area residents for citizens' review boards in most of the city's police precincts."[32] In sum, representatives and organizations of the poor at neighborhood and city-wide levels used CAA resources to develop a base of power with which to influence a wide variety of city policies. The poverty program, and later the Model Cities program—which was at least initially influenced by many NPC members—would become institutional bases of power for an increasingly strong and militant black leadership.[33]

Yet the bureaucratic character of Detroit's CAP placed certain limits on the level of participation in the city. CAA staff members were in every respect employees of the city, not of neighborhood poverty councils. Since they enjoyed the protection of the civil service system, essential control of the program was kept in the hands of government officials. The CPC and NPCs were formally designated as *advisory* committees, and because the committees' approval of programs was not *required,* rushed and harried officials often found pressing administrative reasons to forgo the lengthy process of consulting with the councils. Partly for this reason, attendance at NPC meetings fell to less than half the total membership. The case of the Urban Slums Employment Program illustrates this pattern fairly well. Initially, the relevant proposals in one of the areas were developed with the participation of NPC and Target Area Consultants. But after this proposal had been rejected by OEO, a revised version had to be submitted within two weeks, and CAA officials rewrote the plan without consulting NPC members. Moreover, they limited participation in this program to the actual recipients of its service, thereby excluding most residents with enough experience and skill to articulate client interests effectively.

These limits on participation were a product of Detroit's entrenched, impermeable administrative structure, created by the city's successful reformers generations earlier. While the reform of the party system permitted a strong union and later black community activists to play major roles in electoral politics, comparable reforms of Detroit's administrative structure precluded the translation of electoral power into equally effective control over policy. For one thing, the mayor had only limited control over the administrative structure through which he was supposed to govern. Bureaucrats were so protected by civil service regulations vigorously enforced by a strong, independent civil service commission that the mayor had great difficulty appointing reliable allies within administrative agencies. After the 1967 Detroit riots, the mayor, hoping to take advantage of the city's sense of crisis, tried to capitalize on the report of the city's riot commission when it proposed greater centralization of authority within the office of the mayor. But the bureaucracies were too powerful to be defeated even during this period. As Olson has pointed out: "City agencies successfully prevented the consolidation of the municipal bureaucracy . . . by defending their past performance; petitioning for additional resources and manpower; discrediting the analysis [of the riot commission] . . . through a rigid definition of professionalism with the rules, regulations and standards attendant to that professionalism; and defending existing agency autonomy."[34]

CAP activists also had only limited success in altering policies of other administrative agencies. Even more important, the same civil service regulations were applied to the CAA itself, limiting the level of involvement of community residents. The civil service commission required that the agency be staffed by professionals and that nonprofessionals be hired by supposedly objective tests measuring performance competence. The Cavanagh administration itself was reluctant to allow the program to become an agent of community, rather than mayoral, objectives. The mayor had such limited authority in other policy areas that he wished to keep at least some substantial control over this new federal program. In short, the CAP program, like so many other city agencies, became a professionally run, bureaucratically administered program consistent with the ideals of reformers a generation earlier. But these reform institutions only qualified—they did not entirely negate—Detroit's responsiveness to black pressures for participation. These demands had been articulated so skillfully because of the resources, organizational capacities, and concern for collective political action that the black community had learned from Detroit's labor movement. And, by comparison with most other large cities, black leaders had indeed substantially shaped the poverty program.

NEW YORK CITY: THE POLITICS OF GROUPS

If New York City is the rational coordinator's nightmare, it is the pluralist's dream. It is no accident that every major work on New York City politics has depended heavily on the group approach of Bentley, Herring, and Truman.[35] Although Sartori may be right in claiming that the concept "group," as some group theorists have defined it, refers to everything and therefore to nothing,[36] a more limited definition of this concept provides an approach that works best when examining political activity that is dominated by organized, active, aggressive, conflicting aggregations of people who have combined together to promote a shared interest. Nowhere have such interests been more frequently recognized, have potential groups been most likely to become "real" organized groups, have possible conflicts the greatest likelihood of breaking out than in New York City. If anything, the prominence of this battle among organized interests enables the group approach to order the data all too easily. Sayre and Kaufman's definitive volume, *Governing New York City*, perceptively examines the range of group pressures that constrain the policies of the various bureaucracies and particularly the city's elected leaders.[37] Theodore Lowi's analysis of the appointment process provides an excellent example of the ever-increasing influence of groups on the mayor's selection of his cabinet.[38] In an exhaustive treatment of the politics of school desegregation, Rogers identifies an incredible array of interest groups seeking to shape school policy from both outside and inside the system.[39] Indeed, the group approach has been applied in New York politics to some arenas where its critics usually believe it to be least useful. Michael Lipsky, for example, finds it helpful in explicating his theory of protest politics.[40]

The New York City government is particularly vulnerable to group pressures because city agencies are protected neither by a powerful political organization, such as Chicago's machine, nor by the obliteration of virtually all organizing devices that are at times characteristic of reformed cities. Since La Guardia's administration in the 1930s, the Democratic organization has not been able to dominate New York politics. Tammany Hall suffered its initial defeats by reformers at the turn of the century; met even more severe reverses during the crucial depression years; and received a final, nearly crushing blow in the 1960s with the partial and somewhat temporary defection of Mayor Wagner, followed by the victories of Mayor Lindsay in 1965 and 1969. Yet as late as 1965, the reformers were not able to destroy the organization entirely as an effective political force and thereby establish a reform mayor as the sole center of power in the city. In particular, implementation of the reformers' goal has been frustrated by certain important city institutions, namely the borough presidents and the city controller, who together have great influence on the Board of Estimate, which can effectively check the mayor's policy. To obtain a majority on the Board of Estimate, a reform mayor must elect allies as city council president and city controller or, if not the latter, have support from at least two of the borough presidents, a feat which is not easily accomplished by a hastily assembled, disparate reform movement. The borough presidents, moreover, have certain powers which enable them to sustain party organizations even in the moments of reform glory. This fragmentation of power at the very top levels of government as well as the division of electoral strength between the Democratic organization and the reform coalition frees city agencies from close central direction and opens them up to pressures from the host of civic groups in the city. Inasmuch as both political factions must seek support from interest groups, neither side can effectively eliminate them from their spheres of influence within the governing apparatus. The vulnerability of city agencies to group pressures in turn encourages the formation of even more groups in the turmoil of New York politics.

New York welfare politics offer a good illustration of this pattern, for they were dominated by a contest between two coalitions of interest groups, the sectarians and the secularists.[41] The two major sectarian organizations, Catholic Charities and the Federation of Jewish Agencies, traditionally favored the distribution of welfare services to clients through private (sectarian) agencies. Accordingly, they preferred that public agencies simply dispense funds to eligible recipients, contacting them personally only to investigate their eligibility. All other public welfare programs, they felt, were best conducted through private agencies.

The secularists, on the other hand, favored a larger governmental role in the provision of services to low-income citizens. This faction included notably the Citizens Committee for Children, which raised money from wealthy New Yorkers to lobby for the poor, as well as the Protestant Federation of Agencies. Because the poor of New York have historically been Catholic and Jewish, the Protestant Federation is much smaller than the other sectarian agencies. To meet the needs of Negroes and Puerto Ricans (whose Catholicism has been far less fervent than that of the Irish or the Italians), Protestants joined secularists in favoring an active government role. In order to develop programs outside the control of the large sectarian federations, whose influence was greatest at the citywide level, they supported suggestions that leaders of neighborhood groups undertake the planning of programs for their neighborhoods. The secularists thus helped establish the juvenile delinquency programs in Manhattan both on the Lower East Side and in Harlem.

In contrast to Chicago's juvenile delinquency program, these agencies, Haryou-Act in Harlem and Mobilization for Youth (MFY) on the Lower East Side, quickly became autonomous. At the same time, both organizations conformed to the general New York political climate by seeking to expand their influence and control over governmental programs in their community. MFY, in particular, became involved in such militant activities as criticizing local schools and welfare investigators, registering voters, and promoting the 1964 March on Washington. Both these juvenile delinquency programs, themselves products of New York's extravagant group activity, contributed to the formation of still newer groups. For example, while the war on poverty was still being considered by Congress, citizens in a wide variety of neighborhoods of New York City came together to form new organizations which requested funding under that program. Leaders in other neighborhoods in New York City, such as Bedford-Stuyvesant and Brownsville in Brooklyn, the

Lower Bronx, East Harlem, and the Lower West Side, complained that their areas were at least as needy and deserving of federal assistance as Manhattan's Lower East Side and Harlem. Modeling themselves after the structure of MFY and Haryou-Act, they formed neighborhood organizations that demanded federal and city funding of juvenile delinquency and poverty programs.

At first, the Wagner administration resisted these efforts, asserting the city's right and responsibility to direct CAP. Paul Screvane, city council president, Wagner's personal candidate for mayor in the forthcoming election, and the man saddled with political responsibility for the poverty program, stated before a House committee his strong reservations about future funding of the ever-increasing number of poverty-oriented groups in New York City:

> We have been in the process over the last few years of doling out pieces of the City of New York to various groups that would come to it, such as MFY, Haryou-Act, Youth in Action in Bedford-Stuyvesant, and a number of others that have formed since. . . . And after you would delineate the area, fund the organization—a private corporation—they would say, "Don't come here with any of your services, don't let anyone impinge on our prerogative, because this is our piece of real estate." What would happen ultimately. . . . We would have a number of little private governments in the City of New York. . . . I am not confident at all that we would be able to solve all the problems we have with this kind of approach.[42]

But though city officials did not wish to encourage the formation of still more groups who could influence or even control governmental policy, they were too weak politically to prevent precisely this outcome. The very organizations that had been formed under the juvenile delinquency program, MFY and Haryou-Act, not only inspired other groups by their example, but took the lead in demanding that the CAP provide for the broadest possible participation of the poor, and, in particular, that it fund the variety of community organizations that had been forming in neighborhoods around the city. A wide variety of civic groups supported these demands, including civil rights organizations, secularists in the welfare field, and the reform club movement. Candidates William F. Ryan and John Lindsay, who were running against Paul Screvane, sought liberal, minority group, and reform support by attacking Screvane's conservative policies. Under this pressure, Screvane modified his position, and allowed not only some 40 percent representation of the poor on the city poverty council but also allowed for the selection of these representatives by neighborhood organizations. After taking office in 1966 Lindsay made a number of additional changes which further strengthened the influence of these neighborhood groups at the city-wide level. More importantly, NPCs, which were chosen by community groups, obtained substantial authority over local poverty-program policies and personnel practices, including the capacity to support a wide range of community organization efforts.

Not surprisingly, the autonomy which was eventually granted to the NPCs provoked conflict among competing groups within local communities. In each of the three neighborhoods investigated most closely in this research—Manhattan's Lower West Side, East Harlem, and Brooklyn's Bedford-Stuyvesant—competing coalitions of groups sought to utilize the perquisites that the program offered to strengthen their position in the community. This conflict only gave both sides another incentive to organize the community and to make more demands on city agencies for further community benefits. In the process CAP further enlivened the group life of New York City politics. Within a year or so, these groups began demanding influence and control over a variety of city agencies, including the housing and welfare departments and, most notably, the school system. In fact the poverty program provided the impetus to the community-control movement that eventually shook the New York City school system. "Maximum feasible participation" had the greatest impact in New York, an outcome perfectly consistent with the group character of the city's politics.

THE LIMITS OF CASE-STUDY ANALYSIS

These case studies have emphasized the factors specific to each city which have accounted for the participatory character of its CAP. Clearly, these variables—the power of the Democratic machine in Chicago; Philadelphia's "traditional" political culture; Los Angeles' disaggregated social, political, and governmental structures; powerful class-conscious unionism in Detroit; and group activity and effectiveness in New York—affected in each case the perceptions and calculations of individuals and groups concerned with participation. A comparative analysis, however, needs to identify common variables that operated in all five cities to produce the differential outcomes in participation.

Such an analysis might plausibly begin by considering as independent variables operating in all five cities some or all of the factors identified by the case studies. But when this is done for the five variables identified in these case studies, significant correlations are not obtained. First of all, when we attempted to generalize from the case study of Chicago, we expected to find an inverse correlation between machine strength and participation. In fact in an earlier article we ranked four of the five cities (excluding Detroit, for which adequate data had not at that time been collected) in terms of machine strength.[43] The curvilinear but generally inverse relationship that was identified in that article seemed to provide an adequate "explanation," especially since it was consistent with certain theoretical arguments and empirical data on political processes in the urban politics literature. Further research and analysis, however, has shown this interpretation, though not entirely incorrect, to be inadequate.* For one thing, when all five cities are included in the analysis, the rank order of cities on machine strength is only weakly related (either linearly or curvilinearly) to the rank ordering on participation.[44] See Table 1–2.

TABLE 1–2. Strength of Political Machine and Participation in CAPs in the Five Largest United States Cities

Machine Strength	*Participation*
High 1. Chicago	Low 5
2. Philadelphia	4
3. New York City	High 1
4. Detroit	2
Low 5. Los Angeles	3

The variables identified by the case studies on the other five cities fare little better in such a comparative analysis. If our judgmental rankings of the five cities on the extent of interest-group activity and effectiveness are at all accurate,† this variable which seemed so decisive in New York cannot be generalized without seriously mispredicting the levels of participation in Los Angeles, Philadelphia, and Detroit.[45] Table 1–3 shows the weakness of the relationship. Variation in the strength and class consciousness of the trade-union movement,[46] the factor which appeared so important for Detroit's relatively high level of participation, can be gen-

* Our analysis here differs from that in our earlier article in several respects. We now distinguish between political interests and ideologies, whereas before we talked strictly in terms of political interests; we now distinguish decisively between machine and reform cities; and we now stress the critical importance of authority structures in shaping the conflict. Of course, we are also dealing with the CAP more comprehensively and taking up a broader range of issues than was possible in the earlier article. See citation in Note 43.

† For all of these variables we agreed upon a rank ordering. Little claim to precision can be advanced, but the argument advanced in these pages is mainly heuristic, designed to show empirically problems of comparative research. If a positive rather than a negative argument were being advanced, it would obviously be necessary to justify in more detail the rank orderings of the cities on the independent variables.

TABLE 1–3. Influence of Interest Groups and Participation in CAPs in the Five Largest United States Cities

Interest Group Influence	*Participation*
Low 1. Chicago	Low 5
2. Detroit	2
3. Philadelphia	4
4. Los Angeles	3
High 5. New York City	High 1

TABLE 1–4. Strength and Class Consciousness of Trade Unions and Participation in CAPs in the Five Largest United States Cities

Union Strength and Class Consciousness	*Participation*
Low 1. Los Angeles	3
2. Philadelphia	4
3. Chicago	Low 5
4. New York City	High 1
High 5. Detroit	2

TABLE 1–5. "Traditional" Character of Political Culture and Participation in the Five Largest United States Cities

"Traditional" Character of Political Culture	*Participation*
High 1. Philadelphia	4
2. New York City	High 1
3.5 Detroit	2
3.5 Chicago	Low 5
Low 5. Los Angeles	3

eralized even less effectively than interest-group influence, as can be seen in Table 1–4. It was not possible to distinguish perfectly among all the five cities in terms of deference to traditional elites even in an intuitive, judgmental manner and thus in Table 1–5 Detroit and Chicago are given the same ranking on this variable.[47] Table 1–5 also shows that if the tie could have been broken, this cultural variable, which seemed to account for the rather limited participation in Philadelphia, would still have had only a very weak overall relationship with participation. Finally, the fragmentation of social, political and governmental structures might also be negatively related to participation. Although Los Angeles ranked as the median city on participation, the program developed along basically antiparticipatory lines, as fragmentation seemed to limit the political effectiveness of racial and ethnic minorities. Yet the ranking of the cities on this variable (Table 1–6) gives no support to such a generalization from the Los

TABLE 1–6. "Fragmentation of Social, Political and Governmental Structures" and Participation in CAPs in the Five Largest United States Cities

"Disorganization of Social and Political Life"	*Participation*
High 1. Los Angeles	3
2. New York City	High 1
3. Philadelphia	4
4. Detroit	2
Low 5. Chicago	Low 5

Angeles study.[48] In sum, no single factor identified in the case studies accounts for the variation in participation among the five cities.

Reasonable attempts to compute the effects of the five independent variables taken together do not notably improve matters. If we assume that each of the five variables independently, additively, and equally affected the level of participation (in the direction suggested by the case studies), one obtains the rank ordering presented in the row labeled Total at the bottom of Table 1–7. Yet Philadelphia has a less participa-

TABLE 1–7. Combined "Case-Study Variables" and Participation in CAPs in the Five Largest United States Cities

	Cities (in order of increasing participation)				
	Low participation		*High participation*		
Case study	*Chicago*	*Philadelphia*	*Los Angeles*	*Detroit*	*New York City*
Machine strength*	1	2	5	4	3
Interest-group strength*	1	3	4	2	5
Trade unions	3	2	1	5	4
Traditionalism	3.5	1	5	3.5	2
Disorganization	5	3	1	4	2
TOTAL	13.5	11	16	18.5	16
*TOTAL WITH VARIABLES DOUBLE-WEIGHTED	15.5	16	25	24.5	24

tory score than Chicago, while Detroit scores well ahead of New York. Above all, Los Angeles' tie score with New York City grossly mispredicts the levels of participation in the two communities. As can be seen by looking at the very bottom of Table 1–7, the results improve modestly at best when we double the weight given to the two variables, machine strength and interest-group activity, important factors in the two extreme cases. When they are considered to be twice as important in accounting for the level of participation, Chicago's position is more accurately predicted, but Los Angeles is now the most participatory of the cities, and New York ranks only third. Clearly, one does not obtain acceptable precision simply by adding together the factors that were deemed important in the examination of particular cases.

Of course, even if this attempt to generalize from the case-study variables had succeeded, this analysis by itself would not have offered much evidence for an actual causal relationship. Analyses with such few cases must first specify the processes linking political structures and participation policies and then show these processes to be both theoretically and empirically plausible. It is significant, however, that the quite plausible relationships identified in individual case studies could not be generalized. Indeed, this failure indicates a larger problem than the difficulty posed by the number of cases involved in the study.

This larger problem, we believe, is rooted in cultural differences among cities so great that similar structures and activities can signify quite different things to political participants. For example, machine strength or interest-group activity may have very different meanings to the residents of Los Angeles and Philadelphia: These structures may be regarded so differently that neither one can be used satisfactorily to distinguish cities, at least so long as each is defined simply in terms of the way it operates within a single urban context. It is for precisely this reason that the judgmental rank orderings among the cities were themselves so problematic.

The point can perhaps be illustrated more clearly by reviewing one widely discussed controversy in the urban politics literature. Banfield and Wilson claim to have identified a pervasive conflict in urban politics that is rooted in the political "ethos" of various community groups.[49] This struggle pitted lower-class European immigrants who preferred partisan elections in wards and a mayor–city council governmental structure in order to further their "private regarding" or "individualistic" preferences (e.g., for the patronage politics of the political machine) against middle-class, Anglo-Saxon native reformers, who preferred at-large, nonpartisan elections and a city-manager governmental structure in order to further "public regarding" or "unitary" policies (e.g., planning, urban renewal, and administrative efficiency). Much of the data that will be reported in subsequent chapters testifies to the importance of Banfield and Wilson's distinction between the machine and the reform movement. But in their test of this "ethos theory," Wolfinger and Field, in a comparative analysis of all cities with a population of 25,000 or more, found that within regions in the United States, no significant relationship existed between class or ethnic indicators and the type of electoral or governmental structures the city enjoyed.[50] Others have joined in the debate,[51] but neither side has evidently considered the possibility that similar governmental structures can have entirely different significance to participants in different contexts.

As it happens, three of the Illinois cities that Elazar studies in his careful analysis of varying subcultures within the United States illustrates this situation very well. In Rockford, Illinois, an attempt to establish a city-manager form of government failed, because the community was already so "moralistic" (to use Elazar's term) or "public-regarding" (to use Banfield and Wilson's) that citizens "saw no need to change their governmental structures."[52] In East St. Louis, on the other hand, when reformers promoted the commission form of government, it was quickly adopted since the machine politicians operating within the city's overwhelmingly individualistic political culture realized that they could control this fashionable new institution as easily as the older, machine ones.[53] In Peoria, however, the conflict was much as Banfield and Wilson would have expected; businessmen-reformers sought to establish a city-manager form of government in order to weaken the power of "private-regarding" machine politicians representing the immigrant community.[54]

These three Illinois studies reveal how much the goals that identical political structures are expected to serve can vary with the political culture. Just as "elections" mean differing things in different countries, so the meaning of urban political institutions varies with changes in the network of interpretations and perspectives citizens give to them. Even as Wolfinger and Field's attempt to generalize the "ethos theory" by means of a statistical analysis could not take into account these cultural differences, so we failed to explain the variations in participation by generalizing from our case-study findings.

The answer to this problem, however, clearly does not lie in rejecting comparative analysis altogether. At times, to be sure, cultural differences may be so great as to preclude all but the most trivial of comparisons. But when, as in our case, the focus is on a single program in a single national regime, mandated by one federal law, and primarily concerned with the deprivation of ethnic and especially racial minorities, a strong basis for comparison seems clear. There is, however, enough cultural diversity in the five cities to demand that we confront directly a major theoretical problem, that of satisfactorily formulating concepts that can be applied in varied contexts. In this study, which examines a limited number of cases, careful attention can be paid to this problem, because while the observers are close enough to their material to become familiar with cultural differences they can still specify the comparable social roles whose interests are affected by the policy at issue. We now turn to role-interest analysis, in other words, both because it indicates the necessary constants in social life, and because it recognizes the highly diverse and changing political goals that often are a necessary concomitant of differing urban contexts and differing historical periods.

CHAPTER 2: ROLE INTERESTS AND COMPARATIVE ANALYSIS

The case studies in Chapter 1 relied on factors too idiosyncratic to account persuasively for the observed inter-city variation in community participation. The problem, it seems, lay in the differential meaning of apparently comparable political elements in the five cities. In this chapter we shall seek to identify behaviors that are sufficiently regular, recurrent, and similarly significant among residents of all five communities, so that valid inter-city comparisons can become possible. Regular behaviors that have similar meaning for members of the community are usually patterned by their similar orientations and expectations. We shall call such patterned behaviors "social roles." These roles and, in particular, the interests that are associated with them provide the structural similarities necessary for a genuinely comparative analysis.

For the purposes of political analysis, the point of departure lies in the concept of interest, which is ordinarily used to link individual or group participants to valued elements in their social world. As Flathman has said, "In most of its uses the noun 'interest' denotes a two-termed relationship between someone or something (for example, a collectivity such as a labor union) and a substantive in which that person or thing 'has an interest.' "[1] These two terms in the interest relationship offer alternative means by which comparisons can be made among our five cities. On the one side, there is the substantive policy, a participatory Community Action Program (CAP), which is valued by some and opposed by others. Groups and individuals in the diverse cities can thus be readily compared in terms of their varying preferences with respect to community participation. On the other side, there are such groups as blacks, businessmen, and public authorities, who "have an interest in" (i.e., who would be affected by) the substantive policy of participation independently of their stated preferences. Comparisons among cities, therefore, can be made in terms of these participant's characteristics. For example, it is possible to identify variations in the size of the black community, the unity of economic elites, or the strength of the political authorities. Presumably, these characteristics might produce variations in community participation.

This chapter shows that neither of these approaches by itself persuasively accounts for the inter-city differences; to do so, they must be combined. Specifically, the analyst needs to inquire into the conditions under which individuals in relevant social roles recognize that their interests are affected by such important public policies as a participatory CAP. Such recognized interests are important because they often become the basis for political ideologies, which in turn provide coherence and stability for the individuals' preferences. Indeed these ideologies, as defined at the close of this chapter, are used extensively throughout the remainder of the book to explain the inter-city differences in community participation.

SUBJECTIVE INTERESTS AS POLICY REFERENCES

The critical ambiguity in the concept of interest centers on whether an individual recognizes the value of a substantive policy for himself (so that the interest becomes subjectively recognized) or does not (so that the interest remains solely the objective determination of an outside observer). Flathman notes that this distinction simply represents two polar ends of a continuum, with varying shades of recognition falling somewhere in between. "At the 'subjective' end of the continuum," he argues, "the relationship consists entirely of a psychological or intellectual attitude or curiosity towards or about the substantive. . . ."[2] This sense "is conveyed by the adjectival form 'interesting.' "[3]

According to a number of political scientists, this is the only way in which the concept of interest can appropriately be used. David Truman, for example, notes that examining "interests that are not at a particular point in time the basis of interactions among individuals . . . invites the error of ascribing an interest to individuals quite apart from any overt behavior that they might display. In the scientific study of society only frustration and defeat are likely to follow an attempt to deal with data that are not directly observable."[4]* Indeed, this is one of the grounds that have been given for rejecting the utility of the concept of "public

* Truman goes on to note that "a 'becoming' stage of activity must be recognized as a phase of activity if any segment of a moving social situation is to be understood. There are, in other words, potential activities, or 'tendencies of activity.' " But he regards these potential activities as attitudes; he would not regard as scientifically acceptable the attribution of interest that was not subjectively recognized by the individual at least in the expression of attitudes he holds.

interest."[5] Since, according to this view, interests exist only in the subjective concerns of individuals, there are only interests of individuals in a body politic, not an interest that adheres to the public at large, a diffuse grouping that includes an endless variety of individuals each with differing values and goals.

Political economists also take subjectively recognized interests as the point of departure for their political analysis.[6] Just as economists assume that consumer interests consist of those preferences they have for economic goods, so political economists take as given the political wants and preferences (i.e., subjective expressions of interests) of the members of the political community. Any inquiry into whether these wants and preferences represent the true interests of individuals is rejected as unwarranted intrusion of the analysts' own biases into what should be value-free research. After all, they claim, who is a better judge of a man's interests than the man himself.[7]

It must be conceded that this emphasis on subjectively recognized interests does provide a basis for explaining inter-city differences in participation particularly if, with the political economists, we assume that wants and desires are *action orientations* rather than simple affirmations by the individual of what she or he prefers. Subjective interests, in other words, are revealed by the decisions an individual makes in political life. Specifically, political economists assume that an individual seeks to secure as much of a desired good as possible, until the costs of securing additional units of it exceed the benefits obtained.[8]

If such benefits are understood as action orientations—i.e., as commitments to pursue the goal in an efficacious manner, rather than as mere verbal affirmations—subjective interests do seem to facilitate comparisons of diverse situations. Specifically, individuals or groups can be compared on a policy issue such as community participation by carefully observing, in each city, the position taken by visibly important participants, the alliances they form, and their methods of exerting pressure. These steps would help to determine the size of each coalition, and how skillfully and enthusiastically it fought for its preferences. The observed differences in the pro- and antiparticipatory coalitions could then be used to explain the different policy outcomes. Since the focus is always on policy preferences about a single federally mandated program, it would retain the comparability so difficult to obtain through five case studies.

Such an analysis could explain our community action findings. As the data in Chapter 1 make clear, the proparticipatory coalitions were larger and stronger in cities that had more participatory policies. In Detroit and New York, groups favoring participation had the strong support of the mayor or, at least, of a major mayoral candidate; they had no such support in Philadelphia or Los Angeles where the CAP was less participatory; and in Chicago, where the policy decision was most antiparticipatory, those favoring participation could not even count on consistent backing from the press and private welfare agencies.

Unfortunately, however, these observations are not very illuminating; the assertion that strong coalitions are more successful than weak ones is so obvious as to be almost truistic. The basic difficulty with this type of analysis is its focus on explanatory factors which are extremely close to the behavior that is being explained. The revealed preferences of individuals are all that are used to explain their behavior. It is more useful, surely, to learn *why* some cities had stronger proparticipatory coalitions than others.*

These considerations may explain why, for all its apparent attractiveness as an explanatory strategy, few, if any, notable studies of urban politics follow such a strategy. Most seek to explain the behavior of individuals in terms of one or more social roles that they are performing rather than simply in terms of individual attitudes. Dahl, for example, explains the behavior of politicians in terms of the "powerful incentive" they have "to search for politically profitable issues."[9] "The style of Negro politics," says James Wilson, is "a function of . . . [organizational] maintenance needs which both arise from within and are imposed from without."[10] Norton Long argues that "structured group activities . . . can be looked at as games," which "provide the players with a set of goals that give them a sense of success or failure." He notes specifically that these games provide individuals with "determinate roles and calculable strategies and tactics."[11] And Sayre and Kaufman, to some considerable extent, explain the behavior of bureaucracies in terms of their "aspiration to be self-directing, self-sufficient and autonomous."[12] All these studies thus seek to explain behavior not simply in terms of the

---

* This question might well be answered within the subjective-interest approach by trying to explain the individuals' position on CAP in terms of their total complex of attitudes and the social and political contexts out of which these attitudes developed. This approach, however, is fraught with difficulties. If we concentrate on the participants' shared social context, i.e., the characteristics of each city, we return to the case-study approach which failed to produce useful generalizations. If we look at the particular backgrounds of each individual taken alone, we would have to consider an unlimited number of people, each unique in some respect. Indeed, since no two members of a coalition are exactly alike, the pro- and antiparticipatory coalitions would all dissolve into masses of differentiated individuals. It is in this situation, faced with such complete heterogeneity, that the analyst is forced to group individuals according to whether they favor or oppose a particular policy, thereby homogenizing all the individuals into one or the other group. Such inclusive categories, however, consider as identical the attitudes of individuals who reached their positions by entirely different paths.

individuals' attitudes but in terms of certain roles, i.e., the regular behavioral patterns that the individuals perform which constrain their behavior or give them incentives to act in a particular way.[13] Simply put, the interests which are associated with roles people perform affect their behavior.

SOCIAL ROLES AS THE FOCUS OF COMPARISON

This observation suggests that an alternative method of comparison, yielding more interesting findings, may lie in the identification of objective interests associated with definable social roles in a society. As we noted earlier, Flathman argues that we speak of both subjective and objective interests in ordinary language usage. The term "objective interest," he says, can be "used interchangeably with 'benefited by' and the phrase 'in the interest of' becomes equivalent to 'good for.' "[14] He adds that this use of the concept "minimizes the individual's own evaluation and emphasizes factors and considerations accessible to other observers."[15] Critically, this accessibility to outsiders indicates a set of characteristics which can be reliably observed and compared regardless of cultural differences that might, for example, characterize different cities.

Since the observable characteristics of any individual are very numerous, we encounter an immediate difficulty: assessing all the objective interests necessary for determining what is "good for" an individual is probably beyond the capacities of contemporary social science, at least if one considers more than a few persons. It is possible, however, to focus on particular segments of a person's life, in effect, to look at *social roles.* An interest can then be attributed to each social role that a person performs, and this interest can be the mechanism by which the analyst makes predictions about an individual member's behavior. This, in fact, is exactly what analysts have done when they have talked about the politician's desire for reelection, the police department's desire for autonomy, or the maintenance needs of black organizations.

An issue such as community participation aroused the interest of widely diverse individuals, many of whom were not politicians or members of established civic organizations. Thus, to utilize the concept for issues of this sort, certain characteristics of social roles must be considered. In the first place, social roles are clearly distinguishable from the incumbents who occupy them. Just as a theatrical role designates the part an actor plays in a drama, which he may leave when he is no longer on stage, most social-role incumbents may, more or less easily, leave their roles to be replaced by others. Role analysis thus abstracts a single cluster from the total set of an individual's activities, permitting the grouping of otherwise unique individuals into social categories. Therefore, in determining what interests are at stake, it is not necessary to know all the complexities of any particular individual or group of individuals, but only the main characteristics of the role itself.

Next, it is important to note that a role consists first of a set of regularized behaviors, and second, a set of attitudes, i.e., the expectations that pattern the behaviors. The constant repetitive patterns of interaction with other individuals that constitute a role's *behavioral regularities* permits reliable observation and description by outsiders, and facilitates the objective identification of role interests. These behaviors would lose their regularity unless role expectations, in response to certain cues, told role incumbents when and how to perform the role. Indeed, incumbents can perform their role successfully only if these expectations are mutually understood by incumbents of other roles in the same social structure, i.e., those individuals with whom they must regularly interact. Thus, most incumbents can identify deviants who diverge from appropriate role behavior. Although these normative orientations are often called "role expectations," because others expect role incumbents to perform in designated ways, we shall refer to them as "patterning orientations," because they regulate, control, and pattern the behavior of the incumbents themselves.

Any individual role incumbent, of course, may not approve of the activities that his role demands of him, but, whatever his evaluation, performance in the role requires that he act in accord with its patterning orientation. Over time, the incumbent is so socialized that the orientation is internalized; he or she need not think through anew the appropriate behavior for a particular situation. Thus, by referring to the norms regulating behavior as patterning orientations, we emphasize the impact the role has on its incumbents. And it is this very capacity to structure conduct within certain well-defined limits that makes it far easier to specify the standard for deciding what seems "good for" the incumbents of a particular role than it is to make the same judgment about the total social and psychological well-being of particular individuals.

In order to indicate the substantive policy in which the incumbents "have an interest," it is necessary to consider most roles in relation to others which are part of the same social structure. If the role is subordinate to other social roles in the social structure, we can assume that role incumbents have an interest in the structure's change or replacement. For example, workers may be said to have an interest in the organization of trade unions, or even in the total abolishment of structural arrangements by which others exercise authority over them. Similarly, blacks may be said to have an interest in racial equality. These changes would eliminate or at least reduce the presently subordinate character of the roles these incumbents presently perform. On the other hand, those in superordinate positions, such as employers or whites, may be said to have an interest in resisting these changes.

Significantly, however, a role's patterning orientation only regulates behavior within certain socially understood limits. The patterning orientation operates only within a certain *scope* which defines the role's boundaries; outside this scope, the role incumbents may act in ways which observers may find logically inconsistent with the patterning orientation. For example, even though employers seek to rationalize the processes of production, they do so only within the limits laid down by laws of fraud and contractual obligation. Again, although industrial workers are expected to obey employer commands, workers can systematically ignore formal orders prohibiting smoking or governing their work rate without being regarded as deviant. Employers covertly acquiesce in these practices for the sake of industrial peace.

The specific content of role interests, therefore, typically calls for the narrowing or widening of the scope of the role's patterning orientation. If the role is a subordinate one, the interest is in narrowing the scope of the role orientation. Thus, trade unions, acting in their workers' interests seek to specify clear limits within which managers can issue orders.

OBJECTIVE INTERESTS AND COMPARATIVE ANALYSIS

These social roles are often sufficiently similar to make valid comparative analysis quite feasible even in quite distinctive cultural milieus. In the case of community participation, where race, class, and citizen roles were all relevant, the behavioral regularities and patterning orientations that comprised these roles were relatively similar in all five cities. As a result, we could make relatively reliable assumptions about the objective interests associated with these roles by calculating the apparent costs and benefits the policy would have for each set of role incumbents in the various cities. The analyst might then be able to predict policy outcomes in different locales, on the basis of the differential power relationships existing among members of these roles, without detailed examination of the policy preferences of the role members. For example, the analyst may hypothesize that the more heavy industry and, thus, the larger the number of blue-collar workers in a city, the stronger will be the support for welfare state measures. Indeed, some of the more quantitative approaches to comparative state and urban politics have taken just this approach. Lineberry and Fowler, for example, assume that homeowners are disproportionately disadvantaged by and, therefore, are likely to be opposed to higher property taxes. When they find a larger negative association between the property tax rate and the percentage of homeowners in cities with machine rather than reform governmental structures, they conclude that machine cities are more responsive to group demands.[16]*

In examining inter-city differences in community participation, one might similarly assume that individuals in certain social roles will pursue policies in their interests. One might hypothesize, for example, that those in positions of political authority would be adversely affected by a participatory policy that would lessen their control over CAP development. Inter-city differences, therefore, would vary with the strength of the authorities in each city. There are clear advantages to this hypothesis: It has an initial empirical plausibility, since many participants believed participation in CAP would sponsor attacks on city government. On the other hand, nothing about the concept of authority necessarily implies either opposition to or support for greater participation. Thus, the hypothesis is not obviously correct, and certainly not truistic.

On the contrary, it appears to be empirically false. During the period of our study, the mayors of the two most participatory cities, New York and Detroit, were not noticeably weaker than the mayor of Philadelphia, and commanded many more resources than did the mayor of Los Angeles. Even more troubling, the evidence contradicts the crucial assumption of the objective role-interest approach: that incumbents of the same role have very similar policy preferences. Of the six mayors in office during the period of our study, two (Cavanagh and Lindsay) actually favored greater citizen participation.

The objective role-interest approach has similar difficulties when it is applied to other relevant roles. Almost but not quite all the black leaders in our five cities did favor participation, but the organizational strength of the black community did not correlate well with the actual policy outcome. Chicago blacks seemed better organized than those in Los Angeles and Philadelphia, even though Chicago had the least participatory program. And Detroit blacks seemed better organized than those in New York, even though New York's program was more participatory.†

---

* This is only one illustration from their analysis. They make similar, if less convincing assumptions about income, educational, ethnic, and occupational groups. Wolfinger and Field have faulted this study for making assumptions about objective interests.[17]

† We could also hypothesize that the socioeconomic elites in each city would oppose participation in order to protect their advantaged position, and the outcomes would be less participatory where the elites' position was stronger. Yet this expectation is also inconsistent with the data. These elites were least politically effective in Chicago and Los Angeles, where the program was nonparticipatory. Even more important, elite groups were no more monolithic in their preferences than were the mayors. Many so-

The basic difficulty with the objective role-interest approach is its assumption that the policy preferences of role incumbents are as stable as the roles which these individuals occupy. As we have seen, however, members of the same role in different cities may have very different preferences. Different role members, even within one city, can have varying perspectives on an issue. Moreover, the same role incumbents can have dramatically different preferences at different points in time.

Indeed, what is especially significant and, at the same time, puzzling about the community action controversy is that it developed so quickly into a major political issue. Participation of the poor was not an idea that had been sown decades ago, which slowly gathered momentum, and finally blossomed into a potent rallying cry. Rather, the legislation passed by Congress calling for "maximum feasible participation of the members of the groups and residents of the areas served" was thought to be an ambiguous innocent phrase, vaguely expressing a long-established democratic tradition in American politics. But when the OEO began to implement the statutory phrase, large numbers of both black and white citizens, and both incumbent mayors and their political opponents had no difficulty in quickly assuming positions on the issues posed by community participation. And they adhered in most cases to these same positions throughout the controversy that followed. Given the rapidity with which the conflict emerged in the several cities, we are confronted with a central question: How could a single issue suddenly become so important to so many people?

As the previous discussion has made clear, explanations in terms of objective interests simply cannot take into account such sweeping changes in political attitudes over so short a time span. But neither can a framework which simply covers subjective interests or revealed preferences; for, as already noted, the real question is why the preferences changed so rapidly, resulting in the sudden emergence of a new pattern of conflict. The solution lies in identifying genuine, though contingent relationships between social roles and political attitudes. And it is this solution that latent-manifest interest analysis intends to provide.

LATENT-MANIFEST ROLE-INTEREST ANALYSIS

An analysis that focuses on latent-manifest role interests accepts the argument that interests can be attributed to social roles, even when members of those roles do not recognize them. The patterning orientations

---

cially advantaged individuals and their organizations seemed quite indifferent to the level of participation in community action. Those active in the reform movements in Philadelphia, Chicago, and New York were favorable to participation.

and behavioral regularities that comprise the role are so clearly observable that analysts can make reasonably precise statements about substantive policies that are in the role interest of its incumbents. We shall call such unrecognized interests *latent,* rather than objective, when incumbents of the role do not act in a way to improve their role's social position, so as to emphasize the connection between the content of the interest and the specific observable character of the role.[18] When members do act in ways consistent with these interests, we shall refer to *manifest* rather than subjective interests, so as to reemphasize their close relationship to the latent interests which are defined in terms of the role's observable properties.

As is true of the subjective interests discussed earlier, one can speak of manifest interests only when role incumbents adopt action orientations which search for the most effective method of achieving the goals specified by the interest. Often such methods may involve social conflict. Specifying a goal in this way is not the same as indicating the behaviors most likely to achieve it. On the contrary, to maximize effectively, the role incumbent may have to adjust his strategy and tactics in light of his assessment of the widely varying activities and intentions of allies and foes, both current and prospective, as well as of many other factors.

It follows, however, that to identify a latent interest is always to imply the hypothesis that under certain conditions, which affect the incumbents of the relevant role, these incumbents will not only recognize their role interest, but act upon it to improve their social position. But in contrast to those who restrict themselves to recognized policy preferences as their point of analytical departure, this means that the latent-manifest interest approach identifies *stable* and *uniform* social roles as the source of *varying* and *diversified* levels of political activity. Thus, latent-manifest interest analysis is designed to take into account the fact that in some situations two social groups—the incumbents of two social roles such as workers and employers or blacks and whites—may be living in apparent political harmony, while in other situations incumbents of the same pair of roles may be engaging in intense political conflict. Since the role relationships are identical in the two cases, it is otherwise difficult to attribute the conflict to the structural relations between the two social groups even though the actors themselves may claim, for example, that race or class relations are the point of the dispute. The latent-manifest interest solution to this problem is identical whether one is making synchronic comparisons of several cities at a single point in time or comparisons across historical time periods. The latter, diachronic case was Marx's primary concern, and the resolution he provided was one of his most signal contributions to social science. It will be useful, therefore, to look initially at the problem, as did Marx, from a historical perspective.

As Marx saw it, social analysis cannot adequately account for major instances of social change without considering the way in which existing structures contribute to their own demise. Yet, it is the very stability of roles within structures that creates difficulty for Marxian analysis. Certain role incumbents in some structures (e.g., workers) engage in conflict in order to create qualitatively new structures (e.g., a classless society). At the same time, they continue to operate within the old structure, working in the factory as usual. In other words, structures, while maintaining their own stability, may also "generate" a process of political conflict that, in the end, "produces" changes in the structures themselves. Use of the words "generate" and "produce" as quasi-causal terms suggests that a change in the structure caused the changes in the social conflict and, eventually, in other social patterns. Yet, since the causal agents, i.e., the stable structures, hardly varied, it is difficult to show how they accounted for the resultant change.* Although Marx would not use the language of contemporary social science, he was rather self-consciously seeking to use persisting or very slowly changing structures to account for discontinuities in conflict behavior.

In order to link stable structures to rapid attitudinal and behavioral changes, Marx pointed out that the role incumbents' attitudes about these structures could change very quickly. Moreover, rapid change in these attitudes often coincided with revolutionary changes in conflict behavior. Workers, for example, came to doubt the legitimacy of the role they were performing, and they felt impelled to act on their beliefs. They came to hope, and employers came to fear, that their roles would be substantially altered or even abolished. For role incumbents affected by such developments, it can be said that they acquired a manifest interest, on the one side, in effecting a change, while on the other, they attempted to preserve the structure in question. More simply, they became interested in seeking out the most efficacious way of accelerating or retarding social change. But the conflict between workers and employers that emerged so quickly can be understood only in terms of the latent interests that had always divided these divergent social roles.

Used in this way, the concept of latent interest may seem relatively

---

* It is barely arguable that changes in the structures could have produced changes in the conflict behavior of role incumbents. Marx did observe changes in class relationships which increased class tensions and intensified the conflict. But given the essential stability of class relationships, whatever structural changes were occurring were too small, too incremental, to account for the rapid changes in attitudes and conflict behavior that were a part of the French Revolution and subsequent periods of worker outbursts in the nineteenth century.

obvious to those who accept a Marxian view of false consciousness or a Freudian view of the repression of unconscious material. But it remains controversial for many social scientists[19] who, believing that latent interests are unverifiable, find the attributions of such interests inadmissible in scientific discourse, since such attributions, unchecked by empirical observation, are all too likely to reflect the observer's biases, ideology, and values.

The attribution of a latent interest, however, is not an act of evaluation by the analyst. However much it may grow out of his preferences, it may in principle be utilized by other analysts with different values. Nor is the attribution necessarily a description of existing preferences. Rather, it is an hypothesis about potential preferences, namely, that *under certain specified conditions* the role incumbent will recognize that the preservation or change of a particular structure is valuable enough for him to act with others in that role to pursue certain goals. As Dahrendorf emphasizes, the validity of this attribution depends upon its capacity to generate important and empirically justifiable hypotheses, specifying conditions under which role interests become manifest, and inducing role incumbents to seek newly recognized goals.[20] If the hypothesis is confirmed by the behavior of role incumbents, when the relevant conditions obtain, we have an empirical warrant for accepting the assertion of the latent interest. If the hypothesis is not so confirmed, or if the conditions are never observed, there is empirical justification for rejecting it.*

The conditions under which interests become manifest fall into two categories. *Triggering conditions* are the actual political and socioeconomic developments which induce certain role incumbents to treat the "structure" as problematic rather than continuing to take it for granted. The Great Depression and Franklin D. Roosevelt's consequent election in 1932 had this effect for American workers, as did the Supreme Court's school-desegregation rulings in 1954 for blacks. *Predisposing conditions* account for the greater likelihood of some role incumbents recognizing the interest more quickly than others. For example, those employed in the larger industrial plants in the 1930s or blacks residing in southern cities rather than rural areas in the mid-1950s were more predisposed to articulate their role interests than were other incumbents of these same roles.

---

* There are, of course, other quite obviously empirical components to the latent role-interest concept. The role to which the interest is attached can be empirically described. Similarly, the substantive policies which are asserted to be in the role's interests have a clear empirical meaning and, if realized, observable effects. It is possible, for instance, to describe quite unambiguously what is meant by more equal treatment for blacks by governmental agencies.

To remain "rigorously empirical," one might wish to limit one's analysis of social change to such triggering and predisposing conditions, which are empirically observable variables, whose relationship to attitudinal and behavioral changes can be shown by the usual methods of statistical association. From this perspective, it could be said that the 1954 *Brown* decision by the Supreme Court (a triggering condition) and the migration of many blacks to urban areas (a predisposing condition) are empirical variables that account for demands for change made by black protesters in the late 1950s and early 1960s. Intuitively, however, it is unsatisfactory to ignore the importance of the stable, continuing, and egregiously unequal relationship between blacks and whites when determining why the former so strongly supported the civil rights movement. To concentrate only on these triggering and predisposing conditions ignores three sorts of data: (1) Those individuals seeking changes were not randomly distributed in the population but were concentrated among blacks; (2) these roles corresponded to categories (blacks, whites, races, etc.) in the participants' own speech; and (3) the content of the sought-after change related specifically to the distinctive experiences of blacks, such as the denial of access to certain public accommodations. For these reasons it seems necessary to inquire into the causal connection between, in this case, a quite stable racial structure and rapidly changing rates of racial conflict. Yet, to ask about this connection unavoidably involves using the latent-interest concept or some equivalent to which another name might be attached.

In scientific terms, attributing a latent interest does not designate an independent variable which can account for change in a dependent variable. Rather, it designates a parameter or boundary condition that indicates the individuals, i.e., the role members, who are likely to recognize a certain interest. By specifying the triggering and predisposing conditions that help to make such interests manifest, one can then specify how the stable parameter operates, i.e., how it contributes to the emergence of the manifest interests. By stating the boundary conditions, we have, in turn, a warrant for making nonarbitrary explanations of differential pursuit of policy goals among incumbents of the same role (e.g., blacks), who act in different contexts (e.g., in Philadelphia and New York). If we did not attribute a latent race interest in racial equality, we would have no more warrant for asking why some blacks did not attack segregated institutions much earlier than others, than to ask the question of some other economic, ethnic, or regional group. Yet, clearly, given the content of these policies, we want an analytical framework that can provide a specific explanation for the acceptance or rejection of this goal by blacks in particular. The concept of a latent interest that becomes manifest under certain conditions is basic to the establishment of such a framework.* And only the latent interest concept, or some such equivalent, can relate stable social structures to rapidly emerging conflict over their persistence.

At the same time, identifying a latent interest also designates the dimensions along which the dependent variable, the attitudes and behaviors of the role incumbent, will vary. That is to say, such identification specifies the content and direction of attitudinal and behavior changes by indicating those goals which the role incumbents are expected to adopt. As a result, this approach can account not only for the very dramatic difference between a manifest role interest and an unrecognized or latent one, but for the more subtle differences in the *degree* of manifestness—the exact extent to which a given interest is recognized by the role's incumbents. For example, manifest interests may vary in the breadth of change that the role incumbent seeks to secure. A role incumbent whose interests are only partially manifest may concentrate primarily on the most specific economic consequences of conforming to the role's patterning orientation. Workers primarily concerned about improving wages exhibited an action orientation that Lenin termed "trade union consciousness."[21] Similarly, when blacks were actively interested only in improving their employment opportunities their interests were only partially manifest.

Incumbents with a somewhat more manifest role interest may become interested in changing the political as well as economic consequences of conforming to the normative orientations of their role. Thus some workers and blacks sought, respectively, to form socialist political parties and politically oriented racial protest groups.

Finally, a heightened manifestation of the interest among subordinate groups may mean a concern for a thoroughgoing transformation of social activities and patterning orientations. For superordinate groups, the heightened interest may mean the elimination of all obstacles to establishing a very wide scope for the structure's patterning orientation. The content of this highly manifest interest is as much based on the in-

* Obviously, care must be taken in attributing latent interests to specific roles if one is to be successful in identifying the parameters that will prove fruitful in generating interesting and verifiable hypotheses about the emergence of manifest interests. The attribution of latent interest will have empirical utility only if the role is politically significant, i.e., if it contains numerous or politically powerful incumbents. In addition, the benefit specified by the interest must be sizable enough and the role be of enough importance in the lives of incumbents so that the prospect of structural change or preservation will lead them to take vigorous action. One can attribute a latent interest to stamp collectors but it may not prove to be a terribly useful tool of social analysis.

cumbent's experiences in the role as are the more limited manifestations, but they are based on a broader interpretation of the nature of the role, and even upon its implications for the individual's self-image and self-definition. Marx characterized the consequences for workers of their role as alienation, and the authors of *Black Rage* have identified the consequence for blacks of their role as self-hatred.[22]

Manifest interests may vary not only in their breadth, but also in the intensity and energy with which the incumbents act to achieve them. At some point the individual's commitment may be so intense that no possible success could equal the cost of his efforts in time, energy, money, and even physical health and safety. He is then maximizing benefits more for the role incumbents as a group rather than for himself individually. In crisis situations, this intensity may characterize a large proportion of, say, all workers rather than a small number of devoted trade unionists, which is usually the case. Typically, the class structure is not that important to most workers, and other roles such as father, homeowner, or church member compete for the worker's attention. Clearly, these changes in intensity are relevant in understanding increases in conflict behavior as well as such rapid declines in recognized role interests as occurred among CIO workers in the 1940s.*

The latent-manifest interest approach, then, helps us to understand the remarkably rapid and widespread emergence of the conflict over community participation after the passage of the Economic Opportunity Act. Evidently, the act's passage was a triggering condition which helped make particularly manifest certain important interests, notably those of racial roles (see Chapter 3) and citizen roles (see Chapter 4). This observation, however, is subject to an important objection. It is obvious, that the interests of both racial and citizen roles were at least partially manifest in American politics many years before 1964. To take this fact into account, we must consider the impact of political ideologies based on social-role interests.

POLITICAL IDEOLOGIES AS MANIFEST ROLE INTERESTS

Manifest role interests are often particularly important whenever they have been fashioned into a political ideology. In this study, ideology designates a set of *interrelated, manifest role interests* which form a relatively comprehensive, long-lasting, and (to the ideologue at least) consist-

---

* The extent of the decline in manifest awareness of a role interest may vary with the degree of organization of role incumbents, a point first made to us by the late Michael Kepler.

ent perspective on desired policy outputs, on structural change or preservation, and on the methods of achieving these goals. Chapter 3 discusses factional ideologies, in particular those of racial and class groups, which are typically based upon opposed interests of conflicting roles. The regime ideologies we shall consider in Chapter 4 differ from the factional ideologies in that they explicitly recognize the citizen's regime interest in preserving one or more of the authority structures of the American regime.

This role-interest interpretation of ideology has two major advantages for empirical social analysis: First, it permits us to formulate more precise and complete propositions about the content of the ideology, i.e., the ideologue's support for or opposition to certain public policies; second, it accounts more adequately than do other definitions of ideology for rapid changes in the attitudes of ideologues and for the development of similar attitudes in very different contexts.

Because they embody social-role interests, ideologies, as defined here, evaluate any public policy in terms of its probable or observable effects on the roles encompassed by a particular social structure. By contrast, the political science literature has frequently used much broader definitions of ideology, treating conservatism, for instance, as status quo-oriented and liberalism as change-oriented.[23] Or, to take quite another example, the label "ideology" has been applied to any cluster of attitudes or voting patterns that have high intercorrelations on survey or roll-call data.[24] Our role-interest approach to ideology is far more specific. As used here, an ideology indicates the relevance of a policy for each individual by specifying the role interest that each hopes or fears the policy will serve. By referring to this social role, it is possible to anticipate the ideologue's position even on political issues that have not previously arisen, and to formulate empirical propositions accordingly.

Moreover, because these ideologies embrace manifest role interests, our propositions will refer to the ideologue's actions as well as his attitudes. An ideologue is expected to pursue the benefits favorable to the incumbents of the social role to which he is ideologically committed. Accordingly, to assert that some individual is the adherent of a particular ideology, the analyst must combine behavioral data with information about his attitudes. For example, if the individual engages in bargaining behavior consistent with his articulated political goals, and these goals correspond to one or more social-role interests, we may presume that he or she adheres to a political ideology encompassing these interests. If the individual's subsequent behavior is consistent with the presumed ideology, there is some warrant for using this ideology to account for this second set of behaviors.

As used here, then, ideological analysis does not pose altruistic motivation as an alternative to self-interest. It is not, in other words, a cultural analysis of the way in which an individual's political perceptions and goals embody or affirm the rightness of a particular social and moral order. Rather, because they do encompass manifest role interests, individuals may act self-interestedly in politics, even when they behave ideologically. This interpretation does insist, however, that the concept of "self" cannot always be simplistically equated with either the isolated, atomistic individual or a small group. In fact, as the case of participation in the CAP exemplifies, an individual may identify his interest with that of his family or friends, or with the maintenance of his organization, but he may also identify his interest with the condition of his race, or even with his welfare as a citizen of the political regime as a whole.

Indeed, by focusing on the individual's underlying role interests, this concept of ideology can also account for sudden shifts in the importance of an ideological movement and the similarity of ideologies in different contexts, two phenomena which cannot be explained by regarding ideology as simply a set of related attitudes. An ideological movement can gain many new adherents whenever triggering and predisposing conditions make the relevant role interests newly manifest so that the individual now sees a substantial benefit from pursuing some collective goal. For example, working-class support for industrial unionism from the 1880s to the 1930s varied drastically over time in the number of adherents and the intensity of their commitment. These discontinuities can best be understood if we assume that (1) for a period of years certain ideologues had expressed the moderately manifest interests of some workers; (2) the intensity of this core group's manifest interests markedly increased in a short period of time; (3) the interests of many other workers which had been relatively latent suddenly became more manifest; and (4) both of these changes could be explained by citing relevant triggering and predisposing conditions.

For ideological groups that have been continuously active over a number of years, a similar analysis may help account for shifts in emphasis in terms of the groups' political goals. Thus, Chapters 3 and 4 make clear that upper middle-class reformers and black leaders were able to form a new alliance favoring participation in CAP because this federal program made manifest in a new way those role interests to which their ideologies had been committed.

A conceptually similar stress on social structural sources can also account for the presence of evidently similar ideologies in very different locales. For example, while Chapters 3 and 4 base their specification of ideologies on *The Rulers and the Ruled,* a seminal work by Agger, Goldrich, and Swanson, the role-interest perspective offers a new insight into the reasons why these categories have proved useful in empirical analysis. To take one instance, Agger et al. maintained that some participants both in small towns in Oregon and middle-sized cities in North Carolina had similar Community Conservationist ideologies.[25] Yet this assertion is obviously somewhat inaccurate if it is taken as a purely descriptive statement about attitudes. Social and political differences, notably on the race question, necessarily affected the political preoccupations of the Community Conservationists in the two regions. Yet, as we shall show in Chapter 4, Agger, Goldrich, and Swanson did implicitly select from the complex of issue positions similar manifest interests based on the same social roles. As a result, these authors identified genuine ideological similarities; the two groups did indeed react similarly to certain new issues that arose in the late 1950s.

The relationship between the latent-manifest interest approach and the analysis of ideologies is reciprocal. As shown by the discussion of racial and class-factional interests in Chapter 3, and by the discussion of regime interests in authority structures in Chapter 4, a social role-interest analysis greatly increases the utility of ideology in social research. Yet, as these same chapters will make clear, it was through relatively stable ideologies that these role interests affected the behavior of the important groups active in CAP decision-making processes.

PART II

Interests, Ideologies, and Participation

CHAPTER 3: CLASS AND RACIAL INTERESTS IN THE POLITICS OF COMMUNITY PARTICIPATION

Racial role interests and ideologies directly shaped the struggle over community participation. Despite the confusion among administrators and legislators in Washington about the meaning and political significance of "maximum feasible participation," a diverse array of political actors in many cities quickly formed two coalitions with opposing interpretations of the phrase. Given the stability of the cities' social and political structures during this period, the rapidity with which these actors decided on their preferences, and then acted to implement them, suggests the usefulness of the latent-manifest interest approach in explaining the alliances that were formed. From this perspective, black activists in the various cities saw community action as a new instrument for altering the structure of American race relations. Their actions were taken because of racial interests that had become increasingly manifest as a result of the civil rights movement's campaign against legal segregation in the southern states.

The identification of latent black interests in altered race relationships is consistent with Dahrendorf's analysis of the conflicts or "contradictions" between opposed interests contained within a social structure.[1] In Dahrendorf's example, the conflict between workers and employers in the class structure was the dichotomous conflict that explained basic social change. But the obvious importance of racial concerns in the Community Action Program (CAP) controversy requires that race as well as class interests be seen as sources of social change.* In this study we shall speak of

* Dahrendorf himself noted that contradictions may arise from other social distinctions than those traceable to the ownership of the means of production. Our elaboration of race interests is therefore not conceived as a criticism of Dahrendorf's work.

Race and class interests were not the only ones at stake in the CAP. In Chapters 4 and 5 we will explore how still other role interests affected the course of the controversy.

such opposed interests—whether class or racial—as *factional interests.* Where factional interests exist, superordinate groups (e.g., whites and employers) have an interest in the preservation of the social structure in which they dominate. If they were to seek any change, it would be to extend the scope of activities patterned by the norms structuring role behavior. Subordinate groups (e.g., blacks and workers), on the other hand, have an interest in improving their economic and political positions by abolishing or narrowing the scope of activities patterned by these roles.

The concept of black factional interests thus parallels Dahrendorf's concept of latent and manifest class interests. Because the two concepts are so similar, and because class roles did have some impact on the politics of community participation, this chapter will begin with an analysis of class interests, then indicate the position of class ideologies on the issue of community participation, and finally undertake a comparable analysis of racial role interests and ideologies.

WORKING-CLASS FACTIONAL ROLE INTERESTS

Class conflict in an industrial society can be viewed as the outgrowth of the economic authorities' role interest in economic rationalization. Entrepreneurs continuously strive to increase productive output, efficiency and, above all, profitability, regardless of the adverse impacts on others.[2] Workers have a corresponding, but opposed, role interest in limiting the exercise of this economic authority. Historically, American workers have acted upon three distinct aspects of their role interests; they have sought changes in: (1) the orientation that patterns the worker's role; (2) the economic consequences of that role; and (3) its political consequences.

Patterning Orientation

The orientation that defines appropriate performance for employers is their readiness to exercise authority over what workers do on the job in order to increase the rationality of economic processes. The orientation that defines appropriate performance for workers includes a readiness on their part to obey these orders. Yet, such orientations do not necessarily include the negative or positive evaluations that either group has toward its own role, the role of the other group, or the industrial order. For example, a socialist worker may wish to change the entire industrial system, and may detest his own occupational role, but he could still conform to the role in order to hold his job. We can consider him a role deviant only if he refuses to perform as expected, e.g., a worker who totally fails to follow the appropriate orders of his superior.[3] Consequently, role differences between workers and employers are not a matter of degree, but a qualitative difference of kind. Although there may be marginal cases, particularly during transitional periods, generally one either does or does not exercise economic authority over others: One is either subordinate to that authority or one exercises it.* The sharp distinction accounts for the dichotomous character of class conflict, as it has been understood by Marx and Dahrendorf.

Economic Consequences

Of course, working-class protest has not always been limited to, or even primarily concerned with, economic authority in itself. Often, the economic consequences of their subordination to employers have been of more concern to most workers. "Immediate demands" for reform have typically focused on such specific grievances as working conditions, salary, and the lack of adequate provision for times of great financial need. These factors, in turn, can affect the intensity and scope of class conflict. For example, under some, but certainly not all, conditions, improvement in income and work situation has reduced political protest.[5] But these economic consequences of being a worker or employer make only quantitative distinctions among occupations; they do not divide society into two qualitatively different groups in such a way as to form a social contradiction. Not only are some workers less deprived than others on each such attribute, but some are actually better off than some employers. As a result, workers will differ among themselves, and can be disaggregated into distinct, and often mutually antagonistic, subgroups when these matters become central. If, as Dahrendorf argues, conflict between workers and employers is unlikely to disappear in the near future, he is undoubtedly right in attributing this persistence less to any specific grievance over income or working conditions, than to the employers' continuing economic authority over the workers, which will continue to generate new specific disagreements.

Political Consequences

A second historically important consequence of the workers' economic subordination has often been their exclusion, because of their status as workers, from full participation in the political regime. According to one

---

* Following Dahrendorf, we consider any official in a bureaucratic hierarchy to be such an economic authority if he has subordinates under him—including foremen in industrial factories—even if he is in turn subordinate to still higher officials. It follows that because they do not exercise authority over production, trade union officials are not economic authorities. On the other hand, because both farmers and bankers do exercise such authority, conflict between them cannot be considered class conflict in terms of the concepts used here. Rather it must be considered a clash of interest groups.[4]

influential sociological tradition, originating with T. H. Marshall, this exclusion has in fact been a central source of lower-class, often specifically working-class, protest in Western countries.* Reinhard Bendix, writing within this tradition, sees worker protest as a product of the transformation of Western European authority patterns.[7] In this transformation, the direct relationship between the worker and the state replaced the mediated relationship in which the lord—as the economic authority—also stood between the commoner and the crown. In this earlier phase, the commoner could establish his political identity through the borrowed greatness of his master.[8]

But once this mediated relationship ended for the hired worker, his relationship to political authority became problematic. The denial of the rights of citizens by the upper classes cast aspersions, Bendix argues, on the peoples' "civic reliability." "On occasion, this denial of respectability is tantamount to a denial of the right to existence."[9] The resulting political alienation, rather than economic grievances, fueled much working-class protest. In short, one of the manifestations of workers' interests has been their aggressive fight to secure their political rights.

MANIFEST WORKING-CLASS INTERESTS IN THE UNITED STATES

In the United States, the most significant of organized working-class efforts on behalf of their factional interests during this century can be di-

---

* T. H. Marshall distinguishes three kinds of political rights—civic, political, and social—about which workers were concerned.[6] Civic rights include First Amendment freedoms and fair treatment by the courts; political or voting rights relate particularly to the free use of the suffrage. Marshall's specification of social rights, however, seems to us not quite parallel to the other two. In his terminology, social rights include such matters as guarantees for a minimum level of income and social service. But these rights in fact affect the degree of economic and not the degree of political equality in a society. Social rights, from this viewpoint, refer to the same goals which would follow from the workers' trying to better their economic position. Unlike civic and voting rights, social rights, as defined, do not refer necessarily and directly to the citizen's relations to the political authorities.

With certain modifications, however, the concept of social rights can be focused more clearly on the political grievances of the lower classes. In this new version social rights would call for the equal treatment of all citizens by the political authorities regardless of the social categories—class, race, sex, religion, etc.—to which they belong. Social rights could then be said to refer not to the content of policies, as Marshall would have it, but to the criteria by which they are administered. When a group achieves its "social rights," both the allocation of policy outputs affecting the group, and encounters between the group and public officials, will be governed by impersonal, universalistic, and achievement standards. To stress the strictly political reference of

vided into three phases that correspond to the three aspects of their factional interests. Prior to the New Deal, the American Federation of Labor (AFL) concentrated on minimizing the economic consequences of the working-class role by protecting their members' pay, pensions, employment, and working conditions. As indicated by its reluctance to unionize large industrial corporations, the AFL did not represent a substantial threat to the economic authority of employers, particularly insofar as the federation explicitly rejected the use of governmental power to limit the freedom of employers to run their businesses. Rather, the federation's ideology of voluntarism exemplified what Lenin called "trade union consciousness," a concern with immediate economic gains rather than an attack on capitalist authority relations. Moreover, by concentrating on the needs of the most skilled workers, it did not articulate the shared interests of workers generally.

Given the widespread, persistent, continuing worker support for such trade union demands, these demands appear to be consistent with worker role interests. Yet the coral-like growth of the AFL is the very kind of development that can be explained in terms of socializing processes, a commitment to organizational enhancement, the gradual acquisition of a desire for material success, and other factors that do not require any attribution of latent interests. The utility of attributing a latent interest in mitigating the economic consequences of the role is shown not so much by the persistent pressure for increased salaries and improved working conditions as by the extent to which union leaders can mobilize otherwise apathetic followers to strike for these goals at short notice.[10]

This focus on reducing the economic consequences of the workers' role was supplemented in the 1930s with a broader attack by the new industrial unions of the CIO and the welfare state of the New Deal. Even though these new institutions were reformist, rather than revolutionary, in outlook, they sought to limit the economic authority of employers to rationalize the processes of production and distribution. Sweeping labor legislation, National Labor Relations Board regulations, and the organization of whole factories into industrial unions placed substantial and unprecedented constraints on the scope of authority that could be exercised by management. Worker concern with, and achievement of, goals that had been unobtainable for generations occurred so rapidly that a latent-

---

this modification of Marshall's scheme, we shall identify collectively the three types of rights (civic, voting, and social) as political rights. They correspond to three of the authority structures—constitutionalism, participation, and rationalization—which United States citizens have an interest in preserving. (This argument is developed further in Chapter 4, pp. 100–104.)

manifest interest interpretation, which emphasizes the sudden recognition of worker interests, seems unavoidable.

Interestingly enough, these developments followed a more strictly political phase, during which the workers' activities primarily changed the political consequences of their role. In the American example, formal citizen rights had long been secured for most white workers. But as of the 1920s, these rights were far from fully achieved in practice. The right to vote was frustrated by an unresponsive political system, so that turnout among workers was relatively low; the right to organize or to speak for unions was limited by injunctions and hostile police; and public officials often were less considerate of industrial workers than of other social strata. All of these matters were resolved with some success for industrial workers, although not all the American poor, by the mid-1930s.[11] The Smith-Roosevelt electoral realignment meant that the Democrats had acquired both political power and a distinctly working-class constituency that appealed to many former nonvoters. Legislation had greatly reduced the capacity of the courts to prevent strikes, and the first New Deal had created new governmental agencies which treated low-income workers with unwonted solicitude. Again, these political changes occurred so quickly (but have had such an enduring impact) that voting analysts have spoken of "critical elections," in which stable, traditional patterns of voting and other political activity were suddenly altered, establishing a new pattern. The critical elections of the 1930s cannot be fully understood, however, unless the analyst identifies some hitherto latent interest that surfaced sufficiently so that workers were now willing to act collectively to secure their political rights.[12]

Conflict over the political consequences of the workers' vote does not necessarily occur prior to conflict over the very existence of the workingman's role itself. In revolutionary situations, the two issues may be disputed almost simultaneously, as may have been the case in Russia. Yet, in regimes with strong traditions of political democracy where socialist revolutions have not succeeded, as, for example, in France, Great Britain, and the United States, the working class has generally won its political rights before it effectively curbed the economic authorities through the welfare state and a secure trade union movement. Both social-psychological and instrumental factors may account for this pattern. Since exclusion from the active polity meant "denial of civic respectability," removal of this taint evidently gave workers greater confidence in fighting for such economic goals as more generous wages and fringe benefits, and government-sponsored social insurance programs. And at least as important was the securing of political rights, including both the vote and well-established partisan allies, not only increased the workers' political resources in making demands on the authorities, but signified to the authorities that these demands were legitimate and must be heeded in the bargaining over public policy.

COMMUNITY PARTICIPATION AND WORKING-CLASS IDEOLOGIES

These considerations explain the reactions to community participation of two class-conscious ideological groups: the Orthodox Conservatives, as Agger, Goldrich, and Swanson call ideologues who articulate business interests,[13] and Orthodox Liberals, the term we have applied to ideologues speaking for worker interests. Orthodox Liberals generally favored the war on poverty, including participatory CAPs, because in its broadest intentions, it was an economically redistributive welfare-state program with a low-income clientele that included all races. Orthodox Liberals welcomed the extension of political rights to minority groups, in part because workers had secured the same rights rather recently, but perhaps more importantly because these minorities might vote for liberal, prounion candidates, which, in turn, improved the chances of obtaining legislation beneficial to workers' interests. For example, trade unions in all five cities had at some point tried to increase the number of black voters.

Many labor leaders and their Democratic party allies, to be sure, did not back the community participation idea at all. But their commitment to working-class interests had been so qualified by pragmatic concessions to business and other entrenched interests that they cannot be accurately characterized as Orthodox Liberals.* In particular, unions affiliated with the old AFL continued in the Gompers tradition of seeking, at least in local politics, narrow, immediate benefits for members of specific unions. Building broad-based coalitions through programs such as community action was not always compatible with such goals.

Those within the union movement and Democratic party who were Orthodox Liberals did support community participation. These were the most steadfast supporters of the program in Congress and within the executive branch. Locally, the New York Liberal party, dominated by garment industry unions, had its members attend rallies held by black and Puerto Rican groups; an industrial union in Philadelphia provided a hall and a public endorsement for black activists; two Orthodox Liberal Democrats, Governor Brown and County Supervisor Hahn, supported black demands in Los Angeles for a participatory program; and, in De-

* We shall call these more pragmatic union and Democratic leaders Liberal Pragmatists. Their ideology is discussed in Chapter 4.

troit, the United Auto Workers (UAW) helped train members of the Neighborhood Poverty Councils (NPCs) who belonged to community organizations.

The marginal impact of such activities was not due simply to the general weakness of Orthodox Liberals in American local politics. For one thing, the war on poverty had little direct relevance to the economic condition of employees. Although a massive assistance program for the poor might indirectly raise wages for the lowest-paid workers, the Johnson administration's war on poverty had no such potential. Moreover, as administered, the program was aimed more at racial than class groups; some of the more militant black leaders, who called for participation, were hardly reliable allies for Orthodox Liberals. Indeed, the Orthodox Liberals' typical understanding of social reform was not entirely consistent with the demand for participation in urban neighborhoods. Interested in amassing power for the working class as a whole, these ideologues preferred to build broad national coalitions, to centralize power, to operate through large bureaucracies, and to implement policies without regard to race.

As ideologues committed to defending the superordinate position of economic entrepreneurs, Orthodox Conservatives were opposed to community participation and, indeed, to any antipoverty program. To these business leaders and their spokesmen, the entire war on poverty seemed just another government effort to spend tax monies and perhaps to increase overall labor costs at the expense of profits. In rural areas and southern cities, where Orthodox Conservatives had substantial influence in local politics, even the attack on economic poverty was implemented very slowly. Of course, CAP had an insignificant impact on the actual costs of any entrepreneur. Orthodox Conservatives were ideologues who were opposed to any and all welfare state programs, and they were not enthusiastic about the extension of political rights to black Americans, which would increase the number of low-income voters, or about community control, which might place even some economic institutions under the dominance of black militants.*

But once the program had been implemented by Washington, its economically redistributive character had no further impact on businesses within local communities. On the contrary, the program was largess which if one community did not obtain its share would only go to another. At the local level, even Orthodox Conservatives had little interest in criticizing an economic war on poverty. Moreover, the size of the program was not large enough to threaten directly their interests in any sig-

---

* Even though capitalists are interested in economic rationalization, this does not preclude support for, or tolerance of, racial inequality.[14]

nificant way. Given the pluralistic character of the political systems of metropolitan centers, Orthodox Conservatives could influence policies on participation only through substantial exertions. Given these political realities, the issue was just not sufficiently central to the Orthodox Conservative ideology to merit their actively joining the struggle. Except for a few newspaper editorials,[15] few Orthodox Conservatives expressed their views in the participation controversy.

BLACK FACTIONAL INTERESTS

If class interests seldom became manifest in the participation controversy, the situation was quite the opposite for the racial interests of blacks. During the 1960s, the ascriptive distinction between blacks and whites replaced the conflict between workers and employers as the most visible and intense contradiction having the potential for transforming American life. Just as workers attacked three specific aspects of their subordinate role in the class structure, so blacks focused on three similar aspects of the racial structure in which they were embedded. The elements were, once again: (1) the orientation that patterns the behavior of role incumbents; (2) the economic consequences of that role; and (3) its political consequences. As in the case of the industrial workers, blacks initially concentrated on the economic consequences of their social role; then they sought to achieve their political rights; and finally, they attacked the patterning orientation of the role itself. This last phase emerged during the struggle over community participation.

The Imputation of Negro Inferiority as a Patterning Orientation

The patterning-role orientation in American race relations is the white imputation of Negro inferiority. This attitude has so sharply distinguished blacks not only from whites but from all other racial groups that it has produced a dichotomous cleavage in American society comparable to the possession or nonpossession of economic authority in class relations.[16] Accordingly, scholars such as Gunnar Myrdal have written of a caste division which cannot "be successfully crossed by education, integration into the national culture, and economic achievement."[17] "Caste, as distinguished from class, consists of such drastic restrictions upon free competition in various spheres of life that the individual in the lower caste cannot, by any means, change his status except by a secret and illegitimate 'passing' which is possible only to the few who have the physical appearance of the members of the upper caste. Caste thus in a sense may be viewed as an extreme case of absolutely rigid class."[18]

Traditionally, this caste distinction pervaded all social intercourse and received a uniquely entrenched position in state laws. Segregation laws were "written upon the pretext of equality but . . . applied only against Negroes."[19] By informal custom, titles such as Mr., Mrs., and Miss were reserved for whites, and some whites were reluctant even to shake hands with blacks or to have them enter their front doors.[20] By institutional practice, higher education was restricted, and by administrative order black soldiers, even as late as World War II, were generally kept out of prestigious fighting units and restricted to more "menial" services such as food preparation and support. The resulting social separation has led many black writers to argue persuasively that the meaning of being black in America qualitatively differentiates black experience from that of other Americans.[21]

Underneath this elaborate system of separation lay the whites' belief in their own biologicai superiority, as expressed by their preoccupation with racial identity, purity of blood, and the threat of amalgamation through racial intermarriage. These fears produced a cluster of taboos centering on the sex act and extending in attenuated form to interracial dancing, eating, and even athletics. They were sufficiently strong—and perhaps sufficiently important in reinforcing white privileges in other areas of social life—so that whites who systematically violated them were often considered to be traitors.[22] Even sympathetic whites agreed with this imputation of inferiority. One of the most humane of early southern leaders, Thomas Jefferson, in his *Notes on Virginia* came close to accepting the doctrine outright.[23] In the years before the Civil War, "even where the sentiment favoring emancipation was pronounced, it was seldom accompanied by a view that Negroes were the equals of whites. . . ."[24] And one hundred years later, during the New Deal, "frequently breadlines and soup kitchens were operated on the basis of race."[25]

Just as important, many blacks themselves, under the cumulative pressure of social, economic, and political discrimination, came to accept this white view, at least unconsciously, as indicated by the deference shown toward light-skinned members of the black community and the preference for such Caucasian features as straight hair. In analyzing the sketches of southern black children, Robert Coles was struck by "the feeling of worthlessness or inferiority they acquire, the longing to be white they harbor and conceal. . . ."[26]

Nevertheless, both the belief in racial purity and Negro biological inferiority, although widely accepted, have been riddled with confusions and inconsistencies which suggest another factor at work. As countless observers have pointed out, concern with racial purity was coupled with complacent tolerance for illicit sexual relations between white men (originally slave owners) and black women (originally their slaves). Of course, inequality was preserved in that their descendents, sometimes even those with only 1 percent Negro blood, were uniformly considered Negroes. Yet this practice meant that mixed bloods were never treated as some intermediate category, as is the case with the Cape Coloured in South Africa, which one might expect if biological factors were considered primary. At the same time, visiting Africans, provided they could distinguish themselves by dress or hair-styling, often encountered noticeably less discrimination than did American Negroes of any hue.

It seems, therefore, that the imputation of Negro inferiority is not only associated with physiological differences related to color, but is also linked to the meaning attributed by white Americans to the blacks' specific historical experience as American slaves. From colonial times, American nationality has been defined explicitly, or implicitly, in terms of an "errand into the wilderness" that had as its purpose the establishment of a "city on a hill," a new society where a new man, first (in New England) the puritan saint and then the entrepreneurial liberal, could prove his salvation by exploiting his religious, economic, or social opportunities.[27] By being brought here, by being exploitable capital* in a society so uniquely and single-mindedly devoted to exploiting capital, black Americans constituted the ultimate anomaly.

Slavery, the peculiar institution, distinguished race relationships from the competitive relationships among ethnic groups. Undoubtedly, as Myrdal admits, "Upper class people in all countries are accustomed to look down upon people in the laboring classes as inherently inferior."[28] And this prejudice was applied with particular force at various points in the nineteenth century to the Irish, the Germans, the Czechs, the Italians, and the Poles who were each in their turn regarded as inferior, dirty, stinking, and lacking much in the way of decency and self-respect. Yet all white groups, and even Mexicans, were generally thought to be assimilable.[29] Whatever the ethnic hostilities, no limitations were placed on immigration until 1920, and even then the legislation was passed as much because labor groups feared scabs and competition from immigrants as for ethnocentric reasons. The ease with which immigrant groups captured local political institutions, gained representation in Congress, and preserved many of their European customs dispelled comparatively quickly any notion that they were fundamentally inferior to native-born Americans. After all, no white man could ignore the fact that his ancestors were

* In this sense, because everyone knew that they could eventually participate freely in the social and economic competition, white indentured servants differed sharply from blacks.

at one point immigrants themselves. Differences in degree were obvious, and led to many a political conflict, but they could not be equated with the qualitative distinction that was made between black and white, as the much higher rates of exogenous marriages among ethnic groups indicates. Even more symbolic is the widespread usage of such phrases as "half-Italian," "part-German," or "some Irish blood"; Americans always considered mulattoes as part of the Negro community.

Thus, racial roles had a permanence both for the individual and for his descendants that was rooted in slavery, and had profound consequences for the social interaction between the races. As Pettigrew aptly summarized them: "The white must act out the role of the 'superior'; by direct action or subtle cue he must convey the expectation that he will be treated with deference. For his part, the Negro, if traditional norms are to be obeyed, must act out the role of 'inferior'; he must play the social role of the 'Negro.' "[30]

The Socioeconomic Consequences: Unequal Life Chances

The consequences of this imputation of inferiority extended to almost every facet of life, blighting, and making blatantly unequal, the life chances of most black Americans. Admittedly, this pattern does not apply equally to all blacks, some of whom have greater life chances than many whites. Nevertheless, St. Clair Drake is undoubtedly correct when he describes the overall picture as one of "victimization," i.e.: "A system of social relations which operates in such a way as to deprive them of a chance to share in the more desirable material and nonmaterial products of a society which is dependent in part upon their labor and loyalty. They are 'victimized' also because they do not have the same degree of access others have to the attributes needed for rising in the general class system—money, education, 'contacts' and 'know-how'."[31]

As Carmichael and Hamilton argue, this pattern of prejudice and discrimination, what Drake called a "color caste system," affected both institutions and informal customs.[32] In some cases, the restrictions on black life chances directly benefited whites. Excluding blacks from highly paid craft unions with carefully limited membership increased the number of openings for white workers. Limiting black access to skilled jobs in the factories and middle-level management positions had comparable effects. Partly as a result of these competitive handicaps, Carmichael and Hamilton reported, in 1967, that "a non-white must have between one and three years of college before he can expect to earn as much as a white man with less than eight years of schooling over the course of their respective working lives."[33] As Pettigrew observes in another, equally striking, comparison, "the floor of Negro privation frequently goes below [that of] the most indigent of whites."[34]

Since, in many cases, unequal black life chances do not directly benefit whites, their origins seem to lie in racial prejudice per se. The higher death rates of black Americans offer an outstanding example, and black housing presents a similar picture.[35] As late as 1948, two federal agencies, the Federal Housing Authority (FHA) and the Veterans Housing Administration (VHA), were insuring and guaranteeing housing projects where blacks were contractually excluded. Insurance companies, to take but one set of major private financial institutions, systematically avoided financing homes in black areas, even when the age and value of the home otherwise made it a desirable investment opportunity.[36] These and other policies meant, as Miller observes, that ". . . the black belt never expands as rapidly as the demand for housing for Negroes grows. It is constantly overcrowded and just as constantly expanding. Overcrowding means overuse of available dwellings and a constant decay dependent on that overuse."[37] Since residential segregation prevents the diffusion of blacks throughout metropolitan areas, many whites suffer substantial costs as well. In fact, the block-by-block expansion of black neighborhoods probably causes far more disruption to white communities than would a more fully integrated housing pattern.

Nor are whites significantly advantaged or helped by the severe damage that discrimination has inflicted on the social-psychological fabric of black life.[38] According to St. Clair Drake, "both income distribution and the occupational structure function to reinforce the number of families without fathers and to lower the prestige of Negro males vis à vis their mates, prospective mates, and children."[39] Careful statistical analysis suggests that this pattern may be largely a function of low incomes in contemporary urban settings, rather than any special characteristic of the black family. But whatever the source, this pattern seems to have characterized urban ghetto life since the Great Depression. Although Coles carefully specifies the elements of psychic strength in the black personality, he also reports that the sketches by black children which he examined "revealed their sense of fear of white people, their sense of a lack at not having white skin, their sense of foreboding at what the future held for them as Negroes."[40] Obviously, many of the sources of this psychological damage could be removed or minimized without appreciably diminishing white life chances, even though such changes would require substantial revision of racial attitudes.

Unequal Political Rights

These socioeconomic handicaps were reinforced by a more formal denial of political rights, clearly more disabling than that experienced by American workers prior to the 1930s. Southern blacks faced legal disenfranchisement by a variety of devices including grandfather clauses, white primaries, illiteracy tests, and rank discrimination by voting registrars. In the cities of the North, first the Republican and then the Democratic machines turned out black votes, but the corruption and bribery and threats of violence reached such proportions during the first several decades of this century that the act of voting fell short of free, democratic participation in the selection of rulers.*

This denial of black voting rights paralleled the denial of black civic rights, especially in the South, where free speech was systematically denied, and where black protest organizations were harassed by both public officials and private vigilantes. Even more striking, southern and northern courts alike treated blacks much less well than they did whites in terms of arrests, legal counsel, selection of juries, bail arrangements, sentencing, parole practices, and the imposition of the death penalty.[42] Blacks could justifiably question whether or not Constitutional restraints on law enforcement agencies had ever been regarded as being applicable in their case. Finally, blacks in both regions were denied their social rights in that universalistic and achievement norms did not control the distribution of public goods among races. As Drake observes, governmental expenditures on such services as public education, recreation, and culture were grossly unequal in both the North and South.[43] And when Marvick matched groups of black and white respondents in terms of comparable socioeconomic status, he found that black respondents were less optimistic about their treatment by governmental employees.[44]

MANIFESTATIONS OF BLACK FACTIONAL INTERESTS

If correctly formulated, a "contradiction" identifies two widely shared, but opposed, role interests with the potential for extensive social conflict. By this criterion, black-white role relations in American society clearly could be considered the source of a major contradiction in the mid-1960s. Obviously, the potential for such conflict was heightened by the gross inequality of life chances, by the gross denial of political rights, by the fact that blacks can escape their racial role only by insanity, emigration, suicide, or passing as whites, and by the intensity of white racial fears and taboos. In this situation, blacks could achieve full social equality, acceptance, and participation only by changing their racial role. Accordingly, three aspects of black factional interests have historically

---

* For example, Daniel Elazar notes that in East Saint Louis, though the proportion of blacks in the population has for many years been comparatively high, they had little power because a "boss" used the corrupt tools available to him to control the black vote.[41]

been the focus of black attention: (1) the equalization of life chances; (2) achievement of full citizenship; and (3) abolition of the imputation of inferiority, the expectation that patterns the racial role itself.

Booker T. Washington and Equalizing Life Chances

As in the case of workers, black Americans initially devoted most of their energy in the late nineteenth century to the economic consequences of their role, i.e., improving their unequal life chances. A concern with economic and social self-help, both individual and collective, particularly animated Booker T. Washington, one of the best-known Negro spokesmen of this early period. His emphasis on self-reliance encouraged indifference not only toward social integration with whites but also toward political activism and reliance on the state. Indeed, Washington's doctrines are remarkably parallel to the voluntarism of the AFL's Samuel Gompers. Just as Gompers focused on specific economic grievances to the exclusion of any general attack on the economic authority of businessmen (the orientation that patterned class roles), so Washington concentrated on specific economic gains rather than attacking the imputation of inferiority (the orientation that patterned racial roles). But for all his opposition to immediate social integration, Washington did seek a new pattern of social life in which individual black citizens would have life chances equivalent to those of whites and, as a necessary consequence, the thorough functional or economic integration of the two races.

As in the case of workers, the consistency and persistence with which black groups have sought to improve their disadvantaged economic and social position seems at first glance sufficient warrant for attributing a racial role interest in achieving this goal. The economic attack on poverty, which sought to provide better governmental services and greater educational and employment opportunities, was only the most recent of many economically oriented programs endorsed by black groups. Yet, the very continuity in these demands permits explanations that do not require a role-interest analysis. It could be argued by some observers that blacks have simply adopted American values in seeking economic advancement for themselves, just as every other group in American society has done. And if the attribution of a latent role interest were designed only to explain these readily observable demands for economic progress, its utility would indeed appear rather limited. In fact, however, the role-interest concept proves useful even on the question of economic betterment. Black goals did not simply include a general demand for economic improvement but reflected the particular deprivations suffered by blacks. And this perspective can be understood only by a concept which reflects that distinctive experience, not just a general discussion of the American value system. Moreover, these demands have emerged with special urgency and suddenness at particular points in American history, including Washington's own widespread popularity among his fellow blacks, continuing through Randolph's March on Washington to, more recently, the Poor People's campaign of the Southern Christian Leadership Conference and the riots of the middle and late 1960s. The periodic political eruptions can be more satisfactorily explained as the blacks' sudden recognition of their latent factional interests, rather than by any slow diffusion of stably held values among the black population.

Nonetheless, a struggle focusing entirely on the equalization of life chances could hope to transform American race relations only if it were part of a massive change in the general distribution of life chances. A society such as Cuba's, where blacks under Castro seem to be approaching a full equality,[45] might well eliminate the racial "contradiction" by means of a broad-scale attack on unequal life chances, the hope of such militants as Eldridge Cleaver. Yet, the history of radical movements in the last century suggests to us that a social transformation of this magnitude is highly improbable in an industrialized society such as the United States, with its entrenched traditions of pluralist democracy.

Short of such revolutionary changes, several considerations suggest that concentration by blacks on changing life chances is not likely to liquidate by itself the racial contradiction. In the first place, blacks themselves have differed in terms of their life chances. Moreover, the relatively advantaged blacks, in terms of income, education, or even physical health, may well benefit more from new opportunities than the most seriously victimized. Given the American propensity to recognize those who achieve, presumably equalitarian efforts to help the black community often begin by directing benefits to already successful individuals. Private insurance investment programs in the inner city have primarily aided middle-class blacks leaving the ghetto;[46] fair employment laws have helped only those individuals with economic skills. Even job-training programs were initially directed at workers with enough skills to be clearly employable.[47] Second, insofar as poorer blacks have enjoyed improving life chances, their progress may simply reflect secular trends affecting the entire society such as increased average per capita income, more or less stable levels of employment, and wider diffusion of education and medical services. In comparison, specific governmental or private programs aimed at the black community have had a rather minor effect on the life chances of poor blacks. Third, general programs and regulations designed to alleviate the economic plight of blacks cannot be applied to particular cases without the exercise of some administrative discretion. But if administrators continue to believe, even unconsciously, that blacks are inferior, discrimination may continue in subtle forms almost impossible to punish, prevent, or even detect.

The essential problem with limiting black protest to an attack on life chances is illustrated by an observation of St. Clair Drake. "American Negroes," he writes, "do not set the rules of the game. Unlike Negroes in Africa and the West Indies they do not fight for national independence but rather for 'desegregation' and 'integration,' . . . [which] in the final analysis, also means that the Negro community must increasingly become more middle class in values and behavior if it is to win respect and approval. Negroes do not determine the ends for which they struggle nor the means. . . . Even within the civil rights movement . . . white friends, even in left civil right circles often strive to bend Negroes to their will and not to ask their advice as co-workers."[48] This concern with life chances, in other words, cannot provide full equality, because it leaves too little room for the black community's collective effort under its own leadership. Even Talcott Parsons observed that "the healthiest line of development will be not only the preservation but the actual building up of the solidarity of the Negro community in the sense that being a Negro has positive value."[49]

The Civil Rights Movement and Political Rights

In contrast to Washington and the black businessmen and politicians who followed his lead in trying to equalize life chances, the civil rights movement focused clearly and explicitly on addressing the blacks' political deprivations. The demands for changes in the political regime were powerfully articulated early in this century by W. E. B. DuBois of the National Association for the Advancement of Colored People (NAACP). Beginning before the NAACP court cases against legal disenfranchisement of southern blacks, and continuing with the voter-registration drives of the fifties and sixties, voting rights were always a continuing concern of the movement. Denial of the right of free speech and the right to organize sparked civil-disobedience campaigns and aditional court suits, as the NAACP, in particular, fought for its Constitutional right to exist in many southern states. Blacks also showed concern for their civic rights in their attacks on the white jury system, use of coerced confessions, and denial of legal facilities to black indigents. But, above all, they sought the social right to equitable treatment by public officials through the celebrated *School Segregation Cases* of 1954 and by the continuing manifold attempts to secure its implementation not only with respect to schools but also parks, public transportation, swimming areas, and finally, in all places of public accommodation. And it was on this issue that Martin Luther King, Jr. rose to fame by organizing boycotts in 1955 and 1956 against the segregated buses in Montgomery, Alabama. From there the civil rights movement moved to the North, attacking *de facto* school desegregation by means of boycotts, sit-ins, and public demonstrations.

Clearly, the rapid surge of protest among the black masses after the Supreme Court decision in 1954 cannot be understood without identifying a latent black interest in political rights. Of course, the protests had historical antecedents, most notably the quiet, patient work of a few lawyers in the NAACP since the early 1920s. But this effort by an elite cadre could not have received such massive public support so quickly in the 1950s had not there been a continuing black interest in these rights. Just as the denial of political rights to nineteenth-century European workers generated intense protest,[50] after 1954 blacks protested the state's denials of their civic equality and political efficacy.

To be sure, certain predisposing and triggering conditions were necessary before this latent interest became manifest. And, interestingly enough, these conditions were similar for both European workers and American blacks, whose political deprivations were comparable. In the first place, each group needed sufficient individual and collective resources to permit political activity. John Stuart Mill summarized some of these factors as they applied to the workers:

> . . . of the working men, at least in the most advanced countries of Europe, it may be pronounced certain that the patriarchal or paternal system of government is one to which they will not again be subject. That question was decided, when they were taught to read, and allowed access to newspapers and political tracts; when they were brought together in numbers, to work socially under the same roof; when railways enabled them to shift from place to place, and change their patrons and employers as easily as their coats; when they were encouraged to seek a share in the government, by means of the electoral franchise.[51]

Second, workers needed a leadership strata with appropriate organizational and ideological skills. In Mill's words, again, workers were mobilized "when dissenting preachers were suffered to go among them, and appeal to their faculties and feelings in opposition to the creeds professed and countenanced by their superiors."[52] Third, the history of worker protest also suggests the importance of a prior struggle for political rights by another, probably socially a less-disadvantaged group, and, finally, a precipitating event that identifies the illegitimacy of preexisting patterns.

These same conditions facilitated black protest. The process of industrialization, especially during the labor shortages of World Wars I and II, offered new job opportunities for many blacks and provided an economic base for the emergence of a black middle-class which felt free to support civil rights efforts. And, particularly in large cities, the anonymity of urban life made it much harder to intimidate those blacks who spoke out for civil rights. Moreover, racial segregation in northern cities provided a stable geographical base for civic and political activities which added to the black community's organizational skills. Clearly, the protests launched by the civil rights movement were triggered by the 1954 *School Segregation Cases,* which, for the first time in this century, unequivocally legitimatized the demand for—although it did not by itself secure—black citizen rights. And, finally, just as black protests have generated new demands for recognition by Indians, Puerto Ricans, Mexican-Americans, and women, the black protests themselves were facilitated by the successful efforts of the industrial workers in the 1930s to achieve their political rights. In fact, participation in the efforts of trade unions and Democratic party organizations helped spread invaluable political experience and skills in the black community.

Triggering and predisposing conditions facilitated the rapid surge in demands for political rights. Yet, by themselves, they do not account for the rapid transformation in the political consciousness of black people. Only an assumption that identifies a latent interest in these rights even in quiescent times accounts for the speed of this change in attitude about the long-established pattern of American race relations.

The demand for political rights had a much more dramatic political impact than Booker T. Washington's focus on the economic consequence of the racial role, partly because of the widespread white support that these political protests attracted. The sudden outpouring of public backing for civil rights legislation in 1964 and 1965 can be too easily forgotten; its support went far beyond the usual bounds of the liberal community. This support (and the rapidity with which important segments of white opinion changed) was itself due to appeals to the long-standing beliefs in such values as freedom of speech, the right to vote, and equal treatment by the government. One could describe this change of white opinion in terms of the tension between American ideals and racial practices which Myrdahl characterized as the "American dilemma." But egalitarian and humanitarian commitment to blacks, though long important for some small cadre of white liberals, had for years only a modest impact on the condition of black people. Not until black Americans were able to mobilize and broadcast their demands, by means of court suits and mass demonstrations, did they arouse wide elements of white support, a phenomenon we shall consider more extensively in Chapter 4's discussion of regime interests and authority relationships.

As significant as was the thrust for political rights, it was highly unlikely to eliminate the racial contradiction by itself. If an attempt to eliminate black inferiority by focusing on its economic consequences could succeed only in a Marxian utopia, an attack on its political consequences can eliminate the role only in a liberal utopia, where political participation is so extensive, so all-embracing, so inclusive of all social life, that equality as citizens is tantamount to social equality. During the Eisenhower and early Kennedy years, some such myth helped sustain the great interest in voting-rights legislation. This liberal utopia also sustains those, like Talcott Parsons, who favor the wider application of "universalistic norms" in order to further "the emancipation of individuals of all categories from . . . diffuse particular distinct solidarities."[53] Thus, Parsons demands of all ascriptive communities that they "relinquish certain of the controls over [their members] which they previously exercised."[54] In sum, he says, "these civil rights demands in [their] deep layers [are] . . . not for the inclusion of Negroes as such, but the elimination of *any* category defined as inferior in itself."[55]

The liberal utopia, however, is confounded by the widespread liberal commitment for gradual change. Parsons himself stresses the complexities of any process which improves the blacks' situation. "The activists in such movements are above all likely to become impatient with those who would pay attention to the importance of other factors."[56] But if other factors, other interests, must always remain important, the resolution of the racial contradiction is continuously postponed. As Carmichael and Hamilton argue, black victimization is too substantial a problem for black leaders to be dissuaded by such arguments as " 'granted, things were bad and are bad, but we are making progress.' 'Granted your demands are legitimate, but we cannot move hastily.' "[57] But these observations only reflect a fundamental fact of modern polities, that large areas of social life are beyond the jurisdiction of governmental control. The persistent respect for privacy and diversity of local practices limits the impact that even the most successful demands for equal political rights can have.

Black Nationalism and Black Power

By the mid-1960s, aware of the limited gains that demands for political rights could achieve, many black leaders made a startling shift to a long-standing but often ignored theme in black thought: Black Power and Black nationalism. Not surprisingly, this shift away from political rights to a direct attack on the imputation of Negro inferiority brought on, in turn, a notable decline in white support for black demands.

THE NATIONALIST REORIENTATION OF BLACK POLITICS. The rapidity of this change deserves emphasis. Within months some civil rights activists found that long-time friends were becoming bitter enemies. Stokely Carmichael and "Rap" Brown emerged as influential black spokesmen almost overnight. Established figures such as Martin Luther King, Jr., Roy Wilkins, and Whitney Young suddenly began using "Black Power" language that seemed inconsistent with the old goals and ideals they still pursued. Extensive changes in hairstyling and clothing were readily accepted among men as well as women. Within a few years, indeed, black pride and Black Power themes found extensive treatment in such middle-class black magazines as *Ebony*.

Nationalist movements, of course, had been present among black writers and leaders for decades, but always, in Harold Cruse's term, as a "rejected strain." Although the Garvey movement had enormous appeal, it neither attracted black intellectuals nor developed a sophisticated political strategy. The Harlem Renaissance of the 1920s anticipated the full cultural flowering of black nationalism two generations later, but it had no linkage to political life. Booker T. Washington and his associates recognized the need for independent black economic, social, cultural, and political institutions. But they refused to attack either basic racial attitudes or the pattern of white domination. The greatest black thinker, W. E. B. DuBois, at points embraced nationalist goals, but this complexity in his thought was never appreciated by his colleagues in the integrationist NAACP. Up to the 1960s, nationalist leaders either lacked significant mass support or an orientation toward collective political activity, or both.

The speed with which nationalism did become politically relevant in the 1960s, and the dramatic reorientation of black goals it entailed, suggests the appropriateness of a latent-manifest interest analysis. Even though the race structure itself scarcely changed, many black leaders came to recognize a new political way to attack black subordination. For example, it replaced civil rights idealism (symbolized by the activity of black and white religious leaders) with a far more pessimistic assessment of race relationships. The authors of *Black Power,* for example, dismissed "the premise that political coalitions can be sustained on a moral, friendly, or sentimental basis, or on appeals to conscience . . . . Political relations are based on self-interests.[58]

These new attitudes, indeed, were as notable for the extent and popularity of the break with past social patterns as for the speed with which they emerged. School integration lost its appeal, even for many black activists, so that a black member of the Chicago school board, long attacked as an "Aunt Jemimah" ally of white neighborhood segregationists, found new respect among some black leaders who saw her as an early spokesman for Black Power. Nationally, even though the NAACP continued to support federal government efforts to decrease residential and educational segregation, the integration drive evoked less and less enthusiasm from other black leaders.

These developments led many to blame a conspiracy. The FBI perceived Communist influence, even though, as Harold Cruse has shown, Communists were incorrigible integrationists.[59] Moderate black leaders blamed the press for widely publicizing insignificant individuals who had little political strength, thereby distorting black opinion. Social scientists suggested that white Americans used the nationalists as scapegoats on whom to blame the urban riots of the mid-1960's.

The proliferation of these partial and sometimes simply incorrect theories reflected the confusion of many Americans whose existing categories of social thought failed to account for a new nationalism, which repudiated close collaboration with whites no matter how well intentioned. As Cruse showed, the alliance with white radical groups, such as the New York Communist party, had led in the 1930s to white leadership of the black struggle. A generation later, the same pattern characterized the integrationist and egalitarian Mississippi Summer Project. In an even more fundamental challenge to prevailing assumptions, Black Power adherents asserted a unique cultural perspective based on the blacks' singular experience in the United States, which white allies could not hope to understand. Where black factional and white regime interests had effectively coincided in the struggle for black political rights, whites now found the new nationalist movement insisting on racial autonomy and the importance of a distinctive *national identity*.

The interpretation of this position as the recognition of a hitherto latent interest seems particularly appropriate precisely because it grows out of, and must be understood in terms of, the centuries-old structure of American race relations. Cruse's own penetrating study, *The Crisis of the Negro Intellectual,* shows that the new nationalism (and particularly his own variant) signified a direct attack on that structure's patterning orientation, the imputation of Negro inferiority.[60] As a sequel to the civil rights movement, the nationalist demand for Black Power thus represented a full manifestation of black factional interests.

Insofar as this imputation rested in part on a belief in inherent racial inferiority, blacks had an interest in asserting a *racial* pride in their African heritage, the Swahili language, black history, and typically Negroid physical features. But, insofar as the imputation was also based on the anomaly that, as a group, only blacks had been brought to the new world against their will, full liberation depended on cultural as well as economic and social development.[61] It was this point that Cruse particularly stressed. It was not enough that blacks, like white nationality groups, contribute to the existing culture with which these whites, as descendants of Europeans, could in some general way already identify. Rather, blacks had to make a distinctive cultural contribution that was beyond the capacity of white Americans. For only such sustained, systematic cultural activity by the blacks themselves could demolish the assumption of inferiority which in very different ways had affected the basic thought of both races. For his part, Cruse himself implicitly claimed for blacks a potential cultural superiority which, if fully realized, would not only abolish, but even reverse, accepted notions of racial inferiority. Jazz, America's most influential indigenous musical form, illustrates the creativity of black artists; while *Porgy and Bess,* in Cruse's view, reflected not only the superficiality of the white man's understanding of black people, but the general emptiness of (white) American culture.[62]

CONDITIONS FAVORING THE EMERGENCE OF THE BLACK POWER MOVEMENT. The full flowering of this new nationalism in the 1960s is not accidental. Subordinate groups often depend upon outside allies when they first articulate far-reaching factional interests. Even after the 1954 Supreme Court decision, black leaders did not have sufficient resources of their own to make the vigorous pursuit of this racial interest feasible. If Bendix and Marshall are right, blacks also lacked the confidence bred by secure political rights to mount an entirely independent, nationalist movement. For all his disdain toward the civil rights movement, Cruse tacitly conceded it a place in the South, where political rights were so frequently denied.[63] In fact, however, Cruse may have overestimated the extent and security of black political rights in the North. The ability of northern blacks to elect black public officials, to vote for candidates and parties that directly appealed to black interests, to enjoy equal treatment by the courts and police, and by the bureaucracy, were all still not fully secure even in the early 1970s, let alone in previous decades. And, in any case, the toleration up to 1964 of second-class citizenship for southern blacks by the *national* political authorities cast a fundamental doubt on the civic "respectability" of blacks everywhere.

Industrial workers first attacked the economic and political consequences of their role, and only then attacked the orientation that patterned class relationships. Similarly, the nationalist attack on the imputation of Negro inferiority followed the civil rights activities of young middle-class blacks. Indeed, the civil rights movement's victories achieved a new civic respectability for all blacks which, together with the specific political resource of increased black voting, meant a new base of independent political power. Strengthened by these new resources, northern blacks in the mid-1960s adopted the rhetoric, cultural aspirations, and political ideology of autonomy and collective self-help and then applied them to community action.

BLACK POWER AND COMMUNITY ACTION. This new posture may appear consistent with an established tradition of ethnic politics, and it did take advantage of the importance that Americans attach to privacy and cultural diversity. But the similarity of black nationalism and this older pattern can be easily overstated, for these first groups did not suffer from a pervasive imputation of inferiority which was bolstered by both biological and biblical warrants. Precisely because the mere assertion of a distinctive black social and cultural life in no way eliminated this imputation, the success of white immigrants in ethnic politics did not promise comparable success for the new black nationalism. For blacks, success could come only by explicitly controlling the vital social and cultural institutions of their own community. In this way, cultural achievements undeniably their own could help end the imputation of Negro inferiority by transvaluing color as a symbol in American social thought. In fact, it can be argued that to control these institutions and thus eradicate the imputation of inferiority, blacks had to demand authoritative political power rather than mere influence. At any rate, this interpretation of black factional interests does account for the increasing emphasis of many black community groups on controlling Community Action Agencies (CAAs), rather than merely securing minority representation on the governing boards.

Representation of minority groups on policy-making boards of the war on poverty's CAAs certainly was not a meaningless institutional innovation. It gave certain established and potential black leaders an opportunity to voice opinions and to scrutinize CAP project proposals. Yet, for the growing nationalist strain in black thought during the 1960s, even fair representation of Negroes on city boards or national commissions would not suffice so long as whites remained dominant. Black Power advocates insisted on community control which meant authority rather than simply influence. As the dominant political slogan for black nationalists in the middle and late 1960s, "community control" had decisive implications for the politics of community action. For Black Power advocates, maximum feasible participation came to mean the capture of institutional power to provide the resources for social, economic, and cultural self-development rather than the mere fact of formal representation. Personnel decisions, the CAA's organizational structure, substantive programs encouraging community organizations, and the pressures CAP was willing to bring on other governmental agencies were the critical factors affecting the participatory thrust of the program, as nationalists came to understand participation. And it was this formulation of the participation issue to which both allies and foes eventually responded.

Stated in terms of traditional American pluralism, black leaders therefore sought to utilize the antipoverty program's resources in order to institutionalize black interests within the system of group bargaining, as a way of turning other urban institutions from protecting white influence and control toward promoting black values, interests, and autonomy. Insofar as blacks obtained effective control over CAPs, they did acquire an institutional base that hardly any other bureaucratic institution in northern cities had provided. And the extent to which CAP facilitated the development of community control over the schools (notably in New York) or control over the subsequent Model Cities programs (notably in Detroit) provided a good measure of participation in CAP itself. Indeed, Harlem's Haryou-Act, an autonomous all-black program funded by CAP, became a symbol of participation for black leaders around the country. Yet these very observations suggest the limitations of an understanding of black nationalism based on a model of group bargaining.

BLACK POWER, PLURALIST BARGAINING, AND THE AMBIGUITY OF "MAXIMUM FEASIBLE PARTICIPATION"

The Black Power demand for decentralization, was to some extent, within the pluralist tradition, since decentralization has regularly been the primary technique for establishing interests in the system of group bargaining. Indeed, the "community control" slogan had appeal simply because it appeared to conform to this traditional pluralist pattern. Moreover, American local governments were sufficiently autonomous so that local control did mean control over important institutions in the educational, welfare, cultural, health and safety fields, as well as influence on economic activity. By controlling these institutions, blacks could then bargain effectively for incremental changes in other areas. Thus, by calling for the decentralization of large urban governments, community control promised to create additional pockets of Black Power even in cities like New York where blacks remained a minority of the entire city's population.

The fight for community control, indeed the entire nationalist demand for Black Power, still could not be the only political strategy for black Americans. For one thing, blacks made up only 11 percent of the national population; they lacked the votes, money, or weapons to transform American race relations without some white assistance. In addition they suffered, to borrow a concept from Huntington, from political "underdevelopment";[64] they lacked the institutional resources, such as control over large economic units, to promote and nurture the culture and value systems necessary for a completely successful nationalist attack on the imputation of inferiority. In addition, cities and counties are far from completely independent political or legal units. It is simply not feasible for black nationalists to withdraw into local government enclaves until they have eradicated the imputation of inferiority by building an autonomous Negro culture.

Fundamentally, and it is here that the pluralist interpretation of black nationalism breaks down, black leaders found themselves constrained by certain inegalitarian elements inherent in the processes of group bargaining, which legitimatized their call for decentralization. A newly active, hitherto deprived group, whose interests are basically opposed to those of an already established group, is likely to encounter serious obstacles in asserting its goals. These difficulties are particularly likely to emerge when the new group, as in the case of black Americans, seeks rapid and substantial changes in governmental policy—and it is here that a latent-manifest approach to social interests is necessary.

As with class interests, then, a manifest racial interest is an action orientation which seeks a specific outcome; in this case, improving the social position of black Americans by radically altering the structure of American race relations. These manifest interests, however, prescribe support for sometimes rather different policies, as the groups' political opportunities, possible alliances, and potential opponents change. Thus, it is perfectly feasible to assume that blacks have a continuing interest in seeking to improve their socioeconomic condition, but the obstacles to further progress in this arena make it advantageous for them to concentrate on achieving full political rights. In turn, the limitations on the real gains obtainable from this strategy may lead them to a nationalist Black Power approach. In each case, black leaders acted partly on the basis of practical judgments as to feasibility. But problems of feasibility clearly apply to the demand for community control as well.

On balance, then, a nationalist emphasis on self-development and community autonomy became one of three basic approaches to abolishing the existing racial structure through political action. We can thus profitably assert that black Americans had a role interest in seeking to eliminate the racial contradiction in each of these three ways, since no one way could be expected to dominate the black struggle. These black factional interests proved so relevant to the community action controversy because a participatory CAP was consistent with all three elements of black factional interests.

The war on poverty overtly sought to improve the economic situation of inner city blacks. And many big-city mayors firmly announced their support of participation only to mean the extensive employment of low-income blacks in a variety of nonprofessional positions with the CAA. Moynihan has even attempted to challenge any other understanding of the word,[65] though mere employment in a subordinate role in an agency has hardly connoted "participation" in the conduct of its affairs to any one other than public relations officers. Nevertheless, extensive participation in decisions about the delivery of the CAA's social services did enable black activists to press for more effective efforts to improve the life chances of inner city ghetto residents.

Obviously, participation still more plausibly referred to securing black political rights, including efforts to increase black voter registration, to help them organize politically, and to obtain more equitable treatment by public officials. This interpretation seemed all the more persuasive when the CAP conflict focused on the means of selecting representatives of the poor to serve on the NPCs and, on this basis, blacks effectively recruited white supporters from among the press, reform groups, private welfare agencies, business leaders, and, in some sense, the general public.

Ultimately, of course, participation could also mean black equality based on the black community's control over its own institutions. Since this community control interpretation of participation raised the specter of Black Power and the exclusion of even friendly whites from the affairs of the black community, it was unlikely to attract great white support. But on this point the exact timing of the participation controversy was important. The participation issue in all five cities reached its peak in 1965. At that time, the civil rights movement continued to dominate black politics, and Black Power was only beginning to emerge as a new but rapidly growing political force. It was the year of Selma, Alabama, the Voting Rights Act, and also the Watts riot. In this period of transition—between demonstrations and riots, between civil rights and Black Power, between black appeals to white liberals and black rejection of these liberals' help, between demands for integration and for self-determination—even most political activists were unsure what "participation" meant. Without understanding these confusions of the time, it is impossible to understand both the radical transforming implications (if not always achievement) of the participatory impulse as well as its widespread political support.

COMMUNITY ACTION AND RACIAL IDEOLOGIES

The Black Power ideology which articulated the full range of black factional interests was directly relevant to the politics of community action because it favored all three meanings of participation, including support for community control. Black Power advocates were not only actively involved in the participation controversy in all five cities, but initiated the demand for extensive, autonomous participation in each of the CAPs. But surprisingly enough, participation seemed less relevant to those adhering to an opposed factional ideology, which we shall call *White Power*. As a result, this second racial ideology was only marginally involved in the participation controversy.

Of course, White Power ideologues, who favored retention of the existing structure of race relations, could be expected to oppose the use of public money to support attacks on economic poverty or strengthening of black "political rights," let alone, the turning over of community agencies or local governments to black militants. Indeed, during the 1960s, as Black Power advocates articulated their interest in community control ever more clearly, White Power ideologues became stronger and more explicit in their opposition. Such groups, in fact, had first developed in connection with school controversies in all five cities, and they were courted as early as 1965 by candidates such as William F. Buckley in New York, who asked a white neighborhood-school movement leader to run with him on his Conservative party ticket for mayor. The race riots accentuated these developments, particularly after 1967.

On the community action issue, however, White Power advocates were rather inactive, at least through 1966. The Johnson administration's rhetoric about a war on poverty, which seemed to include some whites, may have been one factor. But, perhaps just as important, the initial stress on the participation issue appeared to make the entire CAP matter one of authority rather than race relations; the implications for white interests did not at first seem direct or substantial. Indeed, White Power advocates became a really major force in the politics of large northern cities only in the late 1960s when they supported important mayoral candidates in Boston, New York, Philadelphia, Detroit, and even Minneapolis. By contrast, in the period covered by this study, of the key actors in the CAP controversy, only Los Angeles' Mayor Samuel Yorty demonstrated an overt concern with white factional interests.

For White Power ideologues, as for Orthodox Conservatives and Orthodox Liberals, the issue of participation did not appear to be immediately relevant to these groups' manifest factional interests. The CAP struggle was "about" race, but it involved directly only one of the two groups in the "racial contradiction" and neither of the major class-oriented ideologies. Indeed, the next two chapters will show that, apart from Black Power advocates, the ideologues most centrally involved in the community participation issue were primarily concerned about its implications for the structures of authority in the American regime. It is the character of these regime ideologies that we shall now consider.

CHAPTER 4: REGIME INTERESTS AND IDEOLOGIES: PARTICIPATION AND THE STRUCTURE OF AUTHORITY

The conflict over community participation presents an obvious anomaly: it sharply increased the manifest racial interests of the black community, but provoked little direct opposition from White Power groups and almost no class-based conflict of any sort. Instead, the war on poverty pitted the black activists against big-city mayors and other urban political leaders, who were primarily concerned about the character of political authority. Overtly, the immediate issue was to determine who would control local public offices. Most mayors were determined to maintain their individual authority as elected public officials, resenting accusations that they did not represent the local community. Indeed, city officials found the activists' own legitimacy, and consequent claim to spend public funds, rather unclear. Thus the executive committee of the United States Conference of Mayors formally resolved: "*Whereas,* no responsible mayor can accept the implications in the Office for Economic Opportunity *Workbook* that the goals of this program can only be achieved by creating tensions between the poor and existing agencies; . . . NOW THEREFORE BE IT RESOLVED that the administration be urged to assure that any policy . . . assure the continuing control of local expenditures relative to this program by the fiscally responsible local officials."

On the other side, community groups emphasized a different principle that reinforced their own claim to authority: that public officials active in any given locale must be genuinely representative of the residents. In East Harlem, where the implications of community action were most fully developed, the leading community organization sought poverty funds "to enable 'legitimate locals' (that is, the area's residents) to assume some responsibility for guiding the destiny of East Harlem." If funded they promised to create "effective and meaningful opportunities for the development of local leadership. Leadership training, participation on boards and advisory committees, the employment of local residents and the utilization of 'legitimate' East Harlem spokesmen, should become the rule not the exception."

The slogans and rhetoric of the competing sides did not probe too deeply into the character of these authority relationships. To do so might have introduced complexities which would have weakened their respective cases, since any appeal to the traditions legitimatizing authority in the United States would not provide clear-cut guidelines. But each side in the conflict did seem concerned about the grounds on which their claim for authority could be based.

For their part, the mayors and their allies saw a threat to the very foundations of urban government. The intensity with which these new community groups made their demands threatened to undermine the elaborate system of bargaining among established groups, making it extremely difficult to negotiate political compromise. In addition, the racial content of the demands threatened to undermine many of the professional, bureaucratic standards by which city officials carried on their administrative activities. In contrast, for black activists, public institutions lacked a legitimacy which could only be acquired by selecting community representatives in a democratic participatory process.

To understand fully the implications of this debate and the rapidity with which it dominated local politics in the mid-1960s, we must examine in some detail the *authority structures* that comprise the American regime. For just as there are factional role interests in the preservation or change of race and class structures, so citizens in the American regime can be said to have *regime interests* in the preservation of these existing authority structures. Paradoxical as it may seem, it was these widely shared regime interests which generated much of the intense conflict over community action.

AUTHORITY STRUCTURES OF THE U. S. REGIME

In complex societies several authority structures govern the command-obedience relationships between rulers and citizens. In the United States four principal structures can be identified: (1) democratic *participation* in the selection of rulers; (2) *pluralist bargaining* among institutionalized interests, i.e., deference to vested groups in the formation of policy; (3) adherence to instrumentally *rationalized* norms in governmental administration; and (4) *constitutionalism,* the safeguarding of fundamental political liberties. These four are all *structures* of authority in that each contains both a patterning orientation and a behavioral regularity. The patterning orientation consists of the principles that both the citizens and authorities expect to shape their command-obedience relationships. The behavioral regularity consists of the practices that conform to these principles. But there is always a potential conflict between principle and practice, inasmuch as principles do not perfectly guide all the interactions between citizens and authorities. As with any other social structure, the scope of the principles can always be widened to include additional activities, or narrowed to exclude some previously included. And this tension among the four American authority structures helped exacerbate the struggle over community action.

Participation

Democratic participation has been widely perceived to be a fundamental characteristic of the American regime. Beginning with de Tocqueville, many foreign observers have emphasized the American commitment to political equality in voting and competition for office, although universal adult suffrage was extended only gradually, as the worker, black, woman, and young adult suffrage issues have demonstrated. Along with universal adult suffrage, citizen participation in the selection of rulers requires accurate vote-counting, protection of the voters from coercion, and the elimination of voter bribery on election day.

Preelection campaigns are also governed by this widely accepted authority principle. In the first place, it is expected that some wider group than a political elite should influence the selection of candidates, a trend accentuated in this century by the still-spreading pattern of presidential primaries. Secondly, it is expected that politicians should be free to compete for popular support. In principle, if not always in practice, the criterion excludes devices restricting organized competition, such as collusive competition between parties in which, for example, a machine dominates or buys off the opposition. A desire to apply the participation principle to such matters led the Progressives to support primary and nonpartisan elections. Significantly, although political scientists have criticized these reforms as counterproductive in that they actually reduce organized competition, the reforms appeared to be so consistent with the participation authority structure of the American regime that neither political leaders nor voters have been inclined to return to earlier practices.

Third, for participation to be meaningful, voters need to have some policy-relevant range of choice in the selection of officeholders, and they need mechanisms which rather easily supply information about these alternatives as they are posed in elections. Radio and television, for example, are expected to provide equal air time for all the major contestants.

Pluralist Bargaining

A second authority structure specifies that authorities *bargain* with a *plurality* of interests as they determine public policies. Banfield's discussion of Chicago politics provides an illuminating statement of the pluralist bargaining criteria: ". . . a policy ought to be framed by the interests affected, not by the political head or his agents. In this view, the *affected interests* should work out *for themselves* the 'best' solution of the matter (usually a compromise). The political head should see that all *principally affected* interests are represented, that residual interests (i.e., 'the general public') are not *entirely* disregarded, and that *no interest suffers unduly in the outcome.*"[1] As our italics indicate, most of those groups which must be consulted are well endowed with material and organizational resources, since they are already strong enough to participate in the process of working out the solution "for themselves." As a practical matter, then, pluralist bargaining requires deferences by the authorities to established organized groups, i.e., to those with sizable material interests which have an already recognized place in a system of political competition and bargaining. Equally important, the stress on compromise means no single policy decision will do serious harm to one of the established bargainers. Only groups excluded from the system of bargaining are expected to suffer substantial defeats, at least in the short run. For example, the Fourteenth Amendment was intended to protect black interests, but since Negroes were poor and largely excluded from nineteenth-century politics, the amendment was used instead to protect the large corporations who possessed property, organization, and the respect of other participants.

An interest in preserving pluralist bargaining is nonetheless not identical to any factional interest, because pluralist bargaining does not preserve the status quo as much as it limits the speed with which it can be altered. Students of public administration, such as Charles Lindblom, have called the practice of pluralist bargaining "incrementalism"; they point out that administrators do not consider all possible alternatives nor fundamental value questions, but start with the existing situation, modifying it, presumably in any one of several directions, as they proceed with marginal alterations.[2] The process is so far from being identical with any particular factional interest that Lindblom, Dahl, Banfield, and others have nearly equated it with rational action in the public interest.[3] By making minor marginal changes, it is argued, the number of options that need to be considered is reduced to manageable proportions so that rational action becomes feasible. By seeking compromises, one is likely to be taking into account the broad range of values that impinge on a policy decision. By negotiating with the organized, established interests, one can avoid the deplorable situation whereby a "relatively apathetic majority" crams "its policy down the throat of a relatively intense minority."[4]

The pluralist bargaining order, moreover, is not always exclusively a province of the bourgeoisie. In recent years, labor relations policies have produced incremental changes that have only marginally affected the vital interests of organized labor. Since the passage of the Civil Rights Act of 1964, southerners have had only marginal success in weakening the position of strength that civil rights groups gained over federal government policies affecting school integration in the South. Once civil rights interests had become part of the federal educational establishment, the checks and balances in Congress and within the executive branches of government inhibited strong efforts to weaken their position, even after public concern for civil rights issues had rapidly declined.[5]

Although pluralist bargaining is not identical with any particular factional interest, it still has differential effects on various social groups. While the principle specifies that the majority may not ignore an intense minority, intensity tends to be measured by the vigor with which groups use channels of communication and their access to the centers of decision-making. Yet access may be denied to some, and others may have few resources and less organization for expressing their intense feelings. As a result, there have been tendencies to (1) favor groups with more material resources at the expense of groups with fewer resources; and (2) defer to previously existing groups at the expense of new groups, seeking to become established.

For all of these inegalitarian implications, pluralist bargaining, as a principle, is deeply rooted in American political thought. When Dahl suggests that "intensity is almost a modern psychological equivalent of natural rights,"[6] he indicates that explicit concern with pluralist bargaining and limited change dates back to eighteenth- and nineteenth-century liberal thought, including, above all, James Madison's argument in *The Federalist,* which recommended constitutional provisions that would protect natural rights against tyrannical invasion. Madison never fully specified these rights, but the prominence of property rights was unmistakable. This emphasis was shared by political figures such as John Taylor of Caroline and John C. Calhoun and, subsequently, by such pluralist scholars as Pendleton Herring and Herbert Agar.[7] The result of this mode of thought, Dahl argues, was "the whole complicated network of constitutional checks and balances" which hindered change and protected socially advantaged minorities.[8] Whatever the defects of this "Madisonian ideology" in its logic, definition, and scientific utility, Dahl concluded that it was likely to remain "the most prevalent and deeply rooted of all styles of thought that might be properly labeled 'American.' "[9]

Rationalization

The third authority structure, rationalization, controls the way in which individuals within groups are treated once policy is formulated. First of all, individuals must be rewarded according to their functional performance, i.e., according to achievement norms, rather than according to ascriptive criteria such as social background, ethnicity, birthplace, sex, or race. Second, where individual performance is irrelevant to the allocation, as in the provision of elementary education and welfare assistance, the distribution of valued things must be made according to some universalistic criteria of eligibility such as age or income.

The significance of instrumentally rationalized procedures has been elaborated by such continental writers as Max Weber, who explicated the legal-rational character of modern bureaucracies. This literature tends to identify rationalization with the efficiency that is the great achievement of modern administrative practice. In fact, the modernization and rationalization of public administration in the United States owes much to the American concern for efficiency, which so dominated economic relationships during its industrializing period. But the concern for *due process,* rooted in Anglo-Saxon constitutional thought, has also contributed to the processes of rationalization, as understood and practiced in the United States. For example, it is expected that those subjected to the administration of criminal or civil justice receive equal treatment, and the judiciary in recent years has spent considerable time and effort to see that this principle does regularly pattern the behavior of law enforcement agencies. Here the focus is as much on fairness and equality as on efficiency. In fact, egalitarian considerations at times take precedence over efficiency per se. For example, one might operate a fire department, police department, or any other governmental agency with a higher level of efficiency by recruiting largely from within one ethnic group, but such policies, and they are not unknown, are clear violations of universalistic and achievement norms that are a mark of rationalized administration.[10]

Constitutionalism

The fourth structure of authority, constitutionalism, limits certain matters from within the authorities' legitimate sphere of command. It protects such First Amendment freedoms as speech, press, religion, assembly, and, by inference, political organization. It also protects the individual's privacy by forbidding unwarranted intrusion into his home or improper tapping of his telephone. The individual's personal property is also protected from expropriation unless it is needed for a public purpose and he is properly compensated. Constitutionalism allows the individual to limit the use of his personal property to his friends and acquaintances, and excludes others from its use for any reason, even the most arbitrary.

This authority structure is guarded, perhaps, even more zealously than the others. Although the other authority structures were also protected in part by the founding fathers, this structure has become so central to court interpretations of the Constitution that deviations are subject to particularly severe criticism. Yet there have been numerous instances in which authorities have quashed political organizations, invaded the privacies of well-known criminals and deviant politicians, and misused the power of eminent domain. No authority principle is so perfectly established in American politics that deviations in practice cannot be discovered. Significantly, however, violaters of the principles do not explicitly attack the authority criteria themselves, but contend instead that their actions, in fact, constitute no deviation from the principle.

Together these authority structures—participation, pluralist bargaining, rationalization, and constitutionalism—may be said to constitute the American political regime. Although it is too much to claim that these empirically derived categories capture all the complexity of authority relations in a sophisticated modern polity, these structures, including their patterning orientations, are certainly essential for any definitive analysis of political authority in the United States.

AUTHORITY STRUCTURES AND REGIME INTERESTS

These authority structures are in fact so basic that they may appear to be unproblematic "givens" which define the situation for citizens.* Yet, because these authority structures fundamentally pattern political behavior, each citizen has an important stake in their perpetuation. We

* Authority principles may well have somewhat differential significance for different citizens. Some may conform routinely to the principles, simply because of habituation or fear of social sanction or physical coercion. Others may view the authority structure as "legitimate" so that commands consistent with the patterning orientations ought of right to be obeyed. But as is true of other social structures, authority structures operate effectively only if the appropriate role expectations are in fact internalized. These and other issues related to our concept of regime interest are discussed in Appendix A.

can therefore attribute a role interest in preserving or extending the scope of authority structures to citizens in the same way that role interests can be attributed to incumbents of race and class roles. In fact, we shall argue that the varying levels of recognition of these interests, called here a citizen's regime interests, contributed directly to the conflict over community participation.

The regime interests that citizens have in their authority structures are rooted in the benefits that all citizens—authorities and nonauthorities alike—share in the preservation of existing authority structures. Of course, authorities obviously have special incentives for maintaining existing authority relations which protect their claim to office and bolster their power to issue commands. Dahrendorf has in fact gone so far as to claim that this interest of authorities places them in "contradiction" to other citizens who do not share in the exercise of authority.[11] But this view ignores that authority structures, even while protecting authorities, place important limits on them. Specifically, they control the succession of authorities by designating the criteria by which an individual obtains the right to issue commands, and they provide criteria that limits the character of commands that can be issued. Only in absolutist political regimes, whose authority structures place virtually no limit on the nature of commands or on the rules of succession, would it be appropriate to identify a "contradiction" between authorities and nonauthorities.*

Far from benefiting authorities exclusively, structures of authority confer important benefits on all citizens. The limits these structures place upon the actions of rulers confer dignity on the citizenship role. In constitutional regimes, the very authors of the authority structure are said to be the citizens. Although the empirical founding of modern governments rarely is consistent with such lofty notions of authorship, such theoretical underpinnings to constitutional societies very likely have important practical consequences for the status of citizens. But the benefits of preserving authority structures are not limited to the questions of self-esteem or self-definition. As Hobbes has forcefully argued, authority structures also foster civil peace. To abolish them or to weaken them through proposed changes is an invitation to anarchy, a war of all against all, that would afflict authorities and nonauthorities alike. Equally important, by patterning political relationships, these structures provide the

---

* Empirically, major conflicts in the United States do not seem to have involved a "contradiction" between authorities and nonauthorities. Neither race nor class conflicts have divided the population along these lines; both authorities and nonauthorities have been regularly found on both sides of these issues.

citizens with stable expectations, which enable them to anticipate correctly the future behavior of both the authorities and other citizens.* Precisely because existing authority structures have patterning orientations, they enable the citizen to avoid the costs of continually deliberating on a command's moral rightness or calculating the personal advantage of obedience. And these costs affect all participants in the regime equally, authority and nonauthority alike.

This explains why, subject to empirical verification, regime interests can be plausibly attributed even to severely oppressed groups, such as blacks in the United States. Some might argue that it is more appropriate to attribute to such groups an "antiregime interest." They could point out that such groups have regularly sought to alter authority structures that operated against their factional interests. For example, they have directly attacked participation as practiced in southern states and challenged pluralist bargaining in all sections of the country as an obstacle to rapid progress toward racial equality. On the other hand, as many black leaders have asserted, blacks seemed likely in the mid-1960s to benefit rather than to suffer from the extension of participation, rationalization, and constitutionalism. But the basic objection to this concept of an antiregime interest derives from the concept of interest. Only if *all* the citizens were harmed by a particular authority structure would it be useful to assert that the citizens had a *shared* role interest in changing that structure. In fact, as Chapter 3 argued, black interests can be much more persuasively and straightforwardly interpreted in terms of the racial structure, which allocates blacks to a disadvantaged role, rather than to a single-citizen role which includes both black and white incumbents.

The status of the regime interest concept within the social sciences deserves a further explication which is provided in Appendix A. But in the end, the validity of attributing shared regime interests to citizens depends on identifying instances where these interests have become manifest in such a way as to have important consequences for political life. If citizens never recognize the benefits that authority structures confer upon them, the concept of latent interest has little utility. But if, under certain pre-

* It is possible, of course, that if the existing authority structures were abolished, the new patterns might provide civil peace, stable expectations, and the dignity of citizenship more effectively than existing structures. But the citizens run some risk that civil peace and a satisfying citizen role may not be reestablished at their previous level. If the new patterns do take hold, the citizens must invest considerable time and psychic energy in learning to conform to new, unfamiliar role expectations. And during the transition itself, the citizen is left without reliable internalized guides to action as well as a clear position in the polity.

disposing and triggering conditions, citizens actively seek to protect these interests, the concept may help to explain important political conflicts. It is to the way in which these interests contribute to political conflict, even to regime strain, that we now turn.

REGIME STRAIN

Although citizens share a latent regime interest in their authority structures, not all citizens are likely to be equally concerned about protecting and enhancing them. Just as blacks do not have uniformly manifest racial interests, regime interests are not uniformly manifest among citizens. As with other role interests, citizens vary both in the extent to which they wish to apply the structuring principles and in the intensity with which they pursue their goals.

In the first place, those citizens with a manifest regime interest are usually concerned not merely with preserving the relevant structure but with extending the structure's scope, i.e., bringing a broader range of practices into conformity with the patterning principle. The pursuit of this goal tends to bring these citizens into conflict with others who, with a less manifest interest, accept the existing practices. Citizens also differ in the intensity with which they actively seek to extend the authority principle. In some cases, citizens merely *prefer* that constitutionalist principles be extended and preserved; others actively *work* for the American Civil Liberties Union. Under appropriate conditions, concern for an interest may sharply increase. A particular event, e.g., the egregious violation of a recognized right, may trigger previously apathetic citizens to pursue vigorously the application of the authority principle. In other cases, this new awareness may be the response of factional groups such as blacks, which invoke an authority principle in protesting the denial of a particular right.

Even these variations in the manifestness of a single regime interest do not fully account for all conflicts over authority relations. Authority structures also contribute to conflict because the authority principles themselves are not logically consistent with each other. They form instead only a partially integrated set of norms and behaviors. Such malintegration makes it possible for one group of citizens to pursue the extension of one authority principle while another defends a second, not entirely compatible structure.

As the inconsistencies between two such authority structures become apparent to more and more citizens, the polity is subject to increasing *regime strain,* in which the two authority principles compete for predominance. Such regime strain will vary in importance over time. Even though union leaders during the 1930s sought to increase working-class voting, the primary issues of that time reflected the clash of economic and class interests. On the other hand, periods of intense conflict over race relations from the Civil War to the war on poverty have always involved just such regime strain. (The case of the Civil War is examined at some length in Appendix A.) Whites favorable to the black cause have asserted manifest interests in participation, constitutionalism, and rationalization, while other whites have resisted black demands in the name of pluralist bargaining.*

It was just such a pattern that developed on the community-participation issue. Unquestionably, participation in Community Action Programs (CAPs) was directly congruent with the participation authority structure. Citizen involvement in the administration of CAP agencies obviously fostered widespread participation in the selection of officials of this agency. And insofar as it increased the political resources of the black community, it facilitated more meaningful activity on the part of a previously rather powerless group of citizens. As a result, a participatory CAP was attractive to those with a manifest regime interest in participation.

But these changes contravened the pluralist bargaining principle. The very fact that participation mobilized blacks and other minority groups disturbed the established institutionalized network within which pluralist bargaining had been conducted. Thus, a participatory outcome was unlikely to appeal to citizens with a manifest regime interest in preserving this authority structure.

The implications of community participation for the rationalization of governmental policy were less clear. On the one hand, blacks claimed that existing bureaucratic institutions were inefficient and ineffective in meeting the problems of blacks and other minorities because their interests were not properly represented in policy-making and administrative positions. Moreover, they argued that racial discrimination had systematically denied these minorities the opportunity to compete for administrative positions consistent with achievement norms. At times,

* In tracing conflict to regime as well as factional interests, the regime-strain approach thus reverses Marx's understanding of false consciousness. Beginning with a working-class interest in social conflict and structure change, Marx asserted that periods of social stability were due to the latency of class interests. The regime-strain approach begins with the shared regime interests of all citizens. Periods of conflict over authority structures are understood to be due to the latency of some regime interests for one group of citizens and the latency of other regime interests for a second group.

however, blacks seemed to reject these very norms, claiming that the Community Action Agencies (CAAs) and other bureaucratic agencies could only be run effectively by blacks, putting the value of community participation ahead of administrative speed and efficiency. Demands for a participatory CAP, then, were likely to meet an ambivalent response from those citizens with a manifest interest in rationalization.

These observed inconsistencies among regime principles did not insure regime strain on the community participation issue. Such conflict occurred only because different groups of citizens had opposite patterns of latent and manifest regime interests. The protest activities of civil rights groups in the early and mid-1960s were a major triggering condition in producing such a pattern. In addition to making black factional interests more manifest, these protests triggered among many whites a new awareness that the participation principle could pattern behavior consistently only if it were extended to include black citizens. The previously accepted limits on black influence over bureaucratic practices in local communities seemed to be at odds with the participation principle. The limited number of blacks at the higher policy-making levels of the city bureaucracies hardly squared with the universalistic and achievement norms of a rationalized authority structure. Finally, it became clear that police and court practices in the inner city were not always consistent with the requirements of the Constitution. Plainly, then, these black protests triggered a rapid change in the manifestness of certain regime interests for a large group of whites, thus creating an important set of potential allies for the black struggle.

But if the civil rights movement triggered newly manifest interests in participation, certain groups in large cities were predisposed to react to the issue in ways consistent with their traditional concerns. On the one hand, community participation received the support of urban reformers, for whom participation and rationalization were manifest regime interests, while machine politicians, more concerned about maintaining the pluralist bargaining structure, opposed them. The conflict between these two political groups had persisted in some form for many decades, and the competing factions had developed stably manifest regime interests that can be called regime ideologies. The presence of these ideological groups helped organize and focus the white response to black demands. Both white supporters and opponents of participation found an already established pattern of local conflict in which it was relatively easy to coordinate allies and mobilize resources. As a result, whites with newly manifest regime interests found themselves part of a long-standing political cleavage.

In sum, the preexisting regime ideologies (a predisposing condition) and the new black protest (a triggering condition) together produced the intense conflict over community participation that emerged in a number of cities. Having considered the emergence of black protest in Chapter 3, it is now necessary to examine the regime ideologies that also helped shape the conflict over community participation in the 1960s.

LIBERAL PRAGMATISM AS A REGIME IDEOLOGY

Studies of American urban politics have not emphasized ideologies in large part because ideology is, with certain exceptions,[12] thought of in race, class, or group terms. Even the most important study of ideology in American local politics, Agger, Goldrich, and Swanson's *The Rulers and the Ruled,* suggests that most big-city politicians are primarily concerned about power, that they are "pragmatists" rather than ideologues.[13] These observations seem to apply most plausibly to the machine politician, the most distinctive figure of American urban politics. According to this view, the machine politician, to maximize his own power and secure reelection, satisfies the particularly salient claims of each interest group in return for its votes, money, and other resources. At this, the machines surely excelled. They recruited as supporters of one organization numerous European nationality groups; Catholics, Protestants and Jews; blacks and whites; and, perhaps most revealing of all, businessmen contributors and working-class voters. As their scholarly defenders pointed out, this characteristic concern for bargaining and compromise, rather than principled adherence to factional ideological causes, enabled the machine politicians to help resolve or to minimize potentially convulsive conflicts among social groups.[14] Their pragmatic method was to satisfy particular group demands (those which least outraged other powerful groups) regardless of, or in open defiance of, any more broadly principled consideration.

This pragmatism of machine politicians was, however, produced by an ideology concerned with maintaining pluralist bargaining among institutionalized interests.[15] The apparently "pure" pragmatism of the machine politicians was itself governed by this authority principle deeply entrenched in American political thought long before the machine emerged.[16] Of course, pluralist bargaining often led the machine politicians to consider the political consequences of their actions, for this was a crucial indicator of the relative strength of institutionalized interests. In these cases their very faithfulness to the ideology made them appear unideological. But under certain conditions this same ideology led machine politicians to ignore the political consequences of their actions in order to defend the pluralist bargaining structure of authority from attack. And rather than minimizing conflict, they exacerbated it. To understand such apparently curious behavior we must consider the origins of the machine politicians as an ideological group.

Disintegrative Forces in the Urban Polity

Machine politics developed as a response to the problems of conflict management and social service distribution in nineteenth-century American cities. The techniques used to minimize turmoil in smaller communities were simply not available in large urban areas. In contrast to small towns, where the fear of social ostracism can dampen conflict,[17] public antagonists in large cities have few, if any, significant private relationships, and none of the actors are likely to find their network of intimate friendships severely disrupted. Even economic sanctions against urban dissidents are less effective than those enforced in rural areas. Both a more elaborate organizational life and an impersonal, complex economy make reprisal against deviants more difficult. Trade unions, civil service regulations, and professional associations usually protect workers against employer retaliation. Minorities in large cities can develop their own economic as well as social institutions. Thus, blacks became a political force in southern cities more quickly than in rural areas, because more blacks had sufficient economic security to defy the white community.[18]

The civic life of large cities, moreover, breeds conflict-oriented political roles. In the small town, the only interest likely to be represented by even a semiprofessional individual is the local chamber of commerce. By contrast, many single-issue "cause" organizations specialize in drawing attention to particular social problems in large cities, while a host of economic and social organizations hire professional staffs to guard group interests. The small-town press primarily supports "booster" or solidarity activities such as annual festivals, "Merchant Days," the basketball team, and the efforts of the chamber of commerce. Big-city papers, on the other hand, also emphasize divisive issues such as corruption, crime, racism, and pollution. Small-town elections are usually either uncontested or low-key personality contests. Campaigns in large cities are conducted by candidates who clash over divisive political issues.

The endemic proclivity of urban areas to political conflict was aggravated by the institutional inadequacies of late nineteenth-century American cities, many of which were relatively new and most of which experienced phenomenal rates of population growth. As Mandelbaum stressed in *Boss Tweed's New York,* basic communication and transportation inadequacies precluded much in the way of unified government.[19] The post office was incredibly inefficient; some twenty-five newspapers each had their own parochial audience; many residents were entirely illiterate; streets were clogged with traffic, jammed with market stalls, and filled with dangerous potholes. Unable to provide for all the city's children, the schools ignored compulsory attendance laws despite absenteeism which regularly ran above 50 percent. Welfare services were left to small private agencies, and private entrepreneurs provided such essential public services as shipping docks, mass transit, and even fire control. One of the few major, but seemingly simple, public services the government did undertake, garbage collection, was notoriously bad.

As a result, the usual urban conflicts were exacerbated by the complaints of morally outraged insurgents against officials unable to provide even rudimentary services. In retrospect, even stronger voter reaction might well have occurred. In fact, the utter collapse of urban institutions, the emergence of radical political movements, or even a population exodus to the hinterland may not have been avoided were it not for the vigor of urban industry and a few integrative forces such as the political machines, which dominated nearly every large American city in the post-Civil War period.

The Political Sources of a Pragmatist Ideology

Machine politics survived and flourished under these conditions because, in the pursuit of their own individual self-interest, the machine politicians did provide a measure of conflict-management and social service that formal government could not provide. Indeed, in such a conflictual, uncoordinated urban society, efficient administration was unfeasible; as Mandelbaum persuasively argues, "The failure to clear the streets properly could not entirely be laid at the door of the politicians." Rather, "precisely because street cleaning under the conditions of that time was doomed to failure . . . the cleaners . . . took their prestige from an outside organization, the political party."[20] By privatizing politics, by appealing to the narrower interests of ethnic neighborhoods or even to the individual and his family, the machine politicians in effect made up some of the deficit of political support for the government which administrative laxity created. They distributed administrative positions according to partisan criteria, buying support directly from individual citizens through corruption, graft, and patronage, rather than acquiring it through popular public policies. In the process, they modeled urban institutions in a congenial fashion. The civil service merit system was anathema except to "blanket-in" party supporters when the leadership feared an imminent defeat. Aldermen were elected from small wards so that men who knew their neighborhoods could assign patronage most advantageously. Many public officials were elected, increasing direct partisan control over the largest possible number of positions. In addition, each elected officeholder could be expected to use his office to promote his own reelection and, in the process, the success of his party's entire ticket.

The particularized benefits thus distributed were sufficient to win the support of actively engaged political participants, but too limited to be made available to all citizens. At the mass level, the machine appealed to neighborhood and ethnic loyalties through careful balancing of the lengthy electoral ticket. In addition, the organization relied on its precinct captains and workers, who held political sinecures, to provide the votes of friends and neighbors simply on the grounds that the captain was "one of them." This appeal to particularistic interests did indeed help secure public order by diffusing and privatizing conflict. For all their problems, urban governments were not bedeviled by chronic large-scale conflicts which would have polarized the population into hostile camps and severely threatened political stability.

Indeed, political conflict was so well controlled that in many American cities a one-party political system emerged. Once in office, a party used available patronage and other material rewards to solidify its political position. In certain "inner city" wards, whose low-income residents were especially receptive to the precinct captain's favors, the opposition became co-opted. In exchange for cooperation on vital matters, including general elections, the ruling party distributed some of its patronage to the minority whose leaders used these resources to insure control over their own primaries.[21] Similarly, when the dominant party itself became severely divided, the fights were often settled within the primary to minimize conflict. As Bryce noted seventy years ago: "In many cities the party majority inclines so decidedly one way or the other (e.g., New York City is steadily Democratic, Philadelphia Republican) that nomination is in the case of the dominant party equivalent to election."[22]

Severe social conflicts were no more appealing, then, to the leaders of the machines than to the heads of the country's large corporations. Indeed, the machine politicians thought of themselves in the same terms as the big businessmen who had become cultural models since the Civil War. They acted accordingly, as Banfield and Wilson have noted: "Business organizations are machines in that they rely largely upon specific material incentives (such as salaries) to secure dependable, close control over their employees. A political machine is a business organization in a particular field of business—getting votes and winning elections."[23] Since workers were paid for their services, they were not expected to criticize the decisions of the company. As best they could, top party leaders systematically opposed dissension and conflict, particularly rank-and-file rebellions. In Boss Flynn's words: "It is essential that no one successfully challenge the decisions of the organization. Every challenge must be met head-on and beaten, if the organization itself is to survive."[24]

Moreover, machines and the new corporate giants shared the late nineteenth-century entrepreneurial values of acquisition and capital development, which overrode older virtues of self-restraint, honesty, and open competition. Not only did the machine provide the bulk of its sizable financial payouts to well-to-do, often unscrupulous businessmen, but it sought to control entry to the political marketplace just as vigorously, and usually as effectively, as the captains of industry discouraged their potential competitors. (The most lucrative alliances often occurred between machines and businessmen "on the make" who sought municipal franchises to provide such monopolistic services as mass transit.) Implicitly and sometimes explicitly, the machine politicians like G. W. Plunkitt recognized the connection and adopted a business metaphor: "I had a cousin . . . who didn't take any particular interest in politics. I went to him and said, 'Tommy . . . can I count on you.' He said: 'Sure, George.' That's how I started in business. I got a marketable commodity—one vote—That was beginnin' business in a small way, wasn't it? But that is the only way to become a real lastin' statesman. I soon branched out."[25]

The more reflective machine politicians overtly adhered to the pluralist bargaining principle, which prescribed deference to entrenched, usually material interests. As the pluralist scholars of the 1950s recognized, partisan ward elections, control of both policy and administration by like-minded politicians, recruitment of partisans to civil service positions, and even corruption and graft could all be defended as ways of maintaining a viable urban policy which respected special concerns and interests.[26] Machine politicians were not prone to conceptualize the significance of their activities in such abstract terms. But many of them recognized that personal gain was not the only basis for defending their actions. They talked in terms of friendship, loyalty, helpfulness, cooperation, harmony among competing groups, and a slow rise to political power after one learned how to accommodate diverse groups. By stressing these values, however, they were only stating more concretely that deference to entrenched interests was an integral part of the American regime, which contributed significantly to conflict management and functional coordination in the disorderly, chaotic setting of nineteenth-century American cities.

As a result, in defending themselves against the reformers' outraged moral indictments, the machine politicians acquired an ideological commitment, just as previously unideological conservatives such as Edmund Burke articulated an ideology in self-defense against liberal-rationalist critiques. By the 1960s the machine politicians came to believe that attacks on, or even disregard for, pluralist bargaining procedures should be resisted as a matter of principle, even at the expense of one's immediate electoral interests, because they threatened the stability of the regime itself. As Chapter 5 shows, this concern led some machine politicians to subordinate their immediate electoral interests when confronted with the demand for a participatory poverty program. In sum, their pragmatism had become principled.

The Liberalization of Machine Politicians

Because of the realignment of the 1930s, however, the machine politicians, or at least those with reasonably coherent belief systems, became Liberal Pragmatists rather than simply pragmatists. Although the machine helped forestall the development of a powerful socialist-oriented labor party, the machine itself was profoundly affected by the shift of its lower-income electoral constituency to the banner of the national Democratic party. To retain these supporters in local elections, machine politicians embraced the domestic social goals of New Deal Democratic leaders. Machine congressmen became steadfast supporters of liberal, welfare state legislation. As the labor movement became an arm of the Democratic party, industrial unions reinforced this trend.[27] Thus, Liberal Pragmatist congressmen provided vital support for eventual passage of both the Economic Opportunity Act and the earlier juvenile delinquency program. Liberal Pragmatist mayors, such as Tate, Wagner, and Daley, enthusiastically endorsed both programs.

Liberal Pragmatists, then, resemble but are not identical to the Liberals described by Agger, Goldrich, and Swanson, who, for greater clarity, are called Orthodox Liberals in this study.[28] Both groups have a comparatively low social status and a relatively low sense of cultural class. Both represent a working-class and minority group constituency and are aligned with organizations such as the trade union movement and the Democratic party. But the Liberal Pragmatists are loyal to an organization which relies on divisible material incentives, and their ideology is fundamentally conditioned by a manifest interest in pluralist bargaining. Accordingly, they stress harmony and cooperation, whereas the Orthodox Liberal is committed to egalitarian, redistributive social policies for which he is willing to initiate political conflct.

Latent Interests of Liberal Pragmatists

If the machine politicians' regime interest in pluralist bargaining was manifest, their concern for other authority structures was much less evident. To be sure, previous hostility to rationalizing local government had been modified in the face of the enormous expansion of public bureaucracies necessary to implement the New Deal programs. Even so, machine politicians could hardly be enthusiastic about enhancing universalistic and achievement criteria which ran contrary to the machine's desire to distribute governmental resources on the basis of an individual's political affiliations. Under the machine, it became extremely difficult to implement laws according to standards which recognized no distinction between black and white, Catholic and Jew, Pole and Italian. Indeed, the machine's strength, especially in eastern and midwestern cities, lay in its sensitivity to the parochial, but nonetheless genuine, concerns of each of these groups.

Similarly, Liberal Pragmatists lacked a manifest interest in extending participation to a wide range of authority relationships. The machine did not oppose electoral participation as such. Instead, machine politicians, anxious to amass reliable supporters, regularly ignored legal technicalities in their efforts to naturalize and then to register the waves of urban immigrants. But the machine did oppose *uncontrolled* electoral participation, particularly if it increased the influence of angry voters whose demands were difficult to compromise.

In fact, the debate between most critics and defenders of the machine has centered on the machine's blithe disregard for the participation principle. With the optimism of nineteenth-century Jeffersonians, critics of the machine argued that widespread political participation would produce good citizenship, vigorous republican government, and sound public policies.[29] To Ostrogorski, its vote-buying, vote-stealing, and sheer organizational strength meant that: "Where the Machine is supreme, republican institutions are in truth but an idle form, a plaything wherewith to beguile children. . . . It is no longer 'a government of the people, by the people and for the people.' "[30] Reflecting the pessimistic twentieth-century theories of mass society, defenders of machine politics have feared uncontrolled mass involvement such as that generated by the interracial tensions of the 1960s. Too often, they felt, such involvement leads to confrontations that not only block compromises among diverse interests but also prevent political leaders from disregarding mass sentiments "at crucial moments when public opinion, or intensely moved parts of it, is out of line with long-term national interests."[31] By contrast, these scholars argue, machine control of the electorate through ethnically balanced tickets and material payoffs to individual voters reduces the accessibility of city officials to mass pressures and any temptation to demagoguery.[32] Insofar as community action sought to break the apathy of inner city residents, it thus directly violated the machine politician's pragmatism. By contrast, it was precisely because of its concern for participation that the reform movement supported black demands for a participatory poverty program.

THE REFORM MOVEMENT AND THE URBAN POLITICAL REGIME

Initially, of course, the urban reformers were overtly committed to both rationalized government and widespread participation as integral parts of the new political order that they sought to substitute for the machine. Believing that the machine's disdain for universalistic and achievement values impeded efficient implementation of public policies and perverted efficient, honest government, reformers sought to implement the principles of scientific management then popular among businessmen. They distinguished between politics and administration and sought to hire for local governments objective, nonpartisan, professionally trained experts in such posts as city managers, school superintendents, and police chiefs. In this way partisan considerations could be eliminated from policy implementation, and policy choices would not be contaminated by the power of political bosses to control public employment.

The reformers also enthusiastically embraced the criticisms of vote-buying, vote-stealing, and the suppression of issue-oriented politics leveled against the machine. For, if the policy choices themselves were to be made rationally, the political sphere would have to be restructured so as to permit the more meaningful, i.e., autonomous, participation of individuals. Only by making it possible for the citizen to participate freely in the political process could dispassionate, intelligent judgments on political issues be assured. Institutionally, therefore, the reformers sought to secure rational, informed, unbiased electoral decisions through nonpartisan city elections, and a short ballot which reduced the number of choices about which the rational citizen had to seek information. Finally, the reformers favored the initiative, referendum, and recall, in order to increase the citizens' channels for implementing their rational judgments.

In this, the reformers' concern for rationalizing administration and broadening participation in politics merged. In order to rationalize government, reforms had to eliminate patronage, expose graft and corruption, and rigorously adhere to the letter of the law. Such steps were also expected to weaken the machine's ability to dictate the citizen's political allegiance and vote. At the same time, reformers were less concerned about pluralist bargaining. To be sure, the reformers did not attack this authority structure any more than the machine politicians explictly rejected participation or rationalization. Indeed, pluralist bargaining among vested interests often flourished in areas such as California where Progressive reformers had eliminated any significant partisan organization. Yet the reformers' manifest interest in governmental rationalization and citizen participation far exceeded their enthusiasm for pluralist bargaining.

Intuitively, it seems reasonable that this ideological commitment would lead reformers to support unequivocally a participatory CAP. But by the 1960s, divisions within the reform movement, which reflected a tension between the principles of participation and rationalization, precluded any uniform response. It is hardly self-evident that broader public participation facilitates rule by experts or that a rational system of public administration furthers broader participation. The link between these two regime interests rested on the reformers' optimistic nineteenth-century assumption of infinite human perfectibility. They believed with John Stuart Mill that the workers' participation in politics would enhance the quality of their own lives and make them better citizens. In Britain this goal required extending the franchise. In the United States the reformers favored institutional devices which freed the citizen to vote rationally and freely. Majority rule and good government therefore were not seen as mutually exclusive but as highly interdependent goals. Once the vested interests, corrupt politics, and vote-buying of the machine were eliminated, once formal education spread, the people and only the people could be expected to support those leaders and policies beneficial to the whole community.

Such leaders, moreover, would rely on the advice of experts in the science of government. The mayors and city managers would justify their extensive authority primarily by selecting the most knowledgeable and technically proficient employees; the voters in return would support these rational executives in future elections. Urban reformers thus sought to establish, in Brzezinski's recent formulation, "meritocratic democracy," which "combines continued respect for the popular will with an increasing role" for "individuals with special intellectual and scientific attainments."[33]

This perspective turned the machine theory of local government on its head. The machine relied on the voters' corruptibility to hold together a polity which, in any case, could not be administered efficiently. For the reformers, it was not the voters but the politicians and the interests that were all too corrupt and incompetent to administer honest local government. If the machine relied on human corruptibility to organize a chaotic polity, the reformers relied on the hope of human perfectibility to improve a corrupt one.

This optimism, however, did not prove to be entirely warranted. On one side, citizens did not always fulfill the reformers' hopes about rational voting behavior even when they could vote freely. Denied partisan cues, the residents of nonpartisan political systems voted for candidates on racial, religious, and ethnic grounds, rather than according to universalistic qualifications. In some cases, they supported political underdogs against the recommendations of almost all the civic leaders and good-government groups. In fact, such rebellions took place in 1961 in both Los Angeles and Detroit, the two cities in our study where reformers had achieved their greatest successes. In the face of such behavior, some reform groups turned against elections for certain positions and even sought to limit the elected mayor's power to appoint city officials. For example, to satisfy reform demands, school board nominees in Chicago, Philadelphia, and New York were, as late as the 1970s, appointed by mayors from a list prepared by blue-ribbon panels of prestigious citizens.

Reformers also found it difficult to argue that the increasing influence of experts in the city administration insured the implementation of the rationalized policies that citizens desired. For one thing, administrative expertise and a theory of scientific management proved of little use in choosing among general policy alternatives advocated by different social factions. Even in the sphere of policy implementation, rationalization proved a complex goal. Rather than faithfully executing policy, officials in administrative bureaus and agencies developed specific organizational interests of their own, which they vigorously defended in bargaining with other administrators. Ironically, the reformers' own innovations encouraged such developments. To preclude machine politics, civil service reforms often protected the job of every member of a bureau save its chief. But this arrangement made it virtually impossible to reshuffle key personnel in order to change policies. In some cases, the mayor did not even choose the heads of important bureaus. In other cases, reform rules forced him to select from among officials who had already served for many years in the agency they were supposed to change. And no matter how the administrator was chosen, the mayor risked accusations of political interference if he then tried to control his subordinates' activities. Urban bureaucracies had become, in Sayre and Kaufman's phrase, autonomous "islands of functional power" free to operate in their sphere with little regard for outside jurisdictions.[34] With no individual or institution having sufficient authority to coordinate the city government's activities, a genuinely coherent, rationalized policy became impossible.

These difficulties led some reformers to place even more emphasis on a rationalized system of administration and policy-making even at the expense of wider political participation. Others, however, reluctantly concluded that participation was a more important goal and were prepared if necessary to sacrifice administrative rationality. Few reformers openly rejected or even tacitly abandoned either of these regime principles. Both types continued to hope that eventually the two principles could be reconciled. But the realities of urban politics forced each group to subordinate one regime principle to the other, dividing the urban reform movement ideologically into Progressive Conservatives and the more liberal Community Conservationists.

COMMUNITY CONSERVATIONISTS AND PROGRESSIVE CONSERVATIVES

According to Agger, Goldrich, and Swanson, these two groups made up distinct, if sometimes cooperative, ideological tendencies in post-World War II urban politics. They point out that both ideologies have in common a concern for the good of the polity as a whole. In our terminology, they are more concerned with regime than factional interests.* But the two ideologies were nonetheless different in crucial respects. Community Conservationists were more concerned about participation than were Progressive Conservatives. As Agger and his co-authors point out, Community Conservationists "prefer to see the masses share in political power through extensive electoral participation in support of the Conservationists and their policies.[35] But Community Conservationists were also concerned with rationalizing government, particularly if this did not conflict with participatory goals. In this respect they "are the most recent of a long line of 'reformers' . . . who stress the need for and the duty of government to provide long-range planning in the public interest by nonpolitical administrators."[36]

Progressive Conservatives, on the other hand, were more conservative and less participatory. In contrast to Community Conservationists, they "prefer a type of power structure wherein power is in the hands of a

---

* We have certain differences with Agger and his colleagues concerning the defining characteristics of these ideologies. According to them, Progressive Conservatives believe industrialists and financiers should govern, while Community Conservationists believe that "elected public officials and professional public administrators must be the guardians . . . architects and builders of this public interest." (Agger, Goldrich, and Swanson, p. 21.) But this concern with the different social groups from which leaders are to be drawn obscures a more important difference between the two ideologies, i.e., the *interests* which such a leadership is supposed to serve. After all, if the "elected public officials" favored by the Community Conservationists should come from the ranks of the industrialists and financiers, the two ideological groups, as Agger, Goldrich, and Swanson have defined them, would substantially overlap. In trying to identify elected and appointed officials as the *strata* from which Community Conservationists would recruit political leaders, they have confused a political role with a social group. Yet there is much in their description of these ideologies that is consistent with our definition.

relatively small proportion of the citizens."[37] Moreover, they tend to identify the interests of industrialists and financiers with the interests of the community as a whole. The "attitude of 'what's good for the X corporation is good for the community' indicates an innate complement of self-interest and the common good."[38] Yet, in contrast to Orthodox Conservatives, who are willing to settle for inefficient, ineffective government as long as it is responsive to business interests, Progressive Conservatives seek to apply business principles of efficiency and a certain entrepreneurial activism to the government. In fact, Progressive Conservatives are willing to cooperate with Community Conservationists as often as they do simply because they share a concern for rationalized governmental activity.

In retrospect these different strands of reform politics can be traced back to differences in the manifest regime interests of the early reformers. The conservative wing of the Progressive movement grew out of the respectable nineteenth-century Republicans-turned-mugwumps who opposed government corruption and gross inefficiency. As one scholar of the reform movement concluded: "Although businessmen wanted to purify democracy, they opposed extending it. In general, they continued the mugwump tradition, declaiming against local bosses and corrupt legislators, and encouraging civil service. At cries for direct primaries, direct election of senators, or the initiative, referendum and recall, articulate businessmen took shelter from the mob under principles of regulated democracy."[39] To the extent that these Progressives supported democratic reforms at all, they did so to strengthen their political position against corrupt, inefficient machine politicians rather than because they were deeply committed to the participation principle.

However, the reform movement found a second, very different source of support among many diverse groups of professionals, including social workers, educationists, journalists, ministers, social scientists, and certain types of lawyers. Although they favored a more rationalized administrative process, these reformers emphasized even more the importance of democratizing American government. Participation may have been a Populist slogan, but as La Follette's following in the cities demonstrated, it had many urban supporters who, as Rogin put it, "saw no contradiction between faith in the experts and faith in the people."[40]

As supporters of popular participation, these liberal reformers generally welcomed working-class influence on elections. Social workers such as Jane Addams and muckrakers such as Lincoln Steffens called for public policies that would improve the position of the lower classes. While not opposing the trade union movement, they went beyond the AFL in supporting child labor, minimum hour, and workmen's compensation laws. In sum, the Community Conservationists were not nearly so concerned that government be more economical as that it be more efficient, and they sought administrative efficiency less to reduce operating costs than to reach the most needy members of the community. Indeed, they succeeded in extending compulsory schooling, providing the first rudiments of a welfare system, and building public libraries and recreational facilities.

PROGRESSIVE CONSERVATIVES, COMMUNITY CONSERVATIONISTS AND COMMUNITY PARTICIPATION

Not surprisingly, these two types of reformers did not give community participation equal levels of support. The Progressive Conservatives saw the poverty program primarily as a way of rationalizing services to low-income groups. They therefore were receptive to participation less as a new way for the poor to make political demands than as a means for improving a welfare system which was inefficient, uneconomical, and used for patronage purposes. But an efficient, patronage-free CAP, closely controlled by a professional bureaucracy, was also perfectly compatible with their ideology. Insofar as the demand for participation came to mean community control, the Progressive Conservatives' enthusiasm markedly declined. They feared that black leaders would recruit staff and apportion benefits on the basis of color rather than competence. Progressive Conservatives were even more concerned when, as in New York City, charges of graft and corruption were made against community-controlled programs. The probable impact of participation on the rationalization of government services was nevertheless sufficiently ambiguous in the early period of the CAP controversy studied here, so that at times Progressive Conservatives supported black demands.

The Community Conservationists' much stronger commitment to participation meant that they did not object as vociferously as did the Progressive Conservatives to the sacrifice of professional standards for the sake of greater community participation. Believing that the poor needed a greater voice in government, they welcomed representation on community action councils and greater efforts to organize the poor politically. In their view, antipoverty-program resources could appropriately be used to stimulate voter registration and turnout drives, and to organize demonstrations against unsympathetic public bureaucracies, schools, or landlords.

The Community Conservationists, nonetheless, differed from Black Power advocates because they were concerned that the program consistently adhere to participatory and constitutional principles. They opposed limiting employment in CAP agencies to Black Power advocates, for this would make political beliefs relevant for public employment and reintroduce patronage practices into local politics. They also feared that the leaders who secured initial control of these CAP-supported organizations might all too readily manipulate their mass following to perpetuate their own control. These implications of the participation issue were not immediately apparent in 1965, however, and, accordingly, Community Conservationists gave participation their sustained and widespread support.

The rhetorical appeals to authority and legitimacy made by the various contestants in the participation controversy thus appealed to the regime interests that citizens shared in the existing principles that patterned authority relations. But these authority principles did not offer consistent guidelines as to the way in which participation policy should be formulated. The pluralist bargaining principle suggested that change should be limited so that existing interests would not be seriously threatened by this new program. But this conflicted with the participation principle, which legitimatized black demands for major changes in the distribution of political resources in big cities. Significantly, the Community Conservationist reformers, who rallied to the support of blacks, had traditionally been concerned with extending the participation principle, while the Liberal Pragmatist machine politicians, always concerned with maintaining pluralist bargaining, became the most potent foe of community participation. The third group concerned about authority relations, the Progressive Conservatives, had a less consistent perspective on participation, for the compatibility of the goals of participation and rationalization was not clear. The conflict among these ideological groups indicated a considerable regime strain, for it pointed up the inconsistencies and conflicts among the principles that had traditionally justified the exercise of authority.

Some might argue, however, that the appeals to authority principles were ad hoc justifications for policy objectives sought on far more narrow grounds. Each of the contestants, it may be said, was pursuing policies that would protect and enhance their own individual or group political interests rather than fighting, on an ideological basis, to preserve one or another of their regime interests. This, we believe, does not adequately account for the positions taken in the participation controversy. But the argument is so powerful that it must be dealt with in detail, a matter we shall turn to in Chapter 5.

CHAPTER 5: IDEOLOGIES VERSUS ELECTORAL AND ORGANIZATIONAL INTERESTS

Although the Progressive Conservative ideology gave no clear guidance on the participation issue, Liberal Pragmatism opposed community participation, while Community Conservationism favored it. This chapter will show how these ideological differences substantially affected the development of the proparticipatory and antiparticipatory coalitions which emerged in our five cities. Such an interpretation contradicts a dominant view in the urban politics literature, which argues that political leaders take positions on policy questions primarily in response to the dictates of their electoral or organizational interests. At times, this widely accepted view is stated so generally that it becomes simply a post hoc rationalization for any decision a politician happens to make. At other times, electoral or organizational interests are defined so loosely that it is impossible to distinguish between these interests and political ideology. But if the two concepts are sharply defined, they provide alternative explanations for the stands leaders take on any given policy question. Neither electoral or organizational interests nor ideology by itself can account for positions taken in all cases. Yet, together, they provide adequate explanations for the particular constellations that the forces involved in the conflict over community action formed.

ELECTORAL/ORGANIZATIONAL INTEREST MODEL

In the urban politics literature, the electoral interest model has been developed most carefully and precisely in Banfield's work on Chicago, Dahl's study of New Haven, and Long's influential article on the "Ecology of Games."[1] As set forth by these authors and by others who have adopted this perspective, the electoral interest model assumes that an elected politician makes key decisions by calculating (with admittedly imperfect information) the best way of insuring his success in the next election.[2] If it is true, as Weber said, that "the politician seeks power alone, power as a source of money, but also for power's sake," it is argued that this may not be as pernicious for democracy as Weber implied.[3] Indeed, the very search for power insures that politicians will seek to please as large a portion of the voting population as possible, simply to protect their base of power. Where suffrage is widespread, and where voters choose among competing elites in free and fair elections, the only way in which politicians can achieve reelection is to implement what is preferred by the majority.

The argument has been formalized into an "economic theory of democracy" by economist Anthony Downs, who argues that in cases where information is perfectly circulated, politicians who seek to maximize votes in competitive elections would certainly implement policies preferred by the majority in every case.[4] In any given policy decision, elites in office will seek to carry out the preference of the majority; otherwise, the competing elites out of office would support the majority position in that case and in all others match the position of the officeholders. Under these circumstances, national voters would then replace incumbent officeholders with the competing elite at the earliest opportunity. Inasmuch as there is not a perfect circulation of information in the political marketplace any more than in the economic, deviations from this ideal can be empirically identified. But even here politicians who are desirous of reelection will follow the course determined by their best estimate of the maximum net advantage (political "profit") in terms of reelection chances from any given expenditures of resources, such as time, money, energy, or policy determination.*

The electoral interest model seeks an explanation that depends on the political ambitions of elected officials. A comparable interpretation of political participants who are not seeking election to political office has not been developed as systematically. Yet Banfield's argument that political issues arise as a result of the "maintenance and enhancement needs" of formal organizations provides a substantial beginning in this direction.[6] Essentially, this organizational interest approach suggests that groups and organizations participating in the political sphere will assume

* Riker has modified Down's model by arguing that politicians do not seek to maximize majorities but only to obtain the minimal coalition necessary to win reelection.[5] To the extent that more than a minimum is included within the coalition, the limited resources at stake would have to be more widely shared. The propensity of politicians to seek only the minimum winning coalition is said to account for the perpetuation of two-party systems.

positions on issues that affect their own organizations' economic or political advantage. Newspapers seek out controversies because controversial issues help to sell papers. Newspapers also oppose party patronage and corruption because where parties are weak newspapers have greater influence. Private hospitals encourage the expansion of public hospitals because they want to reduce indigent usage of their facilities. Civil rights organizations seek to dramatize apparent racial affronts because only by so doing can they sustain and build their membership roles.

The examples could be enumerated endlessly; in all cases, the organizational or group actor, like the politician, chooses according to an amoral self-interested code. Goals are not pursued for their own sake but are simply the by-product of a "game" in which each actor is pursuing his own interest. To be sure, the actors are not likely to undertake activities beyond the range of conventional morality, but this is simply because it would not be in their political interest to do so. On the other hand, analysts rarely condemn this apparently amoral behavior; rather, the pursuit of organizational interests, like the politician's amoral pursuit of reelection, is said to be governed by an invisible hand that insures benefits to the public as a whole. As each organization articulates its own interest, politicians (who are pursuing reelection) work out compromises and mutual adjustments that produce a rough approximation of the best balance among all interests.[7]

Whether or not an invisible hand operates, this model as applied both to politicians and to groups and organizations has proved to be a powerful tool for explaining political choices and strategies. Of course, it is usually very difficult to state precisely the motivation for any particular set of political activities. When properly formulated, these models argue only that actors reach decisions *as if* they were trying to maximize their electoral or organizational interests. Unless he is particularly honest (or foolish), the political actor is likely to give more altruistic reasons as motivation for his behavior. Yet the model both is simple and has predictive power. It identifies a similar motive for all actors, and it enables the analyst to forecast what actors would do in the case of new issues that have yet to arise. It is therefore extremely useful for developing explanatory propositions about political decision-making. Accordingly, in an early publication based on this research we used the electoral interest model to order much of our data.[8] Even now, as we have to come to realize the limitations of the model, its elegance and widespread usage suggests to us that the case for presenting another explanation for the policy preferences of political actors is strongest only when this model seems clearly inadequate.

POLITICAL IDEOLOGY MODEL

To account adequately for the position that key actors took on the community participation issue, however, it proved necessary to supplement the electoral/organizational interest model with one which views actors as if they were making choices in order to maximize ideologically determined goals, drawing on the definition of ideology elaborated in the preceding chapters. Scholars who use the electoral/organizational interest model may not always reject ideology as a useful analytical concept, but they usually circumscribe its significance. Certain individuals may engage in politics for ideological reasons, the model will admit, but they run the grave danger of being ignored, and thus rendered ineffective. At its crudest level the argument holds that ideologues should be shunned as arrogant elitists who are acting on their own views of the general good, rather than by calculating majority preferences. In Downs's more sensitive hands the model admits that even successful politicians may use ideologies, but only to facilitate rational calculation in a system of imperfect communication.[9] An organized ideology enables the politician to guess the opinions of his supporters on one issue by knowing their opinions on others. Thus, on the basis of their general views he can reliably calculate how to win their support on the matter at hand, even though he is unable to consult them fully. But even this sophisticated version of the electoral/organizational interest model subordinates ideology to political calculation. The possibility that skilled and successful politicians consistently pursue polices for ideological reasons, even when such actions violate the best calculations of their electoral interests, is contrary to the model. At best, such occurrences are deviant cases. If such a pattern occurred frequently, the validity of this model would become suspect.

To offer the ideological model as a genuine alternative to this electoral/organizational interest model, it is necessary to give it the same specification. In the first place, this interest model identifies incumbents of certain roles, notably elected officials, who, it hypothesizes, will calculate and act on their political interests. To provide comparable specificity, the ideological model must identify ideologies with a fair degree of ease and precision. It is not enough to take an individual's current attitudes with respect to a certain issue, label them "his ideology," and then use this "ideology" to explain the position he takes on that particular policy question. Such a procedure does nothing more than tautologically use the individual's attitudes to explain themselves.

However, ideologies are not simply points of view; they are action orientations. Consequently, identifying the ideologies of particular politicians or groups can be done most accurately by inferring orientations that are implicit in some observed political behavior. This, together with direct attitudinal information, can be the basis for constructing a presumed ideology. If subsequent behavior corresponds to this ideology, there is some warrant for explaining the second set of behaviors in terms of the initially inferred ideology. For example, when machine politicians consistently bargain among established interests, this warrants the inference that they are committed to a pragmatist ideology. Knowing the politician's commitment to this pragmatism enables the analyst to predict that future behavior will be consistent with the past pattern of pluralist bargaining even when it hurts his electoral interests. Similarly, the analyst expects the Community Conservationist to support community participation in the war on poverty—once again, even if it damages his electoral interests—because he has supported citizen participation previously.

One can also rely on membership in a group which has a clear ideological commitment as a means of identifying an individual's ideology. In most cases, members of such groups may be assumed to have the same factional or regime interests or both. Although the assumption may not always be warranted, usually it can be anticipated that an individual who has been identified as an active, loyal member of the group will act according to the group's ideology. Thus, in the ideological model an individual's past and continuing allegiance to an ideological group becomes an equivalent of a politician's incumbency in a political role in the electoral/organizational interest model. For example, we inferred a commitment to Progressive Conservatism on the part of individuals developing welfare agency policy from the close relationship between private welfare agencies and progressive members of the business community. Although the inference is probably not correct in every case, generally recruitment mechanisms very likely select out as welfare leaders those who are particularly committed to rationalizing governmental services.

The electoral/organizational interest model connects an individual to his policy choice by specifying the content of the interest; i.e., it states how a policy would affect the incumbent of a particular role, as, for example, a policy's effect on an elected leader's chances for reelection. Similarly, to specify the relevance of the policy for an individual's ideology, it is important to state the specific content of that ideology. Here our particular definition of ideology is helpful. As set forth in Chapter 2, we regard ideologies as relatively stable sets of manifest interests in the preservation or change of one or more social structures, whether these be authority structures or the structural relationships between classes or races. This definition enables us to predict an ideologue's stand on an issue once the impact of his ideology on the specific social structure is known. An Orthodox Liberal, for example, can be expected to support a more redistributive tax policy that mitigates the economic consequences of the workingman's role. A Progressive Conservative can be expected to support proposals that coordinate urban bureaucracies in such a way as to rationalize governmental policy.

The electoral/organizational interest and ideological models thus give different, but roughly comparable, bases for predicting and explaining the positions politicians take on policy questions. Yet, unless important distinctions are kept in mind, the two models can be confused, for they share two elements in common. In the first place, both models depend on the concept interest. Ideologies, as we use the term, are manifestations of the regime interests of citizens or of factional interests of races and classes. The electoral/organizational interest model also interprets behavior in terms of interests—in this case, the interests of organizations or of individual power-seeking politicians. Thus, the distinction between ideologies and political interests lies not in *whether* the politician is taking interests into account in making his decisions but rather *what kind* of interests he is considering. We have used the concept of ideology to identify a concern with the interests of broad social groups and/or the interests of citizens in the authority structures of the political regime. Concern for these broad interests is one particular elaboration and specification of conventional usage of the concept "ideology." The word identifies a concern on the part of political leaders with matters that stand in sharp contrast to the comparatively narrow concerns that are the focus of the electoral/organizational interest model.

The two models are concerned with different kinds of interests, but they share a second important similarity: *Both models attribute role interests to members of specified social roles.* Interestingly enough, some scholars, who are highly critical of attributing latent role interests to workers or blacks (arguing that this involves an unwarranted intrusion of the analyst's bias into political analysis), are quite willing to attribute role interests to political leaders.[10] They assume regardless of his expressed attitudes that the role the politician is performing necessarily requires that he seek to enhance his political career or to maximize the returns to his organization. The content of the role to which an interest is attributed in the electoral/organizational interest model differs from roles we have discussed in our latent role interest analysis, but the attribution of a role interest by the analyst is the same in both cases.

The electoral/organizational interest model, however, assumes that electoral interests have a constant rather than fluctuating importance to the actors. Of course, on most issues skillful politicians are probably aware of these electoral role interests. But when an analyst asserts that the electoral interest model by itself can account for all the policy orientations of political leaders, he in effect assumes that all political actors continually recognize these interests throughout a complex controversy. By contrast, we believe it is far more useful to assume that, just as regime and factional interests may be latent, so electoral and organizational role interests may be latent when certain conditions are not fulfilled.

COMBINING THE POLITICAL INTEREST AND IDEOLOGY MODELS

Taken alone, neither electoral and organizational interests nor ideologies account for the behavior of the key actors in the conflict over participation. As the remainder of this chapter will show, the interest model, though it explained the orientations of some participants, could not account for all of them. For example, the responses of the six mayors who served in the five cities during the crucial formative period of the program were quite diverse: Two whole-heartedly supported participation, three bitterly opposed it, and one supported it symbolically but undermined any substantive participation. Yet, the ideological model also was insufficient, for though it accurately predicted Community Conservationist support and Liberal Pragmatist opposition to participation, it failed to give any guidance at all to the likely orientations of the Progressive Conservatives.

The two models, used in combination, more successfully predicted actor orientations and activities with respect to the Community Action Program. If combined, the two models yield four possibilities, as are set forth in Table 5–1. In the first place, neither model may give any indication as to the actor's behavior. The relevant ideology, as in the case of

TABLE 5–1. The Action Relevance of Relationships Between Political Ideologies and Interests

Relevance for specific political activity	*Relationships between models*	
	Models agree	*Models diverge*
	1	3
One or both models irrelevant	Indifference; no apparent motivation to initiate political action	Either interest or ideology is indifferent and the other determines behavior
	2	4
Both models relevant to policy choice	Congruence; behavior jointly or over-determined	Conflict; situational factors determine which model will predict behavior

Progressive Conservatives with respect to participation, may be compatible with either of opposed issue outcomes, and the electoral or organizational interest may be uncertain, difficult to determine, or simply irrelevant to the issue. It is perhaps not surprising that we found no indisputable instance of this case in the politics of community action, for any such individual is likely to be a nonparticipant. But if he is a participant he might well serve as mediator, and it may be that Leroy Collins, who mediated the political settlement in Los Angeles, had no ideology or organizational interests that inclined him either to favor or oppose participation. Second, both models may predict the same course of action. This is the type of situation that Anthony Downs has identified as all-pervasive; actors use ideologies simply to calculate more expeditiously their electoral interests. Where both models predict equally well, behavior is overdetermined, so to speak, and one model is sufficient. Even though in any given case the ideological model might intuitively seem the more plausible, we shall not insist on this interpretation; if all cases were of this type, there would be no need to formulate an alternative to the widely accepted electoral/organizational interest model. In the third place, either this interest model or the ideological model might give no precise guidelines for political action. In this situation, one expects the alternative model to predict the behavior. For example, we shall argue in the case of community participation that Progressive Conservatives are likely to act according to their electoral or organizational interests, and politicians who are unable to calculate the effect of participation on their election possibilities are likely to act according to their ideologies. Fourth, the two models may predict alternative courses of action; in this case, situational factors will determine which model best predicts actor behavior.

With the exception of the first, each of these patterns occurred in the participation controversy. To explain the orientation of the most important actors in the five cities, we can therefore illustrate the utility of combined use of electoral/organizational interest and ideological models. To be sure, for Black Power advocates, this exercise is hardly necessary. Their ideological motivation for supporting participation has already been amply demonstrated in Chapter 3, and the attractiveness of the resources—money, jobs, prestige, power, and legitimization—that the poverty program could provide neighborhood organizations and civil rights groups is so apparent that one need not be a cynic to interpret black demands for participation also in terms of the electoral/organizational interest model. Indeed, the orientation of black participants in the Community Action Program (CAP) controversy was so consistent in all five cities precisely because electoral or organizational interests and ideology decisively reinforced one another. But the application of these models is more complicated in the case of the other, largely white political participants in the community action controversy, and it is to their interests and ideologies that this chapter is devoted.

MAYORAL ELECTORAL INTERESTS AND THE PARTICIPATION ISSUE

The most obvious connection between community action and the electoral interest model was the set of substantial costs that a participatory program would impose on all big-city mayors. Of course, varying conditions in the five cities meant that all the mayors did not, on balance, have the same interests. But in understanding the behavior of all the relevant actors, it is important to understand the common mayoral costs.

A participatory CAP, after all, would necessarily encourage heightened protest by ghetto residents. Charges of police brutality and calls for a civilian review board, however, would clearly arouse the ire of police departments. Public housing authorities would hardly welcome the formation of militant tenant groups. Principals and teachers would generally oppose complaints about traditional educational practices, especially those articulated by slum dwellers with little formal education. Real estate interests would bitterly attack picketing, demonstrations, and rent strikes by tenement residents. And private welfare agencies were sure to dislike the development of autonomous organizations that competed for clients, funds, and staff.

Few mayors desired to antagonize any of these entrenched interests. Independent militant groups sponsored by the war on poverty seemed likely to irritate most of them. For mayors loyal to a regular party organization, such participation might also threaten the political loyalty and reliability of inner city voters. Once having obtained poverty funds, neighborhood groups would acquire a strong incentive to obtain enough power to assure additional funding later. And such power seemed readily available if they could replace precinct captains in influencing the residents' political behavior.

Even for reform-minded mayors, community protests, by directly attacking governmental agencies that had great independent power, might create political difficulties. It is true that reform mayors might wish to capitalize on such protests by using them as an excuse for centralizing power in the mayor's office. Both Lindsay and Cavanagh felt bureaucracies needed more mayoral direction and that community criticisms of bureaucracies might help achieve this objective. The greater centralization that might be a by-product of protest could produce a voter dividend. But the strong negative reaction of electorally potent public bureaucracies to such a strategy suggests the contrary, even in Detroit and New York. Indeed, Piven argues that the great increase in urban expenditures in recent years has been due to political leaders who, in pursuing their political interests, "bought" the support of bureaucratic personnel who were offended at the criticisms articulated by community organizations and civil rights groups.[11] Although mayors might wish to supervise their bureaucracies more closely, encouraging protest is not the politically profitable way of achieving this objective. Even reform mayors had good reason to be wary, in the words of militant community organizer Saul Alinsky, of financing "a group dedicated to fierce political independence and to the servicing of its own self-interests as it defines them."[12]

These obvious political costs did not mean, however, that the mayors had an interest in opposing participation in all its aspects. The very fact that the attack on political poverty had struck such a responsive chord among urban minority groups indicated a political alienation, a sense of exclusion from full citizenship, which presented the mayors an opportunity to minimize their problems. So long as they could keep control over the Community Action Agency's (CAA's) substantive *policies*—so that attacks on the cities' entenched interests were not encouraged—the mayors could respond to this alienation by accepting, indeed embracing, participation as a symbol.[13] At least in the short run, and the short run is where political careers continue or are terminated, it was in their electoral interest to adopt institutional arrangements which were formally or procedurally democratic. Such an arrangement might well have the residents of the poverty areas elect representatives to the City Poverty Council (CPC), provided the representatives did not significantly influence policy.

In the language of economic analysis, the model assumes that the mayors would maximize their electoral interests by "spending" enough of their available resources to secure, if at all possible, reliably antiparticipatory substantive policies. But mayors would not "overspend"; they would not fight OEO's participatory requirements to the extent of trying to achieve a symbolically antiparticipatory program, because the cost in terms of inner city resentment would not be offset by any significant gain in greater support from other groups. Whites in general had only a marginal concern about participation in CAP, and entrenched interests, opposed to black militancy, would be able to distinguish between symbolic and substantive participation policies. Admittedly, this course of action cannot conclusively be shown to a better electoral strategy than opposition to participation at both the symbolic and substantive policy levels. But such an alternative specification of mayoral interests fails to explain the relevant data. Only two of the six mayors considered here categorically and consistently rejected symbolic participation.*

To argue a third alternative, that the electoral interest model accounts for both acceptance and rejection of participation by actors *in identical or substantially similar situations,* seriously undermines its scientific utility. Conceptually, use of the electoral interest model resembles the attribution of a latent factional or regime interest. Its validity does not rest on the actor's observable attitudes or desires, because it refers to what is in fact ("objectively") good for him; its scientific status depends on its utility for generating interesting and empirically valid propositions. But to hypothesize that actors, in such similar circumstances, will at times pursue one course of action and at other times a diametrically opposed one, eliminates any way of falsifying (and therefore of verifying) the model. Since the electoral interest model clearly has difficulties in explaining mayoral responses to participation, we shall return to this problem later in the chapter in order to see if the ideological model fares any better. But we shall begin by examining easier cases, where interests and ideologies suggest congruent political strategies.

AGREEMENT OF INTERESTS AND IDEOLOGIES: AN ATTACK ON ECONOMIC POVERTY

Except for Yorty, all mayors found it both in their electoral interest and consistent with their ideological commitment to conduct an economic war on poverty through both the CAP and juvenile delinquency program.† Liberal Pragmatists such as Tate, Wagner, and Daley acquired a clear ideological commitment to fight economic poverty through governmental activity when they accepted the welfare state programs of the national Democratic party. These Liberal Pragmatist mayors supported passage of these programs at the federal level and enthusiastically implemented them locally. Cavanagh and Lindsay also found the attack on economic poverty entirely consistent with their commitment as Community Conservationists to an active, rationalized government solving the problems of the poor. Moreover, these mayors, like the mayors of other big American cities with substantial poverty areas, found the program equally attractive in terms of their interests as politicians. An antiquated tax structure had created severe burdens on city budgets at the

* Daley and Yorty opposed symbolic participation. Tate, Cavanagh, Wagner, and Lindsay did not. The change in the mayoralty in New York in the midst of the early stages of the CAP gives us six mayors in the five cities.

† Yorty's ideology and interests are considered explicitly on pages 140–141.

same time that the poor and minority groups were demanding costly expansion of such services as education, health, recreation, and welfare. Even though community action provided far too little money to solve such problems, the new federal program at least could satisfy some demands at little cost to local taxpayers and perhaps at the same time act (or appear to act) to prevent civil disorder.

Consequently, except in Los Angeles, mayors formed committees to direct local poverty programs even before June 1964, anticipating that the war on poverty program would focus on the economic problems of the poor. Even earlier, the three Liberal Pragmatist mayors, Daley, Tate, and Wagner, consistently supported the development of the juvenile delinquency program, the attack on economic poverty that preceded the war on poverty itself. Because the juvenile delinquency program was in its early stages not afflicted by the participation issue, it nicely exemplifies the manner in which these Liberal Pragmatist mayors, in attacking economic poverty, conformed almost perfectly to both their pragmatist ideology and their electoral interests. They modified their initial proposals and personal preferences quite readily to minimize opposition among influential groups they did not wish to alienate. In effect, changing conditions in the "market," i.e., the demands and influence of other actors, led these mayors to adjust their own policy positions. But at the same time, the mayors deferred to and compromised among a wide variety of vested interests, thus conforming to their commitment to pluralist bargaining. Let us examine mayoral behavior in each of the three cities.

Pluralist Bargaining in New York City

In New York, Mayor Wagner had first to take into account the sectarian Catholic Charities and Federation of Jewish Agencies which had long favored distributing social services (except for cash payments to eligible recipients) through private, very often religious, agencies. This coalition was opposed by the Protestant Federation of Agencies and secularist groups, notably the prestigious lobbying organization, Citizens' Committee for Children, which urged a larger role for public agencies. In 1961, the secularists accordingly sought better coordination of services within the city government by increasing the supervisory powers of the office of the city administrator—a traditional Protestant bailiwick—over departments responsible for services to children and youth. As a result of these pressures, a deputy city administrator did obtain jurisdiction over the juvenile delinquency program. In order to develop activities outside the control of the large sectarian federations, whose influence was greatest at the citywide level, he encouraged various community leaders to plan juvenile delinquency and related programs for their neighborhoods—a step opposed by Catholic Charities and their close ally in city government, the youth board.

Well aware that these conflicts could endanger his political position, Wagner carefully arranged compromises that reflected the apparent balance of power in the private welfare community. Although the mayor agreed during his 1961 reform campaign to have the reform-oriented city administrator assume a direct coordinating role over youth services, he postponed this step and thus mollified Catholic Charities by initially authorizing only a study of the proposal.[14] By the time the study had been completed, the reform movement, the secularists' ally in welfare politics, had been weakened by the deaths of its most well-known leaders, Mrs. Eleanor Roosevelt and former Senator Herbert Lehman. Reflecting this shift in power, Wagner never implemented the report's recommendation for coordinating youth services. In early 1964, as national discussions of the poverty program began, he assigned supervision of this new program not to the city administrator, but to a staff assistant with closer ties to the sectarian agencies.

Pluralist Bargaining in Chicago

In Chicago, the early struggle over the juvenile delinquency program largely took place between public and private agencies.[15] Daley first asked the director of the youth commission to develop the program. But the private agencies and the President's Committee on Juvenile Delinquency and Youth Crime, believing the youth commissioner would be too sympathetic to the interests of other governmental agencies, induced the mayor to select as coordinator the deputy commissioner for city planning. The mayor also agreed to shift formal control from a strictly public agency to a private corporation, whose board of directors included business and private agency leaders as well as city officials. Reflecting his unusually strong bargaining position, Daley appointed to the new corporation's board a majority of public officials and community leaders closely associated with the city administration. As a result, the mayor could have a decisive vote in formulating policy should he wish to exercise it. Nevertheless, in order to minimize conflict among competing interests, the mayor had made a significant concession with respect to the program's organizational structure and formal lines of authority.

Pluralist Bargaining in Philadelphia

The juvenile delinquency program in Philadelphia was originally shaped by the Greater Philadelphia Movement, an organization of leading businessmen who had supported the reform movement, the city's urban renewal program, and who, in the 1960s, turned to problems of "human renewal."[16] Informed that the Ford Foundation would finance social reform, they sought an organization independent of both the city welfare department and the private agencies' coordinating council.* Their pressure finally induced Mayor Tate to establish an independently controlled juvenile delinquency program (PJDP).[17] The new agency, however, encountered substantial opposition almost immediately. It openly criticized private welfare services in North Philadelphia and developed its own comprehensive plan without consulting experienced professionals in the field. Meanwhile, the welfare department submitted its own plan for a youth conservation corps to the Ford Foundation and when the foundation funded PJDP instead, the department cooperated with its rival unenthusiastically. PJDP also managed to antagonize the black community which it had sought to help, for it had recruited few blacks at either staff or policy-making levels. Indeed, after the outgoing president of the local NAACP resigned, PJDP had no blacks at all on its board.

All of these tensions focused on the selection of PJDP's executive director. The city proposed an administrator from its welfare department. Businessmen reformers, suspicious of city control, favored a university professor who had developed the original proposal submitted to the Ford Foundation. The public and private welfare agencies, upset over the professor's implied criticism of past policies, bitterly opposed him. As a compromise, PJDP selected a Jewish lawyer with no involvement and thus no enemies in the welfare arena, appointing the other two candidates as assistant directors. But the conflict only intensified: Both assistant directors left the program complaining about incoherent, weak leadership; while the new NAACP president, Cecil Moore, unhappy about PJDP's inaction and lack of black personnel, criticized the inexperienced white director as the kind of individual "who pulled out of North Philadelphia when Negroes moved in."[18]

Although PJDP finally managed to finance four separate programs providing services to the North Philadelphia black community, the prospect of a federally funded CAP led to an even greater crisis. Supported

* During this same period, the Ford Foundation began to develop a policy of providing massive philanthropic assistance to transitional neighborhoods in large cities to keep them from adding to the urban slums. A carefully researched but comprehensive attack on the entire range of social problems in these "gray areas," it was believed, might save them from a "black future." Close liaison was maintained between the gray areas and juvenile delinquency programs. Thus, they both funded the same projects in Philadelphia and New York City; in Chicago, however, the program was funded solely by the President's Committee. For purposes of simplicity and comparability, we shall refer to both the Ford Foundation and the President's Committee programs in all of the three cities as juvenile delinquency programs.

by the businessmen reformers, the Ford Foundation threatened to withdraw its financial support unless Tate assigned PJDP the responsibility for CAP coordination. But the public and private welfare agencies adamantly opposed giving this program such power over vast federal funds. Local welfare officials urged the national OEO staff not to give the PJDP staff any information on CAP procedures. Many private agencies sent their projects directly to the welfare department instead, arguing that all proposals had to have city approval. One private welfare leader bluntly told the mayor that his agency was not adequately involved in CAP through mere representation on the PJDP board. And another welfare executive refused to help PJDP review CAP proposals.

Tate's flexibility in the face of these pressures both conformed to the norms of pluralist bargaining and at the same time protected his own electoral interest. He had included representatives of all interested public and private agencies on the PJDP board, had the staff members selected primarily to mollify every important interest; and, in June 1964, despite his own preference for a city-controlled CAP, he had assigned the staff responsibility for the new program to PJDP. It was the opposition of the private and public agencies, not mayoral sabotage, that rendered this compromise unworkable and led both Tate and the Ford Foundation to turn away from PJDP as a vehicle for welfare reform.

Covert Politics of Liberal Pragmatists

In all three cities, mayoral efforts to reach compromises that roughly reflected power relations in the welfare field clearly conformed not only to the three mayors' Liberal Pragmatist ideology but also to their electoral interest in maintaining broad support. In the first place, policy content reflected this consonance of ideology and electoral interest, as mayors found workable compromises that accommodated the vital concerns of all the most powerful participants rather than imposing any settlement in opposition to the demands of an established interest.

Second, the political style also reflected mayoral realism and commitment to the pluralist bargaining approach. Had the mayors wanted to impose their own settlement on the participants, a crusading style with appeals to the public would have been in order. Mayoral interests and Liberal Pragmatist ideology prescribed a more cautious approach: First the power factors that were being brought to bear were identified, and only then did the mayor work out a compromise.[19] Thus, Wagner in New York accommodated the various interests without publicity. Newspaper accounts only reported official events, such as the initiation of a study, the completion of a report, and the formation of a committee to develop a poverty program. The internal bargaining among established interests was kept discreetly confidential. In Chicago, Daley made his concessions to the private welfare community without involving the media at all. Even in Philadelphia, where the conflict was most prolonged and complex, Tate bargained privately. When the new NAACP president sought to socialize the conflict, he received support from neither public nor private agencies. Rather than throw the issue into the partisan electoral political arena, these agencies opposed PJDP, with ultimate success, in private meetings and committee sessions. As will be shown later, only where this political style was itself under open attack and the option of privatizing politics was precluded, did Liberal Pragmatist ideology induce its adherents to overt political conflict.

IDEOLOGICAL INDIFFERENCE AND ELECTORAL/ORGANIZATIONAL INTEREST SALIENCE

Yorty and an Attack on Economic Poverty

If a coincidence in the ideology and electoral interests of Liberal Pragmatist mayors accounts for their consistent support of a war on economic poverty that nonetheless accommodated established interest groups, other actors, whose ideology provided no definite guidance, followed a political strategy that varied with changes in "market conditions," i.e., the strength and activities of other actors. As a result, the extent of their activity and the policies they favored sometimes took an apparently erratic, or even contradictory, course as they made adjustments to newly perceived opportunities, potential alliances, and unforeseen obstacles during the conflict. Mayor Yorty clearly illustrates this pattern.

Yorty's ideology provided no clear guidance with respect to an economic attack on poverty either through the juvenile delinquency program or CAP. His ideological neutrality on this issue reflected his two very disparate manifest interests. He acted as a White Power advocate and appealed to antiblack sentiments by denouncing both the Watts riots and any organized expressions of black militancy. He employed "law and order" slogans which were widely understood as an attack on black violence. He strongly defended his police department against charges of police brutality. In 1969, he narrowly won reelection over a black city councilman with a campaign increasingly marked by racial attacks. On the other hand, Yorty also was committed to rationalizing governmental services. As mayor he allied himself with the governmental bureaucracies which dominated Los Angeles' nonpartisan, fully reformed local politics. In rejecting community control over the police and the schools, he invoked the expertise of the city's professional administrators. He supported activist governmental agencies, which operated according to impersonal standards, and sought to expand their activities and budgets.

Certainly there were tensions between rationalizing government, which required color-blind policies, and the racial animus of a White Power advocate. Yorty's ideology was thus relatively rare among major politicians in the five cities. A Democrat, he consistently supported Republicans in national politics and fought publicly and repeatedly with leading state Democrats, and his ideology was sufficiently peculiar so that he became California's leading maverick in a state known for personality politics. Yet Yorty was not opposed to the city government's hiring individual blacks through the formal, impersonal procedure of a civil service system. The mayor himself appointed a number of cooperative blacks to his administration and made alliances with a few friendly black politicians. Still he was manifestly concerned about defending whites against the rise of a broadly based Black Power movement. He opposed black efforts to obtain collective political power in order to alter standards for hiring public employees, compensate for past discrimination by special programs for minorities, or attack the allegedly racist acts of particular city officials. And often—for example, in defending the police department's response to the Watts riots, or rejecting demands for a participatory CAP—the two elements of the ideology were combined quite comfortably.

The attack on economic poverty, however, was another matter. The mayor's manifest White Power interest hardly welcomed a program explicitly directed in urban areas to benefiting black and Mexican residents, often on a collective basis. Yet his concern for rationalizing administrative practice was entirely consistent with the reform of welfare services and the grant of new federal funds to the city's aggressive bureaucratic agencies. The two components of his ideology gave contrary guides for dealing with an economic war on poverty. As a result, he was left to act primarily on the basis of his electoral interests. His behavior consequently fluctuated with changes in perceived political opportunities, alliances, and threats.

Yorty cooperated in establishing the juvenile delinquency program because he had much the same electoral interest as any other mayor in acquiring federal funds to help potentially restive minority groups and in appearing to act forcefully to solve a difficult social problem. But as soon as maximum feasible participation in CAP emerged as a significant issue, Yorty's electoral interests became more complicated. Despite his continued interest in fostering federal support for social services, even an attack on economic poverty appeared contrary to his overall interests once it seemed possible that the CAA would itself be influenced by residents seeking participatory policies. With this change in the situation, Yorty's behavior shifted accordingly. To be sure, he never actually prevented the establishment of a CAA, which he had the practical power to do. Such a step might have been too costly. And, after negotiation of a satisfactory compromise, he generally cooperated with the new CAA. But during the tortuous maneuvering which preceded this agreement, he offered a series of distinctively different proposals on the composition of the CPC, denounced alternatives proposed by others, and even upset an agreement that all other parties had reached. These tactics so delayed OEO funding that, in its first year, Los Angeles ranked far behind New York, Chicago, and Philadelphia in the per-capita level of federal CAP money received and spent.

Yorty, in short, followed his interests in supporting the economic attack on poverty when there was no issue of participation, but was willing to impede the economic aspect of the program to forestall a participatory program. Since he had few ideological qualms at delaying or reducing CAP's service-delivery component, he refused to allow the program to proceed until the participation issue was resolved to his satisfaction.

Mayors Daley, Tate, and Wagner had equally strong reasons to oppose a CAP in which representatives of the poor had genuine influence over policy. But they favored an attack on economic poverty for reasons of both ideology and political interest. As a result, they took steps to separate the attack on political poverty, with its participatory potential, from the issue of delivering services, so that they could continue to seek federal funding for its economic aspects. Unlike Yorty, their ideology impelled them to maximize CAP's economic activities at the same time that they sought to minimize its participatory component. By contrast, Yorty's electoral interests, uncomplicated by a clear ideological commitment to the war on poverty, helped delay and thwart the development even of the CAP's economic component. Indeed, totally unlike the Liberal Pragmatists, he sometimes reveled in broadening the conflict through a series of attention-getting attacks on his varied political foes.

The Progressive Conservatives and Participation

If Mayor Yorty was ideologically indifferent to an economic attack on poverty, the Progressive Conservatives assumed a similar stance toward an attack on political poverty. Although they took part in the controversy over participation in every city but Detroit, where the mayor and black leaders settled the issue before others could intervene, Progressive Conservatives had no clear ideological position on participation in CAP. They favored greater resident involvement insofar as this might secure a more coherent, better coordinated distribution of social services, which were scattered among a hodgepodge of public and private agencies. And they also favored participation insofar as it would handicap mayoral use of the program for patronage purposes. But even in the early stages of the participation issues they were hardly enthusiastic about any growth in lower-income political militancy that might interfere with rationalized bureaucratic procedures or harm the interests of the business community. Given this ideological uncertainty, the Progressive Conservatives supported or opposed participation as their specific electoral or organizational interests dictated.

The carriers of the Progressive Conservative tradition in big cities have been the institutions that have concerned themselves with the welfare of the community as a whole but at the same time are heavily dependent upon the business community. Three such institutions which became involved in the politics of community action were the private welfare agencies, the urban Republican party, and the metropolitan newspapers. To be sure, these institutions were not always headed by a Progressive Conservative leadership; the very Orthodox Conservative character of the Illinois Republican party in the mid-1960s and Chicago's leading newspaper, the *Tribune*, are well-known cases in point. And we shall note in passing the differences in the responses of Progressive Conservatives, motivated solely by their electoral or organizational interests, and Orthodox Conservatives, who remained in principled opposition to participation. Moreover, the diversity of private welfare agencies make generalization about the ideology of their leadership particularly risky. Yet, in general, metropolitan newspapers depend on the advertisements of downtown establishments, the urban Republican party depends on politically oriented members of the business community, and private welfare agencies not only recruit businessmen as board members but are also dependent upon United Fund drives conducted by businessmen. Significantly, all these institutions are not dependent on the business community as such, but primarily upon the most prominent, the most influential, the most civic-minded, and the most progressive members of that community. Under these circumstances, the similar ideological perspective of most leaders of these various institutions is not surprising.

PRIVATE WELFARE AGENCIES. Although the Progressive Conservatives' ideology provided no definitive guidelines for participation, private welfare agencies had a very considerable organizational interest in influencing CAP. Most obviously, they wanted poverty funds for their own programs, but they also sought to prevent the new program from "duplicating," i.e., competing with, existing activities. They argued that antipoverty personnel should meet the agencies' own professional standards. Finally, it seemed imperative that OEO-funded programs not offer much higher salaries than private agencies could afford to pay for comparable positions. "From the outset [commented one New York agency executive]

I thought that the size of the salaries was too high. Demonstration projects raided us and the public agencies. . . . Besides that, those who were left were dissatisfied with their pay because they knew of the big salaries that people were making with these demonstration projects." In addition, the private agencies in each city belonged to a coordinating council (their titles varied*) to help regulate relationships among themselves and represent their common interests politically.

In pursuit of these organizational interests four coordinating councils excluding Detroit's first offered to assume direct administrative control over the CAP, arguing that the agencies' experience would insure the CAP's prompt beginning and efficient administration.† When all four mayors rejected these offers, preferring to maintain direction of the programs themselves, the councils next sought substantial private agency representation on the CPC. The executive director of the Chicago coordinating council called for "a governing body with balanced representation of the many community interests concerned with poverty and able to contribute to its substantial reduction." The private welfare agencies in Philadelphia not only sabotaged the juvenile delinquency program's control over community action because they felt excluded, but objected to a new plan which relegated private agency representatives to a merely advisory role. The agencies asked instead that the CPC include representatives from all the major sectarian organizations, the settlement houses, and the coordinating council itself.

The New York City coordinating council told Paul Screvane in a memorandum that: "Professional and lay leaders of voluntary agencies . . . [feel that their present] advisory role . . . does not properly position the voluntary sector in the structure to be of maximum service. . . . They urge that representatives of the voluntary sector participate in policy-making and decisions regarding the design of the total program." One private welfare leader put the demands more colloquially: "I said, 'Mr. Screvane, this city is full of some of the top leaders and experts in the field of health and welfare and . . . we resent very much the idea that you people . . . are not drawing in these real experts. . . .'" Screvane responded by giving representation to welfare agencies on the CPC and by establishing a planning and coordinating committee which in-

---

* In 1965, the titles were: Welfare Council of Metropolitan Chicago; Coordinating Council of Greater New York; Philadelphia Health and Welfare Council; United Community Services of Metropolitan Detroit; and Welfare Planning Council of the United Way (of Los Angeles).

† In Detroit, Mayor Cavanagh moved so quickly to establish the city's program that the private agencies had no real opportunity to intervene. In addition, results of recent studies had damaged the agencies' reputation in the antipoverty field.

cluded private welfare agency representatives. In Los Angeles, the coordinating council of private welfare agencies, finding themselves excluded from the CPC as it was originally constituted, sought first to establish their own Economic Opportunity Federation as a CAP delegate agency with no tie to local governments. After attracting support from Community Conservationist politicians in the Democratic party and from OEO itself, they were then able to seek a merger which initially retained a nongovernmental majority on the CPC, though later, at Yorty's insistence, a governmental majority was established.

In the course of these efforts, the private agencies, led by the councils in each of the four cities, formally or informally supported participation during at least one phase of the maneuvering over the CAAs' organizational structure. In Chicago, although the coordinating council itself took no formal position, individuals associated with it did voice their concern about participation to the city administration. One of the council's board members objected to the city's initial plan because it suggested to him that "local grass roots movements are not welcome." A staff member urged that the program encourage "organized and effective request[s] for better police protection, building code enforcements or refuse collection." Later, a council staff memorandum urged the CAA executive director to "state a principle that the local citizens living in poverty areas will be involved to the greatest extent possible." Council staff members even met with neighborhood groups to discuss joint efforts for promoting resident participation.

In Philadelphia, the settlement house movement gave considerable help to the neighborhood organizations asking for greater citizen participation. The private welfare agency representatives on a committee advising the mayor on community action proposed that the CPC include six to ten representatives of the poor. In Los Angeles, the coordinating council included minority group representatives in their proposed Economic Opportunity Federation, and this entity did negotiate a CPC structure providing for some low-income representatives. The private welfare agencies encouraged resident participation most openly in New York City. The president of the coordinating council vigorously attacked the CAP structure because it lacked the support of black and Puerto Rican neighborhood leaders: "This is the biggest double-cross I have ever seen in all my years of dealing with City Hall. The announcement was not to have been made until the proposals had been reviewed and accepted by the neighborhood groups. They had lots of questions, and it was understood that there would be refinement of the proposals."

The private agencies, however, acted in this way only when their own organizational interests were furthered. In all four cities they opposed a program tightly controlled by government officials, and urged instead a large CPC on which they would have significant representation and, subsequently, considerable influence. When faced with exclusion from the CPC, they supported the participation of the poor in order to create a broadly based, more effective coalition. But in every case, resident participation lost its allure when the private agencies achieved the primary goal of significant representation on the CPC for themselves. Typically, in establishing the Economic Opportunity Federation, the Los Angeles coordinating council included direct representation of the poor on the proposed CPC only after the black leaders in the "1122 Group" raised the possibility of a coalition against the local governments. Even then the council allotted only three of the fifteen seats on their proposed CPC to minority group representatives. And they agreed to a reduction in even this ratio when they merged with the government agency, so that only three of nineteen seats were allocated to these representatives. Others outside the private welfare community, notably OEO and certain black leaders, generated the subsequent pressure for the substantially larger proportion of resident representatives, with seven out of twenty-three called for in the final plan. Moreover, once the CPC was established, the representatives elected by low-income residents found that the private agency spokesmen usually sided with the public agencies.

In Philadelphia, as soon as their influence was secured, the private welfare agencies opposed selection of the representatives of the poor by neighborhood groups, favoring selection either by settlement houses or by the other members of the CPC, which consisted primarily of city officials and representatives of the private agencies themselves. The agencies only reluctantly agreed to the election of representatives of the poor as a minimally acceptable compromise. Shortly thereafter, they ruptured their relations with the elected representatives by insisting that the CAP administrative staff have professional training, making it much harder to hire the poor.

Even when the private agencies did not readily secure a strong position on the CPC, as in Chicago, their organizational interests sometimes led them to oppose participation. To protect its position in a community whose civic life was so dominated by the mayor, the Chicago coordinating council never asserted its support for community participation formally and publicly. When a reporter for the *New Republic* published one of the council's especially negative, but highly confidential, evaluations of the Chicago CAA, the council apologized profusely to the CAA director.[20]

The agencies eventually became the most concerned about participation in New York, where they feared that community groups would become a direct organizational threat. Even while the lay president of the New York coordinating council was still attacking Screvane's antiparticipatory policies, certain private welfare professionals quietly took a different position with Mayor Wagner. By this time they had not only been offered a position within the decision-making structure, but they had begun to see the growing number of autonomous neighborhood agencies, such as Haryou-Act and Mobilization for Youth (MFY), as serious competitors for organizational resources.

REPUBLICANS. The electoral interest model can be applied in a comparable way to the behavior of Progressive Conservatives in the Republican party. As the opposition party in Chicago, New York, and Philadelphia, Republicans had a clear electoral interest in fostering participation. A city-controlled antipoverty program might well increase the Democrats' patronage, welding inner city residents still more closely to the machine. Moreover, since black leaders seemed to be thoroughly unhappy with the Democratic mayors' antiparticipatory position, the Republicans had the opportunity, if they supported participation, to encourage dissatisfaction among blacks, undermining the Democrats in their ghetto bastion. Indeed, even if autonomous community organizations were not regularly Republican, they might well compete with their partisan enemy for voter loyalty. Equally important, any resulting resentment among whites was very likely to focus on incumbent mayors, not the Republicans. Given these clear electoral benefits, the progressive Republicans in Philadelphia and New York attacked the antiparticipatory policies which their cities' Democratic mayors followed during CAP's first months. Pennsylvania's Lt. Gov. Raymond Schafer, already planning his successful race for governor in 1966, maintained that: "Certain organization changes are desperately needed in the Philadelphia program if the poor of the city are to receive their just share of opportunity. The Philadelphia program must be expanded to be all-inclusive of representatives of those persons most affected by this blight of modern society." To Governor Nelson Rockefeller, the poverty program was "too important to the people to be turned into a high-pressure machine for narrow political advantage." He consequently vetoed a law designed by Mayor Wagner to prevent neighborhood representatives from acquiring control over administrative functions. Even more bluntly, Sen. Jacob Javits urged ". . . more alertness on the part of OEO and better procedures to insure that federal standards are being implemented to make it unnecessary for the poor to hold mass meetings to protest, instead of participate in these programs."

California Republicans, on the other hand, failed to support community participation. But this, too, was consistent with the party's political interests. Since Republicans in southern California did not have to contend with a significant Democratic party organization in Los Angeles' inner city, they did not share Javits's and Schafer's electoral interests in fostering politically independent neighborhood organizations. On the contrary, such organizations could well have increased the voting levels of lower-income Democrats; and certain units of Los Angeles' CAP did, at one point, undertake a voter-registration program which had precisely this result. Consistent with these electoral interests, Republicans gave no assistance to the black and Mexican-American proparticipatory coalition. For the more conservative Republicans, this stance was as compatible with their Orthodox Conservative ideology as it was with their political interests. But even a more progressive Republican, Sen. Thomas Kuchel, failed to give support to participation in the way his fellow progressives in the eastern states had done.

In one case, Republicans did act contrary to their electoral interests. Chicago Republicans in 1965 had not yet diverged significantly from the Orthodox Conservatism that has traditionally been the strongest among Midwestern Republicans. With an ideology opposed to participation, they refused to attack Mayor Daley's tight control over the program even though they had potent electoral interests in weakening Chicago's Democratic political machine.* But with this Chicago exception, produced by a more Orthodox Conservative ideology, urban Republicans pursued their electoral interests in taking their positions on the participation issue.

THE PRESS. The behavior of the press resembled that of the Progressive Republicans. To be sure, the press had no clear economic stake in the participation issue. As Banfield has pointed out, urban newspapers sometimes encourage civic controversies to stimulate citizen interest and thus high circulation, and they want the central business district to grow and prosper, encouraging reader identification with the central city press.[21] But these economic motivations do not explain why the papers chose to enter a controversy which did not directly affect central city prosperity, nor once involved, why they should favor—rather than oppose —a proparticipatory position. On the other hand, an organizational in-

---

* Some might argue that Chicago Republicans were simply an appendage of the Daley Democrats, and it was in their organizational interest to limit criticism of the mayor. Although in certain parts of Chicago this may be true, the contention overlooks the close contests at the county and state-wide levels. Whatever the interests of lower-ranking precinct captains, the heads of the Republican party have a clear interest in weakening the inner city Democratic machine.

The more progressive Republicanism of Charles Percy had not begun to triumph within the party until 1966, when Percy defeated his opponent for the Republican senatorial nomination. The events described here took place in early 1965.

terest in weakening the influence of Liberal Pragmatist politicians does illuminate the papers' behavior. The influence of the precinct captain over inner city voters limits the effectiveness of the papers' good-government recommendations both in elections and civic controversies. While city control over CAP was likely to add to the strength of the regular organizations, a participatory program, by weakening the machine politicians, would make the papers all the more influential in local politics. As in the case of Progressive Republicans, the positions of the Progressive Conservative papers, because their ideology gave them little guidance, varied directly with these organizational interests.

In Philadelphia and New York Progressive Conservative papers supported participation. The *Philadelphia Bulletin,* an evening paper that had to attract lower-income, substantially black readership, not only assigned a full-time reporter to cover and thus spread the controversy, but editorialized that "business, labor, the churches, the schools, health and welfare agencies, the neighborhood groups and the poor themselves —in short, the total community—must participate as has been done in other communities."[22] The *Philadelphia Inquirer,* with a somewhat more conservative orientation, did not take an editorial position but reported that the city would lose federal money because there was a "lack of community participation in the city's program."[23] In New York, the regularly, but generally Progressive, Republican *Herald Tribune* was somewhat uncertain but finally asserted that "the right way is to emphasize the people's control at the grass roots. Keep the politicians out."[24] And the more independent *Times* observed that "each day brings a fresh complaint that the final product will be dominated by city officials to the almost total exclusion of experts from established social agencies and spokesmen directly chosen by the people of the slums. . . . It is long past time for City Hall to take the community into its confidence."*[25]

In Chicago, however, the Progressive Conservative Field newspapers,

* For some New York papers, organizational interest and ideological position both dictated a proparticipatory position. The *New York Post,* with its primarily Jewish and black readership and some blend of a Community Conservationist and Orthodox Liberal ideology, termed "essential" a CAP which included "authentic community representation and participation."[26] But for two others, the organizational interest in supporting participation was less important to the paper's editorial staff than maintaining ideological consistency. New York's most Orthodox Conservative paper, the *Daily News,* had little trouble making up its mind. "In the Wagner-Powell set-to, we favor the Mayor and Mr. Screvane, and strongly disfavor Representative Powell."[27] The somewhat less conservative *Journal American* saw some virtue in representation but remained skeptical. "There can be no quarrel with the need for the poor to have a voice in the projects to help the poor help themselves. Their very privations equip them for the job. But can they be chosen without political influence?"[28]

like Chicago's coordinating council, felt that on balance their organizational interests precluded excessive criticism of the Daley administration, and accordingly they gave little support to participation. The *Sun-Times* commented that "The very size and complexity of the anti-poverty programs in larger cities makes it necessary that the initial organization be stimulated by whatever political party is in power."[29] The evening *Daily News,* which like the *Bulletin* sought a strong following in the black community, did permit one of its reporters to write a series highly critical of the CAA's antiparticipation policies. But it editorially opposed participation, and after this series did not seriously raise the issue again in its news columns.* If Progressive Conservative newspapers failed to support participation in Chicago because the strength of the machine inhibited criticism, the Progressive Conservative *Los Angeles Times* opposed participation for quite the opposite political reason. Without any patronage-oriented machine whose political influence qualified the power of the news media, the *Times* had no organizational interest in encouraging militant activity in poor areas. In sum, Progressive Conservative newspapers, like Progressive Conservative Republicans, supported participation when and only when it suited their electoral or organizational interests.

SALIENT IDEOLOGIES AND UNCERTAIN INTERESTS: COMMUNITY CONSERVATIONIST SUPPORT FOR PARTICIPATION

When ideologies are indifferent or irrelevant to the issue at hand, the electoral/organizational interest model, as we have seen, can anticipate rather accurately the position of political actors. The reverse is also true. Where electoral interests are uncertain, ideologies appear to motivate behavior. At least this seems to account for the behavior of Mayors Cavanagh of Detroit and Lindsay of New York, who in contrast to the other mayors accepted, and even endorsed, participation.

As a mayoral candidate, Lindsay charged that "City Hall" had set up "a structural monstrosity" to make policy for the poverty program; he favored instead "prompt steps to increase representation of the poor on the Council." Upon taking office, Lindsay abolished the Wagner administration's complicated structure which had prevented neighborhood

* The Orthodox Conservative *Chicago Tribune,* which had both ideological and organizational interest reasons for opposing participation, took an even stronger line against opening up the program to neighborhood organizations. It was openly fearful, for example, that The Woodlawn Organization, a militant black neighborhood group calling for participation, "already had its hooks in $700,000 obtained from the Department of Labor and was out for more."[30]

organization representatives from influencing administrative decisions. Instead, he established a new board with direct administrative powers, half of whose members represented these organizations. And his administration also gave greater operating autonomy to CAP programs already controlled by neighborhood groups.

In Detroit, when black leaders, at a private meeting with the mayor, demanded substantial influence in the CAA for inner city neighborhood groups, Cavanagh readily complied. As we have seen in Chapter 1, not only did black activists in Detroit secure important positions within the CAA from its first days, but the NPCs, controlled by neighborhood organizations, secured more than a third of the seats on the city-wide council. And Cavanagh allowed the CAA itself to provide some meaningful support to the neighborhood groups' own activities.

This behavior was inconsistent with what has already been shown to be the strong electoral interests against substantive policies encouraging participation that any mayor must have. Only if there were special circumstances in New York and Detroit offsetting the general considerations that affect all mayors could it be said that their behavior conformed to the electoral interest model. On first inspection, certain factors can be identified which do make New York and Detroit appear exceptional. Active community organizations, although troublesome for any mayor, are perhaps least threatening to reform mayors such as Lindsay, who are elected over the opposition of still-active machine politicians. Such mayors have depended for support largely on the newspapers, the prestigious civic associations, and middle-class reform clubs. But they lacked a stable organization to mobilize voters in low-income areas where even a weakened, but potentially effective, party organization may revive to regain power as it did in Saint Louis in the mid-1960s. By supporting funds for community groups in low-income areas and listening sympathetically to their demands, reform mayors could hope to expand their own voting constituencies. At least they would create new problems for hostile party organizations.

All of this seems to apply with particular force if the mayor supporting participation is a Republican reformer, opposing Democratic Liberal Pragmatists, as was the case with John Lindsay in 1965 and 1966. The Democratic black and Spanish-speaking residents living in the lowest-income areas often sought increased welfare benefits, more housing, better educational opportunities, and more opportunities for employment as skilled workers. Such demands threatened Democratic Italian, Polish, and Irish groups more than Republicans who lived in silk-stocking neighborhoods.[31] Through the mid-1960s, the machine's distribution of material benefits to particular individuals enabled the Democratic leaders to ignore such black demands at the local level, thus helping to maintain the loyalty of white ethnic groups. But if new community organizations were to make more collective demands for better public services, it would not be so easy to maintain the blacks' Democratic loyalties. In the 1965 local elections an alliance between Republicans and reformers in both New York and Philadelphia led to significant black defections from the Democrats, including leaders of neighborhood groups. And Lindsay did even better in black neighborhoods in his 1969 race.[32] Such political gains might well offset whatever difficulties insurgent community organizations might pose for any city administration.

In nonpartisan Detroit, independent mayoral candidates had no need to fear a patronage-oriented Democratic organization, but the electoral interest model offers another explanation for Cavanagh's behavior. Since the founding of the United Auto Workers (UAW) in the thirties, political conflict often took place among factional ideological groups. In the late 1950s, however, race had become more important than class as a local issue, and Cavanagh first won election with the overwhelming support of a black community outraged at a police "crackdown" in the ghetto. Although Cavanagh also needed, and received, significant white support, he recognized his debt to the black leadership. He had a clear electoral interest, it would seem, in maintaining good relations with them by acceding readily to their demands for participation.

These considerations, then, might appear to outweigh the problems which militant community organizations created for all big-city mayors. In fact, however, Lindsay's and Cavanagh's electoral interests were even more complicated than the preceding paragraphs have suggested. Both mayors also had to consider whether encouraging minority demands for inclusion in the political system might rupture the entire alliance between minority groups and white Community Conservationists on which they depended. In Detroit, the steadily growing black community reached about 40 percent of the total population in the late 1960s, making it feasible for a black candidate for mayor to reach the nonpartisan run-off election. In fact, after Cavanagh had decided not to run in 1969, a black candidate did reach the run-off and lost the general election by less than 1 percent. If one could anticipate such developments in 1965—and the demographic trend was too obvious to be overlooked—developing black political muscle was hardly in Cavanagh's purely electoral interest.

Even though the proportion of blacks in New York is much lower, Lindsay was faced with a comparable problem. Together with Puerto Ricans, blacks in the mid-1960s made up about 30 percent of the New York population, and it was entirely possible that they would coalesce behind a minority group candidate in the Democratic primary. In New

York's uncertain politics he might attract enough minority votes, plus liberal Jewish and Protestant support, to be a strong candidate. As it happened, Herman Badillo, a reform-minded Puerto Rican with substantial black support, only narrowly lost the Democratic nomination in 1969. Had he won the primary, it is not clear whether he would have defeated Lindsay by taking away much of his support or merely have caused the election of the Republican-Conservative candidate by splitting the liberal Democratic vote. But in terms of Lindsay's political career, the result would have been the same; all his steadfast support for participation in the black and Puerto Rican communities only would have strengthened the political position of his liberal Democratic opponent.

These considerations, even when added to the more general problems created by a participatory program, do not mean that Cavanagh's and Lindsay's interests clearly opposed participation. On the contrary, the electoral interests of these mayors were simply unclear. In 1965, a clever strategist for either mayor could have written a very plausible political scenario which dictated either a pro- or an antiparticipatory approach. It is precisely in such cases of uncertainty that politicians may have little alternative to acting ideologically.

Although Lindsay's and Cavanagh's positions on participation can be reduced to the electoral interest model only by ignoring genuine uncertainties in the political game, these same positions seem consistent with their Community Conservationist ideology. Mayor Lindsay, throughout his administration, encouraged in numerous ways the decentralization of city services and the greater involvement of minority groups in their administration. Cavanagh, too, encouraged black participation in the Model Cities program, school-decentralization planning, the program of Detroit's Housing Authority, and other areas of governmental activity. He responded in a more ameliorative, and less punitive, fashion to the 1967 race riots than did the mayor of any other large American city—even though this later would prove costly to his political future.[33] Indeed, it is said that he did not run for reelection as mayor because he believed the time had come for Detroit to have its own black mayor. No better illustration of ideology taking precedence over electoral interests can be provided.

If ideological considerations influenced Mayors Lindsay and Cavanagh, they were equally important to rank and file members of the Community Conservationist organizations that supported participation. Although these organizations varied in name and importance among the five cities, all of them may be loosely referred to as the reform-club movement. The patron saint of the clubs was Adlai Stevenson,[34] whose idealism and rhetoric stimulated certain upper middle-class urban professionals to participate actively in Democratic politics. The reformers soon came into conflict with the professional politicians, usually of immigrant Catholic working-class origin, who typically dominated the Democratic party. In the years just prior to the split over Vietnam, participation in the CAP was one of the major issues that divided these two groups. In 1965, Chicago's only Community Conservationist alderman criticized the Chicago CAP "for not having any poor people on the CPC." In Los Angeles, Congressman James Roosevelt, the reform-club candidate defeated by Yorty in the 1965 mayoral contests, supported participatory demands, as did George Brown, the congressman most clearly associated with the movement. Philadelphia's reform-club organization, the Americans for Democratic Action, demanded that "two-thirds of the directors" on the CPC "come from poverty areas in the city and be elected by their residents." The reform-club movement in New York became so incensed at Paul Screvane's handling of the participation issue that many club activists supported reform Congressman William F. Ryan rather than Screvane in the 1965 primary. Ryan's campaign rhetoric is revealing: "There is a fear that unless the city controls the program, the status quo will be threatened, creating a problem for the city. Because of this political fear and the enticing visions of a new patronage pool, the city administration is attempting to thwart the intent of Congress." Ryan instead called for administration of the CAP by "democratically" elected local boards. Finally, in Detroit, the one city where the mayor immediately acceded to the participatory demands of black activists, Cavanagh had previously drawn heavily on the relatively small group of middle-class Community Conservationists in the Democratic party in staffing both his 1961 campaign and then his administration.

According to the organizational interest model, reform-club support for participation should reflect the organizational maintenance needs of the movement. As Wilson points out:

> The task of maintaining a club based on the amateur spirit is far different from maintaining a machine clubhouse or ward headquarters. The amateur must constantly find ideals, personalities, and causes sufficient to replenish the easily exhausted reservoir of enthusiasm which stimulates him. Club leaders well know that this is not any easy job. As one Manhattan reformer phrased it, "Enthusiasm . . . is a very fragile thing. It can be broken easily. You daren't lose your momentum."[35]

Certainly this organizational interest analysis contributes to an understanding of the issue-oriented style of the reformers, but it does not account for their specific reform goals. The organizational interest model tells us only that the reformers will find some issue or other to stress in order to keep their club a viable organization. It does not tell us the type of issue or its actual content.

Where Cavanagh's and Lindsay's electoral interests on the participation issue were unclear, the interests of the reform club members—at least those who lacked political career ambitions—were neutral. We can explain their enthusiasm for a participatory CAP only in terms of their political commitments, i.e., their Community Conservationist ideology. Indeed, the ideology not only determined the policy position they favored, but it also accounted for the existence of the clubs themselves, and thus their organizational interests. Unless they had been ideologically dissatisfied with the conditions of urban and national politics, it is hard to see why the club members would have joined this political organization in the first place. Only after the organization was established, in response to these ideological concerns, could it have an interest in its own maintenance or enhancement.

INTEREST AND IDEOLOGY CONFLICT: YORTY, TATE, DALEY, AND WAGNER AND AN ATTACK ON POLITICAL POVERTY

Students of the electoral/organizational interest model may feel that the analysis thus far has only elaborated, not seriously qualified, this interest model. Some mayors reached positions consistent with both their ideology and interest, a pattern that Downs had clearly anticipated. Some private welfare agencies, Republicans, and newspapers, for whom ideology had no relevance to the issue, shifted their stance with their electoral or organizational interests, a pattern of behavior that would lead some observers to conclude that they had no ideology at all. Even those mayors who acted in accord with their ideology at times when interests were unclear might be explained away as having used ideology simply as a shorthand mechanism for calculating interests. Although this last line of argument is too simplistic, it is true that our insistence on an ideological model as a supplement to, rather than simply an extension of, the electoral/organizational interest model requires the identification of skilled politicians who reached decisions on ideological grounds even when their electoral interests dictated otherwise. And it was precisely because the response to participatory demands by such successful politicians as Mayors Daley, Yorty, and Wagner could not be easily encompassed within the electoral interest model that we were forced to revise our early analysis of this aspect of the politics of community action. The fact that Mayor Tate's behavior could be explained so readily in terms of the electoral interest model only made the contrasting stance of the other leaders all the more puzzling.

All these mayors, it is true, did resemble each other in their initial opposition to participatory CAP policies. Wagner of New York, for example, told a congressional committee: "When I testified a year ago, I urged that the local governing bodies, through their chief executives or otherwise, should have the ultimate responsibility, for . . . the conduct and operation of the program."[36] An early unpublished document of the Daley administration stated his position in language more convoluted yet more revealing: "Chicago believes the role of active and constructive citizenship cannot be imposed on the poor person by participation in an action committee which has ignored his personal development. That if development is postponed in order to involve the poor person immediately in committee action roles, his involvement may frequently lead to the negative involvement of protest." When the federal OEO insisted on some resident participation in the Los Angeles CAA, Yorty accused the federal officials of "trying to browbeat us and threaten us into removing local government from control" of the antipoverty program.[37] Later he claimed that mayors all over the country were "being harassed by agitation promoted by [OEO director] Sargent Shriver's speeches urging those he calls the 'poor' to insist upon control of local end-poverty [*sic*] programs."[38] In a letter to the *Philadelphia Bulletin,* Tate echoed these sentiments, although, significantly enough, in somewhat vaguer language :"Knowledgeable Philadelphians appreciate the fact that it was the *city's* responsibility [as distinct from that of a body of representatives selected by the poor] to . . . get the beginnings of a program under way. . . ."[39]

Except in Los Angeles, these mayors immediately established a City Poverty Council (CPC) to direct the CAA which included representatives from virtually all relevant governmental institutions, such as the schools, the welfare department, the youth agency, the park boards, the employment agency, and later, in response to pressure, representatives of the private welfare community. In keeping with their expressed sentiments, the mayors excluded representatives from black neighborhood organizations. Similarly, Yorty at first insisted that CAP be administered by the juvenile delinquency agency's board, which was comprised of officials from the state, the city and county, and city and county schools. He explicitly and vehemently opposed the inclusion of any nongovernmental representatives from minority neighborhoods.

These positions may seem entirely consistent with the mayors' electoral interests. Yet, as we noted earlier, the mayors' electoral interests required, at most, only opposition to substantively participatory policies, not opposition to the *symbols* of participation. Indeed, in Philadelphia, Mayor Tate and his close associate Samuel Evans followed just such a politically astute strategy. Admittedly, the mayor provided for no representation of the poor in his initially proposed structures, though he included Samuel Evans as a secretary to the mayor's task force on poverty in order to maintain a clear link to the black community. But once participatory demands were raised, he settled the issue more quickly than any of the other mayors (save Community Conservationist Cavanagh), allowing for representation of the poor in an agreement with OEO in early February of 1965. Evans persuaded the mayor that, provided certain precautions were taken,[40] election of the poor would not endanger the mayor's interests. As a result, the mayor agreed to the election of twelve representatives of the poor to the CPC, 40 percent of the council or more than the minimum required by OEO. Although the representatives never succeeded in becoming a significant autonomous political force, this symbolic concession made it extremely difficult for Community Conservationists to criticize the poverty program. In fact, in the subsequent 1967 mayoral election campaign, when the reformers and Republicans united behind a Community Conservationist candidate, he quite self-consciously ignored the CAP as an issue; although "insiders" were aware that the representatives of the poor had been co-opted, the program could not be attacked without apparently attacking the poor themselves. Whether accidental or contrived, Tate concocted a participatory plan that harmonized a complex set of electoral interests.*

In light of the Philadelphia experience, the deviation of the Wagner administration from the electoral interest model becomes readily apparent. The mayor had assigned City Council President Paul Screvane the responsibility for directing New York's CAP activities, supported Screvane's antiparticipatory position, and, then, after deciding not to run for reelection, backed Screvane in the Democratic mayoral primary. CAP's policies and their apparent impact on Screvane's defeat in the 1965

* Mayor Tate's decision to concede to community demands for participation by allowing for representatives of the poor to be elected could possibly be interpreted as a miscalculation, which potentially could have given rise to far more political conflict than in fact actually occurred. Many observers of the mayor at that time claimed that he, rather than being a shrewd calculator of his electoral interests, was politically inept. From this perspective, Tate was saved from disaster only because the elected representatives were unusually moderate in their orientation.

Conversations with advisers close to the mayor convinced us that the mayor had received politically astute advice at this time, however. In fact Tate proved sufficiently able at calculating his electoral interests so that he was reelected mayor in 1967 and supported the winning candidate in 1971. In light of these facts, the preferable explanation, we believe, is that the mayor anticipated that representatives of the poor, chosen in elections rather than by militant community organizations, would not undermine his administration.

Democratic primary does not conclusively demonstrate that he and Wagner ignored their electoral interests, for it is impossible to "prove" categorically the extent to which the antipoverty program contributed to that defeat. Yet some connection seems unmistakable. As later chapters will show in detail, Screvane's actions very quickly encountered severe opposition from minority groups, newspapers, and the reform-club movement. And, crucially, reform-club members maintain that Congressman William F. Ryan ran in the 1965 mayoral primary with strong club support largely because of the participation issue. Certainly, if Ryan had not taken the reform vote from Screvane, it is very unlikely that Screvane would have lost the primary to Abraham Beame.

Defenders of the electoral interest model often explain such cases where the model appears inapplicable in terms of limited information. Politicians deviate from the model and then lose—it is argued—because information systems are imperfect. Wagner and Screvane, therefore, might have calculated as best they could, but they underestimated the resources and determination of their own coalition and of their opponents. Such an argument, however, ignores the considerable, and at the time very obvious, information that should have warned them to follow a different strategy from the one they pursued. Whereas the Chicago machine was an extraordinarily powerful political organization in the mid-1960s, and the machine politicians had recently asserted their dominance in Philadelphia, Liberal Pragmatists in New York had been severely weakened, at least since the scandal-ridden days of Jimmy Walker. Wagner himself had relied in his 1961 campaign on the reform clubs and a number of the organized bureaucracies,[41] although he had subsequently moved away from the reformers in the latter part of his administration, in part perhaps over the participation issue. He and Screvane must be expected to have known that machine support could not guarantee political victory in New York, particularly since their relationship with the party organization was tenuous at best. They could only court defeat by alienating both reformers and black activists. Yet, for months (until shortly before the deadline imposed by the fiscal year and in the midst of the election campaign), they persisted in openly following a strategy as antiparticipatory as did Daley, who enjoyed a far more powerful position vis-à-vis the proparticipatory forces in his city.*

---

* One friendly critic of this argument has suggested that Wagner and Screvane had no interest in supporting even symbolic participation for fear of alienating Italians, Irish civil servants, and more conservative Democrats generally, who were crucial to a Screvane primary victory. But in 1965 these groups showed little interest in the community action controversy. Although they would later strongly oppose school desegregation and school decentralization, the poverty question was too remote from their

To state the situation in terms of the electoral interest model, each unit of Wagner's resources was much more valuable to him than a comparable unit of Daley's because machine resources in New York were so much more limited. Indeed, Wagner and Screvane had good reasons to suspect that they simply had too few resources altogether to "purchase" any amount of their desired outcome, i.e., a nonparticipatory program. As it happened, they could not prevent the adoption of a number of participatory policies before they left office.

But if the electoral interest model cannot explain this behavior, Wagner and Screvane's actions can be readily understood as being motivated by Liberal Pragmatist ideology, with its highly manifest interest in pluralist bargaining. A participatory CAP threatened the structure of pluralist bargaining because, in the first place, the demands of blacks were too sweeping to be compromised with the interests of the entrenched groups which already supported the Liberal Pragmatists. Indeed, if the blacks succeeded in imposing the policy changes, other groups might well see such governmental actions as nonauthoritative, because they would have violated their expectations of incremental change prescribed by the pluralist-bargaining norm. In the second place, a participatory CAP seemed likely to activate masses of voters untutored in the pattern of bargaining and compromises so familiar to those experienced in American politics, raising the possibility of severe conflict and even violence. Liberal Pragmatist mayors saw such fears confirmed by the riots that began in Harlem in 1964 and extended to every one of the five cities by the end of the decade. Such ideological considerations led Wagner and Screvane to resist a participatory program even at considerable political sacrifice. For them, there was a decisive distinction between incremental demands which were negotiable and those which insisted on rapid social and political change. According to their ideology, the latter had to be repelled with all available political resources.

The same ideological interpretation might seem applicable to Daley, who, as we have seen, shared Wagner's Liberal Pragmatism, and to Yorty, who typically defended white factional interests against Black Power efforts. But in their cases it is by no means so easy to dismiss the alternative electoral interest interpretation, since each of them had enough resources, compared to the proparticipatory coalition, to block a participatory program without suffering any immediate electoral reverse. Yet,

---

immediate concerns for this matter to have any decisive impact on their voting behavior. If one calculates, even roughly, the intensities of feeling of the competing sides to this issue, it seems clear that Screvane's immediate electoral interests lay in placating the proparticipatory, not the antiparticipatory, faction.

this power does not explain mayoral rejection of even the *symbols* of participation, such as direct elections. Clearly, Daley could have used loyal machine politicians to control poverty elections; in Los Angeles militants in the black and Mexican communities suffered from severe organizational weaknesses which did, in fact, leave them unable to control the elections which were finally established.*

In Chicago, Daley and his close associate, CAA Director Deton Brooks, systematically reserved to themselves effective control, through appointment, over almost all CPC and NPC members. Equally important, they made this decision a matter of explicit principle rather than excusing it as mere administrative convenience, thus emphasizing the symbolic rejection of participation. As Brooks explained to one group, "it was decided that persons who were below the poverty line could not successfully be involved in a middle-class decision-making type of committee in the initial stages." When others at the meeting challenged Brooks's argument by pointing to the civil rights movement, he responded that "the civil rights movement [is] a protest movement, while the poverty program is a constructive movement."

As did Wagner and Screvane, Daley acted not to maximize political support but to resist a challenge to the principle of pluralist bargaining. As a good ideologue, he was not concerned simply with the actual level of participation but with the principle of maintaining the existing scope of the bargaining order, and he was willing to alienate some members of Chicago's sizable black community in order to sustain the principle, even though it was not necessary to do so in order to control the program.

Yorty's opposition to the symbols of participation was less clear-cut than Daley's or Wagner's. After first resisting any nongovernmental representation on the CPC, Yorty demanded a governmental majority and endorsed a series of proposals, all of which called for the mayor, the city council, and the county board to appoint the representatives of the poor. Yorty was so generally and publicly insistent on these governmental prerogatives that he could hardly be said to have embraced participation as Tate had done. Nevertheless, when Councilman Mills, one of Yorty's black allies, proposed that the poverty area residents vote for their representatives, Yorty accepted the election procedure even though this step had been previously suggested by his political enemy, Governor

* Although one might argue that Daley was so powerful it was in his interest to concede nothing to his opposition, thereby continuing to isolate it from the centers of power in the city, this ignores the cost of unnecessarily offending black leaders. The negative consequences of such actions might not have been immediately apparent, but by 1972 blacks were becoming an increasingly restless component of the Democratic coalition in Chicago.

Brown. Subsequently, elections were included in the final compromise negotiated by federal conciliator Leroy Collins. By accepting this proposal and thereby agreeing to abandon his power to appoint some of the neighborhood representatives, Yorty, like Tate, helped protect the Los Angeles program from criticism that it was undemocratic and nonparticipatory. OEO, for example, withdrew its opposition to the CAA's organizational structure. Of particular significance, Yorty accepted the proposal partly, it appears, because of Mills's political difficulties in his heavily black district. The councilman's earlier support of Yorty when the mayor opposed any community participation had aroused criticism in his district. Thus, Yorty's concession on this point, coming relatively late in the controversy, substantially eased the political problems of one of his allies.

In understanding Yorty's motivations, however, it is important to note that his opposition to participation continued well into the middle of 1965. His antiparticipatory rhetoric only reached its highest crescendo after he had attended a meeting of the Conference of U.S. Mayors at which the dangers of participation to mayoral authority had been widely discussed. It then continued, even after the end of the 1964–1965 fiscal year, leaving Los Angeles without more than the barest minimum in poverty funds. Had he simply embraced *symbolic* participation early in the dispute, in the way that his alliance with Mills later required, Yorty would certainly have placed himself in a stronger political position in minority group communities without obviously endangering his white support. But Yorty, it appears, was also opposed to participation in principle, and his ideology, rather than his electoral interests, dictated his actions at least in the early phase of the political struggle.

To repeat a crucial point made at the beginning of the chapter, it is possible, of course, to argue that Daley and Yorty conformed to the electoral interest model. But the more the electoral interest analysis explains Daley's opposition to formally democratic elections, the less adequately it explains Tate's acceptance. To interpret the electoral interest model to explain the behavior of all three mayors would broaden it beyond the point of refutation and therefore verification.*

CONCLUSION

At times political leaders are forced to choose between their political ideologies and their electoral or organizational interests, a fact which

* Of course, the same objection also applies to any ideological interpretation which would attempt to explain both Daley's and Tate's behavior in terms of the same ideology. The differences in the response of the two mayors require both the electoral interest and ideological approaches.

makes it possible for even ambitious politicians to write about their courageous predecessors. It is easier to demonstrate that politicians fall into such predicaments than it is to explain the conditions under which they choose one or another factor as their basis for decision. Presumably, the character of the politician in question is not entirely irrelevant. But the most likely explanation for the difference between Tate's response and that of his counterparts in the other cities has little to do with character or courage. Tate continued to pursue his electoral interests, it would appear, simply because there was no obvious reason for doing otherwise. As will be discussed in Chapter 9, black neighborhood organizations in Philadelphia did not make the character of their participatory demands as explicit as those voiced in the other cities. Not perceiving the demands as a threat to the pluralist bargaining order, Tate could accommodate them along with the demands of various other interests, but in the process he eliminated any substance to the participation slogan. In other communities, the militance of the black community made explicit the challenge participation made to the existing regime, and Liberal Pragmatist mayors, ideologically committed to the existing order, responded accordingly. Where ideologies and interests conflict, therefore, politicians are more likely to act in accord with their ideology, the clearer the issue is posed in ideological terms by other political actors.

As the various participants in the conflict over participation revealed their respective positions, it became clear that a central issue in the early critical phase of the participation controversy was the way in which the poor would be represented. Since all the poor could not participate directly in decision-making for the CAP, they had to be represented in one way or another. The different participants had quite different notions about the proper form this representation should take. Here they made no mistake, for, as we shall see in Chapter 6, the forms of representation that were decided upon had an important impact on the subsequent development of the CAP.

PART III

Implementing Participation in Community Action Programs

CHAPTER 6: REPRESENTATION OF THE POOR IN COMMUNITY ACTION*

Whether they were involved for ideological, or more narrowly electoral and organizational, reasons, participants in the community action controversy formed coalitions that determined the policies that were eventually settled upon in each city. The conflict between the competing sides ended in one of a very limited number of ways. Either the pro-participatory coalition won and subsequently shaped the Community Action Program (CAP); or, having influenced policies marginally, it lost in all important respects; or, finally, it was severely defeated by the anti-participatory coalition, which then imposed an unequivocally antiparticipatory program. In effect, each city had a *policy settlement,* which determined whether the program was favorable, unfavorable, or hostile toward citizen participation.

This policy settlement had its most visible impact on the program's subsequent development through the forms of representation for the poor that were finally agreed upon in each city. Because direct mass participation in policy formation by low-income residents in large cities was, and is, clearly impossible, some mechanism for "representing" the low-income citizenry had to be devised. Consequently, to maintain participation at the preferred level, the policy settlement needed to structure the form of representation that occurred. Indeed, the decision in each of the cities on how to select the representatives of the poor was such an important issue in the participation controversy that it not only was a critical institutional mechanism by which individuals expected to implement their policy preferences, but it also served as an accurate indicator of the policy settlement itself.

---

* This chapter is a substantially revised version of Paul E. Peterson, "Forms of Representation: Participation of the Poor in the Community Action Program," *The American Political Science Review,* LXIV (June 1970), pp. 491–507. Copyright, 1970, by The American Political Science Association. Reprinted in revised form with permission.

The federal Office of Economic Opportunity (OEO) quickly understood the importance of the process by which representatives would be selected. Its early administrative rule of thumb, later written into law by Congress, required that at least one-third of the local City Poverty Council (CPC) consist of representatives of the poor, who would be chosen "wherever feasible" in accord with "traditional democratic approaches and techniques."[1] Except for the one-third provision, this administrative guideline was as open to as many conflicting interpretations as "maximum feasible participation" itself. The basic problem is the complexity of representation, a political concept whose meaning has been debated in the Western political tradition at least since Hobbes. This complexity, in turn, poses problems for empirical analysts as well as for the participants in the CAP controversy. Hanna Pitkin, using the tools of linguistic analysis, has clarified, if not resolved, the debate by examining such disparate uses of the term as "formal representation," "descriptive representation," and "substantive representation."[2] In this chapter, we shall adapt and employ her analysis as a framework for examining representation in community action.

FORMS OF REPRESENTATION

The formalistic view, as Pitkin describes it, conceives of representation "in terms of formal arrangements which precede and initiate it."[3] It was Hobbes who used "formal representation" as the linchpin to hold together Leviathan, the state in which all the citizens had authorized the sovereign to exercise for them their political rights. Representation was in no way related to the substance of the sovereign's acts; it inhered only in the prior formal arrangements. Hobbes's view was altered, but not fundamentally changed, by subsequent democratic theory, which focused on elections "as a grant of authority by the voters to the elected officials."[4] According to this view, anyone holding public office is a representative of the electorate who selected him.

This view enables one to specify rather easily *for whom* the individual is acting as representative. Whether an alderman acts out of a narrow, parochial or broad, city-wide perspective, he is still formally representative of the electorate of his ward, and not of the city as a whole. Members of the federal government's farmer-advisory committees are formally representative of the farmers, who elect them, and not of the general public. Individuals appointed to a labor relations board by the president formally represent the president, not the labor movement, even if they are themselves all union leaders.

With such an understanding of representation it seems difficult to speak of an individual as being more or less representative, one of the problems which lead Pitkin to reject as inadequate this definition of the term. This problem, however, exists only when speaking from the perspective of the representative. From the perspective of the constituency it is possible to say which of its representatives is formally the most representative. The criterion is the directness by which the population formally selects its representatives. The more indirect the selection process, the less the formal representation. Thus, the change from electing U.S. senators by the state legislature to electing them directly by the voters provided them with greater formal representation.

Nonetheless, formal representation, by focusing on arrangements for selection, in no way takes into account characteristics of the representative—an aspect of the concept Pitkin considers under the term "descriptive representation."[5]* "Socially descriptive representation," as used in this study, refers to the extent to which the representatives reflect accurately the social characteristics of those whom they formally represent. Since no representative is likely to reflect constituent characteristics in all respects, it is necessary to state which characteristics determine representativeness. Social class, ethnic or racial background, age, and place of residence have all been considered by analysts and politicians as relevant. The social characteristics deemed politically relevant have no a priori standing, however, and, in fact, have changed considerably over time and from place to place. This problem, among others, led Pitkin to reject the socially descriptive definition of representation as inadequate. But in analyzing representativeness in any particular case it seems appropriate to consider those traits of greatest salience to the participants involved. Since our concern is with economic poverty, race relations, and the political exclusion of the socially deprived, we shall consider under socially descriptive representation such traits as the representative's race, occupation, and, above all, his income.

Since neither the formal, nor socially descriptive, understandings of representation refer to the representative's substantive behavior, additional information must be examined in order to develop a typology of "substantive representation," i.e., representation which takes into account the "realm of action."[6] In assessing the character of substantive representation, both the representative's influence and orientation must be considered. First, it can be argued that the effectiveness of each individ-

---

* Pitkin includes accurate reflection of political opinions as well as social characteristics within her definition of descriptive representation. Since we will confine our use of descriptive representation to considerations of social characteristics, we shall call this socially descriptive representation.

ual's substantive representation will depend directly upon his influence. Thus, senior members of Congress argue that their position on influential committees makes them more effective representatives than their aspiring opponents would be.* The degree of "actual representation" is thus determined by the representative's influence.

Influence alone, however, cannot measure the quality of substantive representation: The concept also includes the extent to which the representative's orientation agrees with his constituents' interests. But, as noted in Chapter 2, we encounter at this point a controversy of considerable complexity. Those who believe that constituent interests are equivalent to their stated preferences have debated for generations with those who believe that constituents have interests which they may not recognize. Simply stated, the argument turns on the question: Do people's *interests* include their needs as well as their wants? Although Pitkin's solution to this question is not easily summarized, essentially she argues that "the representative must act in such a way that there is no conflict (between representative and represented), or if it occurs an explanation is called for. He must not be found persistently at odds with the wishes of the represented without good reason in terms of their interest, without a good explanation of why their wishes are not in accord with their interest."[7] Such a position, though far from unreasonable, raises considerable problems for the empirical social scientist. In trying to establish which of two representatives is substantively acting in the most representative fashion, it becomes necessary for the analyst to secure intersubjective agreement on the quality of the reasons the representative gives for his disagreement with his constituents.

In Chapter 2 we elaborated the concept of role interest which can be used here as a way to cut this Gordian knot, at least for purposes of social analysis. One major reason for the difficulty in specifying an individual's interests, independent of his preferences, is the complexity of factors which combine to make him a unique individual. The concept of role, however, selects out from the totality of an individual's social re-

* Actual representation may be distinguished from symbolic representation. As Pitkin argues, "We distinguish practical activity rationally directed toward bringing about 'real' goals . . . from expressive, symbolic actions" (p. 102). This latter form of representation, she says, "need have little or nothing to do with . . . enacting laws desired by the people" (p. 106). Insofar as all formal representatives have the capacity to stimulate some favorable response among their constituents, symbolic representation is, to some extent, always present. Thus, where actual representation is almost nil, as it was in Chicago's CAP, it could be characterized by "only symbolic representation." To avoid introducing still another form of representation into the analysis, we have instead classified Chicago simply as "very low" on actual representation.

lationships those patterns of behavior important for a particular analysis, simplifying the empirical or ethical inquiry. Whereas determining the policies that are in the interests of, i.e. "good for," an individual is indeed difficult; it is a far easier task to specify policies that would enhance the position of incumbents of a particular role, for example, by increasing their wealth, power, and/or prestige. Such policies can be said to serve the role interest in question whatever the preferences of the role incumbents.*

Substantive representation, then, is a function of both the representative's influence and his orientation. If the representative's influence (actual representation) is extremely marginal, the representative's orientation is not significant for determining the level of substantive representation. But when the representative has significant influence, the character of substantive representation depends upon the representative's orientation.† Representatives who articulate or seek to improve the life situation of a few specific members of the role provide what may be called "particularistic representation." The machine politician who affirmed the business ethic but who sought "help" when a constituent needed emergency fuel, shoes for his children, or even a low-paying, but badly needed, job illustrates well this type of interest representation.[9] By particularizing the distribution of benefits to role incumbents, the machine representative, though acting to improve his constituent's situation, obscures the shared character of the role interest, thereby minimizing pressures for social change.

Actions which seek to improve the condition of all incumbents of a social role provide "universalistic" interest representation. As was argued in Chapter 3, for subordinate groups this may take the form of attacking the patterning orientation of the role, alleviating its economic or

* In attempting to identify the public interest with the interests of institutions, Samuel Huntington presupposes an argument along the lines we have set forth. Huntington argues that "Institutional interests differ from the interests of individuals who are in the institutions. . . . Individual interests are necessarily short-run interests. Institutional interests, however, exist through time; the proponent of the institution has to look to its welfare through an indefinite future."[8] But institutions are only complexes of role relations which individuals wish to sustain. To attribute interests to institutions, one must initially distinguish between personal and role interests. Speaking of the interests of institutions independent of the preferences of those with the authority to speak for the institution is thus perfectly parallel to speaking of role interests independent of the opinions of those occupying the social role.

† A representative, who opposes the improvement of certain constituent role interests and who overtly seeks to misguide constituents as to what these role interests are, may be said to provide "negative representation" of the role interests, a category of no empirical importance in this analysis.

social consequences, or mitigating its political consequences by extending political rights to role incumbents. For example, the welfare state, which has promulgated employment, housing, welfare, and health policies benefiting industrial workers, has been the product of working-class interest representation more universalistic than that provided by the machine politician. Clearly, the highest level of substantive representation for a subordinate group would be elimination of the role's patterning orientation. In the case of the CAP, the attack on economic poverty was too insignificant to reduce substantially the economic consequences of the black racial role. On the other hand, a successful attack on political poverty, in the context of big-city politics, could help to "vest" black interests in the arena of pluralist bargaining by bringing important city institutions under autonomous black direction, helping to eliminate the imputation of Negro inferiority. Thus, the most universalistic interest representation involved demands by representatives of low-income blacks for a participatory program. The success with which representatives provided such interest representation was a function of (1) the extent to which CAP, particularly Neighborhood Service Center (NSC), resources were used to organize neighborhood residents for collective action; and (2) the extent to which CPC and NPC representatives of the poor, and CAP institutions more generally, articulated demands aimed at changing the quality of services to the poor.

As can be seen in Figure 6–1, the policy settlement affected the various levels of substantive representation in several ways, two of which were particularly important.* First, the policy settlement explicitly determined the type of formal representation, i.e., the manner in which the representatives of the poor were selected, which, in turn, affected their substantive behavior. Specifically, representatives *chosen by the city administration* provided no significant substantive representation; *elected* representatives, who had little organized relationship with their constitu-

* In some cities more than others, but in all cities to some extent the policy settlement also affected both the character of the bureaucracies administering the program and the residual expectations of the various participants. The connection between the settlement and the bureaucracies, and the complex impact that bureaucratic processes had on participation is elaborated in Chapter 7. At the same time, the participants' behavior was also affected by their general recognition that the policy settlement in each city was either proparticipatory, antiparticipatory, or extremely antiparticipatory. It is very likely that these perceptions structured the participants' behavior in important but subtle ways, although the impact cannot be supported with any direct empirical evidence. Essentially, then, this is a residual category included simply for its theoretical importance. Taken together, the four ways in which the policy settlement affected the degree of substantive representation are illustrated in Figure 6–1.

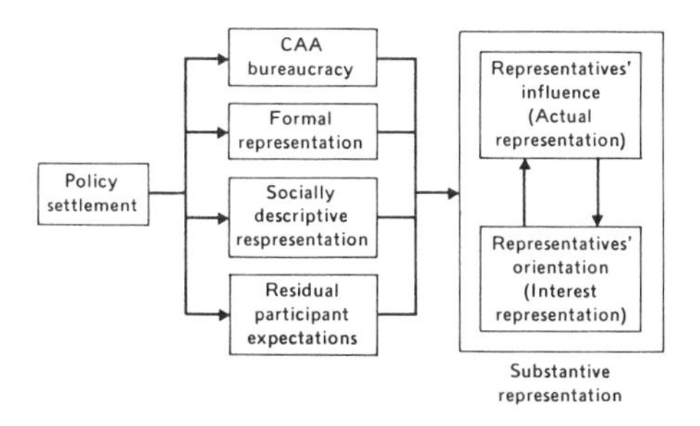

Fig. 6–1. Causal Relationships among Variables, Implementing the Policy Settlement for CAP

ents, provided at most particularistic representation; finally representatives *chosen by neighborhood groups* pursued more effectively universalistic interest representation since their more structured relationship made them more responsive to the collective concerns of the community. In addition, the policy settlement subtly, but nonetheless importantly, shaped the level of socially descriptive representation. Given the low incomes of constituents, the more socially descriptive of the constituency the representative was the more he focused on particularistic rather than universalistic concerns.

The difference between particularistic and universalistic representation is also crucial in part because the two components of substantive representation, the representative's influence (actual representation) and his orientation (interest representation) reinforced each other. And we shall also examine the interrelationships between these two factors. Specifically, where representatives sought to provide particularistic interest representation, their level of influence declined, and where representatives achieved higher levels of influence, the resulting conflicts provoked the contestants to provide more universalistic interest representation. Admittedly, this analysis is complex, but so were the empirical relationships; perhaps by detailing the forms of representation in the five cities, we can clarify the way in which each policy settlement was implemented.

FORMAL REPRESENTATION IN FIVE CAPS

The arrangements providing for representation of the poor in the five CAPs differed considerably, as can be seen in Table 6–1. Philadelphia's and Los Angeles' process of selecting their CPCs provided the most formal representation. In May 1965, the residents of twelve low-income sectors of Philadelphia elected twelve Neighborhood Poverty

Councils (NPCs), each of which elected one of their number to sit on the CPC. The NPC was thus elected directly by low-income area residents, and the city-wide representatives were just one step removed from direct popular election. The Los Angeles process was formally even more representative, inasmuch as residents of the seven designated poverty areas in March 1966 voted directly for a representative to the CPC.*

Because they relied on community organizations to select NPC members, who, in turn, chose representatives to the CPC, the Detroit and New York CAPs had much less formal representation than those of Philadelphia or Los Angeles. During the summer and fall of 1965, community conventions were held in twelve of the sixteen neighborhood areas into which the low-income sectors of New York had been divided.† Neighborhood organizations were invited to send delegates to the convention, which elected representatives to the NPC, and this body, in turn, chose delegates to the CPC. Detroit had pursued a similar method of selecting NPCs even earlier. After the CAA staff informed, by mail and in person, all the major organized groups in each of the four poverty areas of their intention to form an NPC, the staff held a meeting to which these groups sent representatives, and NPCs were elected at that time. The NPCs then selected delegates to the CPC.

Chicago's selection process provided the least formal representation of the poor; the director of each Neighborhood Service Center (NSC) not only appointed NPC members but then selected the one from their number who would serve on the CPC.‡ Since the Chicago CAA executive director, an appointee of the mayor, chose each NSC director, formally, the representatives were indirectly selected by the mayor and not by poverty area residents.

These differences in formal representation were clearly the product of the policy settlement in each city, for most important actors in the political conflict regarded differences in formal representation important

---

* Because of the several months' delay in establishing the Los Angeles program, the residents were formally represented in a much less direct way by seven interim representatives chosen by the mayor and county board from a list prepared by five blacks, five Mexican Americans and the white head of the county human relations commission. This chapter, however, focuses on the activities of the elected representatives.

† Procedures in the other four areas were even less formally representative; community leaders came together, formed an organization, and were recognized by the city as the policy-makers for the neighborhood CAP.

‡ Toward the end of our research, in the spring of 1966, it seemed that at least one representative from each neighborhood to the CPC would soon be chosen by the council instead of the director.

TABLE 6–1. Patterns of Representation and Conflict in Five Cities

Patterns of political activity	*Cities*				
	Chicago	*Philadelphia*	*Los Angeles*	*Detroit*	*New York*
1. Formal representation	Low (indirect via mayor)	High (direct elections to NPC)	Very high (direct elections to CPC)	Moderate (indirect via neighborhood organizations)	Moderate (indirect via neighborhood organizations)
2. Socially descriptive representation	Moderately low	Very high	Very high	Moderately low	Low
3. Substantive representation					
a. Influence of representative	Very low	Moderately low and declining	Moderately low	High	Very high
b. Orientation of representative	(irrelevant)	Particularistic	Somewhat universalistic	Universalistic	Universalistic
4. Conflict	Low	Moderate	Moderate	Extensive and moderately well organized	Extensive and organized

enough to try to determine its specific character. All of the antiparticipatory mayors (Daley, Tate, Wagner, and Yorty) sought personally to appoint the representatives to the CPC. Black neighborhood organizations argued that they should select both NPCs and representatives of the poor to the CPC. Significantly, at no time did neighborhood groups in any city call for direct election of the representatives to the CPC, preferring instead a means of providing formal representation which they could more directly control. Elections in Philadelphia and Los Angeles were a compromise not strongly favored by either coalition. However disconcerting it may be for democratic theory, those directly involved in the struggle expected elections to produce less substantive representation than selection by organized groups. The democratic alternative was suggested by representatives of the mayor in order to forestall influence over CAP by the organized segment of the low-income black community. Accordingly, the neighborhood organizations selected the representatives where the proparticipatory coalition was the strongest, the mayor selected the representatives where the antiparticipatory coalition was the most powerful, and elections were the compromise solution where the antiparticipatory faction was strong but not so powerful that it did not need to make any concessions.

SOCIALLY DESCRIPTIVE REPRESENTATION

By contrast with formal representation, socially descriptive representation was rather uncontroversial. Philadelphia and Los Angeles, as well as having formally the most representative program, had the highest levels of socially descriptive representation—at least with respect to the income of the representatives (see Table 6–1). In Philadelphia, election regulations required that all candidates for the NPC, including those subsequently elected to the CPC, must have incomes of no more than $6,000 annually, the actual limit varying with family size. Candidates for the CPC in Los Angeles could come from families whose income was no more than $4,000 a year. For the other cities, precise information as to the income of representatives was not obtained, but there was no doubt that a majority of NPC representatives were better endowed financially. No more than one-third of those in Chicago's NPCs had incomes that fell within the poverty zone, although the representatives chosen to serve on the CPC had low incomes.

In Detroit and New York, representation on NPCs varied from community to community. In Detroit, the NPCs included many members of public-housing tenants' councils and federations of mothers dependent on welfare assistance. NPC Number 2 on Detroit's West Side, which was socially the most representative, included approximately equal numbers of the unemployed as distinct from businessmen, professionals, and other employed workers. On the whole, however, the largest number of NPC members were homeowners selected by community councils and block clubs organized by the Detroit Housing Commission and the Health Department. And, in contrast to the other cities, representatives to Detroit's CPC were sometimes, but not necessarily always, of low income. In New York, by far the majority of the representatives to the NPCs were middle- or upper middle-income residents, though efforts were made to conform to the requirements that one-third of the membership have incomes within the poverty zone (however loosely defined). And, under the Wagner administration and even more clearly after Lindsay had restructured the poverty program, the CPC contained almost exclusively middle- and upper middle-income representatives.

Given the less controversial character of socially descriptive representation, its relationship to the policy settlement was less obvious. Yet the very noncontroversial character of the issue is evidence itself of the way in which the settlement structured this aspect of representation. Of course, mayors preferred close political and governmental associates as representatives. But once some form of representation of the poor was conceded, mayors and their associates not only tolerated, but actually promoted, socially descriptive representation. In Philadelphia, Samuel Evans, the man whom the mayor had asked to set up the city's poverty program, insisted that the elected representatives be of low income, even when private welfare agency professionals demurred at the idea. In Los Angeles, the mayor readily accepted the idea, once democratic elections had been proposed. Mayor Daley, who balked at anything other than CAA appointment of the representatives, raised no objections to socially descriptive representation on the CPC. In Detroit, too, the CAA staff were quite willing to provide, in a medical proposal sent to OEO, that representation be socially descriptive, i.e., be limited simply to the clients of the program.[10]

On the other hand, neighborhood organizations never offered this solution themselves. They were well aware that it would exclude too many of their members from serving as representatives. Yet, since socially descriptive representation *appeared* to be the most obvious kind of participation by the poor in CAP, they could not very well openly object to it. To have done so would have jeopardized their own claim that they were concerned about a participatory program as distinct from their own organizational interests. After all, who could better represent the poor than the poor themselves? Yet where the proparticipatory coalition was the strongest (in Detroit and New York), the policy settlement provided for the least socially descriptive representation.*

SUBSTANTIVE REPRESENTATION

The Influence of the Representatives

Table 6–1 also shows that these patterns of formal and socially descriptive representation did not vary directly with the pattern of substantive representation, whose two components, the representatives' influence and orientation, are considered in this section. Consistent with its formal representation, the representatives' influence (actual representation) in Chicago was very low, since they had scarcely any effect on the operations of the CAP.[11] The NSCs carried on their activities with little or no direction by the NPCs. Although these councils could "review" and "recommend" programs and policies, they had no authority over center operations or the selection of personnel for NSC's programs. Officially, the NPC could spend $25,000 each year, provided that the money was administered by NSC personnel; but in practice the center staff decided the purpose for which these funds were spent, and the NPC then ratified the decision. Moreover, as of January 1966, small sums had been given to only four neighborhood groups in the city, amounting to but 2.2 percent of the total CAP appropriation.

In Los Angeles, the representatives had slightly more influence. As noted in Chapter 1, all of them opposed the firing of Opal Jones as director of the NSC program, and four of them attended a public protest meeting on her behalf. And one representative, Ursala Gutierrez, was remarkably successful in securing resources and support for her Mexican-American community organization. But these were exceptions that contrasted sharply with the representatives' general ineffectiveness. Indeed, the representatives not only complained about their lack of influence but demonstrated it by their approach to key issues. They actually agreed to the original motion by Mayor Yorty's assistant authorizing Jones's dismissal on March 31, 1966. Only after extensive public protest did they angrily attack CAA Director Maldanado at the next meeting for

---

* Admittedly, socially descriptive representation was also moderately low in Chicago, where the antiparticipatory coalition was the strongest. But this was due to the mayor's capability of realizing, to a greater degree than the antiparticipatory mayors in Los Angeles and Philadelphia, his first preference of appointing governmental and political associates. Yet even in Chicago, the representatives of the poor to the CPC were themselves of low income.

"having misled the Board into believing that he wanted merely to reprimand Mrs. Jones and place her on probation," and then vote unsuccessfully to reconsider dismissal.[12] Significantly, representatives criticized the mayor's assistant "for wording the resolution of dismissal . . . 'so that no matter how you voted it comes out the way he wants it to.' "[13]

The representatives also failed to diagnose accurately certain major obstacles to their exercise of influence. For example, the city and county schools effectively bypassed the CPC and, therefore, a review of their largely nonparticipatory programs. In some cases, after complaining that federal regulations delayed preparation of grant requests, education officials submitted their proposals just before the OEO deadline and, to meet the deadline, sent them directly to OEO officials rather than to the CAA. Yet the schools' representatives continued to sit on the CPC, helping to block any new, more participatory programs in the education field. Furthermore, none of the other agency representatives on the CPC publicly objected to this tactic, not only because of the schools' political power but also because they wanted to minimize the CAA staff members' supervision of their own agencies' programs. The elected representatives had no similar organizational interest, but they evidently failed to grasp the professional bureaucrats' strategy and to protest against it in order to exert pressure for a proparticipatory program.

At first Philadelphia's elected representatives had considerably more influence over the CAP than those in Chicago and perhaps even in Los Angeles.[14] For example, they had been able to revise substantially a planned parenthood proposal so that it included services as well as educational programs.[15] But after the first few months such activities became extremely rare. In the summer of 1965, the newly elected representatives turned down a staff request seeking permission to join a national association of CAAs, formed to lobby Congress and the OEO. However, in the following summer the representatives, who by this time seldom turned down staff recommendations, unanimously agreed to join the national association. Moreover, the Philadelphia school system, in a manner similar to the Los Angeles system, submitted in 1966 its educational proposals only at the last minute when the CPC could do nothing but ratify its provisions before their submission to OEO. The representative from the Congress of Racial Equality (CORE) vigorously attacked this tactic, but the elected representatives of the poor gave him little support.

Admittedly, the representatives had considerable influence over the recruitment of "nonprofessional" employees. They selected hundreds of employees hired both by public and private agencies as well as by their own NSCs. But in the spring of 1966 the representatives relinquished their authoritative control over the director of the NSC in exchange for the possibility that they themselves might be hired to work there. The NSC, which had been under the formal control of the NPC, came under the direction of the CAA staff, much as was the case in Chicago and Los Angeles.[16]

By contrast with both Philadelphia and Los Angeles, the representatives in Detroit exercised and retained substantial influence. Although Detroit's CAA officials sometimes used deadline pressures to avoid consulting CPC and NPC members on proposals, the representatives readily understood this tactic and vigorously pressed their objections at all levels of the CAA. Indeed, they used their positions as CPC and NPC members to reinforce their demands for policy changes in personal contacts with CAA officials. As a result, they exercised a major influence in drafting and revising many of the most important of the CAA's programs, and CAA officials often, though not always, consulted them as a matter of course. Moreover, their influence helped insure that the Detroit CAA provided a variety of different kinds of assistance to local neighborhood groups.[17]

The Detroit representatives did not prevail on all key issues. Mayor Cavanagh rejected their proposal for a majority on the CPC and effectively silenced potential rejoinders by rhetorically asking whether there had been any program which did not provide for participation. Yet the representatives often did use formal meetings to their considerable advantage, most notably perhaps in doubling the number of NPC members on the CPC. In another case, their lobbying efforts, eventually supported by the mayor, secured a change in the ordinarily sacrosanct civil service employment regulations so that CAP was permitted to hire more low-income citizens with limited formal education.[18]

The influence of the representatives in New York was even greater than in Detroit.[19] Initially, more than 46 percent of all CAP funds were allocated to neighborhood and minority groups in the first eighteen months of the program's operations. Also, the NPCs won increasing influence over the operations of NSCs. In two of the three communities studied intensively, the NPCs had the status of independent contractors with the city government, something unknown even in Detroit. With this status, they could disperse funds in accordance with their own objectives, subject only to the provisions of the contract. Even in the third community, where the central CAA staff apparently had more direct control, the NPC interviewed and hired candidates for staff positions, leaving the CAA with only a veto power over the selection of the executive director. In fact, the community successfully protested when the CAA vetoed their preferred candidate on the ground that he had no experience in social work. The NPC also was empowered to remove any executive director with whom they were dissatisfied, although the director could appeal the decision to the CAA. Not only was the staff recruited by the NPC, but the duties of block workers were also determined locally. Eventually, when the Lindsay administration implemented its modifications, this community and the others like it achieved independent, contractual status.

The Orientation of the Representatives

This variation among the five cities in the level of the representatives' influence over CAP correlated very closely with the variation in their orientations (interest representation) (see Table 6–1). Since the representatives in Chicago lacked influence, they were unable to provide any particularistic or universalistic interest representation; the Daley administration operated the CAP in accord with its view that political action in black neighborhoods was undesirable. As a leading local official pointed out, "[It] is through the public bureaucracies with their professional staff that mayors must now build their reputations with the poor and minority groups of the city." Accordingly, the NSCs, though they coordinated a wide variety of governmental services to the poor, trained their employees only to provide services to individuals, and not to community groups. The mission of the efficient, highly bureaucratized NSCs, as stated by personnel throughout Chicago's CAA, did not include strengthening the neighborhood's political resources. Faced with this situation, the representatives were simply unable to protest effectively. Neither the NPC's nor the NSC's employees encouraged voter-registration drives or group efforts directed toward improving education, welfare, or housing facilities.

Indeed, if anything, the NSC dampened political attacks on poverty in low-income communities. In one West Side community, a local organization, which had attempted to prevent landlords from splitting apartments into ever-smaller units, called public attention to the favoritism displayed by the housing authority toward students as opposed to neighborhood residents. The NSC crippled the organization by hiring its entire leadership on the condition that such practices cease. In general, as one South Side minister expressed it, "Civil rights and other community organizations have been weakened since NSC has been in [the] community."

Although the representatives in Philadelphia had greater influence with the CAP, they generally used it to secure particularistic benefits for themselves and their friends, rather than to promote universalistic changes in governmental policy. In fact, the most important issues during the

CAP's first two years were (1) payment of the NPC members for their services, and (2) NPC influence over the hiring of poverty employees in their neighborhoods.

The great majority of Philadelphia's neighborhood representatives felt that they should be paid. Monthly stipends for the representatives were proposed; grants to attend an in-house training institute received the backing of university professors; contrary to regulations, many representatives were actually employed by the CAA; and, finally, generous expense allotments for all the representatives were established. Although the local CAA was receptive to, and encouraged, the demands of the representatives, OEO refused to condone such use of limited poverty funds. Nonetheless, throughout much of the first year elected representatives did hold jobs with the CAA, and only after a major confrontation between the CAA and the federal government did such practices diminish.

The representative's influence over personnel selection was exercised, in many cases, on behalf of close friends and relatives. A minority of representatives objected to this practice in terms such as the following:

> They get mothers, brothers, neighbors, and people they owe favors (for the available jobs). I had my husband apply, because at least he's qualified.
>
> The trouble is that a few of them get all the jobs for their friends. I have recommended people, but they don't get jobs. You can't get a job unless you say the chairman recommended you or something.

A more satisfied representative stated that one of the reasons she enjoyed her position was: "I know what's going on and this way I can help my family and friends." In sum, much as the machine politician provided for the needs of particular members of the immigrant community, the Philadelphia council members sought particularistic benefits that would improve the life chances of specific members of the low-income population.

In Los Angeles, though the representatives were not co-opted in the same way by the city administration or CAA staff, they still provided little in the way of universalistic interest representation. Perhaps because the prevailing norms in Los Angeles so thoroughly prohibited patronage practices, this was not a major concern of representatives to the CPC. Rather, they complained at CPC meetings about their inability to affect program content, lamented the lack of resident participation, and voiced suspicion and hostility toward public and private welfare agency representatives to the CPC and toward certain CAA personnel. Nonetheless, their effectiveness seemed to be limited to personnel issues. For example, they rebelled most dramatically against the CAA leadership when Opal Jones lost her job.[20] But they made no overt attempt to stop the NSCs under her direction from moving steadily away from a participatory approach. Thus, the issue on which they did exercise some influence never directly confronted the participatory policy question.

The representatives in Detroit provided much more consistently universalistic representation than did their counterparts in Los Angeles, Philadelphia, or Chicago. When they intervened to change CAA hiring policies, the representatives altered civil service regulations affecting whole categories of potential employees instead of seeking simply for themselves the power to hire specific individuals. The representatives also favored support for neighborhood organizations serving tenants, welfare recipients, and the like. This same concern informed their efforts to redraft specific CAA project proposals. For example, the NPC members in one area objected strenuously to a medical program that restricted resident participation to those actually receiving its services. The representatives wanted to make sure that the community's most articulate residents, even if they themselves were not recipients of the services, would have an opportunity to affect the delivery of the service.

Representatives in New York also provided more universalistic interest representation. Consistent with the autonomy of NSCs, the extent of such representation differed considerably from area to area. But in all three neighborhoods studied intensively, staff members were charged by the NPCs with organizing tenant groups, block clubs, and other community groups. In Bedford-Stuyvesant, CAP personnel had begun to generate community pressures in favor of major changes in the operations of the welfare department and the school system. But it was in East Harlem that poverty resources were most obviously used to strengthen the political resources of the community. Although two factions competed for control of antipoverty funds, they both tried to organize the local population on behalf of causes which might benefit all neighborhood residents. Their resources helped to maintain a cadre of community activists who continually demanded changes in welfare, housing, and educational policies. Indeed, the political activity in East Harlem generated in time a powerful city-wide movement for drastic reorganization of the city's educational system.[21] Whatever the merits of their goals, these CAP representatives clearly articulated black factional interests more effectively and with greater national repercussions than in any other city. Particularistic interest representation, in the sense that representatives sought payment and jobs for themselves and patronage for their friends, did occur in New York. But, in contrast to Philadelphia, these concerns by no means supplanted the representatives' concern with broader goals.

Relationships between the Representatives' Influence and Orientations

The representatives' influence (actual representation) and orientation (types of interest representation) were closely interrelated. In part this is purely definitional in that a representative without influence cannot provide genuine (particularistic or universalistic) interest representation. For example, in Chicago the representatives failed to promote a participatory program, not only because proparticipatory representatives selected by the CAA were in a small minority, but also because even these representatives had little influence. And in Los Angeles the representatives to the CPC provided little universalistic interest representation primarily because they lacked a power base and the political skills necessary to influence program developments.

The interrelationships between the representatives' influence and orientations were more than simply definitional, however. In the first place, the pursuit of particularistic interests reduced levels of actual representation. This was particularly obvious in Philadelphia, where the pursuit of such interests so dominated the preoccupations of the representatives. The representatives on the NPCs did not promote community organization by their NSCs, and, as a result, only scattered cases of organizational activity by NSC workers, such as forming block clubs and holding neighborhood meetings, could be identified. Moreover, neither the NSCs or their workers actively sought to make broad changes in the operations of other city institutions that claimed to be serving the urban poor. The representatives did appeal to the state legislature in a well-coordinated effort to revise state welfare laws. But this was undertaken with the encouragement of Samuel Evans, who, in acting for the mayor, wished to embarrass the Republican governor and the Republican-controlled legislature. With the exception of one attempt to retard an urban renewal project, the representatives hesitated to criticize local bureaucracies for fear of jeopardizing staff support for their particularistic goals. Indeed, as we noted earlier, they eventually sacrificed their authority over the NSCs in the ultimately vain hope of becoming center employees.

If particularistic interest representation led to declining levels of influence (actual representation) in Philadelphia, high levels of influence by the representatives in New York and Detroit generated intra-neighborhood conflict, which, in turn, encouraged more universalistic interest representation. The greater the level of influence by community representatives over the program, the greater the level of conflict within the community, particularly in neighborhoods of ethnic or racial heterogeneity. As representatives of the poor gained more control over the allocation of poverty program resources, they found more at stake to divide them. But organized and extensive conflict reinforced tendencies toward universalistic interest representation. Competition for power within the community forced the competing leaderships to justify their appeal for community support by representing broad community interests.

The variation among the five cities in influence (actual representation), conflict, and orientation (see Table 6–1) illustrates the relationships among the three variables. Given the low level of influence in Chicago, the major problem for the CAA staff was to stimulate sufficient interest among council members so that a quorum necessary to conduct council business could be achieved. Conflict was sporadic and disorganized when it occasionally arose. In Philadelphia, where the representatives had some influence over hiring policies, conflict revolved largely around the distribution of employment opportunities to claimants sponsored by different members of the NPCs. Conflict was the greatest in the one community where racial factionalism was apparent, as black and white councillors opposed each other over the selection of NSC employees. The animosity was subdued, however, and did not reach the level of public discussion. Although the understanding tended to break down in the heat of the electoral campaign, the two sides had even agreed upon a slate of candidates for the second poverty election. The Los Angeles CAP had no NPCs, and therefore the only intraneighborhood conflicts observable were among staff members themselves. Among these officials, the most significant conflicts were between blacks and Mexican Americans.

By contrast, in Detroit and New York where the representatives' influence was much higher, there was both more conflict and more universalistic representation. Of course, conflicts were not always policy-related. In NPC Number 2 on Detroit's West Side, Rep. Charles Diggs, Jr. had helped form the NPC so as to prevent control by any one organization.[22] Even so, council meetings were marked by a bitter personal dispute between the chairman and the first vice-chairman, partly over the appointment of new NPC members, but partly over the chairman's personal style. In NPC Number 1 on Detroit's East Side a block-club council contested for control with a coalition consisting of a federation of mothers receiving welfare assistance and a public-housing tenants' council, the latter coalition holding the upper hand in the first years of the program. But whatever the source of their internal conflicts, in all four areas of the city NPC members pressed the NSC staff on program and policy issues. Of course, this pattern was caused in part by the separation of powers in Detroit's CAP, which gave influence to the NPCs but kept final responsibility in the hands of CAA officials. Yet the conflicts within the NPCs themselves prompted NPC members to scrutinize carefully staff behavior.

This same pattern was so apparent in New York that it deserves a somewhat more extensive analysis. Conflict was organized in all three New York neighborhoods, as two factions competed for control of the neighborhood's CAP. These factions can be characterized as the traditional community leadership faction and the partisan-oriented faction. The traditional community leadership in the field of welfare was vested in settlement houses, YMCAs, and Catholic, Protestant, and Jewish churches and welfare agencies. Although these groups did not always share a common welfare policy, they buried their differences in order to obtain lucrative CAP funds. On the Lower West Side of Manhattan, memories of conflict between a prominent settlement house and the Catholic Church strained relationships but did not prevent surprisingly close cooperation in the planning of community programs. In Bedford-Stuyvesant, the community had a paucity of traditional leaders, for private welfare agencies had deserted the community as the neighborhood became black. Only the YMCA, supported by local black clergymen, doctors, lawyers, and other middle-class professionals, remained to provide such leadership. In East Harlem a settlement house and a combined church and welfare agency provided basic institutional strength for the traditional community leadership. Despite the diversity of the leadership grouping among these three neighborhoods, they bore in common the burden of being known as "the Establishment," which was the favorite epithet leveled against them by their opposition.

The opposing faction in each of the communities is more difficult to characterize, but inasmuch as they had more overt political ties than the Establishment faction, we shall call them the "partisans." Of course, the Establishment also had political connections, but these were secondary sources of strength, the result, rather than the cause, of their basic institutional importance to the community. The partisans were more vulnerable to the charge of "playing politics," for their base of support appeared to be more narrowly political. On the Lower West Side, the institutional base of support for this faction was the reform-club movement, the predominant partisan force in that area. In Bedford-Stuyvesant the general lack of any stable political force inhibited the development of a strong partisan faction. But the director of the NSC in the community, a politically astute and capable administrator, sought to develop an alternative, more political, base of power in order to free herself from the constraints that the Establishment placed upon her. Within two years, the Establishment, realizing the inherent danger to their own position that her attempts to mobilize a power base on a previously apathetic population would hold, removed the director from her job and replaced her with a more traditional social worker. In East Harlem, the partisan faction rested primarily on an ethnic base. Since the traditional community leadership came from and serviced the black population in this racially heterogeneous community, the partisans appealed to Puerto Rican pride in an attempt to mobilize support from another wing of the community. Led by an attractive and personable young Puerto Rican social worker, they depended on close ties with Democratic leaders in the Robert Wagner administration and in the U.S. Senate.

The extensive character of the conflict was evident both in its duration and in the range and significance of the issues. In East Harlem, both factions had separate access to poverty funds, and each side attempted to secure control of all resources allocated to the community. On the Lower West Side, the debate concerned the method by which council representatives should be selected in the future, and the kind of programs that the NSC should operate. In Bedford-Stuyvesant, the debate centered upon relations with private welfare agencies and the balance of power between the council and its staff. In all three communities, the conflict was detectable at least as early as the summer of 1964, and it continued into the summer of 1966 when this research was completed. During this period, the conflict between blacks and Puerto Ricans in the heterogeneous community of East Harlem became so intense that on more than one occasion physical force was threatened.

Organized and extensive conflict reinforced tendencies toward universalistic interest representation. Both factions, constantly competing for community support, sought to establish their credentials as vigorous defenders of the community's interests. Public officials in East Harlem frequently dismissed community agitation against their agency as simply the by-product of organizational aggrandizement. Their observations, although oversimplified, cannot be dismissed entirely, since the competition for power kept both organizations searching for means by which they could expand their support. In this way, community conflict functioned to generate the articulation of demands for broad changes in governmental services to the poor. By contrast, the lack of conflict in Los Angeles, Chicago, and Philadelphia removed one major impetus for community discussion of the representatives' obligations to their constituents.

THE POLICY SETTLEMENT AND FORMS OF REPRESENTATION

We have set forth the variations in the patterns of representation and conflict observed in the five cities. As can be seen in Figure 6–2, which graphically portrays the most important relationships that have been discussed, the relationship between formal and substantive representation was curvilinear, rather than simply linear as democratic enthusiasts might have hoped. And the relationship between substantive and socially descriptive representation was negative, a finding contrary to the expectations of those who believe that the social composition of decision-makers should reflect the social composition of the general population. Of course, these unanticipated relationships based on the findings for only five cities could be spurious. Possibly, the formal arrangements for the selection and the social background of representatives had no significant effect on their influence or orientation. After all, the variation in representation among the five cities can be almost entirely explained in terms of other political forces operating in the cities. As Part IV will elaborate, the proparticipatory coalition had the strongest position in New York and Detroit, and, compared to the power of their opponents, was weakest in Chicago. The settlement over formal and socially descriptive representation may be understood simply as an initial statement of the power relationships between pro- and antiparticipatory forces. Perhaps these same power relationships, directly produced the variations in the levels of substantive representation. Such an interpretation is persuasive, for it stresses informal, extragovernmental political relationships rather than the technical arrangements of governmental institutions or the personal characteristics of individual representatives.*

However, it would be incorrect to dismiss the significance of formal and socially descriptive representation altogether. To be sure, they were themselves a product of the policy settlement, but this need not suggest that they were not critically important mechanisms by which the policy settlement affected the level of participation in the five cities. For one thing, political actors regarded the selection process by which formal representation would be established as critical, and they invested substantial resources in securing a selection process which they could influence. Second, although the political considerations were more obscure, socially descriptive representation was promoted by those least interested

* And as was suggested in Figure 6–1, we partially accept such an interpretation. Insofar as the policy settlement affected participants' expectations (and consequently their behavior), it structured the level of substantive representation in many subtle ways that only an extremely complicated research design could possibly detect.

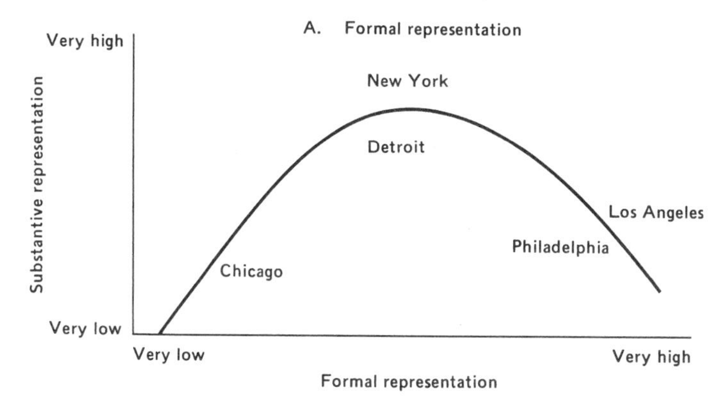

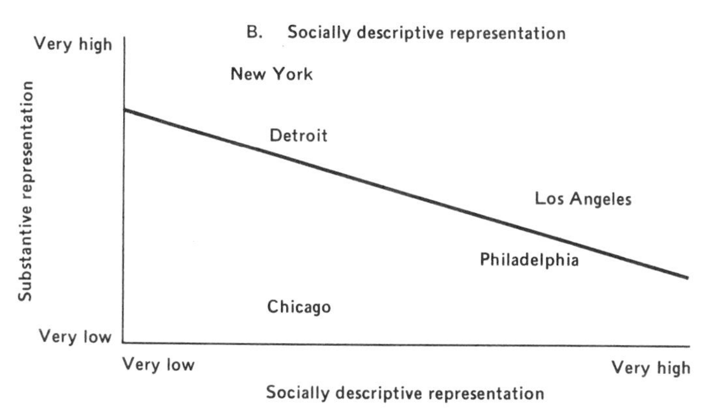

FIG. 6–2. Relationships of formal (*A*) and socially descriptive (*B*) representation with substantive representation.

in participation, suggesting that local political actors also felt that the representatives' social backgrounds would affect their behavior in ways that possibly naïve bureaucrats in the OEO might not anticipate.

Moreover, to assume that formal arrangements and social background have no effect is to argue that participants can expend their political resources equally efficiently regardless of the institutional relationships channeling their activity. For example, had Mayor Daley permitted community organizations to control the appointment of NPC members, would he have been able to as successfully minimize controversy and prevent organizational activity? Or had Mayor Wagner been able to appoint NPC members, would he have had as many autonomous and powerful local groups attacking one city agency after another? We think not, for there are good theoretical reasons which suggest that the representatives' actions were a function of both their social background and the relationship that existed between them and their constituency, as provided by the mechanisms for formal representation.

RELATIONSHIP BETWEEN SOCIALLY DESCRIPTIVE AND SUBSTANTIVE REPRESENTATION

Differences in socially descriptive representation affected both the influence and orientation components of substantive representation. In general, low-income representatives with little formal education frequently lacked the familiarity with complex bureaucratic organizations to operate skillfully in pursuing their goals. The difficulty that representatives in Los Angeles had in influencing CPC policies and CAA activities well illustrates the general pattern. In contrast, middle-class representatives acted with much greater effectiveness. The most independent and aggressive member of the Philadelphia CPC was a male school teacher eligible for participation in CAP elections only because teacher salaries were at the time so low they fell within the income limitations. And, in New York, the victory of the Bedford-Stuyvesant community in its conflict with the city must be attributed in part to the skill with which middle-class lawyers and other professionals used their position on the CPC to protect local autonomy for their NSC.

Of course, not every low-income representative lacked such skills, the individuals with prior experience in community organizations being significant exceptions. The one moderately effective representative in Los Angeles had had considerable experience in the Community Service Organization (she was the sister-in-law of its dominant figure) before winning election to the CPC. And many low-income blacks in Detroit commanded comparable skills. For example, the low-income black woman who figured so prominently in Detroit's NPC Number 1 had become the leader of a federation of mothers on aid to dependent children. In New York's East Harlem, Ruth Atkins, a woman who had for years been dependent on welfare assistance, became one of the most powerful leaders in the community, but she had developed political skills and self-confidence through prior activity in a variety of community organizations. These skilled political actors used their lower-class backgrounds with great effectiveness in bargaining situations, for their claim to represent the poor had a ring of authenticity.

Nor were they taken in by middle-class political tactics. For example, when CAA officials explained to Detroit representatives that time was too short to elicit NPC advice on an employment proposal, NPC members, according to Goodman, "don't quite buy this explanation. . . . [They] remind professionals that a large number of area people spent many long hours in 1966 on short notice going over programs which were to be submitted."[23] And in New York, Atkins and her low-income associates were never fooled in the intricate battles that took place between them and the competing Puerto Rican organization. In fact, the struggle was so intractable simply because both sides calculated closely the impact on power positions that any solution might have. For example, when community elections were proposed, both sides tried to structure them in such a way as to insure victory for themselves.

Low-income representatives were particularly effective, provided they had had prior organizational experience. It may be that this experience itself increased their self-confidence and political skill in bargaining situations. Or it may be that community organizations recruit "deviants" within the low-income community who, for one reason or another, have unusual abilities in this regard. But whatever the causal explanation, the recruitment of this type of low-income representative is more likely to occur where the representatives are chosen by neighborhood organizations. In fact, this may well have been one of the reasons antiparticipatory mayors opposed this manner of selecting formal representatives of the poor.

Socially descriptive representation also affected the orientation (interest representation) of the representatives. Since Chicago's representatives so rarely exercised any influence at all, their orientation had little significance. Generally, where the representatives had even only moderate levels of influence, lower-income representatives seemed more interested in securing particularistic benefits while middle-income representatives were more interested in achieving universalistic changes in governmental services. In Detroit, it was primarily the lower-income NPC members who insisted on changing civil service regulations, so that the NSCs could employ low-income residents, and who advocated payment for the time that representatives spent at CPC and NPC meetings. On Manhattan's Lower West Side, the partisan faction, which agitated for greater involvement of the poor, were repeatedly disappointed by the support which low-income representatives gave to their opponents in exchange for particularistic benefits. But it was in Philadelphia where socially descriptive representation had the most obvious effect on the representatives' behavior. These low-income representatives improved their own economic position by bargaining with CAA officials over particularistic benefits.

Given a tradition of patronage politics in Philadelphia, the pattern is understandable. On a purely statistical basis, low-income representatives are more likely than middle-class representatives to face personal financial difficulties which can be eased by trading power and influence for monetary assistance. More important, such behavior is perfectly consistent with the cultural style of the lower-class community. In Gerald Suttles' anthropological analysis of *The Social Order of the Slum,* he notes that "Slum residents . . . are subject to all the suspicions and bear those disreputable characteristics that turn people away from one another and interfere with joint activities. Seen from the standpoint of the wider community, slum residents do not inspire levels of trust necessary to the usual round of neighborhood activities. Out of necessity, then, they may fall back on local patterns which guarantee their safety and promote association."[24] One of the ways in which "slum residents can assuage at least some of their apprehension" is by "a close inquiry into each other's personal character and past history. Communication, then, should be of an intimate character, and aimed towards producing 'personal' rather than formal relations. In turn, social relations will represent a sort of private 'compact' where particularistic loyalties replace impersonal standards of worth."[25] Under the circumstances, it is hardly surprising that Philadelphia's low-income representatives pursued particularistic goals on behalf of their friends and neighbors.

Thus, the connection between high socially descriptive and low substantive representation obtains only if (1) the constituency includes a predominantly low-income or otherwise socially deprived population, with particularistic communication patterns and little organizational experience and skill; and (2) the criteria established for measuring the extent of socially descriptive representation focus on these same attributes. For constituencies with many middle- and upper-income individuals, or constituencies which include individuals with organizational skills, socially descriptive representation will by no means preclude the selection of effective, influential representatives. Our data do not support the simple conclusion that the Philadelphia and New York CAPs took different directions because lower-income representatives sought material gain, whereas middle-income representatives sought greater influence for their organizations. The impact of socially descriptive representation cannot account for the extremely low substantive representation in Chicago (with its many middle-class representatives), nor for the fact that even lower-income representatives in New York's East Harlem and Bedford-Stuyvesant and throughout Detroit fought for greater neighborhood influence with a vigor unknown in Philadelphia, Chicago, or Los Angeles. To understand these variations among representatives of the same class, we must turn to the direct impact of formal representation on political power relationships.

FORMAL REPRESENTATION, POLITICAL CONSTITUENCIES, AND SUBSTANTIVE REPRESENTATION

The low level of formal representation in Chicago facilitated a low level of actual representation. A powerful city administration, opposed to the political mobilization of low-income groups, itself appointed the directors of the NSCs who, in turn, selected the centers' representatives to the CPC. Thus the representatives of the poor derived their authority from the very source of power toward which demands for change had to be diverted. The representatives found their position too weak, not only to press for broad policy goals but to exercise much influence of any sort. Their very position as representatives depended on the good will of the mayor and his aides.

That high formal representation, indeed democratic elections, did not produce an equally high level of substantive representation in Los Angeles and Philadelphia may appear more puzzling. But in fact these elections exemplify in an unusually extreme form the disorganization in competitive elections typical of "friends-and-neighbors" politics. In *Southern Politics* Key found that such politics are likely to occur when there is "an absence of stable, well-organized . . . factions of like-minded citizens formed to advocate measures of common concern. In its extreme form, localism justifies a diagnosis of low voter-interest in public issues and a susceptibility to control by the irrelevant appeal to support the home-town boy."[26]

One indicator of the low voter-interest in the poverty elections, which was widely broadcast by the news media at the time, was that less than 3 percent of the eligible population participated in the Philadelphia balloting and less than 1 percent in Los Angeles. Closer analysis of the election data suggests that in both cities those few who voted were influenced by localist considerations. In Philadelphia, each of the twelve areas in which NPC representatives were chosen was divided into four sections for polling purposes. To determine the relationship between the residence of candidates and voting behavior, each candidate was classified according to the polling section in which he lived. A voter was eligible to cast his ballot upon presentation of evidence that he resided within that section. Since votes were tallied by voting section, it was possible to determine localist influences on voting behavior.

Localism influenced the voter's decision as to whether he should vote at all. Among all forty-eight voting sections in the twelve NPC areas, there was a strong correlation between the number of council candidates residing in that section and the number of voters on election day. Table 6–2 reveals the sharp increase in the number of voters as the number of candidates increased.[27] The data suffer from our inability to state the voter turnout in percentage terms. But for those twelve voting sections (chosen at random) for which we estimated the percentage turnout,[28] the relationship between the number of candidates and voter turnout was even more dramatic. The rank order of the two variables for these twelve sections was nearly identical, and the product-moment coefficient

TABLE 6–2. Number of Candidates Living in Section and Voter Turnout in Forty-eight Voting Sections

Number of candidates living in section	*Number of sections*	*Average number voting in section*
0–3	(9)	60.9
4–6	(14)	252.2
7–9	(13)	316.5
10–12	(12)	433.1

TABLE 6–3. Number of Candidates Living in Voting Section and Voter Turnout in Twelve Sample Sections

Number of candidates living in section	*Percentage voting in section*
14	5.6
12	5.7
10	2.2
8	1.4
8	1.2
6	2.3
6	0.9
5	2.0
4	0.7
0	0.4
0	0.1
0	0.1

of correlation attained a value of 0.86. (The details are shown in Table 6–3.) In an election having such a low turnout, people did not vote unless there was some particularly compelling reason to do so. In this case, the most powerful force inducing voters to participate was a friend or neighbor running for office; the more candidates in an area, the more people would do a friend a favor by showing up at the polls.

The pattern of support for each candidate within his NPC area revealed that a voter tended to vote for candidates that lived within the same voting section that the voter did. An index of localism was developed in order to state the degree to which localist influences were revealed by the voting behavior. The rationale for this index is stated in Appendix B. Briefly, the index of localism states numerically the proportion of votes received by a local candidate as compared to the average proportion received by all nonlocal candidates, holding constant the general popularity of each candidate. If the local candidate did proportionately no better than nonlocal candidates, the value of the index is

1.00. If his proportion is less than that of nonlocal candidates, the value is less than 1.00.

As measured by this index, localism dominated Philadelphia's poverty election; out of 348 candidates 93 percent ran proportionately better in their home section than did the average nonlocal candidate.[29] Only 6 percent did not do as well, while two candidates ran proportionately as well as did the average nonlocal candidates. The score for the average candidate was 2.07. Thus, the average candidate did proportionately twice as well in his own section as did the average nonlocal candidate in that section. This pattern of voting behavior appears not to have simply reflected racial loyalties, which would appear as localist influences because of segregated housing patterns. If such had been the case, one would have found a lower index of localism in racially homogeneous areas. But, as can be seen in Table 6–4, the racial complexion of an area had little effect on the index of localism.

TABLE 6–4. Proportion of Nonwhites in Community Action Council Area and Area's Score on Index of Localism

Percentage of nonwhites in community action council area	*Number of areas*	*Average index of localism score*
0%–15%[a] (predominantly white)	(2)	2.03
25%–45%[a] (racially mixed)	(6)	2.00
65%–90% (predominantly black)	(4)	2.03

[a] No CAC areas had 16 to 24, or 46 to 64 percent nonwhite populations.

The tendency for the voter to favor the neighborhood candidate, together with the strong correlation between the number of candidates living in a section and voter turnout, suggests that personal acquaintance with one or more of the candidates crucially affected both the decisions to vote and for whom to vote. In this context, friends-and-neighbors politics took on a literal meaning that could not have been quite the case in the southern states that Key analyzed. The NPC areas were so small that nonlocal candidates often lived only a few blocks away. Finding localism in the voting within these supposedly compact council areas reveals an extreme instance of friends-and-neighbors politics. It suggests a lack of issues, disputed by organized competing factions, which usually stimulate citizens to vote. Indeed, during the six weeks before the election, no significant issues and no city-wide organizations contesting the elections emerged. CORE and the NAACP, realizing their own weaknesses, decided to let "the poor people choose their own representatives." The party organizations accepted the decision of CAP officials that party activists were not eligible to participate in this election. Such neighborhood slates as were formed were little more than hastily arranged agreements for temporary gain, rather than a coalition of interests with a discernible policy perspective.

Certain structural characteristics of poverty elections encouraged this issueless, friends-and-neighbors political style. The elections were held separately from other elections. They were electoral contests between politically unknown individuals for an obscure and relatively unimportant post with almost totally undefined responsibilities. The announcement that such an election would be held was made only six weeks prior to election day, an inordinately short period for the selection of candidates, the organization of campaigns, and the development of issues.

The same influences produced friends-and-neighbors voting patterns in the Los Angeles elections, which selected that city's CAP representatives. The index of localism for the average candidate was a high 12.93, which means that of the thirty-two candidates for whom information was obtained the average candidate did proportionately nearly thirteen times as well in his own section as did the average nonlocal candidate in that section.[30] The figures are not directly comparable to Philadelphia, for voters could vote for only one candidate in Los Angeles and neighborhood boundaries were much larger in this geographically dispersed city. But the voting turnout pattern also reflected localist influences. Although it was again impossible to calculate the percentage turnout for each voting section, the sheer number of ballots cast varied substantially, according to whether a candidate lived in the section. In the forty-nine sections where a candidate lived, the number of ballots cast averaged 74.1, while in the one hundred forty-five sections in which there was no candidate, only 23.2 ballots were cast.*[31] As in Philadelphia, Los Angeles voters

* The overall relationship is exaggerated somewhat by the particular circumstances in district area eight, discussed in the text. Nevertheless, in every district there was a greater turnout in local districts, as the following table shows:

	Number of ballots cast	
District area	*Candidate resided in section*	*No candidate resided in section*
I	57.4	17.4
II	33.5	21.7
III	39.5	16.9
IV	45.4	27.9
V	52.7	32.8
VI	48.3	21.8
VII	38.8	21.8
VIII	433.7	14.1

apparently turned out for the poverty election only if they knew one of the candidates or at least recognized him as a member of their particular community.

The conditions under which the friends-and-neighbors pattern of voting flourished in Los Angeles resembled those in Philadelphia. Elections were held shortly after they were announced, no burning issues surrounded the campaign, and no strong community or city-wide organizations contested the elections. The election of Joseph Alexander in district area VIII exemplifies in exaggerated form the forces at work in such unstructured electoral contests. Alexander gained the support of the residents of the Sawtelle Veterans Administration Domiciliary, who technically qualified for the election because they earned less than $4,000 a year. Voters in that section turned out in record numbers, electing Alexander to office. In issueless politics that stir little voter interest, any minimum level of organization, in no matter how small an area, can produce a winner.

The one partial exception to the friends-and-neighbors pattern, interestingly enough, was Gutierrez, who later became the one effective member of the Los Angeles CPC. Although she, too, ran better in her own area, we were unable to identify any one specific section as hers and instead counted as a home section all those where her organization was known to be strong. But even then she only ran proportionately three times as well in these sections as did the other candidates; in other words, her base of support was more broadly dispersed throughout the entire area than was the average candidate's. Although the breadth of her support did not simply and directly account for her political effectiveness, the organization within which she worked may well have been responsible for both dispersed electoral strength and political influence on the CPC.

For the most part, considerations of friendship overshadowed any judgment by the voters in both cities about the representatives' behavior, i.e., the quality of substantive representation, once in office. In terms of the threefold scheme of *The American Voter,*[32] there were no issues, no attributes of particular candidates as potential officeholders, and no partisan or factional loyalties strong enough to undercut the significance for voters of the candidate's residence in his own *immediate* neighborhood.

In Philadelphia, the constituency formed by these arrangements contributed to the representative's particularistic orientation. To the extent that the newly elected representatives had any politically significant constituents at all, it consisted of a few personal acquaintances rather than a strong, organized constituency which could supply future political support or from which they could expect pressure on particular issues. In this political vacuum they sought to develop a small, personally loyal following by distributing particularistic benefits. Therefore, the

CAA staff won the acquiescence of the representatives on larger policy questions by encouraging their interest in questions of patronage and financial remuneration. Friends-and-neighbors politics in Philadelphia, as in the South, extended the power of the dominant political force in the community, in this case, the city administration. As a result, the city fought in subsequent years to continue the elections, even after OEO had lost its enthusiasm for the idea.

In Los Angeles, the election did not so much strengthen the position of the mayor and other public officials, as it helped to ensure that they would not have to contend with a significant challenge from the CAP clientele. Isolated as they were, the representatives lacked both the power which an organized following could provide and a specific interest orientation toward CAP policies. Had they been dependent on community organizations, however, the representatives would have found themselves under pressure to articulate relatively universalistic policy positions that the organizations could use to attract members. And, with the support of these organizations, the representatives might very well have acquired the influence necessary to have some impact on the CAA decisions.

Certainly, the highly organized constituency of the New York and Detroit representatives, as shaped by the formal selection processes in these cities, encouraged universalistic representation. Since the concerns of the organizations in the community did not in general depart radically from the broader interests of the population, their very organization helped them to become effective links binding the representatives to their constituents. And the representatives spoke for, and were accountable to, an organized constituency which could in turn be relied upon in moments of crisis. Whatever their disagreements, the representatives and the community leader drew together to protect the local CAP from city intervention, rather than simply to secure particularistic benefits for themselves.

Instances of such behavior occurred in all three New York neighborhoods we examined intensively and in many others. But events in Bedford-Stuyvesant illustrate the pattern very well. The CAP in that community had been developed by a staff responsive to the interests of the Establishment, but as prospects for funding by OEO improved, a new, more politically oriented director took the helm. The Wagner administration, seeing the growing split within the community, sought to bring the program under more central direction. The community responded with unexpectedly unified political action: community meetings, telegrams, and telephone calls to congressmen (and even to the vice president), and a vigorous defense of the decentralized arrangements in personal discussions with city officials. Representatives from the community on the CPC used their position to increase this pressure. In the face of this opposition, city officials retreated; the availability of the resources of an organized community enabled it to win the local control essential for representation of their universalistic interests.

In Detroit, where the community organizations enjoyed an alliance with the mayor, such a conflict did not emerge. But the resources of the organizations to which their representatives belonged did enhance their influence with CAA officials, while the organizations' expectations about CAP policies pressured their representatives to articulate broad-scale programs, rather than primarily trying to secure particularistic benefits.

As in the case of socially descriptive representation, this relationship between formal and substantive representation may be peculiarly characteristic of representatives of disadvantaged groups in society. The formal process by which corporations, labor unions, and professional associations are selected as representatives on official policy-making bodies probably has little effect on their subsequent behavior. Analyses of group influence in policy-making throughout the federal system in the United States suggest that such groups are capable of providing quite effective interest representation under a variety of formal and informal relationships with policy-makers.[33] The multiplicity of access points available to higher-status groups reduces the significance of any one channel of influence. If a particular representative does not provide effective interest representation, the high-status group will sooner or later find a satisfactory alternative. To guard against loss of position within their own group, representatives tend to be vigorous exponents of the group's interests.

Since low-status groups are likely to have significantly fewer alternative channels, the importance of any one is thereby enhanced. The representative's bargaining position vis-à-vis the agency he is trying to influence is weakened, and his bargaining position vis-à-vis the group he is representing is strengthened. Other factors being equal, he is more likely to make greater concessions merely to maintain his position as formal representative. This pattern can be most effectively reversed by a formal selection process based on organized groups, which strengthen the representative's position vis-a-vis nongroup members. By contrast, selection of representatives by either government appointment or issueless elections without organized competition leaves the pattern essentially unchanged.

CONCLUSIONS: REPRESENTATION AND SOCIAL DEPRIVATION

This analysis suggests two more general propositions about the connection between role interests and substantive representation. First, the relationships among formal representation, socially descriptive representation and substantive representation depends, in part, on the extent to which the constituents' interests are manifest or recognized. Representation of the interests of poor blacks seems particularly difficult, precisely because these are usually so latent. To be sure, at certain historically important times and on certain issues, these interests have become clearly manifest. But by comparison with other groups, the ghetto residents observed in this study tended to be less clear, not only on what public policies were favorable to their racial or economic group collectively, but also as to what steps and techniques they should adopt in order to secure such policies. Indeed, the very deprivation of the poor encourages each individual among them to seek particularistic benefits for himself. Since the poor do not *expect* their representatives to provide universalistic representation, it follows that the extent of the representative's own ideological commitment to securing broadly shared policy outputs becomes decisive. And if he is concerned with universalistic interest representation, the representative of the socially disadvantaged may well differ from most of his constituents at most points in time. If this analysis is right, high socially descriptive representation thus inhibits high substantive representation not just when the constituents are poor but *whenever their collective interests are latent rather than manifest.* Poverty is relevant because it may increase the probability that the constituents' interest will be latent, but interest latency is the decisive variable.

In the second place, the quality of substantive representation is a function of the extent to which the latent interests of a socially deprived group are opposed on crucial policy issues by superordinate groups. The greater the degree of opposition to a specific issue, the more likely it is that the superordinate groups will try to co-opt, i.e., control through particularistic rewards, the subjected groups' nonideological representatives. To maintain influence over such representatives' behavior, it therefore becomes necessary to ask what mechanisms are available to those constituents for whom the shared group interests are manifest. The most important source of control may be an arrangement for selecting representatives that provides substantial influence for organized groups committed to universalistic interests.[34] The greater the conflict of group interests, the more important becomes the inhibiting effect that high formal representation—without intermediate organizations—has on substantive representation. And this relationship would seem to hold not only when the constituents are poor or subjected, but whenever such disparities of interest are very great and one group is superordinate to the other.

This chapter has emphasized the importance of the policy settlement that determined the types of formal and socially descriptive representation, which, in turn, influenced the character of substantive representation in each city. Although extremely important, the terms of the policy settlement were not entirely decisive. Regardless of the way in which the representatives were selected, their impact on CAP policy was influenced by the bureaucratic context within which they operated. A full explanation of inter-city differences in the implementation of the policy settlement also requires an examination of urban bureaucracies.

CHAPTER 7: BUREAUCRATIC INFLUENCE ON PARTICIPATION IN COMMUNITY ACTION

The policy settlement, by establishing a set of shared expectations among important political actors, and by institutionalizing formal arrangements for the representation of the poor, accounted for most of the variation in community participation among the five cities. This correlation between the policy settlement and participation, as presented in Table 7-1, is so high that, except for the small number of cases, statisticians might attribute the unexplained variance to random error. Yet, New York had a more participatory program than Detroit, even though the policy settlement in the two cities was the same. Moreover, Philadelphia had a less participatory program than Los Angeles, even though, once again, the settlements were similar.* The case-study quality of our data enables us to consider these differences in each of these pairs of cities. In the process of doing so, we can identify one way in which reformed institutions have affected policy, at least on the participation issue.

Earlier, we discussed the stance that reformers and machine politicians took on the question of community participation. Machine politicians opposed participation while most reformers supported it. But, in contrast to the proparticipatory *ideologies* of the reformers themselves, the *institutional arrangements* that the reform movement historically favored did not contribute in any uniform manner toward more partici-

---

* One might try to explain these deviations in substantive participation from what the policy settlement predicted in terms of the mayors' ideologies. This does not provide an adequate empirical explanation, however. New York, even under Liberal Pragmatist Mayor Wagner, established a more participatory program than did Detroit under Community Conservationist Mayor Cavanagh. Los Angeles had a more participatory program than Philadelphia, even though Mayor Yorty much more vociferously attacked participation than did Mayor Tate.

TABLE 7–1. Policy Settlement and Participation in the Community Action Program (CAP)

Cities	*Policy settlement (formal representation)*		*Participation in CAP (substantive representation)*
New York	4½	Proparticipatory	5 (High)
Detroit	4½		4
Los Angeles	2½	Antiparticipatory	3
Philadelphia	2½		2
Chicago	1	(Extremely Antiparticipatory)	1 (Low)

patory programs. The cities with the most and least participatory programs—New York and Chicago—were still cities with patronage-oriented, partisan politics, while participation in the two fully reformed cities—Los Angeles and Detroit—also differed substantially. The reform of city government did have an impact on the level of community participation, but it was a much more complicated one than the impact of the reform ideologies.

Two characteristics particularly distinguished the reform from the machine cities in this study. In Los Angeles and Detroit, where reformers had great success, full institutional reform has meant (1) a comprehensive, entrenched merit system which rules out any significant patronage employment (except at the highest policy-making levels); and (2) the establishment of legal and normative barriers to party involvement in city elections, which make them genuinely nonpartisan. These institutional characteristics of the reform cities altered the pattern of political alliances in reformed as compared to machine cities. The consequences this had for the policy settlements is discussed in Chapter 8. In this chapter we focus on a second significant consequence of urban reform, i.e., the autonomy it has given urban bureaucracies. This autonomy did not affect community participation in any simple or direct manner. Rather, it had exactly opposite effects in the two reformed cities. On the one hand, it limited participation in Detroit so that this city had a *less* participatory program than New York, even though the two cities had equally proparticipatory policy settlements. On the other hand, it increased participation in Los Angeles so that this western city had a *more* participatory program than Philadelphia, even though these two cities had equally antiparticipatory policy settlements.

In other words, bureaucratic autonomy weakened the relationship between the policy settlement and participation in reformed cities. In cities where machine politics continued to persist, variations in the policy settlement had a greater effect on the level of participation. Accordingly, Figure 7–1 shows a much steeper line connecting machine cities than the line connecting reform cities. Of course, reliance on data from only five cities and the use of ordinal, not interval, data makes this figure illustrative rather than literally descriptive. But through the use of documentary and interview sources it is possible to specify in some detail the way in which bureaucratic autonomy minimized the impact of the policy settlements in Los Angeles and Detroit.

BUREAUCRATIC AUTONOMY

"Autonomy" is a term fraught with many conceptual confusions. In referring to the autonomy of an institution, we do not mean to suggest that all (or even most) of the "causal" forces affecting its behavior come solely from within the organization itself. Nor do we deny that an autonomous institution is directly influenced by specifically political pressures. In Los Angeles and Detroit, where the CAAs were relatively autonomous, one could still identify extremely important impacts on CAA behavior emanating from state legislators, congressmen, neighborhood organizations, mayors, and private welfare agencies. Indeed, many bureaucracies in reform cities have close, and often primarily dependent, relationships with narrow interest groups highly interested in their specialized activities.[1] Autonomy is used here in the particular sense current in the urban politics literature, in which bureaucracies are frequently said to be independent of the dominant political forces in the community.[2] On the other hand, we recognize that every agency, even in a city like Chicago, has some autonomy; the mayor cannot scrutinize every decision. The question, then, is the relative autonomy among our five cities. Specifically, we use autonomy to characterize those CAA bureaucracies that remained rather independent of the dominant coalition shaping the policy settlement.*

Whenever bureaucratic autonomy was limited, the dominant coalition exercised rather direct control over policy implementation. It did so initially by effectively supervising the recruitment of CAA personnel to insure their adherence to the policy settlement. The coalition also determined the specific decisions which shaped CAP policy in a participatory or nonparticipatory direction. These two elements, control over recruitment and the CAA's ongoing implementation of policy, provided good

* We identify the dominant coalitions in each city in Chapter 8.

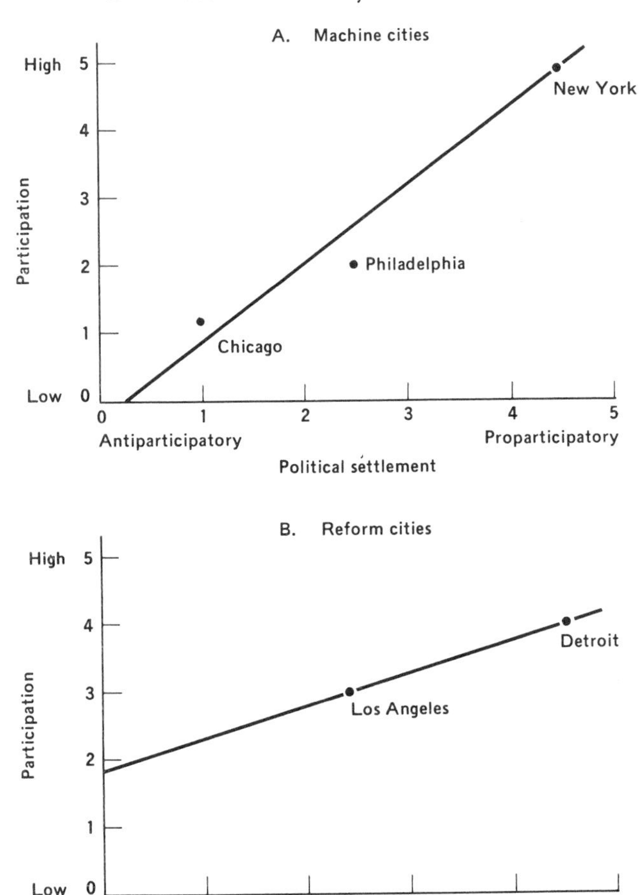

FIG. 7–1. Political Settlement and Level of Participation in Machine (*A*) and Reform (*B*) Cities

indicators of the degree to which the dominant coalition could prevent bureaucratic autonomy.

In seeking to control the program, the dominant coalition was particularly fortunate in the case of the CAP. No existing bureaucratic institution with established traditions and entrenched personnel could claim that the poverty program fell within its jurisdiction. The Office of Economic Opportunity, in calling for coordination among city and private agencies servicing the poor, asked localities to create new institutions with their own administrative staff.[3] Had money been channeled through an established, autonomous institution, such as the school system, control over policy implementation by the mayor or other politicians would very likely have been more difficult. Yet in reform cities, even the CAA, a newly created agency whose personnel was freshly recruited to implement the war on poverty, became autonomous of dominant political forces. In these cities, centrifugal forces in urban politics appear to have been powerful indeed, at least when compared with the machine cities of Chicago, New York, and Philadelphia.

AUTONOMY IN MACHINE CITIES

As might be anticipated, Chicago's CAA did not develop any significant autonomous tendencies. Deton Brooks, its executive director, came from the Department of Public Aid, where he had faithfully assisted its dynamic, but rather conservative, director. Lower ranking CAA personnel were recruited from other city bureaucracies in close consultation with the mayor's office and quickly learned that they had to pursue an economic, not a political, attack on poverty, thus avoiding "the mistakes of the juvenile delinquency program." This program had demonstrated its independence of mayoral control by criticizing the school system, promoting community organization, sponsoring a school boycott, and even leading a group of activists that "booed" the mayor in the midst of the 1964 Fourth of July celebration.[4] The mayor subsequently reorganized the juvenile delinquency agency, fired most of its previous staff, and refused further federal funding unless this was under his firm control. When the CAA was formed, the mayor was determined that this new program should not develop the same independent spirit that had marked its predecessor.

Within the CAA higher ranking administrators ensured that lower level personnel within the organization did not repeat the juvenile delinquency program's "mistakes." Even in Chicago the participatory rhetoric of the national program attracted activist-minded workers into the program, which created some problems for supervisors committed to the Chicago political settlement. A Neighborhood Service Center (NSC) staff member reported that he was refused permission "to conduct a political education class." Other NSC employees, known to have associated with groups critical of Chicago's CAP, reported being told by the NSC director that he was intolerant of "oral and written criticism, pickets, or demonstrations which in any way reflect on the program." The individuals were welcomed "aboard" but sternly warned that the director "runs a tight ship." In still another case, a group of NSC employees participated in a march on the Department of Public Aid led by an activist organization. Attacked by a Democratic alderman, they were called to the CAA's downtown headquarters to explain their actions. Although they were not "fired," no further duties were assigned to the leaders of these internal dissidents. Finally, a private organization, funded by CAA, had permitted one of its employees to organize block associations and hold public meetings. Upon the complaint of the local aldermen, the CAA suspended funding for the organization until it was agreed that the employees would no longer work at community organization. Clearly, a common orientation was imposed on the staff of Chicago's CAA at all levels.

Other high city officials, many of them Community Poverty Council (CPC) members themselves, also made sure that the CAA staff did not initiate controversies with other city agencies. When the CAA staff proposed a health program to be carried out within the NSCs, the Board of Health complained about the intrusion into its jurisdiction. It developed a low-quality counterproposal which the CAA, unable to pursue any distinctive mission of its own, simply forwarded to OEO. The proposal had been so poorly drafted that the federal agency quickly rejected it as inadequate.

In Philadelphia, Mayor Tate could not as easily achieve close control of the CAA by direct administrative orders. Yet, as the process of selecting the CAA's executive director so well illustrates, the mayor shrewdly bargained and maneuvered to prevent any significant deviations from the city's antiparticipatory political settlement. In order to avoid one of the major criticisms leveled at Philadelphia's juvenile delinquency program, Mayor Tate announced in January 1965 that he would appoint a black CAA director.[5] Samuel Evans, the mayor's black adviser on poverty matters, recommended his political associate, Charles Bowser, a young attorney who had some recognition for initiating the lawsuit that had halted "minstrel" parades in Philadelphia. Tate agreed, though he personally seems to have preferred a police captain, who unfortunately had failed to pass a civil service examination when the mayor sought to appoint him deputy police commissioner. Meanwhile, Cecil Moore, the flamboyant head of Philadelphia's National Association for the Advancement of Colored People (NAACP), who had so effectively attacked white domination of the juvenile delinquency program, nominated his assistant in the NAACP. The mayor remained publicly undecided for more than two months, at one point even asking OEO to select the best candidate from a seven-name list. But OEO, wishing to avoid a local conflict, simply declared that they were all qualified.

Tate then decided to enlist the support of the private welfare agencies by appointing an advisory committee consisting of Cecil Moore, Samuel Evans, a personal friend, and two directors of private welfare agencies.

With only one additional vote the welfare officials could thus control the committee. But Tate evidently recognized that their first preference, a professional social worker such as the director of the Urban League, would be politically independent of the city administration. Accordingly, Tate restricted the committee's choice to only five names. Two of the individuals were unknown, and obviously not politically viable, candidates. The mayor's personal friend favored the police captain, Evans favored Bowser, and Moore favored his NAACP associate. The mayor thus deprived the welfare agency professionals of any real options. Their concern for professional qualifications excluded the police captain, and even though Moore had joined them in the juvenile delinquency battle, they did not relish his political style. Rather than increase Moore's influence, they voted with Evans in favor of Bowser, whom the mayor had long since favored. To still Moore's criticism, the mayor then offered the post of legal counsel (at a salary only slightly less than that of the CAA's executive director) to the NAACP candidate, who accepted contrary to Moore's wishes.

Having appointed a directorate politically dependent upon Evans and himself, Tate could expect these two black officials to administer the CAP in a congenial fashion. In addition he could rely on the elected representatives of the poor. Moore of the NAACP (who had broken with his former assistant) together with the representative from the Congress of Racial Equality (CORE) tried to enlist the elected representatives' support for a more participatory program. But given the representatives' desire for both salaries from the CAA and control over patronage positions, they cooperated instead with Evans, Bowser, and the CAA staff. Evans, after all, quickly demonstrated that he could provide them and their relatives—at one point 200 individuals in all—with attractive financial assistance and employment opportunities. Evans even attacked private welfare agencies for limiting the representatives' control over hiring personnel for their programs. This desire to take advantage of existing patronage opportunities in turn led the representatives to recruit staff members to NSCs who would accept CAA leadership. The directors of the local NSCs appointed in this way lacked any administrative experience or expertise, and they were as a result extremely dependent upon instructions from central CAA administrators, even in the first months when the NSCs were formally responsible to the local NPCs. Subsequently, the central CAA obtained formal authority to recruit, supervise, and fire local NSC personnel.

Central control in Philadelphia was never as detailed as in Chicago, for local bureaucracies were not that hierarchically organized. Rather, cooperative relationships were achieved by an elaborate patronage system, which meant some considerable sacrifice in the speed and efficiency with which CAA personnel operated. Nonetheless, Philadelphia's pattern of recruitment meant that organizational personnel looked to local friends and political leaders for cues rather than to any stated goals of the federal CAP. And, consistent with Mayor Tate's preferences, these cues were rarely if ever proparticipatory. It was not that Evans and Bowser directly attacked efforts at community organization but that the processes of recruitment, which they instituted, inhibited any such impulses from emerging.

Although the New York CAP vigorously promoted participation, its bureaucracy was no more autonomous of the dominant political forces than the CAAs in the other two machine cities. In this city, however, proparticipatory forces formed the dominant coalition, and their influence over the implementation of the program helped to preserve its participatory thrust. Initially, Mayor Wagner and his ally, City Council President Paul Screvane, sought to supervise the program closely. They selected an executive director who had no independent base of power, and they gave her definite guidelines within which policy was to be developed. When the mayor expanded the CPC in response to participatory demands, he still sought to supervise administrative action himself by establishing a separate Economic Opportunity Committee, which was to have sole responsibility and direction over the NSCs. Moreover, local poverty funds were allocated through still a third agency, governed by Screvane and a few other government officials.

Yet, these carefully worked out arrangements did not prevent capture of the administrative apparatus by the proparticipatory political coalition, for New York's juvenile delinquency programs had provided another model for conducting CAPs. Haryou-Act in Harlem and Mobilization for Youth (MFY) on the Lower East Side of Manhattan had been established as nonprofit corporations which operated independently of any direct city supervision. They hired their own directors and staffs and established their own program priorities. Although Screvane at one time indicated that he wished to "phase out" these programs as components of the CAP, in favor of centrally controlled NSCs, Haryou-Act's and MFY's political strength precluded any such change.[6] Instead, at least two other neighborhood groups succeeded in establishing similar structures for administering the program in their communities. Even in the remaining areas, where the NSC was formally under central jurisdiction, local groups were able to recruit and dismiss staff members, subject only to the veto of the central CAA. In 1966, after the Lindsay administration came into power, all NSCs were established as independent corporations responsible to their own neighborhood boards. In sum, as the policy settlement became more participatory, administrative control shifted to the proparticipatory forces.

As a result, NSC personnel policies were closely controlled by neighborhood organizations represented on NPCs, who hired staff members, not on their basis of formal training or competence, but on the basis of their organizational affiliations, their racial or ethnic backgrounds, or their personal connections—sometimes in defiance of formal administrative criteria. As in the other two machine cities, the staff had a commitment not to any national OEO program but to local leaders who had been responsible for finding them a position in the organization. And, as in Philadelphia, administrative efficiency was far from ideal. But in contrast to Chicago and Philadelphia, the dominant political force was proparticipatory rather than antiparticipatory, and the NSC staff was frequently diverted from its ostensible duties to engage in demonstrations, protest rallies, school boycotts, and the like.

POLITICAL SOURCES OF NONAUTONOMOUS BUREAUCRACIES IN MACHINE CITIES

Well-established institutions such as school systems, which for decades had sought to isolate themselves from broad political forces, had achieved considerable autonomy even in these three machine cities.[7] Indeed, Sayre and Kaufman's analysis of "islands of functional power" focused on bureaucratic autonomy in New York City.[8] Yet as Lowi's account of appointment practices in New York demonstrates, these agencies won such autonomy slowly against substantial party resistance.[9] When a new program is established within a new agency in machine cities, powerful political actors retain significant incentives and resources to prevent autonomous behavior.

Heads of these party organizations have a particularly strong incentive to control policy implementation in order to respond to citizen and group demands that might affect their (or their successor's) political future.[10] At the same time, they need to reward supporters with policies and positions to secure future contributions to their organizations. Finally, in this case, Mayors Daley, Tate, and Wagner needed to forestall militant activity that might encourage black voters to desert the Democratic party's electoral coalition. On the other side, political opponents eager to challenge these mayors, such as black and Puerto Rican community organizations in New York, had to secure administrative control of governmental agencies in order to sustain their political victory. Otherwise, the gains won in any policy settlement might be subverted over time by the well-organized opposition of the mayor and members of his administration.

Political factions in machine cities also have relatively ample resources with which to limit the autonomy of newly organized bureaucratic agencies. Since political success requires careful coalition building, no single agency head can easily promote himself to a position of power without adhering to implicit agreements reached among political influentials. In Chicago, Deton Brooks did not pursue any distinctive organizational mission, lest he jeopardize any future bureaucratic or political career he might wish to pursue in the city. Samuel Evans and Charles Bowser allied themselves faithfully with even a reputedly weak mayor in Philadelphia, because without mayoral support they lacked sufficient influence in the black community to control CAP. In New York, Mayor Wagner was even willing to delegate responsibility for the poverty program to another *elected* political official, Paul Screvane, knowing full well that Screvane's political future depended on the mayor's strong backing. On the other hand, the very power of the mayor, even in New York, encouraged community organizations to band together in supporting one another's demands for local control of NSCs, since they saw that only through mutual cooperation could the city leadership be defeated. For example, when leaders in Bedford-Stuyvesant united to oppose the replacement of the locally controlled NSC by a centrally directed institution, they won support from other NPC representatives on the CPC.

In addition to their capacity to act in concert in each machine city, the dominant coalition enjoyed a second, somewhat more elusive, advantage: a general acceptance, if not approval, of patronage politics. In Elazar's terms, all the machine cities partook to some extent of the individualistic political culture, which sees politics as an extension of the marketplace.[11] Political activists in such a culture are easily tempted by patronage offers, and those who had divisible perquisites perceived them as a viable mechanism for winning support. To be sure, Daley in Chicago had sufficient resources to implement the policy settlement without using CAP resources for patronage, though even here the poverty program's largess was not an unimportant factor in forestalling criticism from spokesmen for the black community. In Philadelphia and New York, the dominant political factions also discovered that patronage was even more useful in solidifying alliances and insuring the recruitment of lower-ranking personnel responsive to their dictates. Of course, CAP employment opportunities also abounded in the reformed cities, but there was no accompanying sense that a bureaucratic appointment obligated one politically to its dispenser.

AUTONOMY IN REFORMED CITIES

Although Mayor Yorty successfully secured an antiparticipatory political settlement in Los Angeles, he did not entirely control its administrative implementation by the CAA staff. In fact, the CAA director, Joseph Maldanado, had on occasion supported a participatory approach to CAP. Yet given his professional standing among Mexican-American social workers and his directorship of the juvenile delinquency program, he nonetheless assumed the CAA directorship. It is true that he had not played a leading role in the participatory coalition; indeed, the crucial point is that his lack of identification with any particular governmental or political group recommended him for the position. In Philadelphia, a lawyer could head the CAA because of his political connections, but in Los Angeles the applicable criteria, apart from ethnicity, were professional qualifications and political independence. Indeed Maldanado's reputation for independence and professional competence enabled him to hold his job without serious challenge for the CAP's first four years.

Many of Maldanado's subordinates supported participation more vigorously than he, including such members of the "1122 Group" (which had initiated the participation controversy) as the CAA research director and Opal Jones, who became director of the NSC program.[12] These staff members were also recruited for their competence as social workers, rather than for their proparticipatory position. But once on the staff, they felt no particular political loyalty to Maldanado, let alone Yorty, and therefore they continued to pursue their policy preferences.

Before long, this lack of hierarchical control helped produce a major conflict between Maldanado and Opal Jones, who supervised Los Angeles' NSCs. Initially, Jones appeared to adopt a community organization perspective. Although her commitment often seemed mainly rhetorical, it eventually led her to seek a meeting between the mayor and many of her discontented, proparticipatory staff members. Angry at not being consulted, and evidently concerned about Yorty's reaction to a possibly abrasive confrontation, Maldanado fired Jones for insubordination. The response was surprisingly strong. In addition to the predictable protests from community organizations, Maldanado soon faced a proposal by Opal Jones's ally, Congressman Hawkins, to decentralize CAP, thus further weakening whatever hierarchical structure it had. To head off this threat, Maldanado rehired Jones and agreed to turn responsibility for the entire NSC program over to a private agency, the Federation of Settlement and Neighborhood Centers. This step reduced the possibility that Yorty would blame Maldanado for any troubles with the NSC program.

This problem of subordinate independence was not Maldanado's alone. Shortly after she was rehired, Opal Jones herself faced an almost identical predicament when she fired Gabriel Yanez, NSC director in Boyle Heights, after Yanez told his aides not to attend several meetings called by Jones. This dismissal aroused the Mexican-American community, which criticized apparent discrimination in favor of blacks in the entire NSC structure. At first, Jones tried to quiet the dissent by agreeing to split the NSCs between the black and Mexican communities. In turn, this concession infuriated her black staff members and some militant Mexicans, who then felt sufficiently independent to protest their superior's plans publicly. In the complicated maneuvering, which finally alleviated the discontent, Yanez was rehired.

If superiors had difficulty controlling subordinates within the CAA, it was even more difficult for the mayor to control specific bureaucratic activities from the outside. For one thing, Yorty did not share with Maldanado the type of common commitment that united Daley and Brooks in Chicago, Tate, Evans and Browser in Philadelphia, or Wagner and Screvane in New York. Nor could the mayor control the details of CAP policies simply by means of his representation on the CPC. To be sure, the mayor, if intensely dissatisfied, could have threatened, and, indeed, he did threaten to withdraw from the program entirely. In effect, Yorty had a veto power similar to the one that had enabled his assistant to assume a dominant policy-making role within the juvenile delinquency program.[13] But withdrawing support for CAA proved too blunt an instrument for controlling policy details or administrative matters. Yorty's assistant had exercised more influence over the juvenile delinquency agency partly because it was primarily concerned with planning. By contrast, CAP had administrative responsibility for specific on-going programs run by a large number of individuals who inevitably exercised discretion. Yorty was thus confronted with a vast array of administrative actions each relatively insignificant in itself but which, when taken in the aggregate, were difficult to follow let alone control.

If Yorty could have secured a coherent majority on the CPC and, therefore, more leverage on Maldanado, he might possibly have secured tighter control of administrative activity. But such a coalition was impossible given the jealousies among representatives of autonomous public agencies, the wariness of private welfare agency representatives, and the independence of the elected representatives of the poor (who could not be co-opted by a patronage system, as in Philadelphia). The CAA bureaucracy consequently had much more freedom to modify the policy settlement in Los Angeles than it had in any of the machine cities.

Detroit's bureaucracy was equally autonomous, but in this case, it asserted an independence vis-à-vis the city's victorious proparticipatory coalition rather than vis-à-vis an antiparticipatory mayor. Of greatest importance, neighborhood organizations had much less control over the recruitment of personnel than did similar organizations in New York City. The rigid ban on patronage in Detroit politics was vigorously enforced by the Civil Service Commission, which was funded by the Detroit Common (City) Council but otherwise remained almost entirely independent. The commission enjoyed a notable esprit de corps as the self-proclaimed guardian of professionalism, good government, and merit-based personnel policies in Detroit.

This concern for merit as the basis for recruitment led to an early and important struggle over CAA's hiring of community and counselor aides, the agency's two lowest-paid nonclerical, nonmaintenance positions.* At first, the commission insisted on filling these positions, like other city posts, through written examinations, a stand it later took in the case of teachers aides and nurses aides. But these impersonal and apparently impartial criteria, designed for middle-class applicants, clearly threatened the recruitment of poverty area residents, including informal community leaders, placing the Cavanagh administration in a difficult position.

City officials found themselves caught politically between their increasingly influential black allies and a prestigious commission whose good-government stand made it nearly invulnerable. Dissatisfied community organizations tended to interpret any concession to the commission as a barrier to hiring many ghetto residents, and, perhaps, resistance to a genuinely activist orientation for the entire CAP. The commission tended to interpret any agreement with the protesters as a break in the merit principle, and, perhaps, the first step in subverting the entire civil service system. In the end, the commission compromised by adopting a special Federal Economic Opportunity Act Classification for counselors which reduced the weight of the written examinations from 70 percent to 30 percent of the grade, reduced passing scores on the examination from 70 percent to 50 percent, placing greater emphasis on personal characteristics, experience, and place of residence. Equally important, since the community aide positions were considered part-time jobs, it substituted oral, for written, examinations and waived the literacy requirement.

Nevertheless, these concessions did not entirely appease proparticipatory critics. The Civil Service Commission, rather than the CAA, in which neighborhood leaders had substantial influence, continued to make the actual appointments. Some protesters pointed out that under the modified rules, certain community leaders could still be rejected for jobs which essentially involved community leadership. Moreover, employees under this new classification had no transfer rights to other city departments. Even within the CAA, many of the community aides who were recognized

* Community aides, who were hired initially at $1.50 per hour, were to inform residents about available services and to assist community organizations; counselor aides were to deal with problems of community residents who came to the NSC.

by CAA officials as having performed competently could not be promoted until they passed a written examination, a restriction which created additional resentments. In a newspaper article discussing this situation, the CAA director, though he expressed hope that such workers could be promoted, reiterated the importance of adhering to civil service policy.[14]

The insistence on these formal civil service procedures affected higher levels of the CAP staff just as significantly. Only the agency's director and deputy director served at the pleasure of the mayor. All their subordinates had to meet civil service requirements, including examinations. In many cities, of course, skillful administrators have manipulated such regulations to appoint and promote political allies. But such manipulation was rarely practiced in Detroit. Officials moved up through the ranks and sought to transfer from one agency to another as they saw attractive opportunities develop. Rather than politicians influencing the career opportunities of administrators, some career officials made good political use of their positions within the city administration. Thus, the first CAA director later became an important confidant of the mayor.

Since neither the mayor nor his agency heads could exercise the hierarchical, monocratic control that Mayor Daley enjoyed in Chicago, the community organizations found it difficult to insist that the mayor enable local activists to control CAP's day-to-day operations. Indeed, these organizational constraints reinforced whatever reservations Cavanagh as a Community Conservationist already had about such a step, because it would so very probably decrease administrative rationality and efficiency. Rather than having to confess such doubts publicly, Cavanagh could plead the obvious pressures of a widely respected merit system.

Since the civil service system insulated employees from direct political pressures, black activists primarily tried to enforce the participatory political settlement through their representation on the CAP's neighborhood and city-wide councils. Detroit's NPCs, of course, did have much greater influence than their counterparts in Philadelphia or Chicago. By discussing NPC policies with the CAP's Target Area Consultants, who were hired from the local community to give advice on proposals and programming, the representatives acquired some information from a source independent of the professional administrative staff. For this and other reasons, NPC and CPC members could, and did, substantially affect both the shape of CAA proposals and the details of administrative behavior. Indeed, several of the representatives became well-known, articulate spokesmen for community opinion and criticism.

The relevant comparison in this context, however, is not Philadelphia and Los Angeles but New York City, where an equally participatory policy settlement led to outright community control. From this perspective, NPC influence over agency operations was limited. One substantial source of the differences between Detroit and New York was certainly the Detroit NPC's lack of control over staff recruitment. Indeed, the NPCs and CPC in Detroit were formally designated as advisory rather than as governing bodies. As a result, the CAA staff was never *required* to consult with the NPCs. Often the staff, under pressure of time, bypassed NPCs.[15] In sum, if bureaucrats in Los Angeles could act without fearing the loss of their jobs or other severe mayoral constraints, bureaucrats in Detroit enjoyed the same protection vis-à-vis the city's otherwise powerful community organizations.

POLITICAL SOURCES OF AUTONOMY IN REFORM CITIES

Political actors in fully reformed cities do not have the incentives to control bureaucracies that they have in machine cities. Certainly, any mayor wishes to have tight control of his administrative apparatus, and Mayors Cavanagh and Yorty constantly battled to extend their influence over the array of more or less autonomous bureaucracies in their local governments. Yet the expectation in reform cities that administrative practices should be isolated from political influences enables the mayors to hold their supporters' gratitude simply by demonstrating good intentions, even if they fail to exercise effective control. Too effective an "iron hand" may actually evoke charges of "dictatorship" and "one-man rule." So long as Yorty expressed his own opposition to participation, limited participatory activities by a joint-power, county-wide agency was not likely to hurt him significantly among established interests or his White Power and Orthodox Conservative supporters. Similarly, so long as Cavanagh personally supported participation in Detroit, frustrated blacks would direct their anger at the independent civil service commission and CAA officials rather than at the mayor's office. Moreover, mayors in reform cities did not need to be as concerned about the ongoing strength of any party organization. At the same time, activist blacks, seeking to build politically significant organizations, were not as dependent as in New York on controlling patronage, because they did not have to contend with strong party organizations. Electoral campaigns in Detroit and Los Angeles have been traditionally fought by issue-oriented party activists, not by government employees concerned about keeping their jobs. Moreover, broad appeals conveyed by the news media, rather than hard precinct work conducted by such patronage workers, were the campaign tactic most depended upon for a candidate's success.

But whatever their goals, mayors and other ambitious politicians certainly lacked resources comparable to those in machine cities. Most clearly, the limits on patronage in these cities handicapped partisans from staffing the agency with officials having similar policy preferences. Had Yorty sought to replace Maldanado with a close political ally opposed to participation, the political repercussions would have been enormous. Had neighborhood organizations succeeded in obtaining from Cavanagh the authority to appoint whomever they wished, a concession which presumably would have led to the patronage practices detectable in Philadelphia and New York, the Civil Service Commission, with its broad base of political support, would have mounted a powerful countercampaign. But apart from this limitation on patronage, the absence of strong political parties itself contributed to centrifugal tendencies. Maldanado discovered that a most successful bureaucratic career could be pursued by deliberately remaining aloof from any political alliances. Detroit's CAA director similarly refused either to support or to attack explicitly the Civil Service Commission; other civil servants moved in and out of Detroit's CAA in response to changing bureaucratic opportunities without forming political alliances with neighborhood groups or anyone else. Newly organized bureaucracies could achieve a considerable degree of autonomy in these two cities because no single set of political actors, even those that dictated the policy settlement, possessed both the incentives and resources to control their behavior closely.

The greater autonomy of CAA bureaucracies in fully reformed cities does not by itself explain why the two agencies used it in exactly opposite ways, i.e., to reduce participation in Detroit but to increase it in Los Angeles. To account for this apparently contradictory behavior, it is necessary to examine two very different elements of bureaucratic mentality and practice: the need for an organizational mission, and the tendency toward routinized behavior.

THE MISSION OF AUTONOMOUS BUREAUCRACIES

For all organizations directly affected by political decisions, distinctive missions are an important mechanism for survival. Among public agencies such purposes are often legislatively prescribed at the time that the agency itself is created, and the organizational rhetoric justifying its existence only elaborates these statutory provisions. In other cases, organizations may modify their legislative mandate in order to pursue a mission which attracts more stable and continuing support. At one point, the Interstate Commerce Commission, to take a well-known example, transformed its original mission of regulating the railroads for the protection of consumers from monopolistic practices into a mission that sought to protect the interests of railroads against truckers and airplanes within the national transportation complex.[16]

The more autonomous an organization, the more important is a mission for its survival. In the cities where the CAA was closely controlled by the dominant political faction, that faction had a strong incentive to provide the agency with the necessary political support so that the agency could implement the policy objectives of the faction. In a sense, the mission of the agency in the limiting case would be devoted service to the faction in power. But where a CAA or any other organization is independent of a single dominant faction, the organization needs to fend for itself in jurisdictional struggles and competitions for funds. In such conflicts, the claim that it is pursuing a socially valued goal becomes a major weapon. But the agency mission is not only vitally important in the conduct of its "foreign relations"; it is also an important mechanism for maintaining internal cohesion. The identification of a particular mission tends to recruit staff with similar goals and preferences or at least assists in socializing recruits who then adopt such values. The emphasis that organizations place on recruitment from the "inside" and promotion "up the ladder" testifies to the importance of a common staff understanding of its purposes. Selznick even argues that the major responsibility of organizational leaders is to define, interpret, and shape an organization's mission, using staff recruitment as a key weapon.[17]

From this perspective, it is clear that the CAP faced a considerable problem in justifying its existence, for its legislative mandate was unusually vague, general, and overlapped extensively with the jurisdictions of other public organizations. The legislative provision which most nearly defined its purpose was the requirement that it "provide stimulation and incentive for urban and rural communities to mobilize their resources to combat poverty through community action programs."[18] As Solomon stressed, there is "nothing in the title or statute [that] explains what is meant by a community action program. At best, there is the suggestion that a community action program shall be indigenously organized use of resources against poverty."[19] Under the circumstances, it was tempting for OEO and its delegate agencies across the country to latch on to the "maximum feasible participation" requirement as the distinctive legislative mandate for its programs, hoping to justify activities which otherwise could have easily been carried out by any number of more established agencies.

From one point of view, participation might appear to be only a means for achieving other goals, not a substantive goal that could justify an organization's existence. But to CAP enthusiasts, participation was an end in itself, for it would promote the extension of citizenship rights to minorities and the elimination of invidious ascriptive distinctions among social groups. At any rate, the national OEO adopted participation as its distinctive mission, and local CAAs, where their political autonomy required the development of a comparable mission, reflected the national orientation.

This development clearly affected the Los Angeles CAP. Many minority group social workers, who had campaigned for a participatory program, joined its staff even after an antiparticipatory policy settlement had been reached. They concentrated, first of all, in the research arm of the agency, where they wrote participatory CAP proposals. Later, these plans were regularly subverted by either the mayor's office, the school system, the police department, or some other established agency and its representative on the CPC. As a result, the research staff became increasingly disillusioned, and many of them later resigned from the program.

Opal Jones's NSC program also attracted a number of participatory-oriented NSC directors who had a more visible impact. Community organization efforts were probably the most carefully thought out and genuinely sustained in the East Los Angeles-Belvedere area, where the Mexican Community Services Organization was already strong. The first director, Tony Rios, concentrated his energies on the CSO's buyers' club program. In Rios's forcefully articulated view, community organizations working for the broader interests of the poor could succeed in the long run only if they held their members' loyalty by providing more immediate material incentives. But Rios's effectiveness in pushing this program declined after he was promoted within the NSC organization and lost direct contact with his center. Shortly thereafter he, too, left CAP in frustration.

Another active center operated in the Watts area, the heart of Los Angeles' black ghetto. By December of 1965, the center's aides helped organize a tenants' union, twenty-five block clubs, and two buyers' clubs. During much of this period, the chairman of the center's NPC was also chairman of the local Welfare Rights Organization (WRO). But after the first director lost her job, turnover among aides increased and organizing activities declined. The Marvista Center also worked closely with the WRO; the first director was a former WRO president, had participated in demonstrations against the Bureau of Public Assistance, and had close ties to a militant social workers union. Not surprisingly, most of her aides were WRO members, and their employment by the center for work that supported WRO's activities represented significant CAP support for participatory goals. In addition, center aides also helped develop some buyers' clubs. But as in Watts, activity subsided under the much less dynamic woman who succeeded the first director. Similarly, the Los Angeles central NSC at first provided some help to the buyers' clubs, a credit union, four block clubs, and a small businessmen's club. But by 1968, all of these activities had become moribund, except for the work of one aide, who continued to maintain contacts with local organizations.

In sum, community organization activities developed in the first year of the Los Angeles program, where the NSC director effectively mobilized center aides. But as time passed, most of the participatory enthusiasts resigned, left, were promoted, or fired, and by 1968 only a few isolated aides still engaged in liaison work with the community. At least at the beginning Los Angeles had more participation than one would have expected from the terms of the policy settlement. But significantly, such participation developed only to the extent that the CAA was supported by OEO's participatory rhetoric in Washington. When the national OEO was forced to deemphasize participation as its distinctive mission, participatory supporters in Los Angeles lacked the backing necessary to maintain their commitment to the program.

The same pattern of declining participation was not as evident in Detroit, simply because the local policy settlement was proparticipatory. But it was equally apparent that the local CAA recruited to its staff those bureaucrats who were sympathetic to participation. Chapter 1 pointed out the extent to which Detroit recruited its staff from civil rights groups and militant neighborhood organizations. It also attracted black staff members who were sympathetic to participatory goals from the welfare department, the city hospital, the Community Renewal program, and other city agencies. Indeed, one of CAP's functions in Detroit (as in other cities) was to provide a mobility route for black professionals who had reached managerial but not top-leadership positions in city government. But Detroit's black bureaucrats, in contrast to their Chicago and Philadelphia counterparts, not only permitted, but even covertly welcomed harassment of unresponsive city agencies by NPC members, organizations receiving assistance from the NSC, and even their lower-echelon staff members. As emphasized below, these black professional administrators did not have an unqualified commitment to participation, but they nonetheless encouraged it whenever it did not directly conflict with their bureaucratic concerns. The key point, then, is that any negative deviation of Detroit's level of participation from what the policy settlement had determined cannot be attributed to the failure of the CAA to recruit a staff that conceived of participation as a primary mission.

ROUTINIZATION OF THE MISSION

However important an agency's mission is for its organizational survival, it has other organizational needs as well, some of which may conflict with the purposes of the mission. To some degree, organizations in Western industrial societies must rationalize their pattern of internal operations through relatively precise routines, standard operating procedures. Failure to act in this way would prompt accusations of agency inequity and inefficiency. In a regime that expects instrumentally rational behavior from public authorities, organizations could not easily survive if they treated each case without regard to any other. Moreover, the organization could not maintain internal cohesion unless its personnel could expect reliable role behavior from one another. Accordingly, organizations attempt to recruit administrators and professionals with the formal training and proper qualifications that presumably insure at least a minimum of competence in performing their specific roles. One implicitly conveyed component of that training emphasizes impersonal, precise, and reliable administration of whatever policies are determined by organizational superiors. Organizational discipline and promotion must be guided by these norms if an autonomous agency is going to enjoy the esteem of its own staff members. Such esteem is particularly important when outside political backing is lacking.

Bureaucratic requirements are not always consistent with organizational missions, particularly when the purpose of an organization is to foster democratic participation.[20] A bureaucracy whose very structure requires rationalization runs contrary to the requirements of participation, which, insofar as it broadens influence over policy formation and invokes the amateur's enthusiasm, inevitably leads to confusion, delay, inefficiency, and, perhaps, even to outright corruption. In particular, bureaucratic routinization depends on well-defined programs, specific prior training, and well-delineated administrative activities. For if such traits are missing, officials cannot confidently expect to be judged fairly by their administrative superiors. Ironically, therefore, the very bureaucratic procedures which protected organizations from the dominant political forces (by inhibiting patronage and undue control of administrative detail) themselves reduced the level of participation in CAP. The pattern was apparent in both Los Angeles and Detroit.

In Los Angeles, the NSC program had called for both community organization and career development, a program of job training for unskilled, unemployed workers that hopefully would reduce economic poverty. The disjunction between the character of community organization as an activity and the nature of rationalized administrative procedures encouraged NSC to emphasize increasingly career development to the exclusion of organizational activity. Although the genuine effectiveness of a career-development activity is extremely difficult to demonstrate,[21] for bureaucratic purposes it is much more easily and quantitatively evaluated than is community organization. The number of individuals recruited to the program, the percentage of those who continue through to its termination, the percentage placed in full-time positions, and finally the percentage still employed over a one- or two-year time period can all be portrayed as fairly precise measures of bureaucratic performance.

Consequently, adopting career development instead of community organization as a goal had a strong appeal not only for top administrators such as Maldanado and Jones, who had to supply concrete justifications for agency programs to the CPC and OEO, but also for many lower-ranking officials that CAA had recruited from other governmental agencies, many of whom were accustomed to bureaucratic routines and modes of thought.

This tendency was in no way limited to local CAAs, for the same tension between organizational mission and organizational procedures confounded OEO itself, especially given its need to cooperate with the General Accounting Office (GAO). Although the initial NSC program proposal approved by OEO contained participatory rhetoric, it stressed career development. Accordingly, federal accountants from the GAO, consistent with standard bureaucratic practice, expected adherence to the easily documented career-development goals at whatever cost to the achievement of the more vaguely worded participation goals. As a result, pressures to minimize participation increased. And in Los Angeles, where Maldanado carefully guarded his reputation for administrative competence, possible allegations of inefficiency or irregularity by federal officials could be particularly damaging. In the words of the CAA's research director,

> . . . the fundamental constraint is built into the program at the federal level. That is, the GAO carefully looks into programs and demands above all that budgets are followed strictly. Innovation and community originated programs of course go together. The need for innovative programs and flexibility are in direct conflict with the requirements of GAO. Thus only at the outset is there a chance for innovation After the GAO comes through, the community action agency has to tighten up.

In the end, as OEO's funds ran low, the whole NSC program was handed to the Department of Labor, and career development became its exclusive activity.

On the CPC itself, a similar concern with precise standards and expertise rather than spontaneous citizen participation had comparable effects. The staff seemed willing to train the elected representatives on the CPC, but they were also concerned that board meetings proceed as smoothly as possible, which meant that the representatives had to conform to ordinary norms of behavior in meetings, rather than spontaneously asserting their own particular perspective in ways that might well obstruct the proceedings. Thus, with one exception, the representatives proved unable to interact on an equal basis with other board members, who had had considerable organizational experience.[22]

These considerations did not have a noticeable effect on the Los Angeles CAP's level of participation only because the policy settlement itself had been basically antiparticipatory. Pressures for routine behavior simply reinforced the political pressures that Mayor Yorty, various public agencies, and the professionals on CPC were already exerting. Very likely, these political pressures would themselves have been sufficient over time to curb the staff's participatory impulses.

The same tendency toward routine behavior was much more significant in Detroit. First of all, however sympathetic they were to the idea of participation, many of Detroit's bureaucrats nonetheless were professionals who were well aware of the costs in potential nepotism, power-seeking, emotionalism, and waste that could follow from direct citizen control of the program. As one administrator commented, neighborhood participation sometimes appeared to be "mere gamesmanship." "We are committed," he continued, "to try to help these areas through various services which we can deliver to the neighborhood." If only the community would simply stop "gabbing away," he complained, they could accomplish their goals. But the inefficiencies that accompanied "gabbing" or, even worse, the factional disputes among NPC members into which NSC directors were frequently drawn were an almost inevitable concomitant of participation. Given the city's proparticipatory policy settlement, these other activities were certainly not forbidden, but they certainly could not be easily pointed to as the primary accomplishments of the organization.

Second, officials tended to avoid consulting the representatives of community organizations in formulating program proposals whenever this conflicted with administrative convenience. The Urban Slums Employment Program is the most noteworthy case in point.[23] In this case, administrative officials pointed out that rapid changes in federal guidelines made it impossible to consult with the NPC before submitting a revised proposal to the OEO prior to the federal deadline. They argued that lengthy NPC debates, followed by demands for revision, would have resulted in the loss of federal funds. Quite apart from the merits of this argument, the CAA administrators clearly had a quite different definition of the situation than did NPC members. Administrative rationality was crucial for the one, spontaneous participation for the other. That the two goals could not be maximized simultaneously, even with the best of intentions, placed an important bureaucratic limitation on participation.

BUREAUCRATIC AUTONOMY AND DEVIATIONS FROM THE POLICY SETTLEMENT

As stated graphically at the beginning of this chapter, in both reformed cities the level of participation differed from that predicted by the policy settlement, but in Los Angeles, it was higher than that settlement anticipated and in Detroit, it was lower. This finding can be stated in another way: In reformed cities, the variance explained by the policy settlement was less than the variance explained in cities where patronage-oriented, partisan politics had still survived. In machine cities, the policy settlement had a decisive effect on the character of the program; under conditions of full reform the impact, though important, was muted by the behavior of relatively autonomous bureaucratic officials.

The simultaneous concern of independent administrative agencies with both mission and routine accounts for the impact bureaucratic autonomy had on participation. In both Los Angeles and Detroit, the CAP's distinctive participatory mission had clearly attracted idealists and activists committed to this goal. The recruitment of such personnel in no way distinguished Detroit's CAP from New York's, whose participatory policy settlement also enabled the dominant faction to recruit a proparticipatory staff. On the other hand, the proparticipatory mission of the Los Angeles CAA encouraged recruitment of a staff easily distinguishable from the patronage-oriented, antiparticipatory officials in Philadelphia whose own policy settlement hardly acted as an equivalent for the agency's mission.

The Los Angeles and Detroit CAPs were also distinguished from the other three agencies by a concern for maintaining internally rationalized bureaucratic orientations and behavior. Yet in Los Angeles, the limits which bureaucratic rationality imposed on citizen participation were no more stringent than the antiparticipatory guidelines imposed on the CAA by Philadelphia's dominant political faction. Routinization in Los Angeles, then, did not distinguish its level of participation from Philadelphia's, since Philadelphia's antiparticipatory policy settlement had an effect equivalent to that of the routinizing tendencies of the Los Angeles bureaucracies. But this same routinizing orientation substantially differentiated New York and Detroit. In New York, the decentralized control of the program by neighborhood groups meant that the CAA could not scrupulously follow ordinary administrative procedures while it allowed neighborhood groups to use community action funds for political purposes. The Detroit NPCs could not act in this way in large part because Detroit administrators successfully adhered to an internally rationalized bureaucratic structure which precluded "political" control by citizen groups.

To summarize, in Los Angeles where the policy settlement was antiparticipatory, the mission of the bureaucracy insured at least some measure of participation, but in Detroit, where the settlement was proparticipatory, bureaucratic procedures reduced the level of participation favored by the dominant political coalition. In general, where bureaucracies were autonomous, their contradictory impulses with respect to participation insured that perceptible, but ultimately somewhat limited, participatory efforts would be undertaken.

CONCLUSIONS

These contradictory impulses may well have characterized OEO's entire CAP, if one can generalize about a federal program in a country so politically decentralized as the United States. Specifically, it is probably most appropriate to assume that the CAP in the reformed cities of Los Angeles and Detroit was more nearly typical of CAPs nationwide than the CAP in our three machine cities, which are remnants of a slowly disappearing set of political arrangements. Commenting on the impact of the contemporary urban reform movement, Banfield and Wilson have suggested that it has so weakened party elites that national politicians must now consider the voters' immediate concerns to an extent that they may no longer be able to focus sufficiently on long-range national interests.[24] Whatever the accuracy of this assessment, our data suggest that urban reform has had quite another national consequence. Without local reform, national politicians seem to find it administratively very difficult to implement national policies in local communities. As the very different levels of participation indicate, local politicians in machine cities still have the capacity to control local bureaucracies; as a result, federal programs, even when implemented through new local agencies, can easily be modified to accommodate local political demands.

Either the desirability or harmfulness of this situation can be argued persuasively. In terms of the set of American authority patterns considered by this research, these findings do not have clearly positive or negative implications. It can be argued, for example, that the lack of full reform enables the local community to adapt national programs to local needs, or at least to the particular political preferences of voters in each city. In this view the local citizen's regime interest in participation is consequently enhanced by the capacity of his locally elected leader to control not only political symbols, but the actual administrative operations of local government. This interpretation, however, makes the local rather than national electorate decisive. Even in its own terms it depends on at least two assumptions which are by no means always valid: (1) that local politicians regularly face strong enough political competition to force them, for fear of losing elections, to pursue policies the citizens prefer; and (2) that local politicians in any case pursue their electoral interests and therefore cater to citizen preferences rather than to some regime or factional ideology.

It does appear that local administrators in reformed cities are guided more closely by federal legislation and administrative guidelines, even to the point of adopting the national mission as their own. And this result may seem consistent with the citizens' regime interest in rationalizing government, since reformed institutions permit bureaucrats to implement policies efficiently and fairly in the manner determined by the national authorities. But fairness and efficiency are not always clear criteria and, especially when the relevant national legislation itself calls for local "community action," it is not self-evident that federal rather than local authorities should prescribe the standards for fair and efficient administrative implementation. In fact, the federal system was primarily and successfully designed to foster the regime interest in institutionalized bargaining rather than either participation or the rationalization of government. The differences in participation among our five cities demonstrate very clearly the continuing vigor and impact of this constitutional and institutional arrangement.

What the distinctive features of CAP administration in reformed cities show most unmistakably is the continuing dilemma of reformers who simultaneously seek participation and instrumental rationality, two goals which animated the national war on poverty from its first days. As our discussion of Progressive Conservatives and Community Conservationists made clear, the American reform movement slowly split asunder, once it discovered how often the goals of rule by experts and citizen participation were not complementary but incompatible. Particularly when confronting the fundamental problems posed by poverty and racial conflict, reformers at both state and national levels found their nineteenth-century assumptions about this compatibility fatally overoptimistic. Rationality and spontaneity in fact are inherently in tension with each other. As much as OEO encouraged participation, its failure to achieve it was due in part to its own belief in the importance of efficiency, coordination, and precision as necessary elements of an effective social welfare program. Certainly, as Part IV argues, the overall level of participation ultimately depended far more on the distribution of political resources, in effect the structures of political power in our five cities, than on the good works of bureaucratic agencies committed with equal fervor to both participation and administrative neutrality.

PART IV

Political Structures, Policy-Making Processes, and Public Policy

CHAPTER 8: POLITICAL STRUCTURES: CITIZEN PREFERENCES, POLITICAL ORGANIZATION, AND PUBLIC POLICY

In Chapters 4 and 5 we argued that the ideology first articulated by nineteenth-century machine politicians and reformers still affected political commitments of individuals and groups active in the struggle over community participation. In Chapter 7 we showed the impact of urban reform on bureaucratic behavior. This chapter turns to another ramification of the machine-reform conflict, namely, its pervasive effects on the types of political groups actively influencing each city's policy settlement. Perhaps because it was so pervasive, this effect was hardly direct. Although the policy settlement was very antiparticipatory in the preeminently machine city of Chicago, the reform cities of Detroit and Los Angeles reached no more participatory agreements than did the other two machine cities, New York and Philadelphia.* But if institutional reform did not directly determine the policy outcome, it nevertheless changed political preferences and resources so that no single variable affected the policy settlement in the same way in both machine and reform cities.†

This argument parallels that of Chapter 7 which showed the reformed bureaucracy was a basic condition that weakened the connection between the policy settlement imposed by the dominant political actors and the actual level of participation. The consequences of institutional

* We use here the same definition of an institutionally reformed city that we used in Chapter 7; reform cities have a comprehensive, entrenched merit system which rules out any significant patronage employment (except at the highest policy-making levels), and legal and normative barriers to party involvement in city elections, making them genuinely nonpartisan. All five cities have some reform features (even Chicago has legally nonpartisan elections for its city council), but only Detroit and Los Angeles have been fully reformed so as to have both these key reform characteristics.

† In more technical language, reform institutions can be understood as a parameter or boundary condition whose presence changed the entire pattern of observed relationships between independent and dependent variables in our analysis.

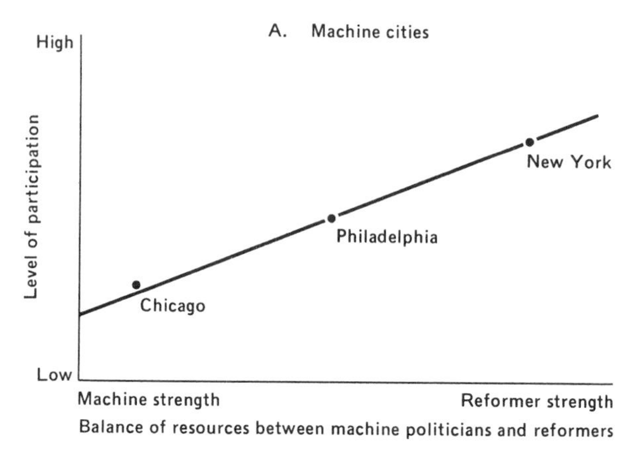

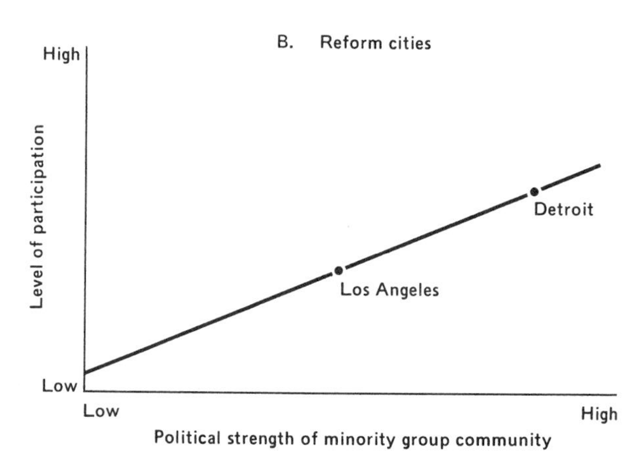

FIG. 8–1. Political factors directly affecting policy settlement in machine (*A*) and reform (*B*) cities.

reform described in Chapter 7 operated in the functionally specific arena of administrative behavior. The present analysis explores the much wider influence of these institutional reforms on the controversy over the policy settlement. Specifically, we will argue that the changes in the way citizens organized politically in the reform cities of Detroit and Los Angeles (as compared to the three machine cities) decreased the recognition of their regime interests, while it increased the recognition of factional race and class interests. As a result, different factors explained the different policy decisions in the reform as compared to the machine cities. Indeed, two very different groups of actors dominated the conflict in the two types of cities. Participation in machine cities varied with the balance of of resources between the machine politicians and their reform opponents, whereas in the reform cities, it varied with the political influence of the minority group community. The relationship is presented in Figure 8–1.

But how did institutional reform operate in this way? What were its specific effects that led to these differential power relationships in the two types of cities? Fundamentally, by changing urban institutions, these reforms limited the significance, i.e., reduced the manifestness of regime interests for key political actors. Reform limited pluralist bargaining by destroying much of the organizational base for the pragmatist political style, which emphasized both compromise and incremental change, thus reducing the number of machine politicians with a highly manifest regime interest in preserving this political style. At the same time, by abolishing machine-style practices, it reduced public concern for the manifestness of regime interests in the rationalization of governmental administration and the extent of citizen participation in political life. Institutional reform had this effect not only by changing public preferences but by altering the capacity of various groups to organize on behalf of common goals. We thus begin our analysis by explicating the way in which the problems of organizing citizen preferences affects policy formation in urban politics.

POLICY PREFERENCES, POLITICAL ORGANIZATION, AND PUBLIC POLICY

Much recent political research has focused on the extent to which citizen preferences influence public policy. On this point, some scholars assume that American politics is sufficiently open, resources sufficiently dispersed, and politicians sufficiently responsive so that widespread and/or intensely held preferences will be effectively articulated and eventually shape public policy.[1] If this assumption is correct, then policy differences among cities, states, or other political units are likely to reflect differential political preferences held by members of different political communities.[2]

We agree that citizen preferences are likely to influence public policy in systems structured by democratic authority criteria. The following pages show repeatedly that the effectiveness of various groups depended in part on the distribution of political preferences in the community at large. But as Mancur Olson, Jr. has shown, the preferences of large social groups may not always be effectively organized so as to influence public policy.[3] Olson notes that if a desired good is truly indivisible or collective, all individual members of the collectivity will enjoy it, as long as it is supplied to any one member. This is the case whether all, half, or only one of the members of the collectivity help provide the good. For example, any individual employee in a factory may benefit from the higher wages, shorter hours, and better working conditions obtained through his union's bargaining with employers, regardless of whether he supports the union's efforts through paying dues, attending meetings, or striking. Any self-interested man acting "rationally" would therefore maximize his utilities by withholding such contributions, thus enjoying the collective benefits without incurring any individual costs. In Olson's terms, such an individual is a "free rider."

If all employees calculate similarly, the union will never be organized and no collective benefit will be secured; even though each individual employee might very much "prefer" the benefits a union could provide. Because any individual employee would be unlikely to establish a union successfully through his own efforts, those who first contribute in effect risk incurring substantial costs without ever achieving any collective benefit at all. This risk is great because, at least in the extreme case, the individual has to assume he will act alone, since everyone else will "free ride"; he must therefore compare his benefits with the *total* cost of supplying the collective good.

Olson sees this problem as endemic to any effort to organize voluntarily large aggregates of individuals. He argues that in order to secure the requisite contributions from their members, organizations have had to use either compulsion or specific incentives, i.e., benefits which are awarded only to those individuals who contribute to the organization's collective action. This requirement accounts for the intense efforts of unions to secure compulsory membership through closed shops, and for the strong support in the business community of "right to work" legislation. And it also accounts for the wide variety of specific benefits that successful organizations supply to those who make contributions. For example, while the Farm Bureau tries to secure better market conditions for all farmers, it provides life insurance and special demonstration projects for bureau members only. The National Education Association fights for higher salaries and better facilities for all teachers, but it only defends association members in lawsuits brought by parents or school boards.

If Olson is right, this raises certain problems for democratic theory. Large aggregates of individuals may prefer a certain collective good but may not be able to organize effectively to demand it from the government. Air and water consumers may prefer public controls that would provide cleaner air and purer water. Yet any self-interested individual, rather than contributing to an organization seeking to obtain these goods, would rationally maximize his utilities by letting others contribute to the cause, hoping to enjoy fresher air and better water without any personal cost. Olson's analysis not only persuasively accounts for the small membership of so many antipollution groups (even at a time when environmental issues are salient for a broad public), but sharply questions any assertion that all political preferences have a more or less equal chance of being articulated. Preferences articulated by organizations that rely on compulsion or specific incentives for their maintenance apparently have a clear advantage.

Yet for all its persuasiveness, Olson's argument requires certain qualifications. First, as the recent upsurge in antipollution activities has demonstrated, when a group's interests are extremely manifest, the mass membership contributes to the collective action of the group out of all proportion to the benefits each individual member is likely to receive from the anticipated policy change. Second, in the longer run, many organizations are sustained by small numbers of ideologically committed individuals who pursue collective ends to an extent far beyond any material benefits they could expect as a result of their efforts. Third, as Frolich and his colleague have argued, even self-interested individuals can rationally contribute to collective action, provided that political leaders convince such individuals that their small contributions will probably be matched by others.[4] Given such effective leadership, the self-interested rational man no longer need compare the utility that the collective good has for him against the *total* cost of supplying it; he only need compare the cost of his own small contribution against the resulting increase in the probability that the good will be supplied. For example, if an individual values pure water very highly, and if he believes that a rather modest contribution to an antipollution campaign will significantly increase the prospects for cleaner water, he can rationally make the contribution. But if he feels that this contribution will have no effect on the relevant probabilities, he can better maximize his utilities by withholding the contribution. More formally, the contribution must not be greater than the contributor's estimate of the increase in the probability that the collective good will be supplied multiplied by the value he assigns to the good itself.

Even this verbal presentation of Frolich et al.'s mathematically formulated argument may be rather obscure to the reader unfamiliar with the writings of political economists. But their point can be usefully illustrated by a well-known, recent instance of remarkable political leadership. In the late 1960s, Cesar Chavez successfully induced many Americans to refuse to buy green grapes until his migrant farm workers' union was recognized by the grape-growers. These consumers may well have received substantial psychological gratification from improving the working conditions of a severely exploited occupational group. Yet for decades these same Americans enjoyed eating grapes, and even if they were concerned about migrant welfare they saw no way their individual actions could help the workers. Chavez succeeded because he supplied the political leadership that convinced each individual consumer that his contribution, not eating grapes, would in some small way increase the probability of supplying the collective good, i.e., an effective boycott which would force the growers to capitulate. Fortunately for Chavez, the contribution each individual had to make was very small. Housewives could easily substitute some other fruit. But before Chavez appeared, even well-intentioned white liberals would have seen such a step as pointless. It would have irrationally deprived them of grapes without helping the migrants. Chavez's leadership thus substituted for the use of compulsion or selective inducements to individual contributors, an achievement that Olson's argument by itself could not account for.

Frolich and his colleagues have qualified, but not entirely destroyed, Olson's argument, and the consequent problems it raises for democratic theory. For it is by no means certain that groups who lack powers of compulsion or selective inducements will find leaders as effective as Chavez. Empirically, in other words, it may be hypothesized that variations in public policy among cities (or any other political units) will be a function of at least three factors: (1) variations in preferences among individuals in these cities; (2) the differential availability of selective incentives or compulsion to induce individuals to join particular organizations; and (3) the differential availability of skilled, effective political leadership.

Let us see how these three factors affected the variations in the strength of the minority group communities in Detroit and Los Angeles, and the relative positions of machine politicians and reformers in the other three cities.

POLITICAL RESOURCES IN MACHINE CITIES

The political strength of machine politicians and reform organizations varied widely among Chicago, Philadelphia, and New York. Liberal Pragmatist machine politicians dominated Chicago politics. The mayor was the chairman of the Democratic party organization. Reformers were chronically ineffective, while Republicans had been an insignificant force in city politics since the 1930s. The situation in Philadelphia was similar, but it was by no means identical. The city's once powerful Progressive Conservative reformers faced a resurgent Liberal Pragmatist party organization which had revived under Mayor Richardson Dilworth in the late 1950s and by 1963 elected as mayor one of its own ward committeemen, James Tate. The city also had a fairly united congressional delegation.

But the party regulars lacked the Chicago organization's cohesiveness; indeed in 1965 a public dispute broke out between Mayor Tate and the Democratic party chairman. Moreover, in that same year a Republican-reform coalition elected the city's district attorney who two years later nearly won the mayoralty, and in 1966 an independent gubernatorial candidate almost carried Philadelphia in the Democratic primary.

New York City, meanwhile, had become a hotly contested battleground, with the reformers gaining strength, as evidenced by the growing number of reform congressmen elected in the city. Machine politicians, on the other hand, had so much less cohesion than in either Chicago or Philadelphia that their reform opposition attacked the "bosses" rather than the "boss." Liberal Pragmatist Wagner even had to desert his party organization in 1961 in order to be reelected, though later in his term he reestablished his relationship with party leaders. In 1965, of course, a reform coalition elected John Lindsay as mayor.

One rough quantitative indicator of these inter-city differences in the mid-1960s is the capacity of the Liberal Pragmatist machine to control Democratic primary contests. As James Wilson once noted, "the absence of real primary contests is probably as good an indication as any of the power—both actual and imputed—of the machine."[5] In fact, both the number of candidates per available Democratic nomination to the lower house of the state legislature and a proportion of the vote the losing candidates obtained described the very core of the machine's political power—its capacity to monopolize the path to public office.[6] The data for this index came from the four primary elections (1958–1964) preceding the initiation of the Community Action Program (CAP).

This measure of Liberal Pragmatist strength vis-à-vis its reform opposition sharply differentiates the three machine cities, as is shown in Table 8–2. Chicago's powerful organization so discouraged insurgent candidates that less than one-fourth of the races were contested compared to about a third of the races in Philadelphia and just under two-fifths in New York. Even more striking, in less than a tenth of all races did losing candidates in Chicago receive 20 percent of more of the vote, while this figure doubled to over one-fifth in Philadelphia and reached almost a third in New York.*

Differential Political Preferences

These power relationships can be interpreted to some rather limited extent as a function of the varying citizen preferences in the three cities.

* For Detroit and Los Angeles, this quantitative measure of machine strength no longer accords with intuitive judgments of informed observers, and in Chapter 1 we

Admittedly, there seems to be no survey research that has systematically examined the exact amount of citizen support for the Liberal Pragmatist, Community Conservationist, and Progressive Conservative ideologies. Yet if Banfield and Wilson's understanding of the social bases of support for "public-regardingness" is at all accurate,[7] and we think it is insofar as it applies to support for reform candidates, there should have been more reform supporters among upper middle-income, better-educated Jews and Protestants in the mid-1960s than among lower-income, more poorly educated, Catholic immigrant groups. And in these terms, reformers were apparently strongest in New York City and weakest in Chicago. For example, New York had proportionately many more Jews than Philadelphia, which in turn had proportionately more Jews than Chicago. Moreover, the politically important business community seems to be more oriented toward Progressive Conservatism in the East than it is in the Middle West. Chicago businessmen, even in the 1960s, seemed more wedded to the economic

---

did not rigidly follow the rank ordering it produces, for this would consider Los Angeles' Democratic party more centralized than Detroit's—a conclusion that seemed quite unwarranted. It is true that both Los Angeles and Detroit have fractionated Democratic parties that have lost any cohesion that patronage might provide. Yet, the result seems to have been slightly different in the two cities. Given the alternative bases for political organization in Detroit, frequent primary contests appear. But in Los Angeles, the lack of alternative organizational devices gives the incumbents an advantage relative to those in Detroit, thereby reducing the number of contested elections. In sum, this is a valid measure of machine strength only where there in fact is some Liberal Pragmatist organization of machine politicians which systematically tries to control primaries. The data for the two nonmachine cities is presented in Table 8–1:

TABLE 8–1. Percentage of Vote in Reform Cities for Candidates in Democratic Primaries for Lower House of State Legislature (1958–1964)

Percentage cast for losing candidates[a]	*Possible contests (percent)*	
	Los Angeles	*Detroit*
No opposition	51.7	5.9
1–19	5.2	3.3
20–39	20.7	24.7
40–59[b]	12.1	42.9
60–	10.3	23.0
TOTAL	100.0	99.8
Number of possible contests	(58)	(152)

[a] See note *a*, Table 8–2 for special calculations employed for Detroit which like Philadelphia and Chicago had multimember districts.

[b] See note *b*, Table 8–2.

TABLE 8–2. Percentage of Vote Cast in Machine Cities for Losing Candidates in Democratic Primaries for Lower House of State Legislature (1958–1964)

Percentage cast for losing candidates[a]	*Possible contests (percent)*		
	Chicago	*Philadelphia*	*New York*
No opposition	77.5	67.1	61.2
1–19	14.5	9.9	6.1
20–39	8.0	20.4	16.5
40–59[b]	0.0	2.6	16.2
60–	0.0	0.0	0.0
TOTAL	100.0	100.0	100.0
Number of possible contests	(138)	(152)	(260)

[a] Special calculations were required in the multimember districts in Philadelphia and Chicago. Here the number of candidates running was calculated in terms of the available Democratic nominations. If three candidates ran in a two-member district, only one race was said to be contested. If four or more ran, both seats were considered contested. In calculating the percentage vote for losing candidates in these two-member districts, the procedures were as follows: Where three candidates ran, the opposition's percentage was calculated by taking the vote of the losing candidate as a percentage of the combined vote of this losing candidate and the weakest winning candidate, where four or more candidates ran, the percentage for one race was calculated by dividing the vote of the strongest losing candidate by his vote plus the vote of the weakest winning candidate. The opposition's percentage in the contest for the second seat was the following ratio: the total vote of all losing candidates, except the strongest, over this numerator plus the vote of the strongest winning candidate. In this way, contests in multimember districts were compared to those in single-member districts.

[b] In contests involving three or more candidates, the losers together can receive more than 50 percent of the vote.

individualism of an earlier period than to the sense of public responsibility characteristic of the Philadelphia economic elite. In adidtion, New York had many more national organizations and foundations, which attracted unusual numbers of Community Conservationist-oriented professionals, than did either Philadelphia or New York .

But without an attitude survey, which determines these differences rather precisely, the analysis just offered is essentially speculative. It must rely on the very uncertain procedure of explaining the variation in machine-reform strength by inferring different distributions of preferences from apparent differences in the demographic makeup of the three cities. One difficulty with this procedure is indicated by the fact that in the mid-1950s Philadelphia's reform movement seemed at least as successful, if not more successful than New York's, while ten years later New

York's reformers were clearly in the stronger position. Such a change cannot be explained by the demographic variables which remained relatively stable.

Even if these demographic differences do accurately indicate voter preferences, it seems very unlikely that the differences indicated are substantial enough to account for the wide differences in the machine-reform contest. For example, the large proportion of Jews in New York City cannot be taken at face value, at least in the 1960s. Many lower-income Jews, notably in Brooklyn, loyally supported party regulars. Moreover, the differences in Liberal Pragmatist strength between Chicago and Philadelphia were much greater than the differences in the proportion of Jews living in the two cities.

In short, the speculative and sometimes dubious character of the inferences made about citizen preferences from urban demography suggest that the differences in machine and reform strength also depended on the extent to which the citizens with these preferences *acted collectively* to further them. Indeed, there is solid rather than merely speculative evidence that New York, Philadelphia, and Chicago differed on precisely those variables that both Olson and Frolich et al. identify as crucial in making such collective action possible.

Availability of Selective Incentives

Certainly, political organizations differ substantially in their capacity to provide, or withhold, selective incentives attractive to individual members. Liberal Pragmatists in particular depend upon city and state patronage to sustain their political organizations. In Chicago, the organization has been estimated to control tens of thousands of patronage positions throughout the city and county governments. And from 1961 through 1968 Democratic governor Otto Kerner controlled thousands of additional state jobs. By contrast, Philadelphia's party organization had to contend with the much more effective civil service system instituted by reformers in the early 1950s, though by the mid-1960s, Liberal Pragmatists had opened up some patronage loopholes such as newly available jobs in programs like CAP. Moreover, in the late fifties and early sixties Democrats controlled the Pennsylvania state government which had available substantial numbers of patronage jobs.

By comparison even with Philadelphia, New York's Liberal Pragmatists had the smallest supply of selective inducements. Certainly, patronage had not entirely disappeared, particularly since party loyalists in the courts retained control over a substantial number of positions. Yet reformers had succeeded in extending civil service provisions over more and more of the city's administrative positions, and equally significant, they so changed the normative expectations in New York civic life that even the positions as department heads, appointed "at the pleasure of the mayor," went increasingly to technicians and bureaucrats rather than to party loyalists.[8] Finally, with the exception of one term in the mid-1950s, Republican governors had controlled the state house, and thus the state payroll, continuously since 1942. As Olson's argument suggests, the political strength of the Liberal Pragmatists in the three cities varied consistently with their supply of selective inducements.

Less obviously, the same factor also affected one of the major political resources of the reform coalition. Even though the reformers themselves have consistently spurned patronage as a selective inducement with which to sustain political organizations, they often made electoral alliances with Republican party organizations which embraced it, and therefore had the considerable organizational incentives to be a sometimes valuable ally. In Chicago, however, the Republicans were so orthodox in their conservatism that they were unable to work with reformers in city politics very effectively. As late as 1971, when the Republicans finally endorsed a Community Conservationist for mayor, they failed to give him much support.

The Philadelphia and New York Republicans included fewer Orthodox Conservatives, and more readily welcomed alliances with reform organizations. In 1965, Philadelphia Republicans, the Americans for Democratic Action, progressive businessmen, and the press united to elect Alan Spector district attorney and then supported him for mayor in 1967. Lindsay, of course, symbolized the same pattern in New York City.

These differences in the behavior of local Republicans may of course account for much of the Chicago reformers' frustrations and isolation, but this factor does not explain the much greater success, by the mid-1960s, of reformers in New York as compared to Philadelphia. It is not entirely obvious, for example, that in early 1965 New York City Republicans were in a significantly stronger position than were their Philadelphia counterparts. New York reformers had nonetheless outstripped similar groups in Philadelphia in level of activity, number of members, rank-and-file enthusiasm, and success in Democratic primaries. These differences cannot be easily explained by any set of selective inducements such as patronage which reformers in all three cities abhorred. However helpful Olson's analysis for understanding political machines, it fails to consider sufficiently the importance of political leadership, a factor which not only helps explain differences in reform strength but even some of the variation in the capabilities of the machine politicians themselves.

Differences in Political Leadership

Reform leaders claim to offer their supporters the collective good of honest, efficient government and the opportunity to participate freely in the political process. But "rational" individuals will contribute to securing this collective good only if such contributions appear to increase the probability that the good will be supplied, in this case through a reform victory. And as Frolich et al. indicate, no single factor is more likely to affect the reformers' estimates of the probability of victory than attractive, prominent, and talented leaders. In this regard, Chicago reformers once again had the weakest position. Admittedly, Adlai Stevenson, the very inspiration for the reform-club movement nationally, had been governor of Illinois, and his running mate in 1948 was Paul Douglas, whose distinguished senatorial career attracted enthusiastic support from reform Democrats.[9] Yet, neither of these leaders provided any direct help to the Community Conservationist cause in Chicago. The Liberal Pragmatists in Chicago, particularly Mayor Daley, tolerated almost any position that Stevenson or Douglas took on national issues, but they might well have declared open political war had either of these national figures seriously interfered in local politics or jeopardized the organization's sources of local patronage.

Philadelphia reformers, by contrast, won many local victories during the 1950s by rallying around two intelligent, resourceful politicians, Joseph Clark and Richardson Dilworth. Significantly, both politicians received substantial backing from businessmen, the press, and middle-class Protestants and Jews in large part because their socially prominent backgrounds seemed likely to help them defeat their machine opponents. Such expectations can quickly become self-fulfilling, and both men won even higher offices until Clark became Senator and Dilworth narrowly lost the gubernatorial election in 1962. Once they left local politics, their reform followers' dependence on these two leaders became painfully clear. Except possibly for Alan Spector, the able prosecuting attorney who won election as district attorney in 1965 but who failed to oust Tate in 1967, the reform movement in the 1960s did not produce any leader even close to Clark's or Dilworth's stature. In fact, when a series of scandals made it possible to reform the school board in 1967, the reformers turned once again to Richardson Dilworth.

By contrast, New York reformers had no shortage of attractive leaders in 1964 and 1965, partly because the city had a much better established reform tradition than either Philadelphia or Chicago. New York's first reform victories began shortly after the founding of the modern city at the turn of the century, and the greatest triumphs before Lindsay were under Mayor Fiorello La Guardia's leadership during the 1930s and early 1940s. In the decade which followed, Liberal Pragmatists reasserted their strength, but by the late 1950s, reformers enjoyed the active support of two leaders with unsurpassed liberal reputations, Eleanor Roosevelt and former Senator Herbert Lehman, and they once again became a major political force. Having recruited Mayor Wagner as a temporary ally in

1961, the movement actually defeated the bosses in the Democratic primary, only to find that Wagner and his associate, City Council President Paul Screvane, had begun a rapprochement with the party regulars. As a result, most reformers turned in the 1965 mayoral primary to Rep. William F. Ryan. Although Ryan did not have a city-wide following, he did attract so much reform support that Screvane lost the primary, and in the general election the reformers, by backing Lindsay, successfully reestablished the fusion with Republicans that had elected La Guardia.

Differences in leadership qualities also account for much of the variation in the organizational strength of Liberal Pragmatists, and for a reason consistent with Olson's analysis: the machine politicians' use of selective incentives does not do away with the free-rider problem altogether. It remains rational for the self-interested party member holding a patronage position to withhold his contribution to an electoral campaign unless the organizational leadership not only can accurately assess his efforts but then withdraw the incentive if he fails to make a substantial contribution. Effective Liberal Pragmatist leaders, then, must not only correctly assess their subordinates' activity but also punish any attempts to free ride. The leaders' capacity to do this depends not so much on their electoral attractiveness as their ability to maintain cohesion and discipline among the various segments of the organization. Without cohesion, rewards cannot be properly assigned and withdrawn; patronage resources cannot be distributed most efficiently; and a divided leadership may even use its resources to engage in intraparty battles rather than defeat Republicans and reformers.

On this score, Liberal Pragmatists had a particularly strong position in Chicago, where Mayor Daley, as Democratic party chairman, controlled the diverse elements of the Democratic organization with an effectiveness unequalled by any of his contemporaries. Whenever he passed the word, all the party regulars in the state legislature voted together; the city council never acted in opposition to the mayor's publicly stated wishes,[10] and until 1966 the Chicago congressional delegation acted with marvelous unanimity.[11] Liberal Pragmatists were not so harmonious in Philadelphia. In fact, the party chairman feuded with Mayor Tate in 1965, unsuccessfully running a candidate against him in the next mayoral primary. In some ways, this conflict was itself but a continuation of the battles between party leaders and Tate's predecessors, Clark and Dilworth. Yet even these struggles were not as debilitating as the continuous factionalism within the New York party organization which dated back to the Brooklyn Democrats' famous battle cry that Tammany's "Tiger shall not cross the bridge." Above all, by decentralizing some key patronage to borough party leaders, the borough system of government preserved considerable autonomy for local party organizations, which led, as Boss Flynn reported, to frequent conflicts in city-wide primaries.[12] Thus, in 1965, when most reformers backed Ryan, Screvane secured some support from party regulars (as well as a modicum of reform backing), while other regulars worked for the eventual primary winner, Abraham Beame.

The New Deal and Urban Political Leadership

These inter-city differences in the relative effectiveness of reform and machine leaders themselves reflected a critical historical development: the different power relationships between Libereal Pragmatists and their reform opponents during the New Deal. That historical epoch was so significant that the balance then prevailing affected political life for many subsequent decades. For one thing, the Democrats established their durable majority among urban voters during this period, and the voters' national party preferences strongly influenced their preferences in local elections.[13] Secondly, since Roosevelt's New Deal also funneled many new governmental programs through the mayor's office, whatever group controlled the mayoralty secured numerous new resources to enhance its position. At the same time, because both Liberal Pragmatists and Community Conservationist officials supported and helped administer the new federal programs, the local politicians in power shared the President's popularity. In sum, the faction which won recognition as the national Democrats' local representative could monopolize both the prestige and perquisites controlled by the national party.

In Chicago, the machine Democrats profited enormously from the fact that Republicans held office locally as well as nationally when the depression hit. As a result, Democrat Anton Cermak had the opportunity to win such a sweeping victory that he could unite his hitherto divided party for the first time in decades.[14] Since Cermak had opposed Roosevelt's nomination at the 1932 Democratic convention, the president had initially been cool toward Chicago's Democratic regulars, and he invited nonmachine Democrats, such as Harold Ickes, to join his administration.[15] But Cermak's assassination, by a bullet aimed at the president-elect, precluded any significant national support for Chicago reformers. Not only was Cermak visiting Roosevelt in Miami in order to "make peace," but more importantly, Kelly, Nash, and the other Irish leaders who replaced Cermak had been closer than Cermak himself to Roosevelt's supporters during the preconvention manuevering. From that point on, Roosevelt routinely channeled all patronage and perquisites to party leaders, and from then through 1968 no active Chicago reformers ever secured close access to the national leadership; on the contrary, Mayor Daley effectively established himself as a leader in national party circles.

In New York City, the situation was almost the reverse. Discredited by the depression and the scandals of Jimmy Walker, machine Democrats lost power locally for almost all of Roosevelt's presidency. Since the pragmatist politicians were still the local party leaders, however, Roosevelt could not entirely ignore them; and men like "Boss" Flynn handled much of the national patronage flowing into the city. Nevertheless, Roosevelt valued both La Guardia's liberalism and his popularity, and the president treated him accordingly. Subsequently, national party leaders such as Stevenson and Kennedy, having failed to achieve local unity, followed Roosevelt's lead by insisting that reformers as well as machine politicians share in the largess that flowed from the national party. And in the late 1950s, Eleanor Roosevelt and Herbert Lehman openly exploited their reputations in national politics to support the local reform movement.

Unlike New York which had a reform mayor, or Chicago which had a Democratic machine mayor, Philadelphia was controlled by Republicans throughout the depression and, indeed, most of the 1940s. As a result, no Democratic party faction established clear title as local representative of the national party. Indeed, the reformers did not establish a clear liberal image until the late 1950s when Clark entered the U.S. Senate. Even then, he did little more for Philadelphia reformers than Paul Douglas had done in Chicago. On the other hand, because of the Republican's local hegemony, the city's Democratic Liberal Pragmatists did not expect their leaders to become major party figures—and none of them developed a national reputation comparable to that of the Chicago leaders. Rather, it was Pittsburgh's David Lawrence, mayor of the state's *second* city, who became Pennsylvania's leading Democrat even before he won election as governor. Philadelphia Liberal Pragmatists were consequently unable to combine control of federal perquisites flowing through the mayor's office with those from state and local offices traditionally in the hands of a single local party leader. A persisting bifactional struggle between party leaders and the mayor was almost unavoidable.

In machine cities, then, the relative strength of the pro- and antiparticipatory coalitions was far from simply the product of differences in the citizens' political preferences. Although voter preferences were not irrelevant, they seem less important than the availability of organizational resources for each coalition and the prominence, magnetism, and unity of their political leadership, which were in turn influenced by the city's political history since the New Deal. But whatever the sources of the differential power relationships between the two factions, they did shape the character of the CAPs.

LIBERAL PRAGMATISTS, REFORMERS, AND PARTICIPATION

Certainly, power relationships between the Liberal Pragmatists and the reform coalition had a critical impact on the CAP policy-making process in Chicago. Once the Daley administration made clear its opposition to a participatory CAP, unhappy neighborhood and civil rights organizations won the support of a Community Conservationist alderman, earned a friendly newspaper series in the Progressive Conservative *Chicago Daily News,* and received episodic backing from certain private welfare agency leaders. But these pressures were too weak to force any participatory concessions. Indeed, as Chapter 9 will show, their public protest may, in fact, have made the mayor more adamant than if they had intervened much less openly.

In Philadelphia, the reform coalition more cautiously supported civil rights and neighborhood group demands for more representation of the poor. The *Philadelphia Bulletin* and leaders of private welfare agencies, together with the reform-club movement, generated enough pressure so that Mayor Tate included Progressive Conservative reformers on the committees which selected the CAA's executive director and helped determine both the composition of the CPC and the compromise election method for choosing the representatives of the poor. But the dominance of the Progressive Conservatives within the reform coalition was decisive. In effect, the electoral compromise reflected private welfare agency suspicions of mayoral appointments, mayoral suspicions of settlement house appointments, and their shared opposition to letting neighborhood groups make the choice. The relatively close balance of power between the mayor and his reform opposition, together with the Philadelphia reformers' more conservative orientation, precluded a really participatory political settlement.[16]

In New York City, Liberal Pragmatists Wagner and Screvane were too weak to ignore the reform coalition's support for the neighborhood groups' participatory demands. Newspapers gave these groups widespread coverage and editorial support, the reform-club movement endorsed a participatory program, mayoral candidates Ryan and Lindsay repeatedly attacked the city administration, and the president of the welfare agencies' coordinating council publicly endorsed majority representation for the poor on the City Poverty Council (CPC). After several months, Wagner and Screvane recognized that rejecting significant concessions would jeopardize the whole New York CAP and their remaining liberal credentials.

The power relationships between the Liberal Pragmatists and the reform coalition decisively shaped the outcome in machine cities. The dominant position of the machine politicians in Chicago produced an extremely antiparticipatory policy settlement; the independent resources of Progressive Conservative reformers enabled them to moderate, though not eliminate, mayoral control in Philadelphia; and the still greater strength of the reform coalition in New York produced a participatory settlement.

With only three cities, these observations do not prove conclusively that the actions of the Liberal Pragmatists and their reform opponents were decisive. But it is clear that the actions and resources of the Black Power faction of civil rights and neighborhood organizations did not account for these different settlements. Instead, these factions had rather similar impacts in all three cases. In each city they publicly criticized the antiparticipatory proposals of the mayor, formed a broad group to coordinate complaints of disparate organizations, and appealed to the Office of Economic Opportunity (OEO) in Washington to enforce its participatory guidelines. In all three cities, they placed the participation issue on the political agenda. But these similarities cannot explain the differences in outcome. To be sure, in certain black neighborhoods in New York, community organizations were better organized than those in the Philadelphia black community. But this difference, particularly considering the effectiveness of the black consumer boycotts in Philadelphia, was by no means as dramatic as the differences in the two political settlements. The critical factor, then, seems to have been the much greater vulnerability to liberal reform pressures of New York's Liberal Pragmatists. Moreover, although Chicago's civil rights groups and activist neighborhood organizations did not mobilize all their resources in an attack on the mayor's antiparticipatory plan, it is unlikely that Daley would have made important concessions even if they had made such a commitment. Such was the strength of the machine that a sustained black attack on a segregated educational system had had little visible impact on school policies in the previous five years.[17]

It is significant in this connection that the participatory character of the policy settlement in the three machine cities was far from positively correlated with the size and unity of their minority group populations. According to the 1960 Census, black residents in Chicago made up 22.9 percent of the population, less than the 26.4 percent in Philadelphia, but much more than New York's 14 percent. And during the decade of the sixties, Chicago's black population grew more rapidly than Philadelphia's, so that by 1970 both cities had almost exactly a one-third black population. Of course, taken together, blacks and Puerto Ricans (8 percent of the population in 1960) made up 22 percent of New York's population. But the possibilities of joint action between blacks and Puerto Ricans were limited, as the bitter controversy in East Harlem has demonstrated (see Chapter 6). In demographic terms, then, one would have expected New York to have the lowest rather than the highest level of participation.

The conclusion that differences in the policy settlements reflected not the political strength of blacks and other minorities but the strength and aggressiveness of their reform allies seems reasonable if we assume that at least until 1965, minority groups had little power to impose changes in public policy. In his analysis of rent strikes in New York City, Lipsky offers a model to explain the strategy of relatively powerless groups, as exemplified by the situation where "A would like to enter a bargaining situation with B. But A has nothing which B wants, and thus cannot bargain. A then attempts to create political resources by activating other groups to enter the conflict. . . . In response to the reaction of [these other groups], or in anticipation of their reactions, B responds, *in some way,* to the protesters' demands."[18]

Consistent with this model, blacks in the three machine cities protested the lack of participation in the antipoverty program, but the authorities paid little or no attention to their demands until another group, the reform coalition, entered the controversy. The authorities then responded in a manner consistent with this coalition's political resources and actions. In Chicago, the coalition was so weak that the blacks suffered a crushing rebuff. In Philadelphia, the coalition's dominant wing was stronger than Chicago's reformers but did not vigorously challenge the mayor's antiparticipatory preferences. As a result, the mayor made some, but not major, concessions. In New York, the reform coalition was strong enough to force a much more participatory arrangement. In the final section of this chapter, we shall examine the particular reasons for the Black Power advocates' dependence on reform allies in machine cities. But to make this concluding point adequately, it is necessary to consider first the contrasting situation in the reform cities of Los Angeles and Detroit, where the political strength and activities of the Black Power advocates did shape the cities' policy settlements.

POWER RELATIONS IN REFORM CITIES

Blacks had much greater political influence in Detroit than in Los Angeles. In 1961, the black community was the single most influential bloc within the coalition that elected Detroit's Mayor Cavanagh; in 1965, it helped reelect him by a wide margin; and in 1969, it came very close to electing a black mayor. By comparison, in Los Angeles, Samuel Yorty could successfully run for mayor by vigorously supporting tough police policies and articulating other still less subtle appeals to White Power. In 1969, black City Councilman Thomas Bradley did run a strong campaign for mayor. But Bradley gained much of his white support, and 47 percent of the final vote, because of Yorty's right-wing White Power appeals, his frequent trips out of the city, and the widely circulated allegations of corruption in his administration, factors which four years later led to his election. By contrast, the black defeated in Detroit that same year ran against a relatively liberal politician who explicitly shunned a "law and order" White Power campaign and accepted most of Cavanagh's policies; the candidate closest to Yorty's ideology and political style ran a rather poor third in the Detroit mayoral primary.

Nor was the Detroit black community's greater ability to act collectively limited to electoral politics. Two of the most violent urban ghetto disorders in the mid-1960s occurred in Detroit and Los Angeles, and both ended with thousands arrested and hundreds in local jails. This mass of defendants made it difficult for the two black communities to provide even minimal legal representation. Yet, by comparison with Los Angeles blacks, the Detroit black community responded with a much more extensive, coordinated, and sustained effort.[19]

Differences in Citizen Preferences

These differences in political strength reflect, first of all, the fact that blacks were proportionally twice as numerous in Detroit in 1960 (28.9 percent of the population) as they were in Los Angeles (13.5 percent of the population). Consistent with population trends in all big cities, the percentage of black residents did increase in Los Angeles during the following decade to 17.5 percent, but it increased much more dramatically in Detroit to 43.7 percent. Of course, Los Angeles had a second significant minority group, the Mexican Americans, who made up 10.6 percent of the population in 1960 and about 15 percent in 1970. Yet, even added together, the proportion accounted for by the two minorities in Los Angeles was substantially smaller than that of the blacks in Detroit (by about 5 percentage points in 1960 and 10 percentage points in 1970). At least as important, blacks and Mexican Americans in Los Angeles had even more difficulty in uniting politically than did the blacks and Puerto Ricans in New York. Mexican-American areas of Los Angeles County rarely voted heavily for a black candidate, e.g., substantial numbers of Mexican Americans cast their votes in 1969 for Yorty.

Differences in Selective Inducements

Yet these demographic differences may not account entirely for the greater strength of Black Power advocates in Detroit. Much of their success can be traced to the efforts of the United Automobile Workers (UAW) to build a precinct-level electoral organization committed to Orthodox Liberalism. Admittedly, the UAW met with only mixed success in local elections. Although it gradually and unevenly made the city council more liberal, it failed to support the winner in any highly competitive mayoral campaigns for almost three decades. Yet, in participating in these campaigns, in organizing to bring out the prolabor vote, the union's activities provided excellent political training for large numbers of its black members at every level from doorbell ringing to formulating general strategy. And this training was reinforced by the black union members' participation in the UAW's own intense political life, which included numerous campaigns for local union offices.

As a result, black leaders could rely on a core of able, experienced workers who covered lower-income ghetto precincts with an efficiency exceeded only by the most effective patronage-oriented party organizations. In both nonpartisan city elections and national and state partisan contests, these activists worked very harmoniously with other union members. But they defied the formal union endorsement to engineer Cavanagh's 1961 upset victory, making clear their ability to act independently of white-dominated groups in future campaigns.

The black community developed these indigenous resources with the assistance of the UAW, which through union-shop contracts could compel members to contribute to its maintenance. In most reform cities, the elimination of patronage makes it particularly difficult for low-income groups to maintain any political organization as effective as that of the political machine. Without the machine's selective incentives, it is especially difficult to obtain contributions to prospective collective action because would-be leaders have to convince each individual follower that his contribution would materially increase the probability of collective success, a particularly severe task in the initial stages of political organization. But in Detroit, even though the unions did not *directly* rely on selective incentives for their political activities, the UAW's political activists profited from its massive organizational strength in the industrial relations area. Because it was the workers' sole bargaining agent and could count on their dues, the union began its political activities with certain contributions to its collective political actions already in hand. These contributions came both from those leaders already on the union payroll (or otherwise subject to various selective incentives) and from those members who were especially grateful to the union leadership because of its industrial achievements.

Certainly, in the absence of such organizational assistance, blacks and Mexican-Americans failed to develop any comparable level of organization in Los Angeles. Southern California's more diversified, less heavily industrialized economy meant smaller, weaker industrial unions which simply lacked the organizational resources with which to mobilize minority group members for political activity.[20] To be sure, in the mid-1960s, organized labor made some rather modest efforts to register and turn out minority voters. But labor-minority group coalitions, though sometimes successful (notably in school board and council races), were episodic at best. No well-organized, independent army of precinct workers regularly mobilized minority voters. Together with the often visible tensions between the black and Mexican communities, the absence of such a strong organization clearly differentiated minority politics in the two cities.

Political Leadership

If strong political leadership is available, organizations which use selective inducements or compulsion are not absolutely essential. Such leadership was particularly important for blacks and Mexican-Americans if they were to attract at least some white support. Once again, Detroit blacks enjoyed the more favored position. As a result of UAW activities, black community leaders had been integrated into the liberal political coalition led by the UAW's Walter Reuther, which made the Democratic party the dominant force in Michigan politics throughout the 1950s. In the process, black leaders developed a stable working relationship, including the mutual exchange of favors, that enabled them to build alliances across class and race lines, even when they began to assert their own political strength more independently. And this relationship proved strong enough to withstand the occasional strains produced by disagreements on particular electoral races. In Los Angeles, by contrast, liberals were simply unable to build a stable political faction with which minority group leaders could ally. On the one hand, there were the professional politicians within the Democratic party, often incumbent officeholders, who sometimes worked together but who frequently ran quite independent campaigns. On the other hand, the Community Conservationist reform-club movement was so oriented toward national issues and its middle-class constituency that it made little effort to strengthen blacks and Mexican-Americans politically.[21] Fundamentally, both regular Democrats and reformers, although sympathetic to the plight of minorities, had few spare political resources with which to mobilize low-income groups. Both groups were too busy fighting among themselves to form a durable coalition with other political groups.

Black Power and Participation

These differences in the political strength of the black community appear to have been decisive in producing the different policy settlements in Los Angeles and Detroit. Even taken together with Mexican-Americans, Los Angeles blacks were clearly weaker than blacks in Detroit, in terms of numbers, cohesion, and organizational resources necessary to develop effective alliances with sympathetic groups in the white community. In these two reformed cities this difference was reflected in the CAP decision-making process itself in which Black Power advocates played such a predominant role. Cavanagh broadened participation in the Detroit CAA as a direct response to the complaints of black leaders and ghetto neighborhood groups.* The Los Angeles policy settlement reflected the limited strength of minority groups. Governor Brown, for example, could have vetoed the antiparticipatory Los Angeles proposal if he had the support of a united black and Mexican-American community. But these groups had such difficulty working together that Mexican-American leaders only cooperated with black Congressman Augustus Hawkins' proparticipation campaign after it had been well under way. Even then, they formed a separate Mexican-American committee which demanded only one-third representation of the poor, instead of the 50 percent sought by the Hawkins group. Yorty then took advantage of this split by proposing a compromise which came close to satisfying Mexican-American demands. Subsequently, the Mexican Americans, who preferred bargaining to protest, refused to participate in demonstrations at City Hall.

Black leaders, meanwhile, found it almost as difficult to maintain unity within their own racial group as it was to cooperate with the Chicanos. In typical Southern California fashion, each leader had his own personal following and proved reluctant to work together with others on behalf of group goals. After Hawkins assumed leadership of the proparticipatory coalition, the black social workers, who had initiated the struggle for a participatory CAP, retired from the political arena, partly out of unhappiness with Hawkins' ineffective tactical skills. Several of them accepted positions as CAA officials in order to work for resident participation within the agency. This strategy made some sense given Los Angeles' autonomous bureaucratic agencies, but it left Hawkins with only two or three active supporters and several paper organizations. One consequence was that a black minister, appointed by Yorty to his Committee for Economic Opportunity, successfully challenged Hawkins to let him and his followers attend a meeting of Hawkins' group. They then packed the meeting with other conservative ministers, and eventually voted down Hawkins's own proposals. After this defeat the congressman's effectiveness rapidly declined.

Although Hawkins and his followers were weak and divided, they did win a limited compromise from Yorty (i.e., the election of low-income representatives rather than their appointment by public officials) simply

---

* For a discussion of this sequence of black demands and concessions by Mayor Cavanagh, see page 267–268.

because Yorty himself had such limited resources. Even the clumsy, poorly coordinated attack of a handful of black and Mexican-American leaders could capitalize on the rivalry between the mayor and the governor and the mayor's inability to control his city council. As Chapter 9 will show in detail, Yorty particularly needed the support of a black councilman who could safely back his proposals only if they included some concession such as democratic elections. Thus, although the actions of black leaders had some impact on the outcome in Los Angeles, they secured only the most limited degree of participation.

Groups with regime ideologies played almost no part in the conflict in these reform cities. Precisely because urban reforms eliminated patronage and partisan labels, they did, as their authors hoped, eliminate Liberal Pragmatists as an organized force in local politics. But at the same time the reformers, deprived of their traditional opponents, concentrated on state and national issues. Thus, in Detroit, the newspapers, Republicans, welfare agencies, and white Community Conservationists outside the government took little part in the participation issue. Of course, Cavanagh himself was a Community Conservationist; it could thus be argued that his ideology, and not black resources, influenced program developments. But to explain the Detroit program entirely in these terms ignores the crucial role that blacks played in Cavanagh's election in 1961.

Even as the number of blacks and their organizational strength were poorly correlated with community participation in the machine cities, the strength of the reform movement was negatively, rather than positively, correlated with participation in the reform cities. If one examines the demographic variables thought to foster reform efforts, one finds that in the mid-1960s Los Angeles' population was better educated and wealthier than Detroit's.[22] Partly for this reason, perhaps, and partly because of the UAW's often principled Orthodox Liberalism, Michigan's middle-class liberal Democrats did not develop a substantial organizational base of their own during the 1950s when Community Conservationists elsewhere were organizing on behalf of Adlai Stevenson's presidential effort. In fact, these developments had been most extensive in California, where the reform-club movement became one of the few organized political forces within the Democratic party in the 1950s and 1960s, often succeeding in electing their candidates to state-wide offices. Although they had more difficulty in nonpartisan mayoral elections, they remained the strongest organized opposition to Mayor Yorty; but they did not seek to exercise significant influence over the policy settlement affecting participation. To be sure, some reform Democratic congressmen did verbally support Hawkins's efforts, and the chairman of the private welfare agencies' proposed CAP structure was a former president of the California Democratic Council. Yet Representative Roosevelt, in his campaign for mayor against Yorty, only occasionally mentioned the antipoverty program. And in contrast to Screvane, who made concessions partly because of the upcoming mayoral campaign, Yorty felt free to stall any final decision until after he had soundly defeated Roosevelt.

Progressive Conservatives were even less active in the political maneuvering over the settlement. As noted in Chapter 5, neither Progressive Conservative politicians, such as Senator Kuchel, nor the fairly Progressive *Los Angeles Times* supported demands for participation. The Progressive Conservative private welfare agencies formed a temporary alliance with proparticipatory minority group social workers, but it evaporated as soon as government officials included the welfare agencies in the CAA. In sum, the strength of the reformers could vary inversely with the participatory character of the political settlement because the reformers, while not opposed to participation, left the entire issue to be settled by the cities' various racial factions and government officials.

DIFFERENTIAL PATTERNS OF POLITICAL INFLUENCE IN MACHINE AND REFORM CITIES

The importance of two quite different political factors—the strength of the Black Power faction in reform cities and the balance of power between Liberal Pragmatists and Progressive Conservative–Community Conservationist reformers in machine cities—accounts for our failure in Chapter 1 to find a single variable or set of variables which explained the variation in participation in all five cities. It remains to spell out more explicitly why institutional reform operated so as to differentiate sharply the pattern of relationships in Detroit and Los Angeles as compared to the machine cities. Such an analysis returns us to authority structures, regime and factional interests, and their corresponding ideologies discussed in Part II.

We argued there that although machine politicians operated the levers of government to their great personal advantage, they came to understand what some might call their public function, i.e., their capacity to modulate the tensions among competing interests within the city. Since few political organizations can survive without some public justification for their existence, the machine politicians pleaded the great public necessity for readily available side-payments, willingness to compromise, responsiveness to a wide variety of competing interests, and flexibility in formulating policies. By so doing, they emphasized to themselves, their followers, and to the electorate more generally, the virtue of the pluralist-bargaining authority relationship, thereby making manifest in cities this particular regime interest. In their response to this public justification of their practices by machine politicians, reformers could effectively challenge the machine only by emphasizing those authority structures and corresponding regime principles that it so blatantly violated. As a result, reformers, too, communicated to citizens the need for preserving authority relationships, but in their case they emphasized participation and administrative rationalization.

Urban politics at the turn of the century was thus a conflict over two competing ways of organizing the political community, a conflict that sought to make manifest one or another set of regime interests that citizens shared. To be sure, racial and ethnic tensions in local politics did not thereby disappear, though class conflict was remarkably muted during the rise of industrial capitalism. Yet these appeals to ethnic groups, indulged in by both reformers and machine politicians, were subsumed within the larger issue over the way in which the polity should be governed. And the positions that the contestants took with respect to these authority principles, far from being spurious or merely a rhetorical cover for factional interests, gave practical guidance to government officials once they took office.

In the case of machine politicians, this was not surprising, given the personal returns to themselves for exercising power according to their expressed principles. Yet their openness to at least the particularistic demands of new immigrant groups and the ease with which they adapted to even militant labor organizations suggests that the commitment to pluralist bargaining was for the most part genuine. And reformers were no less willing to carry out their platforms once in office. Whenever they gained power, they instituted civil service reforms, passed nonpartisan election laws, hired city managers and other bureaucratic experts, etc., in order to widen the scope of political behavior patterned by the two authority criteria they felt were particularly important, participation and rationalization. Where reformers succeeded in implementing their goals, as in Detroit and Los Angeles, voters were less influenced by party organizations, and local bureaucracies at least overtly conformed to achievement and universalistic norms. At the same time, these reforms reduced the scope of pluralist bargaining as a patterning orientation, for they removed from Detroit and Los Angeles politics precisely those politicians most committed to incremental, negotiated change. As a result, conflict in these reform cities was usually more programmatic and intense, if less well organized than in Philadelphia, Chicago, and New York. These changes in the scope of the authority structures significantly affected two other factors which influenced political life: The extent to which citizens' regime interests became action orientations rather than mere preferences, and the extent to which individuals were able to act collectively to achieve their widely shared citizen interests. As Mancur Olson would expect, changes in this second factor had the most apparent and dramatic consequences.

Urban reformers had their greatest long-run effectiveness against machine politicians where they could almost entirely eliminate the selective incentives, i.e., patronage, kickbacks, and various other side payments, available for enlisting contributions to the party. Precisely because Liberal Pragmatists were concerned about deference to diverse vested interests and, at most, only gradual change, they could rarely obtain mass enthusiasm for their efforts and had to depend heavily on material rewards. Moreover, these Liberal Pragmatists primarily relied on the poor, the working class, and certain ethnic segments of the lower-middle class—groups which had shown relatively little interest in political participation as an activity desirable in itself. Without patronage then, sources of support dried up, and Liberal Pragmatists declined rapidly as a major force in the politics of such institutionally reformed cities.

Their demise, in turn, directly affected the degree to which regime interests were manifest throughout the community. Apart from their own concern for pluralist bargaining, Liberal Pragmatists encouraged other citizens to recognize it as well, since such recognition meant general support for the machine's system of distribution of material benefits to established interests. Thus, from the highest level to the precinct captain, machine politicians in effect preached moderation, attention to narrow but intensely felt demands, and gradual change. The admiration which Mayor Daley has enjoyed among businessmen, professionals, and even the academic community in Chicago, occupational groups the least susceptible to Liberal Pragmatist appeals, indicates the extent to which distinguished Liberal Pragmatist leadership could make citizens aware of their interest in pluralist bargaining. In Chicago, even those with only limited sympathy for Mayor Daley admitted that at least the city held together and the garbage was collected. Elsewhere, once Liberal Pragmatists were severely weakened, effective and vocal support for pluralist bargaining declined.

Institutional reform also adversely affected Progressive Conservative and Community Conservationist reformers. For one thing, by removing party labels from the ballot, and stripping the parties of any substantial local patronage, the establishment of "good government" made it almost impossible for reform politicians to forge valuable alliances with the opposition party, as they had in machine cities. Historically, reformers had come to power in New York by allying with the Republicans (under La Guardia and Lindsay) and with the Democrats in Philadelphia under Dilworth and Clark. Even Lindsay's victory in 1969 depended significantly on the help of the Liberal party as well as fragments of the two major party organizations, for these party organizations provided a familiar party label and a reliable core of campaign workers which reformers generally lacked. Equally important, the end of patronage politics took a major collective incentive away from reformers hitherto interested in local politics. Precisely because these reforms provided at least the appearance of efficiency in public administration, the regime interest in rationalized government became less manifest simply because it seemed so secure. Similarly, Community Conservationists, content with at least the observance of the most obvious norms prescribed by their regime interest in participation, turned their attention from local to national and international issues. Of course, the reformers' abstract commitment to these principles did not decline. But because the scope of the authority structures had been changed, these interests were no longer so obviously threatened, or rather, were no longer patently inconsistent with urban political practice. Since outrageous abuses became much harder to identify, the erstwhile reformers no longer were so intensely concerned about local politics.

This decline in concern for the preservation of these authority principles was far greater than any changes in the scope of behavior the principles themselves patterned. Although pluralist bargaining did decline in reformed cities, as race and class conflict became more visible and uncontrolled, entrenched interests were still given deference. Similarly, although participation did increase to the extent that no party organization in a low-income area could effectively control the residents' votes, the elimination of the party label hardly ensured widespread citizen participation in urban policy formation. Finally, although reform clearly reduced the importance of political connections as a criterion for public employment, it is by no means true that local governmental agencies in reform cities operated without ethnic and racial prejudice or that they achieved a highly efficient, coherent, hierarchically coordinated administrative system. Given the organizational maintenance needs of bureaucracies, their greater autonomy in many cases may actually have increased goal displacement.*

* The major effect that institutional reform had on the extent to which regime interests were manifest even with only marginal changes in the authority structures themselves emphasizes once again the utility of the latent-manifest interest approach. Clearly, one cannot understand the changing political relationships without considering the structural impact of institutional reform. But on the other hand, the structural changes were so modest that they can be said to explain changes in attitudes and behaviors only by assuming that citizens have an interest in these structures which may rapidly become more or less manifest, depending on circumstances.

As groups concerned about the structure of the urban regime disappeared from the politics of reform cities, they were replaced by factional interest groups, at least in cities whose large size favored the expression of social tensions. First of all, Liberal Pragmatists were replaced by Orthodox Liberals. Since the New Deal, the trade union movement has provided assistance to politicians seeking a lower-class electoral constituency. When united with those Community Conservationists who were still interested in local politics, union-based Orthodox Liberal politicians offered low-income voters in reform cities a left-wing substitute for the Liberal Pragmatists whom these voters frequently supported in machine cities. But this alliance lacked the specific perquisites that machine politicians could offer campaign workers, and it usually failed to win business support or respectability in local newspapers. In most reform cities, it ordinarily remained a rather suspect political minority.

Meanwhile, in the absence of machine politicians as possible foes, Orthodox Conservatives succeeded in winning businessmen away from the Progressive Conservatives by making straightforward appeals to their specifically business interests. Equally important, Orthodox Conservatives at times could make convincing appeals to working-class populations which voted Democratic in partisan elections. Their ideologically conservative attack on governmental spending, governmental intervention in the private sector, and welfare payments to the unemployed poor happened to articulate the complaints of many white homeowners opposed to increased property taxes, urban renewal programs in their neighborhoods, black in-migration, and the snobbishness of the upper-middle classes who insisted on making decisions in terms of the "good of the whole community." Of course, these Orthodox Conservative politicians lacked the organizational resources of unions, but they did have money, talent, enthusiasm, and, often, media support. In cities where they faced no competition from patronage politicians, these resources were often sufficient to appeal effectively to white workers.

Agger et al. identified precisely this type of political transformation in Oretown, a nonpartisan suburb on the Pacific Coast.[23] In the early 1950s, the trade union movement supplied enough organizational resources (even without much patronage) to sustain working-class support for Orthodox Liberals, whose most potent political issue was the municipalization of the local electric plant. But as this organization weakened, Community Conservationists began to dominate the city's politics, cooperating with downtown businessmen on urban renewal and related issues. In the meantime, working-class voters turned to a new leadership, that used rhetoric similar to that of the Orthodox Conservatives, to fight expansion of city services, increased taxes, and annexations. This working-class electoral behavior, which to an outsider seems ideologically erratic, reflected not only the absence of familiar party labels as a guide to voting behavior, but also the much smaller stock of organizational resources available in reform cities. Even politicians able to attract lower-class support in a given election could not easily maintain political organizations that might stabilize lower-income voter loyalties. As a result, these voters supported whatever group happened to best articulate their most immediately pressing grievances at a particular election.

This distinctive pattern in reform cities became still more obvious once the race issue emerged. In machine cities two factors encouraged both black and white working-class voters to continue their support of Liberal Pragmatist candidates. First, the party retained selective, easily divisible incentives. Second, the continued presence of partisan labels on the ballot enabled Liberal Pragmatists to identify all their candidates as members of the Democratic party, thereby capitalizing on the popularity of the national Democratic party in urban areas. These advantages helped the machine politicians maintain a biracial alliance as late as the mid-1960s in Philadelphia and Chicago. Even in New York, where the party organization was much weaker, the alliance held relatively well below the mayoral level. By the early seventies, of course, the alliance came under increasing strain, even in Chicago. But overtly racial cleavages appeared much earlier in the reform cities of Detroit and Los Angeles, focused initially on far less substantial policy issues, and polarized low-income voters more completely. Blacks in such cities, for example, would not vote for any Irish or Italian candidate simply because he was an endorsed Democrat, as Chicago and Philadelphia blacks did as late as 1965. A candidate had to prove his sympathy for the black community by word, and once in office, by deed. In fact, in 1969 the mayoral candidate supported by black communities was black himself, a phenomenon which had not yet occurred in the three machine cities. While Orthodox Liberals, sometimes in alliance with Community Conservationists, sought support in the black community, Orthodox Conservatives in reform cities appealed with increasing success to the white factional interests of the majority racial group.

In retrospect, it can be seen that institutional reform had one consequence—the nationalization of urban politics—which would have thoroughly surprised and distressed the reformers. The emergence of the factional ideologies, so important in local politics after 1950, can be traced originally to the greater salience of lower-class interests after the New Deal. The New Deal's assistance to unions made lower-class local campaigns much more feasible. Later the pro-civil rights actions of national political authorities increased the black communities' recognition that local politics was a field in which they could achieve racial goals. Finally, the New Deal, by inaugurating federal programs with city government participation and by establishing a tradition of governmental intervention in social and economic life, created precisely those grievances—high taxes, official concern for unemployed blacks, and urban renewal—which led some white workers to support Orthodox Conservative politicians. In sum, the reformers, who sought to isolate local affairs from national politics by excluding national parties, succeeded in opening up reformed cities to the influx of national ideologies, which had been contained in machine cities by the focus upon issues touching on regime interests.

CONCLUSION: THE MOBILIZATION OF BIAS IN MACHINE AND REFORM CITIES

If institutional reform changed citizen preferences and the availability of incentives for organizing collective action, it presumably also affected the distribution of power within the community. Indeed, it has often been argued that urban reforms have had a middle-class bias. Nonpartisan elections, it is said, have increased the influence of middle-class areas in elections; business associations and city-wide newspapers have acquired added influence over the recruitment of candidates in at-large elections; and lower-class voters are much less likely to organize as a political force in the absence of patronage and other selective inducements.[24] Yet, the truth of the matter, if any generalizations can be based on our obviously small sample, suggests that the situation is rather more complex.

In the first place, it was in the machine cities that black and Puerto Rican influence was limited to placing the participation issue on the political agenda. Using their specific incentives, and the national Democratic party's popularity, Liberal Pragmatists were often able to limit the ease with which black factional interests could be organized. Chicago blacks in particular had strong, militant civil rights organizations in the early and mid-1960s, which could effectively mobilize enthusiastic supporters for demonstrations and boycotts. Indeed, for this reason Martin Luther King, Jr. chose Chicago as the locale for his major move against residential segregation and poor housing in northern cities. These organizations still had no impact on the loyalty of the low-income black voters to their precinct captains, even though Dr. King's actions seemed to portray the Daley administration as the enemy. Admittedly, Black Power groups in machine cities did have potential allies among Progressive Conservatives and especially Community Conservationists, whose manifest regime interests led them to support at least some, though certainly not all, minority group demands. Yet this dependence on white allies was itself debilitating for blacks, reaffirming subtly the historical relationships between white and black.

In reform cities, by contrast, organizations articulating such black or other minority group interests can more easily voice electorally credible threats themselves, and many politicians have recognized the need to make policy concessions to keep their support. Since political leaders in reform cities tend to become individual political entrepreneurs, the minority group, where it is of any significant size, is likely to find at least a few leaders in official positions who can help bargain for at least minimal concessions. Such minority groups, then, can count on some success if they are willing to struggle vigorously in the policy-making process.

On the other hand, not all political leaders in reform cities will so eagerly seek the support of every minority group. Some, such as Yorty, may conclude that they can win elections without black support, and indeed gain more votes by explicitly opposing black demands. In any case, minority groups in reform cities will attract few allies among the more socially advantaged, largely because Community Conservationist groups are so weak. This problem may be unimportant in cities such as Detroit, where there are so many black voters that they can directly influence policy or even capture the entire local government. But in cities where blacks make up a somewhat smaller proportion of the electorate, or where they are internally divided, this lack of allies may be an insurmountable handicap.

Whereas the allegation of upper-class bias directed against urban reform exaggerates the deference to disadvantaged interests in machine cities, the opposite assertion would be equally oversimplistic. In Schattschneider's terms, lower-class interests are not "mobilized out" of the reform cities' political life to any greater degree than they are mobilized out of politics in machine cities.[25] The difference is only in the mechanisms by which this occurs. In reform cities, by eliminating regime oriented ideological groups, the conflicts become factionally based, permitting those factional groups with the most political resources—in terms of money, organizational cohesion, prestige, control of communications, and sheer votes—to dominate urban politics. When inequalities in these resources cumulate, as they have done in the case of whites vis-à-vis blacks in most American cities, then institutional reform fosters white-dominated structures of power. But machine cities do little if any better by their minority groups. By forcing the conflict over regime interests to the center of urban politics, the structure of machine cities works against the active articulation of all factional interests, subjected and superordinate alike. This means that such interests are dealt with within the pluralist-bargaining arena, where deference is given to established, vested interests. If black interests have become vested, the politics of machine cities may accrue to the advantage of blacks. But in most cities, where black interests are excluded from the pluralist-bargaining arena, the very elimination of factional conflict from urban politics blocks their successful promotion.

If both machine and reform cities tend to be black-exclusive political regimes, then it is appropriate to inquire into the fundamental matter at the heart of the community action controversy, the manner by which urban regimes can be transformed so as to include black interests within the pluralist-bargaining arena. Since this cannot occur without conflict of a scale not typically found in urban politics, the matter directs our attention to the processes of conflict and negotiation that attended the framing of CAP's policy settlement in machine and reform cities alike.

CHAPTER 9: POLICY-MAKING PROCESSES: CONFLICT, CONSENSUS, AND REGIME TRANSFORMATION

Although the character of the Community Action Program (CAP) policy settlement had a very high correlation with the distribution of resources in our five cities, the limited number of cases suggests the possibility of a spurious relationship. The actual settlement might well be the result of any one of countless factors not explicitly considered, e.g., the mayor's control over his administrative subordinates, the character of the city's economy, or the geographic source and the timing of black migration to the city. Of course, Chapter 8 has identified a number of specific activities taken by Progressive Conservative and Community Conservationist reformers in the machine cities and by Black Power advocates in the reform cities that indicated the way in which these political forces seemed to have affected community action policy. Moreover, we were also able to reject the possibility that either Black Power strength or machine-reform power relationships accounted for the variation in CAP in all five cities. But to reject other possible explanations one must show theoretically and systematically the way in which the policy settlement and the relevant distribution of resources were actually linked together by the policy-making processes.

Demonstrating such a linkage is severely complicated by the substantial differences among the five cities in the character of the processes themselves. While blacks in Detroit relied on private conferences to make demands on Mayor Cavanagh, their Los Angeles counterparts resorted to angry demonstrations. Similarly, Community Conservationists protested publicly and even made a campaign issue out of participation in New York, but acted through much less public channels in Philadelphia. On the other side, Mayors Yorty and Wagner, but not Lindsay, Cavanagh, or Tate, publicly condemned the challenge to the authority of local government posed by minority group leaders.* There were, then, two types of political processes—conflictual and consensual—which provided two distinct paths through which groups used their political resources to affect the policy decision.

These differences in themselves did not either produce or reflect the differing policy settlements in any simple or direct manner. One might have expected, for example, that where mayors resisted Black Power demands and implemented an antiparticipatory settlement, conflict would ensue.[1] Alternatively, one might have expected a participatory settlement only where blacks vigorously and openly campaigned (i.e., fully mobilized their resources) on behalf of this goal.[2] But neither pattern occurred in all five cities. Conflictual bargaining preceded the extremely antiparticipatory policy in Chicago, and the antiparticipatory decisions in Los Angeles, and the proparticipatory outcome in Wagner's New York. Consensual bargaining produced a proparticipatory settlement in Detroit and Lindsay's New York, but also the antiparticipatory outcome in Philadelphia. And each type of process could be found in the reform as well as in the machine cities. Clearly, these diverse types of policy-making patterns cannot be accounted for by the categories and typologies elaborated thus far.

Given these complexities, an advocate of the "process" interpretation of political life might reject the entire connection between resources and policy outcomes, arguing that power is too changeable and elusive a phenomenon to establish any constant relationship between a group's resources and a policy outcome.[3] He might well argue that a number of accidents or coincidences rather than resources or stable structural factors shaped the outcome. According to this view, the 1965 Watts riot in Los Angeles motivated all the local authorities to resolve the conflict quickly, considerably strengthening Mayor Yorty's position. Mayor Cavanagh's early responsiveness to black demands in Detroit closed off contentious conflict, thus blocking the mobilization of antiparticipatory forces. In New York City, City Council President Screvane's resistance weakened with the imminent prospect of the mayoral election campaign. By contrast, Chicago's strenuous antiparticipatory stand may have been simply a function of the "accidental" booing of Mayor Daley by the politically naïve leaders of Chicago's juvenile delinquency program. Finally, Samuel Evans could impose his personal, perhaps idiosyncratic, "brainstorm"

* Mayor Daley did not himself publicly attack the opposition, but neither did he negotiate with it. His unyielding stance showed his recognition of the basic challenge the participatory movement offered to Chicago's pluralist-bargaining order.

about elections in Philadelphia, because he happened to have recently established himself as Mayor Tate's favored adviser in the black community.

Since none of these important events were wholly determined by the city's structure of power, the process analyst can plausibly maintain that a structural interpretation is bound to oversimplify complex causal patterns. Yet it is remarkable that each of the settlements seemed finally consistent with the more enduring, structural characteristics identified both by the case-study analyses in Chapter 1 and the analysis of resource distributions in Chapter 8. Moreover, these elements may help us understand key aspects of the accidents: why the ghetto riots strengthened Yorty's antiparticipatory position but left Cavanagh's proparticipatory policy unchanged; why Daley felt he could afford to rebuff the booers, rather than make limited concessions; why Evans' brainstorm was accepted so readily by so many key actors; and why imminent mayoral elections made Screvane, but not Yorty, more vulnerable to black demands.

A more structural interpretation can still be offered in lieu of an extreme process one by showing that the two quite different types of processes— conflictual and consensual—were in some sense equivalent. In other words, it must be demonstrated that despite their apparent differences groups used their resources in comparable ways in both conflictual and consensual policy-making processes. In developing such an interpretation, the first concern of this chapter is to show how both types of processes linked resources to policy. Establishing this process linkage, however, does not resolve all our problems, since it remains unclear why participants in the consensual processes did not always fully mobilize their resources in order to maximize their policy goals. Rather than attribute such nonconflictual behavior to random error (accidents, mistakes, poor estimates of the consequences and the like), we shall assert a structural view that accounts for the type of policy-making process in terms of the relationship between the particular factional interests manifest in each city and the institutionalized bargaining order.

PROCESS LINKAGES BETWEEN STRUCTURES OF POWER AND PUBLIC POLICY: THE ELECTORAL INTEREST MODEL

The most influential model linking structures of power and public policy is the electoral interest model (discussed previously in Chapter 5) which finds it useful to assume politicians will favor policies that will enhance their prospects for reelection. The model links resources to policy decisions by assuming an open competition among self-interested actors, each seeking to influence policy-makers, with the outcome of such competition reflecting the distribution of resources among these actors, and their willingness to activate their resources for political purposes.

Chapter 5 argued that such an interpretation could not explain all the relevant policy preferences with respect to CAP. In some cases, it was more useful to assume that certain actors pursued ideological goals (i.e., the role interests of a very broadly defined group) even when it proved electorally or organizationally costly. In these cases, the political effectiveness of groups reflects not simply their numbers or their social prestige as they operated in a given policy conflict, but their success in using such resources to elect one of their number to relevant positions of authority. Group resources used in this way will influence policy primarily by electing ideologically allied authorities to office, not by threatening them once they have attained office. By contrast, according to the political economy model, group resources can influence policy at the time it is being decided, primarily by suggesting to authorities that it would be in their electoral interest to pursue a policy the group prefers.

In fact, groups pursue both strategies in trying to influence public policy, creating very different policy processes. In some cases, groups will try to influence policy by generating a major controversy in order to alter an authority's policy. In other cases, groups concentrate on elections and refrain from vigorously attempting to influence specific policy decisions, particularly if they anticipate that the authority's ideology has already committed him to a specific approach. Groups may accept this ideology and simply try to influence policy details. In these cases, a pattern of consensual politics will emerge.

CONSENSUAL POLICY-MAKING PROCESSES

Consensual politics can be termed pluralist to the extent that bargaining occurs among a variety of disparate groups and organizational interests, rather than between representatives of two broad social factions such as races or classes. Cross-cutting cleavages are probable, shifting alliances can be detected, actors mobilize no more resources than a prudent cost-benefit analysis would suggest is proper, and compromise among interests is usually inevitable. But these behaviors are pluralist in a particular way. They involve low-intensity conflict, the participants use private communication, and they seem to search for compromises for their own sake as much as out of a concern for power considerations. The sources of this type of low-intensity pluralist conflict will be examined later; but first we shall illustrate the pattern as it appeared in Philadelphia, Detroit, and Lindsay's New York.

Policy-Making Processes in Philadelphia

In Philadelphia, the dominant actors included representatives of the major institutionalized interests at stake in the poverty program, including governmental agencies with related jurisdictions, private welfare agencies, civil rights organizations, and the mayor. None of these actors expended more of their political resources in pursuing their goals than the most prudent calculation of material costs and benefits would have suggested. To begin with, the mayor did not dictate a structure for the CAP without taking into account the preferences of the other major actors. Admittedly, in the initial stage of program development he did attempt to establish a City Poverty Council (CPC) limited to governmental officials. But shortly thereafter, in response to criticism from private welfare agencies and civil rights groups, he gave program responsibility to the Philadelphia Juvenile Delinquency Program (PJDP) with which he had had considerable trouble. After complaints continued he later asked a representative committee to frame their own program proposal, which he then accepted. Moreover, he allowed representatives from these various groups to determine the mechanism by which the representatives of the poor would be chosen, the number of representatives that would be so chosen, and the selection of the executive director of the program—a matter which in the other machine cities had been decided solely by the highest city officials. Mayor Tate need not have been so flexible on these matters; at some political cost he could have imposed a settlement that accorded exactly with his preferences instead of tolerating the compromises produced by this pluralist bargaining. But, since the issues being negotiated did not go beyond the limits established by the mayor's antiparticipatory ideology, he apparently saw no reason for incurring those political costs.

If the mayor was rather permissive in letting other groups influence the decision, they in turn participated in an equally restrained fashion, risking no more in the bargaining than was reasonable considering the impact of the outcome on their material interests. Significantly, both civil rights and private welfare organizations behaved in this fashion, even though they could have allied themselves with the Citizens Emergency Committee (CEC), a hastily formed coalition of neighborhood organizations which protested the lack of participation in CAP. The CEC managed to secure office space and staff assistance from the Americans for Democratic Action, a meeting hall from an industrial union headed by a friendly black leader, and even fairly good coverage in the *Philadelphia Bulletin* (though not in the *Inquirer*). Moreover, Progressive Republican politicians seemed to support CEC's demands when they attacked the "political" nature of Tate's CAP. Under the circumstances, one might have expected that civil rights groups and private welfare organizations also would have supported the CEC, even if this had jeopardized their relationships with the mayor, particularly since the mayor refused to negotiate or even meet with the CEC. Yet the CEC never managed to disrupt or to secure a place in the quiet discussions that occurred among the institutionalized interests that were consulted in the decision-making process. Even the Community Conservationists' candidate for mayor, Alan Spector, later found it difficult to campaign for participation without attacking the economic war on poverty that was popular among blacks and white liberals alike. In the end, the CEC had to adjust to an antiparticipatory settlement upon which the other groups had agreed.

Of course, it is not difficult to give reasons for the little attention that was paid the CEC by the other groups. The private welfare agencies wanted funds for their programs, and an open alliance against the mayor might well have jeopardized them. The National Association for the Advancement of Colored People (NAACP) was interested in obtaining control over CAP by securing the appointment of one of its own staff to the CAP directorship. And the Urban League could not support CEC without white businessmen on the board of directors questioning such controversial use of League funds. (In fact one staff member for the Urban League was nearly fired for giving assistance to CEC without the board's approval.) Yet, it is significant that it was these private, organizational interests that affected behavior, rather than any ideological concern for regime or factional interests.

Consequently, policy-making patterns remained consensual. Except for the complaints of the CEC, communications among the participants were private and confidential. The group that developed the proposal for the CPC pledged itself to secrecy, the differences of opinion among established interests over electing representatives of the poor were never leaked to the press, and the executive director was chosen behind closed doors.

The decisions that were reached were compromises. The mayor did not directly control the program, as he had preferred, but he was conceded overall direction of program policy. The private welfare agencies were not allowed to select the representatives of the poor nor were they able to make the agency a nonprofit corporation independent of the mayor's authority; however, they did secure influential representation on the CPC. The civil rights groups did not control program policy, but they, too, obtained representation and an understanding that the executive director would be black. Indeed, the compromise arrangement on selecting the representatives of the poor even enabled neighborhood groups to try to elect their own leaders. Yet these organizations in Philadelphia were too weak to compete successfully in elections, especially when their more prosperous members could not be candidates. As a result, black interests in local participation and control could not be included in the range of interests deferred to, and accommodated by, the bargaining process.

Policy-Making in Detroit

Although it led to a proparticipatory policy settlement, the policy-making process in Detroit also lacked any overt, intense struggle. Eager to establish a CAP quickly, Cavanagh appointed a twenty-three member CPC in June 1964, even before Congress had passed the Economic Opportunity Act.* From the beginning, he included, in addition to government and private welfare agency officials, several black leaders, such as a board member of Detroit's activist NAACP, the executive director of the Urban League, and a relatively militant Baptist minister. This action clearly recognized that blacks had a legitimate interest in poverty policies. Interestingly enough, no other mayor in the five cities had voluntarily appointed to the CPC such prominent civil rights leaders by the summer of 1964 (before national pressures for participation had been mobilized).

A number of black activists, however, were not satisfied and asked the mayor for a private conference. At that meeting, and without further agitation, they persuaded Cavanagh to establish six inner city Neighborhood Poverty Councils (NPCs) whose members would be selected at meetings largely composed of neighborhood organization representatives. These NPCs, limited by available poverty funds to only four, each sent two representatives to the CPC, who together made up only about a fourth of its membership. Shortly thereafter one of the NPC representatives called for doubling their number on the CPC, and Cavanagh quickly agreed.

Most noteworthy is what did not happen. There were no proparticipatory ad hoc committees, so prominent initially in Los Angeles, New York, and even Philadelphia. No Community Conservationists felt compelled to rally to the cause of participation. No complicated negotiations took place between private welfare agencies and black community groups. Indeed, these agencies suffered a great loss of prestige when a study by an outside research organization indicated that these welfare groups were servicing hardly 1 percent of the poor. Consequently, with the major exception of the Catholic Church, governmental agencies administered all CAPs. Detroit's substantial and politically muscular black community extended its close working relationship with Cavanagh to the poverty program.

The most important communications about these matters proceeded privately. Cavanagh's discussions with key black leaders, as well as Cath-

---

* The shape of the proposed legislation was already known to informed observers.

olic leaders, were as little noticed by the public as were the mayor's private consultations on CAP matters with his own subordinates. Newspaper publicity was confined to announcements of new programs and appointments of personnel. Indeed, there was little conflict which could generate headline treatment by the media.

The decisions in Detroit were clearly compromises. On the one hand, community groups did not demand direct control of program operations nor did they break with the mayor even when the city's civil service commission balked at foregoing the usual standards for employment in CAP. Blacks also accepted a highly professionalized, bureaucratized program, even though this placed clear limits on participation. Nor did they protest when the mayor refused to give neighborhood groups a clear majority on the CPC. On the other hand, Cavanagh agreed to substantial black influence through strong representation on the CPC, recruitment to policy-making positions of the administrative staff, and extensive participation in Neighborhood Service Center (NSC) policy formation by neighborhood organizations.

Policy-Making in Lindsay's New York

Under Wagner, as we shall see, New York's decision-making process was extremely conflictual. But just as Cavanagh's inclusion of blacks in the Detroit bargaining process precluded controversy there, so Lindsay's deference to the opinions of blacks and Puerto Ricans quelled preexisting controversy in New York. During the early days of the Lindsay administration, discussions took place with hundreds of community organizations; groups that had confronted Wagner and Screvane in angry public discussions were consulted in serious but nonetheless rather quiet bargaining sessions. As a result, no participatory political opposition felt impelled to try to discredit the Lindsay administration's plan by making it a political issue. With the change in administration, groups and political leaders all spent many fewer resources in bargaining over community action policy.

At the same time, the final decisions were compromises. To be sure, the mayor incorporated NPCs in all the poverty neighborhoods, giving them more autonomy in handling of funds and personnel recruitment. And the representatives of the NPCs were given greater representation on the CPC, which in turn acquired more direct control over poverty operations. Yet the Lindsay administration, while pursuing participation as a goal, also sought greater rationalization of governmental operations. The poverty program administrative staff was incorporated into a larger Human Resources Administration that had responsibility for the operations of the welfare department and a host of other welfare-related agencies. Suspicious observers could plausibly argue that the independence given to neighborhood groups with one hand was being taken away—or, more likely, carefully circumscribed—with the other. Thus, it is significant that neighborhood organizations accepted this rationalization of governmental services by the mayor without intense opposition.

Consensual Processes and Control of the Mayoralty

These consensual processes emphasize what the electoral/organizational model too often underplays: the very great importance of formal authority in urban policy-making. By setting the limits within which policy alternatives are to be selected, the ideologies and specific preferences of the authorities do not constitute just one element in the structure of power. Very often they are the single most important link between the distribution of resources and the final decisions.*

For several reasons, the mayor proved to be the decisive local authority relevant for the poverty program. President Johnson's publicized emphasis on the war on poverty made it so salient to partisan politics that the mayors themselves were strongly motivated to take a major interest in the program. Largely because the federal government contributed 90 percent of all CAP costs and allowed the localities to contribute the rest in kind, e.g., through the rental value of space provided CAP in city buildings, the mayors faced few financial obstacles to establishing the program. Nor were they constrained, except in Los Angeles, by the veto power of their city councils. Although a few aldermen in each city complained about inefficiencies, financing of radicals, patronage abuses, or lack of participation, most council members focused primarily on the impact that particular CAA programs had in their immediate constituencies. In fact, key policies were usually enacted by executive order or administrative decision rather than by passage of a city ordinance.

Moreover, at least initially, the mayors were not constrained by the functional power of autonomous public bureaucracies. In calling for coordination among city and private agencies serving the poor, Congress had allowed the establishment of a new coordinating body with its own administrative staff, a possibility strongly encouraged by OEO's official guidelines. As a result, no one agency and no one local official, not even the director of the welfare department, could assert a convincing claim to controlling all CAP activities. The mayor was thus relatively free to mold

---

* The electoral interest model does, of course, recognize that those in authority make the decisions. But they see the authority under such intense pressure from competing groups that he becomes little more than a billiard ball responding to the pressures playing upon him. Thus his own ideology becomes of little significance for policy-making.

CAP according to his own preferences. As a result, only Yorty of Los Angeles had to share significant formal authority over the program with other officials, and even he was clearly the most important single actor in Los Angeles.

In sum, the mayor's ideology and preferences set the agenda for discussion and policy formation. In the consensual cases this dominant role of the mayor was accepted by the other actors, who recognized that his ideology would shape the general contours of CAP policy. Thus, to see the way in which the distribution of resources among ideological groups affected public policy, it is necessary to examine how these groups expended their resources lavishly and over a considerable period of time in a struggle for control of the mayoralty.

This pattern was most obvious in New York where Lindsay had just won a hard fought election against both Liberal Pragmatist and Orthodox Conservative opponents in November 1965. Even though he was a Republican, Lindsay received substantial if sometimes discrete assistance from the Democratic reform clubs, as well as the backing of Liberals and Republicans. This victory followed more than a decade of sustained reform insurgency which included an ever-widening series of victories, first in Manhattan and then in other boroughs, notably the Bronx. These gains had already forced Mayor Wagner, despite his Liberal Pragmatist sympathies, to make a relatively short-lived alliance with the reformers in 1961. After Wagner later abandoned the alliance, most reformers opposed Screvane in the 1965 Democratic primary and then supported Lindsay in the final election.

A similar pattern with an opposite outcome characterized Philadelphia politics. In the late fifties, James Reichley observed that reform Mayors Clark and Dilworth had failed to end machine politics in Philadelphia.[4] On the contrary, Democratic Liberal Pragmatists increasingly asserted their control not only over the party machinery but over a variety of elected offices as well, including the city council. They finally came to power as City Council President Tate succeeded Dilworth to the mayoralty when the latter resigned to run for governor in 1962. The following year Tate solidified Liberal Pragmatist control by defeating a Republican reformer in a general election.

In Detroit, the black community, with somewhat erratic help from its Orthodox Liberal allies in organized labor, also gradually accumulated political power. In the late 1940s and 1950s it successfully supported white liberals and black city council candidates and secured enough influence in the late 1950s to push Mayor Miriani away from the White Power-Orthodox Conservative position of his predecessor. In 1961 black activists used their substantial electoral resources to help elect Cavanagh, and, in the first part of 1965, they helped launch his successful campaign to win reelection and secure a black-Community Conservationist majority on the city council.

In all three consensual cases, then, there was a relationship between resource distribution and the policy settlement for CAP. In Philadelphia, the reform coalition was not as strong as in Lindsay's New York, while blacks had accumulated considerable strength in Detroit. Admittedly, since some actors did not obviously pressure other actors to pursue a certain policy goal, it was not obvious from the policy-making process itself how the resource distribution affected policy. But by seeking to control the mayoralty, groups did expend their resources in a way that indirectly, but no less significantly, affected CAP, i.e., through the election of a mayor with one or another ideological or policy orientation.

CONFLICTUAL POLICY-MAKING PROCESSES

However important, the preferences of the mayor could hardly be the only factor affecting variation in participation. Although Chicago, Philadelphia, Los Angeles, and Wagner's New York all had mayors similarly opposed to participation, they had quite different policy settlements. This pattern could occur because (except in Philadelphia) other political actors tried to secure a policy settlement that was beyond the bounds established by the mayor's ideology. To do this, the mayoral opposition had to suggest either explicitly or implicitly that unless the mayor made prompt concessions, his political future (or at least that of one of his significant associates) would be endangered. Such threats, of course, might not work, for the mayor might prove too strong or too stubborn to yield. Yet the threats themselves could be made plausible only by a public, open controversy which appealed directly to the voters who would decide the next election. Such a public conflict might well force a mayor to estimate the relative electoral resources of the two sides to the dispute and perhaps make concessions to his ideological opposition. The CAP policy process itself could in this way constitute a second channel by which participant resources might influence the policy outcome.

This type of influence channel can at times be identified in national policy processes. During the Eisenhower administration, for example, Democratic majority leader Lyndon Johnson often asked the Senate liberals if they wanted a bill or an issue. If the bill was to be passed, it had to be acceptable ideologically to the president, who, having an effective veto, was the relevant authority. If this were done, there was little in the way of large-scale conflict, although considerable bargaining over details might continue. Such was the consensual politics Johnson valued. But at some points, the Democratic liberals insisted on legislation which they hoped would force Eisenhower to choose between his convictions and his electoral interests, since it was hoped a veto would hurt Republican candidates at the next election. To make this threat credible, the liberals attempted to make both the original passage and the subsequent veto of such bills as controversial as possible.

Generally, in this conflictual policy-making arena, actors represent, or at least claim to represent broad social groups such as races, classes, nationalities, or consumers. The resolution of the resulting conflict is not likely to be a compromise designed to placate the largest number of participants. Rather it reflects the ideological perspective of the most powerful political coalition, be it the authorities and their allies or the insurgent opposition. More specifically, the outcome will be as the authorities prefer, moderated only by those concessions intended to ward off serious political damage. As a result, the pattern of conflict will become bipolar rather than multisided, in which open, public communication patterns involve more and more varied participants, some of whom initially had little direct interest in the issue. The relevant authorities will make concessions only if they are politically ambitious and recognize that their opponents are strong enough to damage them electorally. In such cases, the authorities' specific response depends in part on their assessment of the distribution of the relevant resources, though these concessions are often made so belatedly and so grudgingly that some electoral costs will follow. As a result, even though mayoral ideologies are similar, this conflictual pattern can produce different policy settlements.

Policy-Making in Chicago

From the beginning, Mayor Daley opposed a participatory poverty program. When the OEO and others objected that his CPC did not include representation of low-income groups, Daley was willing to alter its composition and establish NPCs only if the representatives were appointed by city officials, rather than selected by neighborhood groups or in poverty elections. Neighborhood organizations criticized the mayor-dominated program and received newspaper coverage in the *Daily News,* the backing of a reform alderman, and some token assistance from private welfare agencies.

Because these reform groups were too weak to alter Daley's policy, their demands primarily served to make participation another issue in the continuing machine-reform struggle in Chicago politics. And it is in terms of this struggle that the mayor's reaction to these demands is easiest to understand. During the early and mid-sixties, civil rights groups had demanded further racial integration in Chicago's housing and schools.

Given the great opposition to widespread, systematic integration of the city on the part of white voters, this political attack was probably the greatest possible threat to the white-black coalition that sustained the Democratic organization in the postwar period. And reform support for civil rights demands only accentuated their political significance.

In this regard, the events surrounding the juvenile delinquency program were particularly important, for they indicated to many actors the connection between participation and the racial tensions in the city. Reform groups at the local and city-wide level had supported a participatory program that had severely chastised mayoral policies and important city bureaucracies. The mayor responded to this attack on Chicago's pluralist bargaining order by dramatically restructuring the juvenile delinquency program, so as to eliminate "agitators" (even though this cost him several million dollars in federal money). When reformers supported demands for participation in the CAP, the mayor saw these protests as simply an extension of the issues surrounding the juvenile delinquency program. Consequently, he ordered his CAA staff not to make the "mistakes" of the juvenile delinquency program, and one of his loyal allies, Rep. Roman Pucincski, informed a witness testifying in support of the poverty program that the OEO would be ill-advised to model CAP on the juvenile delinquency program.[5]

Given both the electoral and ideological significance of participation to the two sides, communications between the disputants were primarily through public channels. Public meetings produced angry demands directed toward the mayor's representatives. Chicago's program was attacked by a neighborhood organization in testimony before a congressional subcommittee headed by Rep. Adam C. Powell, and local officials publicly squared off with the regional representative of the OEO. At the same time, Mayor Daley, apparently uninterested in working out a "deal," showed no interest in a private meeting with neighborhood groups.

The outcome did not reflect a pluralist compromise but was instead consistent with the mayor's first preferences. The shape of what could have been a compromise decision is not difficult to construct. OEO had suggested that representatives of the poor in all cities be selected in some more or less democratic manner, and the regional office had criticized Chicago's insistence that a city official appoint the representatives. A Chicago mayor interested in compromise might have suggested selection of representatives by neighborhood organizations but then ensured that the organizations involved were closely coordinated by the Democratic machine, or election of the representatives could have been managed in a similar way. The outcome might not have been exactly as the mayor preferred, but such minor accommodations are the price mayors are often willing to pay to avoid major conflict.* Clearly, then, the mayor was not interested in consensus but in defeating the challenge to his pluralist bargaining order that had manifested itself in civil rights agitation and the juvenile delinquency debacle. The opposition, in trying to make the matter a conflicutal issue, evidently provoked Daley and thus made their own defeat more decisive.†

Policy-Making Processes in New York City

New York's Mayor Wagner opposed a participatory CAP because he, too, perceived through the juvenile delinquency program the threat to the pluralist bargaining order posed by participation. Wagner also wanted a CPC completely dominated by city officials, or at least by individuals appointed by a city official. Neighborhood groups, civil rights groups, and representatives of already existing juvenile delinquency programs called for participation. And they acquired vigorous support from reformers, Republicans, Community Conservationists, newspapers, and even leaders in the private welfare community.‡

Again, demands were made in public meetings and through the press. As in Chicago, black leaders from New York City also testified critically before the Powell subcommittee (in contrast to Philadelphia where neither side gave public testimony). The intervention of Republican and reform politicians emphasized the electoral significance of the issue. And when Paul Screvane tried to arrange a compromise in a meeting with a few black and Puerto Rican leaders, they invited forty representatives from a variety of neighborhood groups to the "negotiating" session, which erupted in a flurry of charges and countercharges.

Initially, it appeared as if the city administration would not bend under pressure. In April 1965, Screvane, testifying before the Powell subcommittee, made a strong defense of the mayoral prerogative and ex-

---

* In fact, such would have been the solution that the Mayor Daley portrayed by Edward Banfield would probably have followed; a compromising politician, considering the intensity of the various claims that were made, would have sought to accommodate at least to some extent the civil rights demands.[6]

† Of course, this turn of events undermines the argument that mobilization of resources necessarily increases one's power to shape a policy settlement. At least in these cases, the system had little "slack."[7]

‡ In terms of news coverage, the Community Conservationist-Progressive Conservative papers in New York, *The Times* and *Herald-Tribune,* gave the controversy much more publicity—876 and 1,138 column inches, respectively, than did the Chicago newspapers—the *Tribune, Sun-Times,* and *Daily News,* which only devoted 253, 474, and 765 column inches, respectively, to the matter. The reader should not attribute this simply to the greater news coverage of local politics by New York papers. If anything, it is the reverse.

plicitly lamented the difficulties produced by the juvenile delinquency programs.* The testimony only increased the acrimony in New York, and Powell himself may well have sought to block OEO funding for the city's programs until Wagner made concessions. Since unallocated funds would revert to the U.S. Treasury at the end of the fiscal year (June 30), the issue became exceedingly crucial. Screvane, who had valiantly ignored the electoral consequences of defying the reform-civil rights alliance, now risked being charged with losing sizable antipoverty funds, a heavy burden for any liberal politicain aspiring to higher office. At the last minute—but too late to prevent electoral defeat the next September—Screvane yielded to almost all of the participatory demands by giving nearly a majority of the seats on the CPC to representatives of the poor, and permitting neighborhood organizations to select their representatives. Against the desire of the mayor and his chief lieutenant, participation came to New York City.

Policy-Making Processes in Los Angeles

Polarized conflict also characterized the politics of participation in Los Angeles. Various black professionals in the social welfare field led the first protests, which won important, but temporary support from Progressive Conservatives in the private welfare community. Together they publicly sought to establish a structure for the administration of a CAP distinct from any governmental agency. Later, Rep. Augustus Hawkins joined the fray, using his contacts in Gov. Edmund Brown's office and his membership on the House Labor and Education Committee to press for changes in the CPC. Although some Community Conservationists verbally supported Hawkins's efforts, the strength of the attack came from the combined efforts of black and Mexican-American leaders.

Initially, Mayor Yorty appeared to pay little attention to participatory demands. Because he was preoccupied with his electoral campaign, or, more likely, because the juvenile delinquency program in Los Angeles had not pointed out the significance of community participation for

* "We have been in the process over the last few years of doling out pieces of the City of New York to various groups that would come to it, such as MFY, Haryou Act, Youth in Action in Bedford-Stuyvesant, and a number of others that have been formed since," Screvane observed. Then he went on to argue, "And after you would delineate the area, fund the organization—a private corporation—they would say, 'Don't come here with any of your services, don't let anyone impinge on our prerogative, because this is our piece of real estate.' What would happen ultimately . . . we would have a number of little private governments in the City of New York. . . . I am not confident at all that we would be able to solve all of the problems we have with this kind of approach."[8]

white interests, Yorty allowed subordinates and other actors to work out arrangements without any public intervention on his part. Under these conditions, the pluralist bargaining process seemed to be working toward a rather antiparticipatory settlement. Lower-ranking government officials, private welfare agency representatives, and a few black leaders had agreed that less than one-third of the CPC would consist of representatives of the poor, and these were to be selected by governmental bodies. Admittedly, there were more interest group representatives and representatives of the poor than governmental officials on the CPC, but since the interest group representatives spoke for the business community and established welfare agencies, this plan hardly constituted a strong participatory thrust. Moreover, the representatives of the poor were to be appointed by government officials, hardly a mechanism that would recruit political deviants.

Nonetheless, Yorty rejected this compromise since government officials would be a minority. Having heard complaints about participation at a session of the Conference of Mayors, he launched an attack that seemed designed to bring the program under more direct mayoral control. Indeed his intransigence prevented an agreement before the end of the fiscal year, which lost the city millions of dollars in poverty funds. As a result, the conflict became much more heated, even to the point where civil rights groups, with Martin Luther King, Jr.'s blessing, actually picketed City Hall over the issue, a tactic not utilized in any of the other cities.

The outcome of this conflictual process was less favorable to Yorty than the agreement reached through the prior consensual bargaining. But this settlement was not due to Yorty's desire for compromises, as his refusal to accept one illustrates.* Rather, the policy settlement that eventually emerged resulted from the fact that Yorty, alone of the six mayors, lacked the power to impose a settlement unilaterally. In Los Angeles, the city council acted as a quite independent political force, and it could not be expected to promulgate automatically any arrangement that Yorty himself decided upon. Rather, it was influenced by the expressed concerns of black councilman William Mills. Moreover, Governor Brown, who had the authority to veto any poverty program, had shown considerable readiness to veto a plan that was not minimally acceptable to the black community.†

* Although Leroy Collins was dispatched as a federal mediator to resolve the CAP controversy after the Watts riot, the terms of the policy settlement had in fact been arranged before the August 1965 riot, and it only waited ratification when the disturbances broke out.

† As a concession to southern Democrats, the Economic Opportunity Act provided that governors could veto any CAP project within their state within thirty days after

Consequently, Yorty needed to make some concessions to win council and gubernatorial acquiescence. He therefore formed a Committee for Economic Opportunity, with prominent black and Mexican-American leaders, which was to consult with committees to be established in each of eight poverty areas in the city and could veto all poverty programs. Yorty also announced that he would endorse a plan which provided for the democratic selection of six representatives to a nineteen-member council. These steps secured the endorsement of Councilman Mills, thus facilitating the plan's passage in the council. It is true that Mills's support was due in part to his alliance with Jesse Unruh, the powerful state legislative leader, who at the time shared Yorty's opposition to Governor Brown. But Mills, as a black political leader, could not afford to back Yorty's plan without some concessions to black demands. At the same time, these steps helped neutralize Governor Brown. Once the plan had been modified in such a way as to divide black leaders, the governor, instead of vetoing Yorty's plan as Representative Hawkins wished, merely withdrew from the arrangement, stating that the state should not participate in the development of proposals it might have to veto. Evidently, the disunity within the minority group community made Brown reluctant to intervene, afraid that he might be accused of slowing the flow of poverty funds to Los Angeles. The policy settlement thus was a compromise among authorities based on their immediate goals and resources rather than a compromise among vested interests valued for its own sake.

Group resources were expended far more lavishly in the policy-making processes in the conflictual cases than in the consensual cases. Consequently, events in the conflictual policy-making process itself had a clear impact on the policy settlement. Of course, the mayors' own ideological preferences affected these conflicts and their eventual resolution. But if the bargaining had been consensual, one would have anticipated much the same policies in all the cities where mayors shared similar orientations. And if the bargaining had been consensual, the outcome would

---

the project had been approved by OEO. Ironically, this aided proparticipatory forces in certain northern states. Governors Nelson Rockefeller in New York and William Scranton in Pennsylvania both threatened to veto the programs of New York City and Philadelphia, respectively, if they did not provide for sufficient participation. The point in these cases, obviously, was to embarrass urban Democrats.

Still, the veto in northern states was not a potent weapon, for the governor by vetoing a program would assume the burden of denying the state sizable federal funds and jeopardizing a plan for improving the plight of poor minority groups. Consequently, a governor needed strong support from the affected minority groups in order to veto the project. Brown had every incentive to embarrass Samuel Yorty, his political rival within the Democratic party, but he could veto the plan only if reasonably unified black and Mexican-American communities asked him to do so.

probably have been quite different than what eventually occurred. Clearly, Yorty had obtained a more favorable agreement before he generated conflict by a bitter tirade against the prior arrangements. It is also obvious that Wagner and Screvane would have never made so many concessions if they had not been pressed to do so by the opposition. Given Mayor Daley's general style in Chicago politics, it is dubious that he would have taken such a negative, uncompromising stance on participation had it not been for the implied, indeed at times explicit, threats made by neighborhood and reform groups. In the conflictual cases, then, policy was affected not only by group resources utilized in the election of mayors. It was also influenced on the one side, by the resources expended by an opposition trying to force concessions from the mayors through public, bipolar confrontations and, on the other, by a mayor vigorously defending his political views and prerogatives.

POLICY-MAKING PROCESSES, ACTOR EXPECTATIONS, AND PUBLIC POLICIES

If the resources of various groups determined the policy settlement in the consensual cases, they did so primarily through the effect they had on the selection of the mayor, for in these cases it was his ideology which so clearly shaped the policy settlement. In the conflictual cases group resources influenced the policy settlement more directly as well, as groups mobilized their strength in the course of the CAP policy-making process itself. But to show that these two very different types of processes linked actor resources to policy decisions does not by itself demonstrate the nonspurious character of the empirical association between resources and policies observed in Chapter 8. In addition, we must show that the two types of processes were in some sense equivalent, that though resources appeared to be expended differently they can be reasonably understood to have affected the outcome in some similar ways in the five cities. The linkage that Lowi identifies between actor expectations and public policies provides an excellent point of departure for such an argument.

Lowi differentiated: (1) redistributive policies which involve outputs to broad categories of individuals, approaching in size, social classes; (2) regulatory policies which by directly regulating individual activity provide "a direct choice as to who will be indulged and who will be deprived," thereby generating conflict among the specific often comparatively narrow interests affected; and (3) distributive policies, which involve outputs to very small groups or even individual firms, each of whom can be benefited without obviously depriving other individuals or small groups—typified, in a word, by patronage.[9] In each case, the character of the policy helps to determine the types of policy-makers. Since the way actors behave reflects their understanding of the situation, it is not the policies themselves but actor expectations about policies that critically affect interrelationships among political participants. For example, where policies are perceived as redistributive, representatives of large social groupings will participate in policy-formation, but where an issue, which may have redistributive implications, is understood largely in patronage terms, only those seeking the patronage will be involved.

As Lowi concedes, it may be impossible in the long run to distinguish among the three types of policies, since all policies eventually distribute, regulate, and redistribute, thus affecting all three types of interests.[10] But he persuasively argues that, in the short run, expectations with respect to policies are sufficiently diverse to differentiate effectively among types of policy processes.[11] Of course, not all political actors have identical expectations about the same issue. For example, some communists may orient themselves toward all policies according to their expected impact on the perpetuation of capitalism. White and Black Power ideologues may focus on the influence each policy may have on race relations. On the other side, extreme machine politicians may reduce all issues to their distributive content, i.e., their impact on the stock of available patronage and other selective inducements. To understand the character of the policy-making process, Lowi's analysis need only account for the expectations of the preponderance of influential actors rather than the expectations of every citizen.

Once the analyst knows the character of the policy, Lowi argues, he can predict the type of politics associated with that policy. Distributive politics is marked by logrolling among diverse interests ("mutual non-interference" in Schattschneider's words), and the relationship between elite decision-makers and the affected interests is co-optive rather than the product of overt conflict.[12] Regulative politics consists of shifting coalitions, compromises among competing interests, and a fair degree of uncertainty as to the precise outcome, given the variety of possible coalitions which might occur. On the other hand, it seems that since majorities must be built out of a host of discrete interests, policy changes are likely to be incremental. Although the exact policy cannot be easily predicted, the outcome is likely to fall within the limited range of alternatives having an incremental character. Redistributive politics is marked by active executive involvement, dominance by groups representing broad interests of classes, races, etc., considerable cohesion within each of the two sides engaged in the given conflict, and heavy use of ideological language.

Significantly, Lowi is talking about other attributes of political relationships rather than the degree or intensity of the conflict. He does see limited conflict over distributive policies, though obviously two or more individuals could battle furiously over a particular patronage position.[13] But more importantly in this context, he offers no clear propositions as to whether regulative or redistributive politics are more intensely conflictual. In the regulative arena, Lowi accepts certain pluralist analyses which find intense bargaining and conflicts that require resolution by congressional floor votes rather than by committee decisions.[14] Yet he does not entirely rule out the possibility of more amicable settlements. In the redistributive arena, Lowi's interpretation does not focus on conflict, probably because "very few case-studies of redistributive decisions have ever been published."[15] But references to Marx, ideology, and class do suggest intense, unmitigated conflict.[16] On the other hand, his reference to C. Wright Mills's theory of the power elite; his finding that "the legislative process was extraordinarily quiet" with respect to the redistributive Social Security issue because group efforts "were mainly expended in the quieter proceedings in the bureaucracies," and his comment that the lack of redistributive studies "itself is a significant datum," all suggest that Lowi sees covert, consensual politics in this policy arena.[17]

In our opinion, analysis of the CAP participation issue suggests that Lowi's caution on this matter is well taken. Clearly, such participation had a redistributive potential in terms of both political power and social services, which could affect such broad social groups as races and classes. Yet with respect to the same policy, mandated by the same law and administered by the same federal agency in each city, the level and type of conflict varied considerably. Thus, we found the consensual pattern in Philadelphia, Detroit, and Lindsay's New York to be rather more pluralist in terms of the diversity of actors, rather more like the pattern of politics in Lowi's regulative arena than we had anticipated. But we also found intense conflict over this redistributive issue in Chicago, Los Angeles, and Wagner's New York.

We nonetheless agree with Lowi that the way in which a policy is formulated will substantially affect actor perceptions of that policy. It is possible that CAP was seen by participants as simply a patronage issue or a matter to be handled by groups and agencies active in welfare politics. But because participation had become so controversial nationally, it is doubtful that its redistributive potential would be recognized in some big cities while unperceived in others. Evidently, it was not actor expectations about the type of policy that distinguished consensual from conflictual cities, but actor expectations about other matters which were peculiar to that city. This observation suggests the utility of reformulating the relationship among policies, expectations, and political processes that we have taken from Lowi.

In cases where actor expectations set rather clear guidelines to the dominant participants about the degree of redistribution *actually* involved, the conflict is likely to be of the pluralist variety, even when the redistributive *potential* is widely perceived as substantial. The decision-making process is not necessarily limited to a small power elite or a small number of authorities; many groups, organizations, and prominent individuals may participate in the process, provided they follow the normative rules that the game requires. But the narrow groups and other participants involved in pluralistic conflict on such issues are constrained to pursue a covert, compromising bargaining style in order to prevent the larger, redistributive issue, or, more precisely, major changes in the degree of redistribution, from complicating the political game. The set of mutual understandings functions in such a way as to keep hidden from the view of the broader public the nature of the issues that lie beneath the surface.

For participants in consensual politics on redistributive issues, the pattern of marginal policy changes, which take into account the most vital of all the institutionalized interests, constitutes a collective good. If the consensual bargaining breaks down, not only would their expectations about the exercise of political authority be violated, but their present share in the existing pattern of policy outputs would be endangered. Accordingly, representatives of such vested interests had good reasons for cooperating with each other through give-and-take negotiations, rather than trying to maximize their specific factional or organizational interests through escalation of the conflict. Of course, provision of this collective good is constantly endangered by the possibility that any individual participant may decide to violate the norm by pursuing his goals without restraint. Yet, other groups can retaliate by harshly punishing departures from the pluralist-bargaining principle. Thus, unless some outside interest introduces overt, intense factional conflict, powerful constraints protect the low-intensity, pluralist process from potentially disruptive tactics on the part of major participants.

That such low-intensity, pluralist politics occurs frequently on redistributive issues is clear from numerous cases in national politics. The Social Security program, for example, even though it was (and is) perceived as affecting broad social groups, lost its bitterly contentious character relatively quickly. More recently, changes in the Medicare program, which generated intense conflict until 1961, have been settled by negotiations that involved a limited number of organizational, administrative, and legislative elites. The bitter bipolar conflicts that accompanied passage of the Wagner Act contrast sharply with the prominence of specific, organized interests and relatively little social agitation over decisions of the

National Labor Relations Board, which was established to administer that act. And this pattern holds when board decisions affect many employers and employees. Although the pattern and intensity of conflict in these cases hardly approximates Marx's version of class conflict, no small elite obviously controls the process. Instead, conflict could best be characterized as pluralist. And as our case analyses have elaborated in some detail, it was exactly this type of conflict which occurred in consensual politics over participation.

Crucially, the low-intensity and pluralist character of the conflict persisted only when mutual actor expectations on the redistributive aspects of participation were rather clearly established. In all three cases, it was the mayor's ideology which appeared to be decisive in shaping these expectations. In Detroit and Lindsay's New York, key actors recognized that black interests would almost automatically receive sympathetic consideration on the part of the mayor. Other actors simply took this into account in developing their own influence strategies; they made no serious efforts to prevent inclusion of black interests in formulating policy. In Philadelphia, on the other hand, the influential participants acquiesced in a pattern which ignored the black interest in participation. But within this constraint, a pluralist, low-intensity bargaining process ensued. The distribution of political resources affected the political outcomes not through the policy-making processes themselves but by affecting the outcome of preceding political elections. In other words, the electoral struggles were resolved in favor of the ideological group that had mobilized the most political resources, producing an overall political settlement which shaped actor expectations. It was these widely shared perceptions which subsequently facilitated consensual, pluralist-bargaining processes.

Of course, not all actors need agree with mayoral preferences in order for the consensual style to prevail. Some private welfare groups in Lindsay's New York and Cavanagh's Detroit, as well as certain civil rights and Community Conservationist groups in Philadelphia, had little enthusiasm for their respective mayors' positions on the issue. Yet all these groups recognized that the mayors had perhaps the right and certainly the power to impose certain broad limits on policies consistent with the overall political settlement that had been reached in the city.

Actor expectations about what is possible within the terms of the city's political settlement structure relationships in a crucially important way. They predetermine not only the broad outlines of the policy, but also the type of conflict through which policy details will emerge. Of course, the exact outcome may remain quite uncertain, even for the actors, as a variety of possible coalitions on policy details may emerge from the consensual bargaining process. But the basic political resources of ideological groups are not particularly important in explaining these policy details, for bargaining skill, timing, "accidents," etc. can all affect the outcome. Yet the policies are no less structured by group resources, because the policy settlement that emerges occurs within the limits imposed by the political settlement determined by the preceding election.*

A lack of such a political settlement produced the quite distinctive set of policy-making processes typical of the conflictual cases. In Chicago, Los Angeles, and Wagner's New York, significant participants in the political process simply did not accept the mayor's ideology as having established the limits within which the policy would be determined. Instead, they mobilized their political resources as best they could to fight directly over the specific policy decision on participation, thus producing a broad, bipolar, public ideological conflict that might well be expected in the redistributive policy arena. As a result, the dominant coalition could be confident about securing its goals only by insisting on its own specific version of the policy settlement.

The policy-making process was thus less structured by mutual actor expectations and understandings about the accepted character of CAP participation policy. Each side seemed to believe that it could affect the outcome by mobilizing its political resources, anticipating that they would have a measurable effect on policy outcomes. The process that ensued also had no predetermined outcome; it could have been affected by accidents, mistakes, skillful maneuvering as well as any number of random variables. Yet group resources, exercised in such a policy-making process, are still likely to have an important effect on the outcome. Given the fact that both sides to the conflict appeared committed to their ideo-

* We are distinguishing here between a "political" settlement, which is usually shaped by elections that determine who will be the governing authorities, and a "policy" settlement, which determines more specifically the limited range of activities that will be carried on in a specific governmental program. The two are in a hierarchical relationship to one another, as follows:

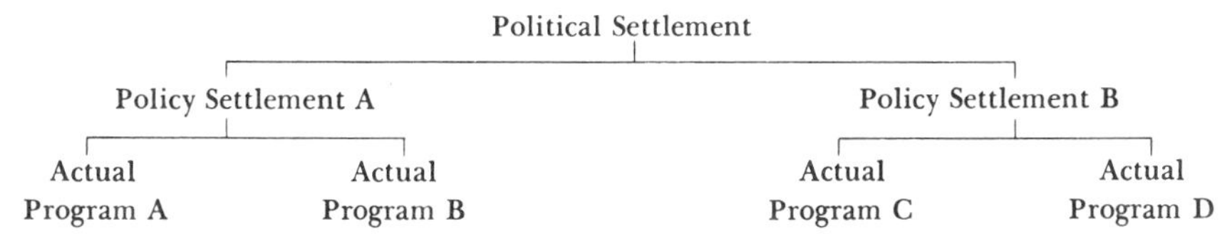

In other words, several policy settlements may all be consistent with any given political settlement, and a variety of actual program activities may be consistent with a policy settlement. On the other hand, certain program activities are excluded from a particular policy settlement and certain policy settlements are excluded by the terms of a political settlement—unless some groups challenge the political settlement itself, thereby introducing conflictual politics.

logical goals, were willing to mobilize considerable resources, and saw the opposition as a political enemy, naked power was likely to be important in resolving the dispute. Only after the crude exercise of power in such a policy-making process could a policy settlement, i.e., a set of mutual expectations, then emerge which would effectively govern the administrative operations of the program. In the consensual case, political resources operated before election day; in the conflictual case, political resources were extensively mobilized even after the election. But in both cases, these resources shaped a shared understanding that structured the development of the CAP. It is in terms of these structuring elements that resources can be said to have an equivalent impact in both consensual and conflictual processes.

It is true that this argument can be rejected if one attributes the differences in levels of conflict to the strategic and tactical decisions of key groups, with respect to the deployment of their resources. In some cities, groups decided to engage in conflict, whereas in other cities, comparable groups refrained from doing so. In general, this approach expects that actors will pursue the strategy that best maximizes their goals. Thus, both the outcomes and the levels of conflict might be said to reflect simply the different patterns of correct and erroneous calculations by groups in different cities. Specifically, it might be argued if the groups do not maximize their political effort, their behavior is accounted for as an "error" in political calculation.

This interpretation, however, ignores the fact that in the present case there were no systematic errors by either the pro- or antiparticipatory factions. Yorty encouraged conflict when he would have obtained for himself a better, i.e., less participatory, settlement without it. Chicago blacks and reformers generated conflict even though they might have secured a more participatory policy through conciliatory behavior. Conceivably, but certainly not necessarily, blacks in Philadelphia, and whites in Detroit and Lindsay's New York might have won further concessions if they had utilized more of their potential resources. Finally, Wagner might have worked out a less participatory settlement if he had not resisted black demands so strenuously. In this situation, then, the assumption of erroneous, as opposed to correct, approaches in the different cities produces not an explanation but a descriptive concern with essentially random errors. Such a conclusion—an admission that the observed data remain unaccounted for—should be accepted only if no pattern of systematic differences emerges. But to reach this point would ignore, like too much of the community power literature, the possibility that the type of strategy must be seen, not simply in individualistic or even group terms, but as a function of system or contextual properties. In many cases, actors are constrained to pursue the strategies they choose, given the character of the regime in which they act. But constraints that limit strategic choices are resources that benefit one or another set of actors in the polity. Specifically, in the case of participation, the particular relationship between blacks and the urban regime, the connection between manifest racial interests and the pluralist-bargaining order in each city, did indeed shape actor behavior.

THE SOURCES OF CONFLICTUAL AND CONSENSUAL POLITICS: FACTIONAL INTERESTS AND PLURALIST BARGAINING

Consensual politics on a redistributive issue can occur only when all manifest interests significant for the issue are included within the pluralist-bargaining process. In Detroit and in Lindsay's New York, consensual politics reflected the fact that black interests had been included in the bargaining on the CAP issue—so that these key groups did not feel the need to protest their exclusion. In Philadelphia, on the other hand, the consensual process reflected, not this inclusion of black activists, but the general latency of black interests in that community. Of course, Philadelphia blacks had not entirely ignored the currents of opinion stirring within the national black community. Black Philadelphians participated extensively in the 1964 March on Washington. NAACP president Cecil Moore had attacked the juvenile delinquency program for not recruiting a black director. A Negro minister, Leon Sullivan, had increased employment opportunities for blacks through a nationally publicized boycott and a government-supported job-training program. Yet by 1965 these activities had not produced an aggressive black leadership which continuously articulated community demands. The Reverend Sullivan, for example, studiously avoided using his training program resources to build a base of political power. The juvenile delinquency program did little to strengthen the resource base of the black community. Not only was the NAACP weakened by the division between its traditional moderates and Moore's more militant followers, but Moore himself seemed willing to sacrifice intense criticism of CAP for patronage opportunities. Finally, the coalition of neighborhood groups that tried to generate a conflict over participation was too small and included too many "paper organizations" to be regarded by Tate as a real threat.

Under these conditions, Philadelphia's more moderate blacks successfully became their community's most important spokesmen on the participation issues (in contrast to the more ambiguous success of Yorty's moderate black allies). Indeed, the leader of Philadelphia's contingent in the March on Washington was Samuel Evans, Tate's ally in achieving a nonparticipatory policy settlement. As a result, rather than having to confront insistent demands for a major change in race relations, the mayor, city agencies, private welfare organizations, and moderate black leaders could ignore the admittedly redistributive content of the participation issue while emphasizing the CAP's effect on more narrow, organizational interests, a matter easily worked out through pluralist, but quiet, bargaining.

Conflictual politics occurs when an interest excluded from this process becomes manifest and seriously tries to maximize its political influence. At this point, the active political participants no longer have any set of mutually shared expectations about the possible limits of policy change. The conflict may become still more intense because the issue now involves, not simply incremental changes on the margins, but the "vesting" of a new interest which could constitute a redefinition of the regime's pluralist bargaining order. Indeed, Liberal Pragmatists particularly concerned with continuing pluralist bargaining, defend the existing order, even at the expense of their electoral interests. The excluded group also seeks allies who are concerned about authority relations, notably those whose ideology embraces regime interests in participation. The recruitment of these allies further escalates the conflict on such redistributive issues, so that compromise for its own sake becomes unimportant to the actors involved. Each side tries to maximize its interests and defeat, perhaps even crush, the opposition.

Thus, the intense conflict observed in Chicago, Los Angeles, and Wagner's New York reflected: (1) a struggle to secure a manifest, i.e., widely recognized and shared collective interest; and (2) the exclusion of that interest from the pluralist–bargaining order, and a resulting struggle over authority issues. At times, the pluralist-bargaining order includes both sides of a set of opposed factional interests, e.g., those of blacks and whites, labor and management, or consumers and producers. In such cases, policy could possibly be determined by leading representatives of the opposed interests who would be able to reach some arrangements that accommodated the vital concerns of both sides. But the vesting of socially subordinate or disadvantaged interests is inhibited by the inegalitarian feature of the pluralist-bargaining norm, which requires special deference to property rights. As a result, the successful vesting of the interests of the working class, blacks, and consumers has ordinarily been slower, more arduous, and more conflictual than the vesting of either broad commercial and industrial interests or those of special producer groups.

For example, the inclusion of broad working-class (as distinct from narrow, more economically privileged craft union) interests in the national political regime occurred only after great economic, social, and political turmoil in the 1930s. Politically, the voting patterns of the American electorate were significantly altered, and such important institutions as the presidency, the Supreme Court and the nature of the federal system were altered in critically important respects. A struggle over the inclusion of black interests has lasted into the 1970s (with the outcome not yet decided in most parts of the country). Social turmoil during this period is clearly evident, and, if Burnham is right,[18] another transformation of the American party system may accompany this attempt to vest a subjected interest. Certainly, after 1964, the conflict over the relationships between minority groups and authorities began to dominate the politics of most large cities with substantial black and Spanish-speaking populations.

Although by 1965 this conflict had not become fully manifest in Philadelphia, in the other cities, mayors, reform leaders, private welfare and city agencies all recognized the political potential of the black-white conflict. Consequently, they appreciated the fundamental issue at stake in a participatory CAP. In particular, the mayors who battled participation with great fervor and apparent ideological conviction were quite aware of the linkages between participation and the broader question of race relationships. Chicago politics had been severely disrupted by civil rights agitation over both schools and housing issues. Moreover, Chicago's juvenile delinquency program had indicated the direct connection between a participatory governmental program and the racial issue. New York civil rights groups had been equally aggressive in local politics, and in this city, too, the juvenile delinquency program had clarified the way in which the call for participation was linked to broader racial issues.

The significance for race relations of a participatory CAP also became apparent in Los Angeles, although perhaps somewhat more belatedly. At first Mayor Yorty remained aloof from the conflict probably because the connection between participation and racial conflict had not been explicitly drawn by the juvenile delinquency program, as it had in New York and Chicago. But after having attended a national conference of mayors, at which the participation issue was a major concern, Yorty vigorously opposed participatory demands, escalating and prolonging the conflict. But since Yorty, unlike Tate in Philadelphia, lacked patronage resources to co-opt black leaders, even a comparatively weak black leadership cadre, once invited to do so, was able to focus public attention on the issue and generate a conflictual decision-making pattern.

Although manifest black interests were necessary for conflict, it was not a sufficient cause. In Detroit and Lindsay's New York, black factional interests were vigorously promoted in CAP discussions, but the conflict was as low-keyed and pluralist as in Philadelphia. The explanation for this pattern is that black interests had become a vested part of, rather than having been excluded from, the bargaining order. Of course, white challenges to black interests in these cities were sometimes effective. Yet more frequently, these challenges required extensive mobilization of white resources, for, at least in the case of participation, the pluralist-bargaining order protected black interests. Both Cavanagh and Lindsay, as they developed CAP policies, consulted closely and regularly with even militant black leaders. And the black interest in participation was clearly, if not perfectly, recognized in the final policy settlement. Moreover, recognition of black interests in these two regimes seems not to have been limited to the CAP.

Studies of Detroit politics have noted that city's comparative deference to black interests. David J. Olson found that, after its major 1967 riot, Detroit officially, in terms of both the recommendations of the city's riot commission and actual policy changes in law enforcement, housing, and education, was clearly more responsive to black interests than were Milwaukee and Newark.[19] Isaac Balbus identified much stronger legal defense efforts for blacks accused of riot-related criminal acts in Detroit than in Chicago or Los Angeles.[20] Alan Rosenbaum noted that, by comparison with Chicago, Detroit had more citizen participation, not only in CAP, but in the Model Cities program as well.[21] Marilyn Gittell found the Detroit school system among the most innovative and open to community participation (including that of minority groups) of the six cities she studied.[22] Finally, Aberbach and Walker have found since 1967 heightened political self-consciousness among blacks and increasing political distrust and unrest among Detroit whites, perhaps the consequence of the inclusion of black interests as part of the pluralist-bargaining order.[23]

Comparable policy innovations can be found in New York under the Lindsay administration as well. During the late 1960s, community control of schools, designed in part to increase black influence over their schools, went farther in New York than in any other major city in the country. Alterations in welfare policy were so substantial that the state legislature intervened to prevent too many concessions to black interests. The city administration also sponsored a civilian review board for the police, although this proposal was reversed in a referendum.[24] Moreover, the mayor formed an Urban Task Force to give priority attention to problems in low-income areas and encouraged a variety of other plans for participation and decentralization.[25]

These policy changes were first stimulated by and then provoked major changes in the two cities' patterns of political alliances. In New York, Lindsay split the coalition between certain machine and reform

Democrats which had supported Wagner. But Lindsay's efforts to woo reformers and minority groups alienated right-wing Republicans. In 1965, the Conservative William Buckley opposed him; in 1969, Lindsay lost the Republican primary to a Conservative-Republican John Marchi. In 1965 and 1969, the Democrats backed first Abraham Beame and then Mario Procaccino, candidates who had only modest liberal credentials. Opposed by both major parties, Lindsay depended for his 1969 victory upon the smaller Liberal party, which since La Guardia had fairly faithfully supported Democrats in mayoral elections. By 1969, then, he had shattered past political alignments.

Cavanagh also came to power through the formation of a new political coalition. After two decades of often bitter conflict, labor and business in Detroit had reached a tacit truce which recognized the vested character of union interests in local politics. They joined together to support the Miriani administration. In 1961, Cavanagh and a few Community Conservationist supporters exploited high unemployment and a police "crackdown" in the black community to defeat Mariani, despite his seemingly invulnerable coalition of supporters. Cavanagh himself gained the support of labor and business interests in his 1965 reelection effort, but that support supplemented, rather than substituted for, Cavanagh's backing in the black community.

The 1969 election presented a somewhat different picture. In a pattern similar to New York's, three strong candidates sought to succeed Cavanagh; one was black, one a Community Conservationist, and one definitely more conservative. Unlike New York, where the Puerto Rican candidate narrowly lost the Democratic primary, the black candidate in Detroit survived the nonpartisan primary election. But in both Detroit and New York, the Community Conservationist was elected mayor in 1969, thus ensuring the perpetuation of the black-inclusive regime for several years—while the black and minority proportion of the electorate continued to increase in both cities.

The predisposition of all actors in a given city to engage in conflict was a function of the relationships between race interests and the pluralist-bargaining order. Indeed, whether black interests had been included in that order affected the relationship between group resources and the policy settlement. In the machine cities, for example, the importance of the balance of power between the machine and the reformers for CAP policy depended on this relationship between black interests and the system of bargaining. The weaknesses of the reformers in Chicago would not have been so completely devastating for participation if black factional interests had not become manifest and therefore relevant to the city's politics. Similarly, the strength of the reformers in New York had so great an impact on participation only because manifest black factional interests provided the basis for political conflict. In Philadelphia the reformers might have prevented a Chicago-type defeat for participation had the process become more conflictual. Indeed, certain weaknesses in the mayor's position might have led to a somewhat more participatory policy settlement. Yet, because black factional interests were relatively latent, reformers affected participation only insofar as the Progressive Conservatives among them were included in the vested interests which the mayor felt compelled to consult.

At the same time, in the reform cities the relative strength of Black Power groups so directly affected the policy settlement only because white interests had not become fully manifest, i.e., were not fully mobilized, on the participation issue. Mayor Yorty felt compelled to fight participation, but in 1965 he did not have enough active backing in the white community to strengthen his bargaining position significantly with the city council or the governor. In Detroit the Civil Service Commission and other agencies may not have been as responsive to black and mayoral pressures had an active White Power opposition emerged—as it did later on educational issues.[26] The possibility that white factional interests might become more fully manifest suggests that black interests cannot easily be included in the bargaining order in any particular city.

"DEVESTING," INSTITUTIONALIZATION, AND RESISTANCE TO CHANGE

Vesting excluded interests is a slow, arduous process, as organized labor discovered even after Roosevelt restructured American politics. Success in one policy area, such as governmental regulation of collective bargaining, did not guarantee speedy acquisition of comparable influence for the working man in all functional areas. For example, major changes in medical policies did not occur until the 1960s, more than a generation after the great political realignment. If this was true for labor in national politics, blacks could expect at least as much difficulty in city politics, if for no other reason than the comparative autonomy of large urban bureaucracies. In fact, only because CAP was generally less autonomous from political forces than more established agencies did the inclusion of black interests come comparatively easy in New York and Detroit in this particular policy area.

Given the slow, arduous process of including disadvantaged interests in a wide number of policy areas, characterizing regimes as "black inclusive" or "black exclusive" may seem to have little utility. Perhaps the participatory policies in Detroit and Lindsay's New York reflected, not a change in the bargaining order, but simply the ideological preferences of Community Conservationist mayors. Perhaps only the authorities changed, rather than the pluralist-bargaining order itself. Presumably, these participatory policies might be overturned, or limited quite specifically to the CAP. Moreover, certain factors peculiar to the poverty program account for the ease with which city administrations in Detroit and New York could respond to black demands.

Black interests, after all, could be included in the CAP without arousing direct, open white resistance that could be expected in other cases. First of all, CAP did not pose as an immediate and obvious threat to vital white interests, as did changes in the residential boundaries of black neighborhoods or changes in school-attendance boundaries in communities undergoing racial transition. Second, the CAA did not directly regulate such government activities as police, fire, or education in which white interests were often strongly entrenched. The poverty program did offer financial incentives to encourage other bureaucrats to accept change. But such bribery was too indirect, perhaps too ineffective, a method of securing change to provoke ideological conflict on the part of White Power groups. Third, in the mid-1960s whites were seldom organized as whites per se but rather as Italians, Irish, Jews, labor unions, welfare agencies, civic groups, etc. With perhaps the exception of the neighborhood school movement and some homeowners associations, the organizations in the white community were not specifically oriented toward the defense of white interests. In black-exclusive regimes where consensual bargaining among established agencies, groups, and institutions effectively excludes favorable consideration of black interests, this makes little difference for white interests. But the suddenness with which black interests became manifest over community action and successfully appealed to the regime interests of certain white groups meant that, in 1965, those opposed to the inclusion of black interests in welfare politics were relatively weak. They lacked the organizational resources to reverse participatory policy, even though survey data suggest the white citizenry may have been ready to support them.[27]

As these observations imply, once an interest has been included in the bargaining order, there is no unbreakable rule that prevents that interest from being "devested" at some later point. Even after working-class interests had been vested, labor unions correctly recognized that certain "reactionary" movements, including some supporters of Taft-Hartley and right-to-work legislation, sought to exclude worker interests from the area of industrial relations policy. The even less-entrenched black interests in New York and Detroit could also be excluded at some later point, just as leftist governments have often been overthrown in Latin American republics. Yet, to say that interests can be devested only points out the significant change that has occurred in these cities.

The question can best be clarified by distinguishing between the vesting and the institutionalization of interests. Although black-inclusive regimes existed in New York and Detroit in the late sixties, they were still very poorly institutionalized. And the capacity of such regimes to survive changes in leadership remained doubtful even as late as 1971. As Huntington points out, "So long as an organization still has its first set of leaders, so long as a procedure is still performed by those who first performed it, its adaptability is still in doubt.[28]* While new, insecure institutions are still developing, new regimes are often dependent for their legitimacy upon distinctive, even "charismatic" personalities. The relative instability of these new regimes, nonetheless, involves the permanence, not the quality or extent of the change, and it should not obscure the obvious distinction between these regimes and their predecessors. New coalitions can form, regimes can change, and policies can turn in a new direction before that direction is firmly established, i.e., institutionalized. And in fact, the process of institutionalization is quite different from the process of vesting.

If the vesting of broad social interests may involve intense and decisive conflict, institutionalizing these interests mainly follows the consensual bargaining pattern. This pattern held in the case of the industrial relations policy with the passage of the Taft-Hartley Act, after which it became clear that labor policy could be altered only marginally. One reason for this has to do with the connection between institutionalization, as described by Huntington, and the development of organizations representing factional interests. Once the interest has been vested in the plural-

* We differ from Huntington, however, in that we believe that political institutionalization can be equated with political "development" only within the framework of a particular regime. Huntington notes that the extent to which organizations become institutionalized, i.e., contribute to political stability, is a function of their "adaptability, complexity, autonomy, and coherence" (p. 12). The equivocation lies in the concept adaptability. "A governmental organ that can successfully adapt itself to changed functions, such as the British Crown in the eighteenth and nineteenth centuries," says Huntington, "is more of an institution than one which cannot, such as the French monarchy in the eighteenth and nineteenth centuries" (p. 17). But of course, if the British monarchy would have been overthrown, i.e., not contributed to stability, it would not have been adaptable. The measure of adaptability is so closely tied to stability, the theory is close to a tautology. In fact some otherwise highly institutionalized organizations—complex, coherent, autonomous—simply cannot adapt to rising social forces and revolutionary action is the consequence. When a new regime is established, however, the old institutions do not contribute to but undermine its stability, and the problem of institution-building begins once again. Huntington's ideas are helpful but only if one first appreciates the significance of changes in regimes.

ist-bargaining order of the American regime, it ordinarily is represented in the consensual-bargaining process through a set of elites in relatively stable roles. In effect, as Huntington has pointed out, institutionalization involves the building of complex, coherent, autonomous, and adaptable organizations. Of course, these organizational elites may be aggressively concerned with their own enhancement and even the maximization of their constituents' factional interests. But the danger in pressing expansionist aims is that basic maintenance needs will be threatened by the negative reactions of others. As a result, organizational maintenance concerns encourage once hostile interests to bargain with each other amicably, even on broad redistributive issues. For, if organizations are autonomous in so far as they "are not simply expressions of the interests of particular social groups,"[29] the process (at least in American politics), by which an organization develops and asserts autonomy from the interests it was originally designed to serve, involves negotiating compromises with other political institutions and interests. In effect, development of the organization thus moderates or limits its commitment to maximizing specific interests. In the American case, it becomes committed to pluralist bargaining and incremental change.

Consequently, even though an issue may affect broad social groups, both administrative agencies and organized pressure groups come to worry more about their specific organizational interests. Under these conditions, such norms as communicating covertly and accepting compromises effectively control behavior. Organizations speaking for factional interests do not challenge adverse decisions publicly, because of the potential risks to their present position. They seek to reduce the uncertainties of a broad political conflict by limiting the process to negotiations among elites who are oriented toward making compromises. Thus, the character of the conflict over Social Security, Medicare, and aid to education has changed with the institutionalization of these programs.

These considerations favoring compromise affect, not only the organization speaking for the newly vested interests, but the organizations with which it interacts. These organizations, too, acquire a stake in preserving established relationships. For this reason, the longer the interest has had to institutionalize itself in the bargaining process, the more difficult it proves to be to devest that interest at a later date.

These observations explain why black interests in Detroit and New York may soon become institutionalized, at least in the antipoverty field, despite the continuing opposition of some prominent White Power-oriented politicians and groups. Yet, the difficulties in achieving initial inclusion emphasize the extremely grudging way the American regime makes policy concessions to the substantive interests of the disadvantaged. Despite the regime's sometimes considerable toleration of protests by less privileged groups, it is extremely hesitant before making major policy concessions to their substantive interests. Vigorously articulated black demands, after all, were effectively rebuffed in two cities. Even where the power of minority groups and their allies helped them win acceptance in Detroit and New York, vesting by no means extended to all policy areas. Community action, even when it had the greatest impact in reducing political poverty, was but one limited episode in the long struggle over race relations that has so preoccupied the American Republic.

CHAPTER 10: A POLICY ANALYSIS: RACE, POLITICS, AND COMMUNITY CONTROL

Policy analysis is typically written for those in power. We offer here a public policy analysis of participation in Community Action Programs (CAPs) from the perspective of those relatively disadvantaged groups seeking political power. Normatively, we are not primarily concerned here with the stabilization of American democracy, which in fact has successfully withstood many seemingly formidable challenges over the past century. Nor do we try to devise the politically most advantageous or feasible policy strategies for those presently in official positions—unless, of course, they should seek to share power with emerging groups, as Sen. Robert Wagner of New York did on labor relations issues in the 1930s. Rather, we will try to demonstrate the relevance of a participatory CAP for eliminating America's racial "contradiction" between opposed racial interests, a policy more immediately important for black Americans than for those in authority.

Although this normative concern contrasts with the predominantly empirical focus of earlier chapters, it usefully complements the preceding interpretation of the different levels of participation in the five cities. To rank CAPs in terms of participation, we assumed throughout our earlier discussions that participation was highest, not where it meant mere representation on a CAP board, but where it meant more, or at least made more probable, community control—in practice control by specific representatives of black and other minority group organizations over certain governmental institutions. It is appropriate now to examine the policy consequences of community control, although black activists in community action made very limited progress toward achieving such control, even in the two cities where participation was greatest.

We have concluded that in the late 1960s and early 1970s community control proved to be the most promising policy strategy open to black leaders in their efforts to secure racial justice and equality. But this emphasis on the importance of community control, as distinct from pursuing other political and economic goals, differs markedly from four sometimes contradictory, but influential, bodies of political science literature. Each of these scholarly perspectives has been openly skeptical about "maximum feasible participation" as a public policy—and very little interested in black Americans' distinctively cultural aspirations, a point of no little consequence. Writers on *social stratification* see participatory policies as only co-optive mechanisms for incorporating black masses within a pseudodemocratic polity, thus forestalling real mass protest. Writers concerned about the problem of *mass society* fear that such a participatory policy would unleash dangerous discontents which government officials will be too weak to pacify. Certain *pluralists* object that meddling, even if well-intentioned, elites will substitute their own values for those of the poor and in the process forestall genuine racial progress. And *liberal progressive* writers anticipate that decentralized, locally controlled institutions will create, and then benefit, new but nonetheless conservative elites, rather than representing and fostering the interests of their mass constituents.

Any defense of community control needs to meet these objections. However, our intention here is not simply to explicate and then rebut the various arguments, but to demonstrate the way in which the disagreements among these mutually contradictory arguments can be understood and perhaps resolved, once the racial contradiction in the American context is properly understood. Moreover, this analysis will clarify the way in which these writers' common rejection of participation and community control is at the same time a rejection of communal, ascriptive social categories as proper considerations in the formulation of public policy. In order to offer a theoretically grounded policy analysis for the black community, we believe it is necessary first to appreciate the theoretical grounds for the four most important criticisms that have been leveled against the policy we propose.

Admittedly, no single writer can be perfectly characterized by any of the four labels we have used. Clearly, some of the ablest critics of CAPs have voiced more than one of these objections. We are concerned here less with classifying individual scholars than with distinguishing among the divergent policy implications of these different analytical traditions. In illustrating these contrasting objections to community action and community control, we have therefore tried to identify the primary—not the exclusive—thrust of the authors' critiques.

FOUR CRITIQUES OF PARTICIPATION

Mass Society Critique

Daniel Moynihan has undoubtedly made the notable use of analyses of mass society in critically examining community action.[1] In fact, Moynihan elaborates the intellectual roots of the CAP itself by pointing directly toward the work of Goodman, Oakeshott, and especially Nisbet, who in one way or another all worried about the intrusion of mass behavior and mass organizations into contemporary political life at the expense of older, liberal values.[2] Reacting to the horrors of Nazi Germany and Stalinist Russia, and affected at least in part by the rise of McCarthyism in the United States, American writers in the mass society tradition question the Populist assumption that mass participation and social progress were necessarily mutually supportive. Moynihan notes that community action originally meant the restoration of a sense of community among an anomic, alienated population.[3] But he maintains that this goal was undermined by misplaced theorizing, mistakes, confusions, misunderstandings, as well as by the conscious intentions of those who had more radical ends in mind. Moynihan then appeals to community activists within the terms of their original intellectual framework, quoting favorably Arthur M. Schlesinger, Jr.'s perhaps too dramatic observation that President Kennedy had "an acute and anguished sense of the fragility of the membranes of civilization, stretched so thin over a nation so disparate in its compositions, so tense in its interior relationships, so cunningly enmeshed in underground fears and antagonisms, so entrapped by history in the ethos of violence. . . ."[4] Indeed, "the repeated message of contemporary social science is," for Moynihan, "that of the scarcity of social opportunity. . . . The consequence of such a sensibility is not so much great *caution* as great *care*."[5]

As a practicing political activist, Moynihan does not hesitate to put the issue in its most concrete form:

> Desire for order, and anxiety about change . . . are commonly enough encountered among working-class and lower middle-class persons. . . . During the 1960s, for the first time in the history of public opinion surveys, crime emerged as the principal issue of domestic concern.
>
> The reaction among many of the more activist social scientists . . . was not to be appalled by disorder, *but almost to welcome it.* "How grand to live in interesting times." This began in earnest with the Negro riot in Watts in 1965, which was promptly declared not to have been a riot at all, but rather

a revolt, an uprising, a manifesto, any term that suggested the masses were on the move.[6]

Thus Moynihan concludes, "if a populist, illiberal conservatism began swelling to ominous proportions in the late 1960s, the middle-class advocates of expressive violence and creative turmoil had something to answer for. Indeed it is directly to them, the professors and 'pseudointellectuals' that Governor Wallace and others like him, addressed *their* critique of the power structure, and *their* challenge to the forms of civility and social stability. . . ."[7]

Moynihan, for one, rejects participatory CAPs because they at least have the potential to breed discontent to the point where social reform becomes impossible, as race is pitted against race. Such developments may lead at best to a right-wing reaction, and at worst, if the European concerns of these writers are recalled, to authoritarian or even totalitarian movements, which may come to control such bursts of mass behavior.

Pluralist Critique

The failure of pluralist theory to produce a critique of the CAP as sustained and thorough-going as Moynihan's is not altogether surprising, since their analytical posture contains a potentially important ambiguity vis-à-vis community control. On the one hand, pluralists believe that public policies should be formulated by democratically elected leaders, who respond to the demands of competing groups and institutions in society. As Robert Dahl, perhaps the most eminent of American pluralists, contends in his basic American government text, "whenever a group of people believe that they are adversely affected by national policies, or are about to be, they generally have extensive opportunities for presenting their case and for negotiations that may produce a more acceptable alternative."[8] Simply because leaders must seek political reelection, they cannot afford to ignore such group opposition; consequently, the more that duly elected leaders are directly responsible for policy, the more it is likely to be acceptable to a plurality of interests. In our opinion, Chapters 8 and 9 have cast severe doubts on the empirical accuracy of this argument. Normatively, however, this view appears to suggest that, insofar as community participation leads to the formulation of policies outside the direction of elected public officials, the democratic character of the policy process is diminished.

On the other hand, Dahl and other pluralists also believe that public policies are, and should be, especially responsive to the intensely held preferences of minorities, particularly when majority sentiment is indifferent. Indeed, they favor insulating certain policy areas from competitive, electoral politics simply in order to satisfy the desires of specific groups most directly affected by the policy. In Dahl's words, "uniform policies are likely to be costly, difficult or troublesome" so that pluralist democracies may be well advised "to find ways by which these policies can be made by smaller groups of like-minded people who enjoy a high degree of legal independence."[9] These considerations seem to suggest pluralist support for community control. Indeed, Kramer applauded the participation experiments which he studied in the San Francisco Bay area on the grounds that "a democratic pluralistic society sanctions and benefits from the creation of new structures for the organized expression of diverse interest groups."[10]

On the other hand, pluralist support for such group influence seems to apply only where the group in question actively demonstrates its intense desire for a particular policy.[11] From this perspective, granting control of CAP policy to indigenous black groups is appropriate only when poor blacks actively demand such a participatory program. And it is precisely at this point that Banfield makes his brief but pointed attack on participation in his controversial defense of "The Unheavenly City."[12] Banfield's entire analysis of lower-class culture rejects any contention that the poor themselves actively demanded participation in CAP or any other program. Because of their present-orientedness, low-income citizens give no more thought for tomorrow than the "lilies of the field." Consequently, the poor may be expected to be politically quite passive with respect to large social institutions, even though these may vitally affect their daily lives. The poor have never activated themselves to form an interest group which might assume control over policy in a specific functional or geographic area. Indeed, says Banfield, they did not even participate in poverty elections when invited to do so.[13]

On the whole, our empirical evidence has supported Banfield's argument. Participatory CAPs were not the result of the poverty residents' own efforts to bring about social change, but the product of black and white middle-class "do-gooders," who "imposed" these institutions on the low-income black community for what they thought was its own good. Those pluralists who consistently reject the latent or objective interest analysis must with Banfield accordingly reject participatory CAPs.

They do so, however, not because they share the mass society theorists' concern for the masses' destructive rage but because they suspect elite meddlesomeness. In fact, Banfield argues that elite do-gooders, rather than aiding the downtrodden, only block programs that might be to their genuine benefit.[14] For example, the educated elite's negative reaction to the Johnson administration's report on the deteriorating Negro family is said to have effectively blocked the efforts of government officials to establish a job-employment program for black males.[15] More generally, pluralists fear that the elite's emphasis on black rage and white racism can become a self-fulfilling prophecy, as blacks and whites come to hold the opinions that are daily attributed to them.[16]

Social Stratification Critique

But, if pluralists and mass society theorists see participation accentuating societal problems, another case against community action rests on an entirely opposite expectation: CAPs will quell, rather than exacerbate, civil strife. The early social stratification literature, to use Nelson Polsby's characterization of a theoretical perspective that was most notably pioneered by Floyd Hunter and C. Wright Mills, developed a radical critique of modern bourgeois societies that diverged significantly from the Marxian tradition. In particular, these writers attributed control of the critical decision-making levels in the United States, not to a social class, but a small "power elite."[17] More recently, this literature, recognizing the variety of political forces operating in both national and local communities, has moved somewhat closer to a class conflict perspective.[18] But both versions reject the pluralist argument that political power is importantly differentiated from economic wealth or social prestige in a democratic society. Indeed, they argue that power is instead almost entirely a function of the social stratification system, the distribution of wealth and status in the community.

Accordingly, public bureaucracies are not seen as neutral agents executing formal policy produced by compromises among diverse interests, but as an institutional apparatus that implements the interests and values of economically and socially dominant groups. Even bureaucracies ostensibly concerned with the plight of minorities and the poor will actually serve instead the interests of dominant groups. In the words of Marris and Rein: "Bureaucracy, as the instrument of power, can be taken to reflect the interests of the dominant social classes. . . . Those who pay for, control, and staff the bureaucracies may well be reluctant to tax themselves more heavily, so that slum schools may compete with the suburbs for the best teachers, and their pupils for college places or the skilled jobs already decimated by automation. . . . As long as service to the poor is not highly regarded, resources will be attracted from their needs by more prestigeful activities."[19] And, in *A Relevant War Against Poverty,* Kenneth Clark and Jeannette Hopkins show the relevance of this interpretation for community participation:

> The insistence on a certain proportion of poor in board or policy positions, which became OEO's verbal criterion and the battle cry of many protest

> groups (e.g., "participatory democracy"), seems to be irrelevant in practice as an index of observable change in the lives of the poor. . . . A vote on a board is not a guarantee of independence. The poor are still poor and financially, as well as psychologically, vulnerable.
>
> The total context of deprivation tends to lead to passivity . . . [and when] the president of the First National Bank or a college president, a spokesman for city hall, or a pastor with high status from a financially powerful church speaks on a community action board, he is listened to. . . .[20]

As a result, Clark and Hopkins conclude that "the actual implementation of these programs . . . [is] likely to reinforce the dependency and powerlessness of the poor."[21]

Of course, an extreme social stratification interpretation cannot account for the very existence of a war on poverty, to say nothing about community participation. But in their subtle and provocative study, *Regulating the Poor,* Piven and Cloward do account for these developments in ways consistent with a social stratification analysis.[22] In their view, welfare policies in modern capitalist societies reinforce a society's work norms. Payments are kept very low, recipients are often publicly degraded, categorical programs (for the old, the blind, and the disabled) are used to induce the marginally paid worker to stay on the job and off "the dole."[23] This is the case, at least, during periods of political stability (however much business fluctuation creates economic distress). But in times of political unrest, such as the early Roosevelt years and the uproar of the late 1960s, welfare policies are altered so as to accommodate the demands of the restive masses, thereby restoring social control and political stability.[24] Crucially, the poverty program financed community workers who, in attacking local welfare bureaucracies, enormously expanded the relief rolls in major cities;[25] in turn, this expansion provided for these masses the minimal economic security necessary to depress the political turmoil in riot-torn urban areas.[26] In Piven and Cloward's view, CAP was thus a brilliant stratagem, intended or not, for maintaining capitalist institutions in a time of crisis, and the effectiveness of a participatory CAP in performing this activity made it all the more important in reducing unrest. Community control in general would have a comparable, indeed, reinforcing impact, by providing a palliative for minority groups that gives them at least a symbolic stake in the existing order without fundamentally altering the existing pattern of wealth and status and, therefore, of power.[27]*

---

* We do not mean to state here Piven and Cloward's general assessment of community control, for elsewhere they have applauded black power and black separatism. How-

In sum, the social stratification literature sees political power rooted so firmly in dominant social and economic institutions that significant social change is unlikely to occur through government-sponsored activity. However much attention is paid to minority group needs, significant change can only occur through major alterations in the structure of capitalist society by means of broad-gauged, perhaps even revolutionary, mass activity. And this is only forestalled by poverty programs designed to pacify those masses.

Liberal Progressive Critique

Liberal Progressive writers also see community action as a conservative policy. But they emphasize its effect on local elites rather than on the masses of the black community, a position consistent with their general emphasis on the independent, autonomous significance of political structures and activities. In contrast to social stratificationists, Liberal Progressives believe that national political leaders, building a base of mass support that includes workers, minorities, consumers, and the poor, have at least the potential to act independently of the dominant groups in the stratification system, in order to achieve greater measures of justice and equality. Provided centralized institutions supply clear guidelines for policy implementation, governmental leaders can produce significant, deliberate social change even in a modern capitalist society. Bureaucracies are the agent of such change, provided that Weberian principles of hierarchy, internal consistency, and lateral impermeability are not subverted by cooperative alliances between lower-level administrators and specialized, highly organized private interest groups.

Grant McConnell's study of *Private Power and American Democracy*, perhaps the major contemporary statement of this perspective, particularly emphasized the dark side of group politics.[28] Agreeing with the literature of mass society that organized groups are often a stabilizing force in society and politics, McConnell maintained that this stability comes at considerable cost in liberty and equality whenever these narrow, highly organized groups are incorporated into semiofficial organs of the state. Such groups prefer that government programs be decentralized, thereby lowering the visibility of their political activities and facilitating stabilized relationships between them and low-level government officials.

---

ever, *Regulating the Poor* interprets race conflicts in class categories and emphasizes the political stabilization functions of co-optive mechanisms for the black poor. For their defense of Black Power, see Frances Fox Piven and Richard A. Cloward. "What Chance for Black Power?" *The New Republic* (March 30, 1968), pp. 19–23.

Specifically, McConnell argues that decentralized public institutions share many of the same oligarchic characteristics that typify the private internal government of the interest groups themselves: they can exclude their members from effective participation in group decisions, demand conformity from those subject to their jurisdiction, and recognize narrow, specific interests at the expense of broader, more diffuse, and simply less-advantaged interests. Indeed, when organized groups and public officials establish co-optive relationships in many decentralized governmental units, power relations in the society, taken as a whole, are regarded by Liberal Progressives as being just as beneficial to the dominant economic and social groups as these are portrayed in the social stratificationist literature.[29] On the other hand, Liberal Progressive writers such as McConnell believe this inegalitarian pattern can be changed without resort to radical social movements. In their view, alterations in governmental arrangements can by themselves have important consequences; the activities of political parties, the presidency, highly centralized bureaucracies, executive authority all may promote desirable social change.

In his study, *The End of Liberalism,* Theodore Lowi amplifies this Liberal Progressive analysis and applies it specifically to the case of community action.[30] Lowi argues that this program, like so many contemporary government activities, substitutes process for a policy. The Economic Opportunity Act, instead of declaring certain policy objectives and precisely stating the mechanisms for achieving these goals, set up "representative" local groups that could consider any and every way of attacking poverty, while defining this key term in the vaguest possible way. The legislators thus delegated their own responsibility to frame policy, not just to local officials, but eventually even to private groups, thereby raising all of the problems that McConnell identified.

The inclusion of representatives of the poor only accentuated the conservative implications of this process-oriented nonpolicy, since "delegation of the program to private groups requires official recognition of groups and representatives."[31] Lowi recognizes that "in the first round we may be impressed by emergence of new groups—and at least impressed by the amount of effort expended to bring new groups about."[32] But he emphasizes that "once the situation is stabilized by official recognition of groups and representatives, the situation tends to militate against emergence of still newer groups. Official level, federal recognition becomes a valuable resource with which some groups [those initially active in the CAP] can demoralize others."[33] This is all the more serious because, "as Peachum and MacHeath teach in *The Three Penny Opera,* the poor are the easiest of all to intimidate, especially with symbols of authority."[34]

In the end, the civil rights movement, by becoming involved in CAP, lost its cutting edge, and black leaders substituted special interests for moral appeals, thereby losing one of their crucial sources of power.

In the view of Liberal Progressives, the CAP and the movement for community control that it foreshadowed, suffered from their dependence on organized neighborhood and community elites within a highly decentralized governmental structure. CAP is dangerous, not for its co-option of the black masses through minor improvements in governmental services, but for its co-option of black elites who will use governmental authority to buttress their own positions, rather than promoting significant redistributive policies.

POLITICAL THEORY AND THE RACIAL "CONTRADICTION"

Relationships Among the Four Theoretical Perspectives

These negative judgments against a participatory CAP cannot be quickly dismissed, in part because they reveal an impressive negative consensus among analysts whose own policy commitments range from radical and liberal to moderate and conservative. Despite their differences, the critiques are in agreement that, at best, a participatory CAP offered the black community and other urban minorities short-lived, illusory gains. Yet it is striking that these four critiques rely on such different, even opposed, expectations about the probable empirical consequences of participation, as is set forth in Table 10–1.

TABLE 10–1. Relationships Among Policy Perspectives Critical of Community Control Innovations

Sources of pressure for political change as a result of community control	*Desirability of the rate of probable change*	
	Too fast	*Too slow*
Mass behaviors are decisive	Mass society analysts	Social stratification analysts
Elite behaviors are decisive	Pluralists	Liberal Progressives

The mass society and pluralist literatures obviously agree that the potentially radical changes, promoted by community control policies, would occur too quickly to the detriment of the minority community and society as a whole. They differ markedly, however, in the importance they assign to elites and masses in producing this result. Mass society theorists believe that community control would help raise popular expectations about rapid social gains which, when frustrated, would arouse mass rage, increase racial conflict, and eventually, perhaps threaten the entire system. Some pluralist critics, on the other hand, expect selected elites to use program resources to make demands which would have a limited relationship at best to the actual preferences of the poor, interfere with policy alternatives genuinely favorable to lower-income groups, and perhaps generate ultimately damaging resentments—indeed racial backlash—by other groups.

Social-stratification and Liberal Progressive theorists believe community control would retard, not accelerate, the pace of social change. But they, too, differ in assessing the impact of elite and mass behavior. Social-stratification writers view community control as a mechanism which at best gives the masses a stake in the existing, if now somewhat reformed, system, encouraging them to moderate their demands, lest they lose newly won gains. Community participation thus becomes an institutional device for the social control of the group presently most susceptible to appeals for broad-gauge, perhaps even revolutionary social change. By contrast, Liberal Progressive analysts regard community action and community control as devices that can co-opt emerging political leaders in the black community.

The Race Structure, a Peculiar Institution

Although each of these interpretations is of interest, we believe their mutually contradictory criticisms reveal a common weakness. Of course, the mere fact that contradictory criticisms are made does not by itself justify rejecting all of them. One interpretation could be correct, and the others wrong. But each is supported by enough evidence and argumentation to make this conclusion rather dubious. Rather, we think that this somewhat confused debate in the academic literature has flourished because each view is partially correct but all ignore the significance for participation of the racial context in which conflict over community action took place.

This oversight should not be especially surprising, for the race problem has confounded every general interpretation of American society and politics for more than a century. Certainly, explaining the outbreak of the Civil War provides the most painfully obvious difficulty both for Louis Hartz's analysis of *The Liberal Tradition in America* and the pluralist emphasis on the compromising, consensual style of American politics.[35] Similarly, race relations in general seem plainly inconsistent, not only with Marxian categories of class conflict and Tocqueville's understanding of a new egalitarian democracy, but also with later, Progressive notions of homogenization, universalism, and the melting pot.

The peculiar character of the racial issue explains, first of all, why mass society and social stratification theorists could have such contrasting, yet comparably plausible, empirical expectations about the inhibiting or reinforcing effect of participation on rates of social change. Given the depth of black outrage at racial inequality, mass society writers can persuasively argue that increased governmental power awarded to the black community will encourage demands for rapid change. But they get into more serious difficulty when they then maintain that on this issue large numbers of blacks will abandon the typically rational behavior that even mass society theorists concede to citizens as long as they are concerned about specific, immediate, daily problems. Whatever the probability of irrational, extremist, and unreliable activity that sometimes accompanies an orientation toward broad, diffuse, and distant political goals, we believe that the race issue is very unlikely to generate such unstructured mass movements among black Americans. In fact, a social analysis which expects such abstractedly motivated behavior from the black movement is itself too abstract and general—ignoring the particular history and context of American race relations which makes this issue concrete and personally salient. After all, black demands have always involved such specific goals as equal employment opportunities, the right to vote, and the election of black officials in particular black communities.

A similarly concrete goal orientation characterized even the most intense conflict over CAPs in our five cities. Of course, the implementation of the poverty program coincided with the urban riots of the mid-1960s. It is difficult to establish whether the program stimulated or helped to quell these outbursts, but it is relatively clear that community residents active in CAPs worked to focus and to make concrete those demands which rioters articulated. As the evidence from Newark seems to suggest, there were circumstances in which an organized black leadership, spawned by federal programs, could use the riots to obtain substantial political power.[36] But that shift to a black-dominated political system in Newark did not destabilize the American political regime more generally, nor even totally transform Newark's own political system.

CAP also apparently failed to foster a new, right-wing white "backlash" authoritarian movement. Indeed, there is little evidence that whites opposed to black demands were any more "irrational," "authoritarian," or prone to undermine liberal values than were the blacks themselves. Of course, many urban whites effectively opposed any meaningful racial integration in housing or schools. Yet, relatively liberal politicians who endorse integration have won white voter support provided they are otherwise in the "mainstream" of American politics. Ironically enough, race is too focused a political concern, too obviously and immediately related to particular aspects of the lives of some individuals—e.g., those whites who live next to expanding black ghettos—to have become an effective vehicle for gathering in all societal discontent.*

These very traits, of course, help us understand why social stratification analysts insist that participation and community control are mechanisms for co-option rather than social change, why participation in and control over vital community institutions might well help stabilize the larger society. Certainly, the vesting of black interests into the institutionalized bargaining order cannot be a happy prospect for advocates of a social revolution. Of course, many social-stratification writers recognize that blacks, who number only 11 percent of the population and command disproportionately few social resources, cannot make a comprehensive social revolution by themselves. But we believe these same writers err seriously in assuming that, without "co-optive" structures like CAPs, blacks would be particularly prominent recruits to a broader, radical coalition.

Blacks are, of course, likely to seek major social changes; they can be expected to express their factional interest in eliminating the imputation of Negro inferiority, and thus transform the most enduring and inegalitarian of American social relationships—much as social-stratification writers expect. But they are unlikely to reject in the process the greater part of the American regime. So long as the prevailing authority structures permit, and even encourage, the mobilization of Black Power, revolutionary activities oriented toward broad-scale change by a large united group of black and white insurgents will face substantial, perhaps insuperable obstacles. Certainly, the activity of the relatively large number of blacks involved in the more participatory CAPs involved concrete demands articulated within the framework of the existing *political* regime, even though these activists sought a major *social* transformation, namely, the elimination of racial inequality.

If understanding the nature of the racial contradiction within the context of American authority relations clarifies the mass society-social stratification debate about mass behavior, it may help to resolve the dispute about elite behavior between the pluralists and Liberal Progressives.

---

* In the early 1970s whites in industrial areas did become increasingly angry over federal court orders which required compulsory busing of school children to achieve racial integration. Significantly, however, this step reflected *integrationist* values which were by no means identical to the central commitments of those seeking community control.

Liberal Progressive writers view elites from an explicitly Michelian perspective.[37] They argue that elites (particularly those with low-income constituents) tend to concentrate on maintaining the organizations which give them their elite status. And by using their oligarchical position within their organizations, they can divert attention away from their stated mission of benefiting their organizational membership to the narrower, moderate enterprise of bargaining and compromising with more politically entrenched and socially advantaged groups. Revolutionary fervor is transformed into bureaucratic meticulousness and regularity. Lowi is surely right in applying this expectation about the "iron law of oligarchy" to these institutions which come under community control. Indeed, our own data show that organizational leaders won power in CAP by promising to fight for radical improvements, but once in office they often became bogged down in detail, found it harder to deliver their promises, and consequently sought to focus popular attention on comparatively limited gains, such as improvement in reading levels, increases in the number of blacks employed in local governmental agencies, and expansion of programs like black studies designed to enhance the dignity of black people. Crucially, we refer here, not just to the elected poverty representatives in Philadelphia, but also to the much more militant and effective organizational leaders in New York and Detroit. Clearly, in both cases, activists benefited much more as individuals than did the residents of the poverty areas collectively. For this reason, Banfield's concern about excessively ideological community activists seems to require qualification.

His argument, however, cannot be rejected entirely. He certainly seems correct in stating that the great bulk of the programs which are directed toward the poverty residents generally, from rent strikes to welfare protests, can largely be attributed to organizational activists, who can be plausibly characterized as do-gooders establishing programs for a community, most of whose members do not actively demand them. To be sure, Banfield's emphasis on the low turnout rates in poverty elections exaggerates the lack of interest in participation among poor blacks and other minority group members, for rational citizens cannot be expected to vote unless they can hope to gain some benefits that exceed the cost of voting.[38] But the poverty elections in Los Angeles and Philadelphia were nearly devoid of any issues, or organized competing elites, or well-known personalities, since the elections had little or any clear relevance for public policy. As a result, low-income voters could hardly be expected to see much benefit in casting their ballots. Yet, stated more carefully, Banfield's point appears more persuasive. If the black masses had been overwhelmingly enthusiastic about participation in CAP, even such inefficiently designed structures for participation as were made available would have been utilized more fully. Clearly, whatever pressure for participation that did emerge came from elites, rather than directly from the black masses themselves.

After all, the most pointed response to Michels was Lenin's argument that the masses, if left to their own spontaneous protests, could not formulate the sophisticated demands which might lead to major social change. Even if formulated, the demands were unlikely to be sufficiently focused or long lasting to succeed. This Leninist analysis seems clearly substantiated by the failure of the American race riots of the 1960s, a clear instance of spontaneous mass protest, to produce in most American cities significant political or social change. For American blacks to maximize their interests, their organizationally sophisticated leaders must thus "do good," at least insofar as they point out to others the most effective techniques for realizing shared goals. To use a Leninist phrase, these leaders must become the organizational vanguard for the movement, even if the movement is for racial equality rather than total social transformation.

Equally important, a reliance on these elites makes some sense in the case of American racial conflict, because there is no reason for assuming that black organizational elites will typically abandon the racial cause. The very nature of racial inequality in the United States—the fact that the "stigma" of blackness has been applied to every American even slightly Negroid in ancestry—has unified and continues to unify black voters of all classes. Indeed, the notable black successes in Detroit and New York politics, as well as in other smaller cities, derive in large part from the tendency of blacks at all economic levels to vote together. This argument, of course, cuts in two directions: It suggests that the black masses share more policy concern with black activists than Banfield seems to admit, but it also suggests that, as he fears, the middle-class activists may not be easily co-opted. Indeed, as our analysis of the racial contradiction in Chapter 3 suggests, black leaders seeking to arouse their followers have some precedent for expecting mass support to emerge eventually, sometimes in one great upsurge of activity. In a sense then, these elites are doing good by working for goals their followers cannot specifically articulate, or will not work for; but their actions are more constrained than what the term *doing good* suggests. For the elites can win mass support necessary for success only if the institutions they build serve some of the economic, political, or cultural needs which prove appealing to the black community. And, significantly enough, in Detroit and New York, where participation was greatest, black leaders focused their attention on bringing additional institutions—Model Cities programs, schools, housing bureaucracies, and the welfare system—under greater client and community influence.

At this point we can state our difference with all four of these critical assessments of participation at once more generally and more precisely. Despite their very different, if in each case partially valid, perceptions of community control, all four critiques suffer from a common defect. Each is ultimately committed to a modernistic view of social life which dismisses primordial or ascriptive ties, such as race, as illegitimate, improper, or ineffective criteria for formulating public policy.[39] Instead, these four perspectives agree that modern society, in general, and political activity, in particular, is and properly should be dominated by functionally defined, occupational roles, based on a largely economic division of labor.

For social-stratification theorists, the key roles may be those of workers and their political leaders acting on their interest in abolishing industrial capitalism; for mass-society writers, the key role may be that of the rational leaders of various economically oriented interest groups; for pluralists such as Banfield, it may be professional politicians skilled at compromising group differences; and for Liberal Progressives, it may be public authorities who frame and enforce Lowi's "juridical democracy." But in each case, these literatures all assume that the specific functions assigned that role in the society's overall division of labor will lead the role incumbents to follow or to work for rationalized political policies. Of course, the various analytic traditions disagree vigorously among themselves about which actors should seek which political goals. But the underlying agreement about a functionally specific, instrumentally rational division of labor as the legitimate basis of modern society—the source of interests or values which do, and should, motivate political behavior—had led all of these perspectives to a similar position on American race relations. Each typically endorses integration as the solution to racial conflict, both as an ultimate ethical ideal, and as an immediate criterion for current public policy.

It is not surprising, then, that in a 1970 article significantly entitled "The Failure of Black Separatism," Bayard Rustin, for over two decades a leader in the black struggle for integration, could utilize themes and arguments from all four perspectives in a single rather consistent and coherent argument.[40] Like Moynihan, Rustin begins with a warning against extreme, passionate conflict as a threat to these political forces most likely to frame reasonable public policies for the amelioration of racial strife. "Our country is polarized as never before . . . the forces of liberalism are in disarray."[41] "The black [separatist] rebellion," he observes later, "is an enormously expressive phenomenon which is releasing the pent-up resentments of oppressed Negroes."[42] The result is an indulgence in "moral" not "political or economic demands."[43] But the consequence of this rebellion, as theorists of mass society fear, is likely to be repression: "if Negroes engage in violence . . . they will be met with oppression . . . if they follow a strategy of racial separatism, they will be isolated . . . if they engage in anti-democratic activity . . . they will provoke a reaction."[44]

At the same time, Rustin, along with most social-stratification theorists, does not rule out mass collective action provided it invokes class rather than racial loyalties. Despite the many charges of racism against it, Rustin insists that "the trade union movement is essential to the black struggle."[45] And any movement for a "revolutionary reallocation of political or economic power" cannot be racially based.[46] "What is needed more than ever," he contends, "is a political struggle which offers the real possibility of *economically* uplifting millions of individuals black and white."[47]

Rustin is also concerned, however, about local elites. Like the Liberal Progressives, he warns that black elites may be seduced by the potential gains that separatism and community control offer. He approvingly cites E. Franklin Frazier's warning that the black middle class supports separatism so that black businessmen can effectively monopolize the Negro market, and concludes that local black elites in a decentralized system would in the end provide social stability and peace for the whites, without seriously attacking the basic problems of "poverty, deteriorated housing, unemployment, terrible health services, and inferior schools."[48] But like Banfield, Rustin suspects that black separatism is all too much the work of an elite—black students and their white liberal sympathizers—who impose these slogans and goals on a nonseparatist majority, perhaps 85 percent, of the black population.[49] Here surely is a group of personally advantaged do-gooders, as Banfield might call them, with little sustained interest in serving the essentially economic interests of the black masses.

By so effectively borrowing from all these perspectives, Rustin's article thus makes clear their shared hostility to race as a legitimate source of pride, anger, and even solidarity in the struggle for equality. Indeed, he accurately characterizes the view of Cruse and other writers when he argues that their new nationalism "bespeaks a fervent hope that the poverty-stricken ghetto [note his economic categorization of black communities] once thought to be a social problem crying for rectification might now be deemed a social good worthy of acceptance."[50] Discounting the hostility of his evaluation, he may also be right in suggesting that, "As if to obliterate the trace of racial shame that might be in their souls, . . . [these nationalists] have enhanced racial chauvinism."[51] The decisive point, of course—and the reason we dissent from Rustin's argument—is that neither he nor any of the four analytic perspectives we have just considered seriously and explicitly considers this question of "racial shame" or, put less provocatively, the particularly severe assumption of inferiority imputed by white Americans to the black slaves and their descendants. But, as Chapter 3 argued, it is precisely because of this imputation that cultural self-development, and consequently control of communal institutions, directly attacks racial inequality.

The Problem of Institutional Racism

Although the policy analysis offered here rejects Rustin's argument as ill-conceived, and even though we endorse community control as at least an intermediate term objective of the black community, we do not believe that the movement to secure this goal is likely to achieve racial equality in the near future. Paradoxically, perhaps, the main source of both our pessimism and our endorsement of the community control objective can be indicated by a single term, "institutional racism," provided this term is properly understood. In political polemics, institutional racism has often been used to accuse whites of harboring secretly racist sentiments, somewhat disguised by a polite public rhetoric. Given our contention that American race relations have been patterned by a deeply entrenched white imputation of black inferiority, we would by no means deny the importance of white prejudice. Nevertheless, white Americans today are at least verbally much more receptive to integration than they were twenty years ago,[52] and some of the comparatively liberal white elite may actually fraternize with individual blacks. Precisely because black interests can still be neglected, even when white attitudes have changed in this way, it is useful to examine the anti-black implications of key institutions. In other words, if institutional racism is to make a useful distinction, rather than merely become a redundant label for anti-black prejudice, it should refer not to personal attitudes but to the constraints imposed by certain social structures. Specifically, the concept designates the unintended, unanticipated consequences of social structures not primarily oriented toward racial concerns.

Of course, many social structures affect American race relations. In Chapter 7 we examined the complex impact of reformed bureaucracies on participation in CAP itself. And the impact of corporate businesses on American blacks can hardly be exaggerated. But in the examination of black efforts to influence policy formation we find authority structures to be the most interesting and relevant, primarily because any insurgent group which seeks to violate them risks increasing the size and strength of its opposition. In such cases, those who oppose black insurgent goals will try to acquire new allies by appealing to regime interests in preserving existing authority patterns that all citizens share. As a result, the implications of each of these structures for black goals, in effect its level of institutional racism, must become a major concern of the black movement in framing its public policy strategy.

Of the four American regime structures, constitutionalism presents the fewest obstacles to black demands. Of course, constitutionalism has been used to protect the freedom of White Power advocates to organize, speak, petition, assemble and get on the ballot, but it has been appealed to far more often to protect the rights—in both civil and criminal cases—of blacks seeking to criticize and agitate against white domination. In general, then, blacks will benefit to the extent that official behavior conforms to constitutionalism as a patterning orientation.

The other three authority structures present much more complicated pictures. Participation, of course, encouraged the rise of the civil rights movement, gave it an opportunity to appeal for broad support in the white community on the issue of voting rights, and by giving blacks some influence in electoral politics, it helped reduce some of the political consequences of the blacks' social subordination. But the principle of participation operates against the establishment of somewhat autonomous institutions responsive to black interests without regard to the concerns of whites, who may be called upon to finance them. Above all, since whites are a majority of the electorate in every state, this principle, if rigorously applied, would regularly limit black aspirations to achieve political self-determination.

The principle of rationalization also partially supports black goals. For example, it opposes the exclusion of blacks from jobs for which they are qualified. And the equal protection clause of the Fourteenth Amendment, one of the most important expressions of this principle, fostered desegregation in education and public accommodations in the 1950s and 1960s. Yet these same achievement and universalistic principles can also complicate the redress of earlier inequalities and discrimination. Equal treatment for those with currently identical achievements does not compensate for the handicaps imposed by past economic discrimination, inferior social services, and political inequality, which together have left many blacks without the requisite formal qualifications.

As in the case of democratic participation, *rigorous* application of the principle of instrumental rationalization thus works against certain kinds of black demands. Chapter 7 showed that the reformed, rationalization-oriented CAP bureaucracies in Detroit and Los Angeles allowed their concern with efficiency, honesty, and standardized operating routines to reduce the level of resident involvement. In Los Angeles, the CAA's limited participatory thrusts were snuffed out by demands for clearly delineated goals and rationalized procedures, so that the program increasingly became an employment agency. In Detroit, the CAA faced constant pressure from the Civil Service Commission to hire workers according to their performance on written examinations, even though this criterion would have blocked hiring both needy inner city residents and certain community leaders. Certainly, as New York City teachers argued in their 1969 strike, universalistic and achievement norms work against the desire of black community groups to hire only black staff members in carrying out their activities.

If participation and rationalization turn out to pose some obstacles to black demands for equality, the principle of pluralist bargaining, has been used even more obviously to defend racial inequality in America. Even while racial integration and equality became explicit federal policy, pluralist bargaining meant that the government worked only slowly and inefficiently to implement its new goals. And as we pointed out in Chapter 9, the vesting of black interests, when it occurs in local politics, is likely to proceed slowly, only gradually spreading from one field to another.

The pluralist-bargaining structure, however, need not always work to the disadvantage of blacks. For one thing, as the puralists have pointed out, the *direction* of change, however incremental its speed, can favor black interests. Moreover, once these black interests have been recognized as legitimate and become vested, the principle may then work to the blacks' benefit. For example, in the New York CAA, blacks have used the control of decentralized units to evade the requirements of rationalization and democratic participation, which favored continued white influence in their communities. For these reasons, the success of the black struggle for equality depends in part on vesting black interests by controlling certain important community institutions, and then legitimatizing this new influence by appealing to the whites' regime interest in preserving pluralist bargaining.

In Chapter 3 we argued that community control was vital for the development of an autonomous black culture which, in turn, was necessary, as Cruse implicitly asserted, for a frontal attack on the white imputation of black inferiority. Here, our discussion of "institutional racism" has suggested a second argument for endorsing community control policy strategy as advantageous to blacks: the relationship of political authority to the realization of specific black factional interests. Precisely because so many vital institutions and structures resist their demands, blacks can benefit from taking over important local institutions where their numbers or other resources make it feasible to do so.

Nor is it accidental that this analysis of American authority structures and our earlier emphasis on black cultural self-development should suggest this same policy strategy. Black culture, as a part of the nationalist revival of the 1960s, appealed directly to the black Americans' sense of peoplehood—the sense of a unique experience based on the ascriptive racial criteria of birth, rather than on the achievement criteria of economic or social function. Despite their homogeneity in political and economic beliefs, Americans have always been extremely diverse in nonpolitical, noneconomic spheres of religion and cultural traditions. Yet, of the four American authority "structures" considered in this study, only the pluralist-bargaining structure helped the political system accommodate to this cultural diversity by allocating to such groups the opportunity, or social space, to develop their own institutions and activities. This pattern has been historically related to the pluralism of competing economic interests. When Madison asserted the value of such an economic competition in the Tenth *Federalist* paper, he explicitly likened it to the Americans' already successful privatizing of religious differences through the norm of toleration. And just as certain economic groups have dominated governmental policies relevant to their interests, certain ethnic and religious groups have effectively dominated, not just key social institutions, but sometimes important units of local and state governments. More frequently, they also have performed for themselves certain communal functions such as educating the young, caring for the poor, and ministering to the sick. One of the indicators of black subjection, in fact, has been their extremely restricted "space" or opportunity to act in just this way. One of the best political examples of this practice in the black community is the restriction placed upon the black administrators of state-controlled black schools and colleges in the South.

The establishment of genuinely independent cultural as well as political and social institutions, as part of a policy strategy which exploits pluralist-bargaining norms on behalf of black interests, is thus consistent with the traditional American approach to cultural diversity among whites. For blacks, this policy has the advantage, unlike demands for social integration, that it does not directly attack the validity of other minority cultures or even, except indirectly, the dominant largely white Protestant culture of the whole society. Moreover, this policy would have the blacks rely more on their own gradually increasing resources rather than on the wisdom, generosity and benevolence of white American elites.

Although racial oppression and inequality often seems virtually intractable, the policy most likely to eradicate it must follow the path of collective self-development that other ethnic groups utilized to establish themselves in a society that was at once white Protestant in its dominant cultural orientation, capitalist in its economic values, and only partially egalitarian in its political aspirations. Community control, for all its faults, can facilitate the forward thrust of black power in the American regime.

APPENDIX A: STABILITY, CONFLICT, AND REGIME INTERESTS

As we have shown throughout this volume, the prospect of community participation immediately injected the question of authority relations into the war on poverty. In order to explicate the resulting conflict, we have introduced the concept of citizen regime interest in Chapter 4, and applied it in our subsequent analyses. Because this concept appears to be a new one in the social sciences, it may be helpful here to discuss its sociological status more fully, and then to illustrate its usefulness in accounting for important political phenomena.

REGIME INTERESTS AND MACRO-SOCIOLOGY

The concept of regime interest, like our treatment of the factional interests of various races and classes, draws in part upon the sociological images of society that Dahrendorf describes in *Class and Class Conflict in Industrial Society*.[1] In Dahrendorf's account, the conflictual image, most obviously associated with Marx, views society as repressive, inegalitarian, and at times subject to rapid changes in conflict behavior which, in turn, may produce sudden changes in important social structures. The integrative image, summarized by Talcott Parsons, seeks to explain functional coordination, cooperation, social integration, and gradual change. Rather than the potential for society-wide conflict seen by the conflictual perspective, the integrative view concentrates on cohesive mechanisms and technological progress. Perhaps it is for this reason that Parsons looks on hierarchical power, rational discipline, and the stratification system far more favorably than do most Marxists.[2]

As a number of authors have pointed out, these two perspectives actually resemble each other in several crucial respects. Each image, for example, is basically holistic, macro-sociological, and comparative in its assumptions about social life, focusing, not on individually generated beliefs, but on extraindividual sources of attitudes and activity such as cultural values or patterns of interaction among socially shared roles. Both images also share a normative commitment to scientific progress, opposition to inherited distinctions, and a concern with the impact of the division of labor in industrial society.

Dahrendorf, to be sure, maintains that "The work of Parsons displays a conspicuous bias in favor of analysis in terms of values and norms . . . while many of those who have been concerned with problems of conflict . . . emphasize not the normative but the institutional aspects of social structures."[3] This difference, however, can be easily exaggerated. Marx's work was far more concerned with norms and values than Dahrendorf seems to indicate,[4] and Dahrendorf himself recognizes that Talcott Parsons, at least on occasion, supplements "his analysis of normative integration by an analysis of the integration of [the] . . . institutional substratum."[5] Indeed, within the integrative tradition, Durkheim focused on the division of labor as much as Weber stressed the concept of authority. Quite apart from Marx's own concerns, certain later conflict theorists, including Barrington Moore, Dahrendorf himself, and perhaps even Lenin, regarded authority relations as central to social conflict.

Our regime interest approach, however, does not use these shared elements in the conflictual and integrative approaches in order to synthesize some general interpretation of industrial society. On the contrary, we believe that both the integrative and conflict traditions make the unwarranted assumption that entire societies can be characterized monolithically in terms of a single, society-wide tendency. For the conflict tradition this tendency is a "contradiction" (e.g., between labor and capital); for the integration perspective it is often an equilibrium, a tendency toward stable integration (among functionally differentiated, but mutually dependent, social sectors).

But it is this shared notion of some unfailing interconnectedness among all major social elements that we reject. Latent role interests, as they were defined in Chapter 2, affect only a limited range of behavior even when, as in the case of authority structures, they encompass almost all members of a society. Even when we attribute such an interest there is no reason to assume that, when manifest, the result will be a complete social transformation. Similarly, we hold that even if one were willing to posit an adaptive response to strain, one could not simply extend that assumption to all the important relationships within the entire society.

Both methodological and substantive considerations lead us to take this position. At this point in the development of the social sciences, these holistic perspectives are only *images;* operationalizing them for empirical testing and application seems extremely difficult at best. As David Easton so cogently argued a generation ago, it is in practice impossible to specify all the relevant variables that are necessary to characterize the equilibrium point heuristically asserted by some integrationist theories.[6] It is equally difficult to specify, even heuristically, the single opposition or contradiction between social groups or structures that has the capacity to transform a society in one and only one direction.

Even if we could solve these methodological difficulties, it would remain the case that complex societies almost always display elements of both change and stability. There are some elements of continuity in almost all revolutions.[7] In apparently stable situations, whether based on repression or integrative co-option, socially subordinate groups may eventually, and in unanticipated ways, encourage substantial change. Indeed, the secondary, tertiary, and still more remote, effects of any individual's or group's activity depends on the reactions of, and subsequent interactions with, other actors. As these developments stretch out in time and involve more and more individuals, they become too complicated to be understood by the observer or anticipated by the participants themselves. Activities oriented toward stability may well have some long-term transforming effects; transforming activities may well have some long-term stabilizing effects; and the ultimate balance between them—for the society as a whole—is difficult to anticipate reliably.

Still more fundamentally, we reject these holistic, monolithic images as overly simplistic, reductionist efforts to explain complex political behavior in terms of a single cultural or economic factor. It is just as reductionist to assume that cultural integration will produce a functional integration for the whole society as it is to assume that class conflict based on the division of labor will wholly transform all vital social relationships.

Regime interest analysis avoids these monolithic assumptions, because it posits the importance of authority as well as class and race structures. On the one hand, by accepting the notion of latent interests, the concept assumes that conflict-producing attitudes may in fact emerge, breaking apart the society's cultural cohesion. On the other hand, because this approach recognizes the independent importance of a variety of latent interests, it necessarily rejects the notion of a single contradiction between two mutually opposed factions.

These considerations do not mean, however, that regime interest analysis falls outside the macro-sociological tradition. It still assumes that individual behavior is patterned into roles by socially shared expectations, and that the role incumbents may, in concert, recognize a shared role interest. The focus is always on socially shared situations, not, as in much of the political economy literature, on clusters of individual behaviors and attitudes. In fact, the regime interest notion does rely on clearly macro-sociological elements from both the conflictual and integrationist traditions of analysis.

THE TWO FACES OF REGIME INTEREST ANALYSIS

The regime interest concept is Parsonsian in two important respects. First, it is voluntarist insofar as it emphasizes role expectations or patterning orientations. By contrast most, though not all, conflict theory stresses external structural constraints. For example, many Marxists hold that the constraining impact of impersonal market factors leads to the exploitation and alienation of workers. But we believe that these particular constraints on workers as a class operated only insofar as the actors accepted the premises of a capitalist free-market economy, including the underlying world view considered by Weber in *The Protestant Ethic and the Spirit of Capitalism.*[8] The behavioral regularities produced by such market forces would not persist without widely shared orientations that pattern behavior into roles.* Dahrendorf himself sees, for example, that routinized collective bargaining has just this consequence.†[9]

These remarks apply, of course, to the factional class and race interests as well as regime interests considered in this volume. But the regime interest concept is also specifically Parsonsian in its stress on the beneficial character of authority relations in that citizens can be expected to defend these authority structures when threatened. Clearly, both these themes are far more congenial to integrationist than conflict-oriented writers.

But, if our concept of structure and role is Parsonsian, the idea of a *latent* regime interest draws very clearly upon the conflict tradition. In particular, the concept of regime strain elaborated in Chapter 4 holds that citizens with one manifest regime interest may openly oppose citizens for whom a second regime interest is manifest. Regime interest analysis thus shares with the conflict tradition the expectation that political

---

* It should be emphasized that the orientations that pattern such role behavior are social and cultural elements rather than simply matters of individual psychology. For example, only some incumbents of a role will readily articulate an understanding of the role's expectations. Others may do so if pressed, or at least can repeat some traditional formula specifying appropriate behavior. Still others, who cannot articulate the expectations, may conform to them *as if* they were understood, and at least intuitively recognize role deviance.

† These considerations lead us to reject Dahrendorf's view of role deviants as those incumbents who do not recognize their role interests.[10] This argument fails to distinguish between two sets of attitudes: patterning orientations, whose violation constitutes a clear departure from what is expected and can indeed be identified as deviant, and, on the other hand, maximizing orientations. The latter do not dictate any specific behaviors, inasmuch as the proper strategy for maximizing interests depends upon situational factors. Even if the role incumbent lacks any maximizing orientations at all, it is sufficient to identify his interests as latent; it is not only redundant, but misleading, to call him a role deviant.

conflict and consequent social change may grow out of a presently stable social situation.

It may be said that regime strain is itself only another term for "cultural strain," i.e., the conflicting values, beliefs, attitudes and ideologies encompassed by a single political culture. If so, regime strain could fit neatly into an essentially integrationist view. For example, reform support for participation and machine politicians' support for an incremental pattern of policy change could be understood as simply the particular political beliefs that certain Americans happen to hold, rather than the manifest expression of certain latent regime interests. However, the identification of latent regime interests provides a tool not available if one simply refers to present, observable values, preferences, and ideologies. Only the use of the latent-manifest interest concept —or an equivalent employing different terms—enables the analyst to analyze the contingent empirical relationship between the relatively constant role behavior and the political development of a manifest concern with the relevant economic, social, or authority structure.

This difference between regime interest analysis and a focus on such cultural elements as observable political attitudes is well illustrated by the thorny problem of the stability of Western democratic regimes. For example, in *A Preface to Democratic Theory,* Robert Dahl emphasizes the significance for democratic stability of widespread, consciously held beliefs in democratic values.[11] But somewhat later, in *Who Governs?,* he observes that, although Americans had a general belief in a "democratic creed," very many of them were uninformed on details and that, at the level of more specific action orientation, "many citizens opposed what some political philosophers would regard as necessary implications of the creed . . . [and] the way the creed is actually applied. . . ."[12] Accordingly, Dahl suggests that the system's stability is partly a function of the citizens' apathy or indifference,[13] and partly a function of certain qualities of the creed itself, which allows "legitimists" to argue effectively against antidemocratic or anticonstitutional groups in political crises.[14] But apathy, which may come and go rather easily, seems to be a weak explanation for the long term stability of American democracy. And Dahl does not specify exactly how the creed limits antidemocratic developments: "no appeal is likely to succeed unless it is framed in terms consistent with the creed—which is perhaps not so small a constraint."[15]

Dahl's argument, however, can be restated in regime interest terms to parallel, point for point, a latent manifest interest analysis of working-class interests typical of the conflict tradition. Although workers belonging to a trade union may accept a general "creed" of working-class solidarity, they are often so critical of their leadership, uninformed about union policies, or even verbally hostile to what both scholars and union leaders might regard as the creed's implications, that one might doubt the capacity of the union movement to survive. Yet it remains useful to assert that the stable employer-employee relationship continues to provide workers with a latent interest in altering their economic position. This interest seems only vaguely expressed in adherence to the creed of solidarity; it can easily become more manifest for many of the rank and file during a strike or economic crisis, leading usually apathetic workers to show an unwonted militancy.

Analogously, the vague democratic creed can be understood as being a limited recognition of the latent interest citizens have in existing authority structures, an interest whose latency is indicated by widespread confusions, contradictions, and outright opposition to specific implications and applications of the creed. But in a political or constitutional crisis, these same citizens might well be motivated to seek the preservation of the existing authority structures. Democratic stability, in other words, cannot be understood as being entirely the result of consciously and continuously held affirmations by citizens during constitutionally stable periods (when attitude questionnaires can be most safely distributed). It must also be seen as the product of interests that become manifest only if the regime is actually threatened. Interviews with citizens in such crises might indicate more widespread and readily activated citizen understanding of, and support for, the democratic creed. For this reason, the character of the regime and its authority structures may do more than just limit the kinds of appeals that are made, as Dahl has suggested; it may under certain conditions generate a manifest interest in preserving itself—together with conflict behavior consistent with that goal.

The regime interest approach, then, takes distinct social and political structures as the key units for political analysis and sees them as possible, but not necessary, sources of diverse patterns of political conflict. This expectation is clearly inconsistent with the monolithic, interconnected view of society held by both the integrationist and conflictual sociological images discussed here, but we believe it does conform to the character of American social life. American politics has been fundamentally affected by at least two significant social conflicts; one between races, another between classes. At the same time, assumptions about a tendency toward stable integration in American society have equally little utility. Not only are there economic and racial tensions which have produced substantial conflict, but, as our discussion of regime strain in Chapter 4 indicates, great discontinuities and conflictual relationships exist even among the authority structures that most members of the society do share. Indeed, when regime strain occurs, the four authority principles overtly contradict one another. Far from generating a single contradiction, far from simply integrating diverse elements in the society, authority structures have thus contributed to a multifaceted and bitter conflict, not only over the war on poverty in the 1960s, but even more spectacularly over issues that lead to the Civil War. This domestic conflagration may in fact provide the clearest case of regime interests contributing to social conflict.

REGIME INTERESTS AND THE CIVIL WAR

Any interpretation of the coming of the Civil War must recognize the fact that northern opinion adamantly opposed slavery in the federal territories only during the middle and later 1850s. This rapid shift in opinion, with its obvious consequences for social conflict, seems immediately relevant for a latent interest analysis, since changes in the relevant social, economic, and political structures were occurring much more slowly. Certainly, some familiar explanations, which only focus on the manifest attitudes and overt behavior of the key political actors, fail to provide a satisfactory interpretation. To be sure, abolitionist agitation admittedly had some impact on northern attitudes; and compromise-oriented politicians such as Stephen Douglas evidently miscalculated in framing the Compromise of 1854, thereby exacerbating tensions. But clearly, these observations by themselves leave several important questions unanswered. After having encountered such frustration and hostility in earlier years, why did the abolitionists so quickly acquire widespread support at least on the territorial question? What was it about northern attitudes which meant that the Compromise of 1854 would so inflame feelings? Why did northern voters refuse to reinstate the Missouri Compromise line of 1820, hoping to win over southern moderates, and instead elected Abraham Lincoln who was openly opposed to any compromise on the territories?

Barrington Moore's *Social Origins of Dictatorship and Democracy,* which focuses on both authority and class relationships as sources of basic social conflicts, provides materials with which to answer these questions about the Civil War.[16] The sweep of Moore's argument, the importance of the issues, and the mass of information relevant for the analysis prevents us, in this short discussion, from making any assertions as to the validity of his general argument, or even his argument with respect to the Civil War. Rather, we shall simply accept his data as given, but reanalyze his facts and recast his argument in regime interest terms, hoping to make more apparent the conceptual status of class and authority relationships which are largely implicit in Moore's own analysis. In the process we shall more fully illustrate the use of the regime interest concept.[17]

Moore's analysis clearly points out the weakness in latent interest interpretations specifically based on race or class structures. For example, a sudden recognition by blacks and their sympathizers of a hitherto latent factional interest in ending slavery might conceivably be thought to account for a rapid change in northern opinion. In fact, however, the few northern abolitionists and freedmen who supported outright black emancipation remained a small and weak minority throughout the 1850s and into the war itself. Most northern whites indicated in personal correspondence, referenda votes, legislation, and in their urban residential patterns no serious concern with emancipation and little desire to have blacks move North.[18] Lincoln himself, of course, promised Horace Greeley to free only as many slaves, and no more, as would be necessary to preserve the union. His emancipation proclamation was a military, rather than humanitarian, measure which left slavery undisturbed both in the loyal border states and conquered areas of the Confederacy.

As Moore observes, it was precisely these difficulties with the "moral" explanation, relying on a principled opposition to slavery, that led Charles Beard to an economic interpretation of the North's position. To put this view in latent interest terms, the agrarian South's hindering of northern capitalist development activities finally led the entrepreneurs to stand firm on the slavery question in order to break the South's political power through war. Intuitively, however, it is unclear why the class interests of so advantaged a group as northern capitalists should move them against slaveholders who had already contributed directly to northern economic development. As Moore notes, the Prussian Junkers, who used serf labor somewhat the way American planters used slaves, did forge an alliance with German capitalists.

Other specific considerations reinforce this conclusion. Moore argues persuasively that the economic issues between the sections such as tariffs, banks, railroads, internal improvements, even taken together, could have been effectively compromised to leave essentially undisturbed the interests of the economic elites. And as Stampp shows, eastern capitalists had the most conciliatory attitudes toward the southerners. Of all the important northern socioeconomic groups, the western farmers, for all their economic quarrels with these northern industrialists, most adamantly opposed their fellow agrarians from the South.[19]

Having disposed of narrowly economic explanations, Moore asserts what he considers to be a broader economic explanation: "The South had a capitalist civilization, then, but hardly a bourgeois one. . . . Instead of challenging the notion of status based on birth . . . southern planters took over the defense of hereditary privilege. Here was a real difference with the North and a real issue."[20] In effect, Moore places great emphasis upon bourgeois politics and society generally, rather than bourgeois economics in particular as the element which fundamentally divided the sections. But this formulation, given the rather similar economic position of the southern planters, northern industrialists, and western farmers, makes it difficult to specify the *class* interests which led to the conflict. It is possible, however, to reformulate Moore's bourgeois-capitalist distinction in terms of regime strain, specifically the latency and manifestness of the four regime interests, which does specify the relevant role interests at work.

Significantly, the direct sectional clash over slavery issues first surfaced in the generation before the Civil War on a civil liberties issue, a southern-sponsored "gag rule" in the House of Representatives which automatically laid on the table all petitions about slavery. Within the region, an interest in preserving constitutionalism became increasingly latent for white southerners, as the possibility of open debate on slavery faded and as religious freedom for blacks noticeably declined. By contrast, this same regime interest became increasingly manifest among northern whites as their concern over these developments mounted, and the arrest of presumed fugitive slaves became a major civil liberties issue. It must be emphasized, however, that the authority structure of constitutionalism itself continued to operate in the South, even if in a somewhat narrowed range. For example, as late as the 1860s, the southern war effort was, if anything, more openly criticized by dissenters than was the effort in the North.

A similar picture applies to participation and rationalization. Both were left undisturbed as authority structures in southern politics. Southern white males retained at least the formal right to vote and even poor white men voted in some numbers. At the same time, southern state governments continued policies which rewarded newly successful planters with wealth and affluence, however low their social origins or, even in some cases, how heavy their foreign accent. Nevertheless, southern attitudes and rhetoric shifted. Special patterns of deference for the poor, economically unsuccessful cousins of the elite, arguments for the enslavement of poor whites, and rejection of the principle of political democracy all became fashionable among southern planters and intellectuals and among the region's spokesmen who debated the issue in the North. By openly challenging the three regime structures which northerners had hitherto taken for granted, this rhetoric in fact helped to make the latter's regime interests in retaining them more manifest. (Indeed, by the end of the war these interests had become so manifest that at least the radical Republicans among the northerners actually sought to transform southern society by breaking the power of the wealthy landowners.)

By contrast, the South's interest in the preservation of pluralist bargaining as an authority "structure" became extremely manifest, enabling the region to argue passionately its fidelity to the constitutional principle of compromise embodied in that charter's references to slavery, and further recognized in the established customs of the three branches of the national government. To be sure, the incrementalist principle of pluralist bargaining permitted admission of a new free state from time to time, or abolition of slave trading in the District of Columbia. But excluding slavery from all the territories—and more generally, turning the federal executive over to an outright sectional enemy—violated their fundamental expectations about the incremental use of authority. In the North, the manifestness of the other three regime interests together with the specific economic differences between the regions combined to make many northerners increasingly insensitive to southern pluralist appeals, in particular the claim that property in human slaves, should remain a vested interest. Yet, as in the case of the three other structures in the South, conformity to pluralist bargaining as an authority structure did not break down in the North. Slavery itself was not directly attacked until after 1861, and other established material interests were carefully respected by Republicans in their formulation of public policy.

This account does argue that social factional interests did play an important role *in triggering* regime strain. Taken together, the southern white stake in Negro slavery, the ex-slave and abolitionist agitation in the North, and differences over the economic issues, reinforced by the North's much more rapid economic growth, combined to make the federal government's attitude toward slavery increasingly important. In terms of the predisposing conditions discussed in Chapter 2, the active defense of instrumental rationalization and political democracy seemed more appealing to men on the make, or men who hoped to be, notably the family farmers, artisans and laborers in the North and Northwest, than to established capitalists in the East, whose fortunes were already made.

It deserves reemphasis, however, that the specifically economic interests of these farmers resembled those of the southern planters on many key points. Moreover, southern rhetoric and policy about the territories—all of which were unlikely areas for extensive slave farming—appear much too indirect a threat to the purely socioeconomic position of the western farmers in the free states to motivate them to fight a civil war. What did threaten the western farmers more immediately was the South's defiance of prospective federal policy, which was to be universalistically formulated and imposed by freely elected rulers after a free and open debate. Not only, as Lincoln put it, would the South's success have made the Constitution "a rope of sand," but it would have undermined the *principles* under which rulers issued authoritative commands. Significantly enough, their battle cry was based neither on economic equality nor black freedom, but preservation of the union. In the end, northern capitalists, who as citizens shared this regime interest, but who as entrepreneurs had very different socioeconomic interests from western farmers and western workers, supported the president. Only regime interests, in other words, can account for the unity of these diverse socioeconomic classes.[21]

As each section came to recognize that the other represented a threat to the regime interests it most explicitly adhered to, each side looked more closely at the other's overt commitment to particular authority patterns, even though the patterns themselves continued to operate in both regions. As a result, the North's political commitments, its manifest regime interests, became much less pluralist than the bulk of northern practice; while southern commitments became much less democratic, universalistic, and libertarian than the bulk of southern practice. Lincoln put it most incisively: the war was fought on the North's part to determine if "any nation," which was "conceived in liberty and dedicated to the proposition that all men are created equal" in fact "could long endure."

This motivation illustrates the extent to which American politics defies any monolithic interpretation. By freeing the slaves, the Civil War set in motion the racial politics of later generations, including those of the 1960s. Yet, because the regime and racial issues were and are very different, because the war was fought over authority and not race relations, southern blacks were left to fend for themselves after Reconstruction. The northern whites' concern for political democracy, not racial equality, in fact, explains all too well the tragic fate of black Americans in the century which followed their emancipation.

APPENDIX B: METHODOLOGICAL NOTE ON THE INDEX OF LOCALISM*

Any measure of friends-and-neighbors politics or localism must be based on votes cast for various candidates in various constituencies, which in this case were called sections.[1] These data may be arranged in a matrix whose rows correspond to candidates and whose columns correspond to sections. Thus we define as an entry in the data matrix: v_{ij} = The number of votes cast for candidate i in section j. Then, let:

S_i = the sum of the votes cast for candidate i in all sections.

T_j = the total of the votes cast for all candidates in section j.

V = the sum of all votes cast for all candidates in all sections.

From this an index of overrepresentation R_{ij} for candidate i in section j can be calculated.[2] R_{ij} simply states the ratio of the actual proportion of candidate i's total vote that he received in section j to his expected proportion, or:

$$R_{ij} = \frac{v_{ij} \text{ (actual)}}{v_{ij} \text{ (expected)}}. \tag{1}$$

The expected proportion is the proportion candidate i would have received in section j had his vote been distributed in equal proportions among all sections, or:

$$v_{ij} \text{ (expected)} = \frac{S_i T_j}{V}. \tag{2}$$

Substituting the right-hand of Equation 2 for v_{ij} (expected) in Equation 1 and dropping the no longer necessary desgnation "actual" from the numerator in Equation 1 yields:

$$R_{ij} = \frac{v_{ij}}{\frac{S_i T_j}{V}} \tag{3}$$

which equals

$$R_{ij} = \frac{v_{ij} V}{S_i T_j}. \tag{4}$$

For purpose of measuring localism this index suffers from the overlap between the data upon which both the "expected" and actual proportions are derived. T_i is the

---

* This appendix is a slightly revised version of the appendix to Paul E. Peterson, "Forms of Representation: Participation of the Poor in the Community Action Program," *The American Political Science Review,* LXIV (June 1970), p. 507. Copyright, 1970, by The American Political Science Association. Reprinted in revised form with permission.

column summation of all cases of v_{ij}, including the instance of v_{ij} which is the basis for determining the actual porportion of candidate i's total vote that he received in section j. As a result, the index of overrepresentation tended to measure not only localism but also the concentration of candidates among sections, a variable which conceptually has nothing to do with localism. This difficulty is eliminated by dividing the index of overrepresentation for local candidate l by the index of overrepresentation for nonlocal candidate m. This yields an index of localism L_l for local candidate l:

$$L_l = \frac{R_{lj}}{R_{mj}} . \tag{5}$$

Substituting from Equation 4,

$$L_l = \frac{v_{lj}V/S_lT_j}{v_{mj}V/S_mT_j} \tag{6}$$

which reduces to:

$$L_l = \frac{v_{lj}/S_l}{v_{mj}/S_l} . \tag{7}$$

To reduce the effect of random error, an average of all values v_m/S_m may be an improvement on the denominator of Equation 7. Thus:

$$L_l = \frac{v_{lj}/S_l}{av(v_{mj}/S_m)} . \tag{8}$$

Thus, the index of localism as stated in Equation 8 is simply the proportion of a local candidate's total vote that he receives in his own district divided by the average of the corresponding proportions for all nonlocal candidates. Note that this formula includes no T_j term, which frees the index from distortions resulting from an overlap between v_{ij} and T_j. However, the S_i term (visible in Equation 8 as S_l and S_m) was not eliminated from the formula upon which the index of localism was based. Consequently, variations in the size of the vote among sections has affected the index to some extent. It is extremely unlikely, however, that any resulting imprecisions in the measurement of local influences in the elections were so great as to affect the substantive argument of Chapter 6.

NOTES

NOTES FOR INTRODUCTION

1. The major theoretical work setting forth this perspective is Lloyd E. Ohlin and Richard A. Cloward's *Delinquency and Opportunity* (New York: Free Press of Glencoe, 1960). Their analysis drew upon Merton's argument that there is a disjunction between American myths and realities. See Robert Merton, *Social Theory and Social Structure* (New York: Free Press of Glencoe, 1957), pp. 131–160.
2. Mobilization for Youth, Inc., on the Lower East Side of New York City, was the most renowned example of this approach. Not only have its actual programs of community organization been important, but the lengthy, sophisticated proposal written to secure funds for the project has been basic reading for students of community organization in the social-work profession. Mobilization for Youth, Inc., *A Proposal for the Prevention and Control of Delinquency by Expanding Opportunities* (New York: Mobilization for Youth, 1962).
3. See Chapter 8 of this volume.
4. The term "potential group" is drawn from David Truman, *The Governmental Process* (New York: Knopf, 1965), pp. 511–516.
5. U.S. Congress, *An Act to Mobilize the Human and Financial Resources of the Nation to Combat Poverty in the United States,* Public Law 88–452, 88th Cong., 2nd Sess., 1964, p. 9.
6. This is not the place for an analysis of the legislative history of the war on poverty. Useful accounts can be found in Daniel P. Moynihan, *Maximum Feasible Misunderstanding* (New York: Free Press, 1969); Sar A. Levitan, *The Great Society's Poor Law* (Baltimore: Johns Hopkins Press, 1969); James L. Sundquist, *Politics and Policy* (Washington, D.C.: The Brookings Institution, 1968), pp. 111–154; John Bibby and Roger Davidson, *On Capitol Hill: Studies in the Legislative Process* (New York: Holt, Rinehart & Winston, 1967), pp. 219–351; Isaac Balbus, "The Evolution of the Community Action Program" (unpublished M.A. dissertation, Department of Political Science, University of Chicago, 1966); Brian Smith (unpublished M.A. dissertation, Columbia University, 1966); Frances Fox Piven and Richard Cloward, *Regulating the Poor* (New York: Pantheon, 1971), Chapter IX; Elinor Graham, "Poverty and the Legislative Process." In Ben Seligman (Ed.): *Poverty as a Public Issue* (New York: Free Press, 1965), pp. 251–271; Sar A. Levitan, "Planning the Anti-Poverty Strategy," *Poverty and Human Resources Abstracts,* II (January–February, 1967), pp. 5–15; Daniel P. Moynihan, "What is 'Community Action'?" *The Public Interest* (Fall 1966), p. 4; Daniel P. Moynihan, "The Professionalization of Reform," *The Public Interest* (Fall 1965), pp. 6–16; Daniel P. Moynihan, "Participation of the Poor . . ." *Yale Law Journal,* vol. 75 (March 1966), pp. 602–605; Richard W. Boone, "What is Meaningful Participation?" *Community Development,* vol. 1 (June 1966), pp. 27–32; Roger H. Davidson, "Poverty and the New Federalism." In Sar A. Levitan and Irving H. Siegal (Eds.): *Dimensions of Man-*

power Policy: Research and Programs (Baltimore: The Johns Hopkins Press, 1966), pp. 61–80.

7. Office of Economic Opportunity, *Community Action Program Guide* (Washington, D.C., 1965), vol. 1, p. 18.
8. Office of Economic Opportunity, *Community Action Workbook* (Washington, D.C., 1965), vol. 3, A.7.
9. Floyd Hunter, *Community Power Structure* (Chapel Hill: University of North Carolina Press, 1953). Nelson Polsby in his *Community Power and Political Theory* (New Haven: Yale University Press, 1963) provides a strong critique of this literature; he also provides a detailed listing of other works in this tradition. See in particular, Chapters 2 and 3.
10. We shall not document here the precise sources for the various components of pluralist theory mentioned in this paragraph. For those points considered in detail throughout the text, the pluralist argument is presented more fully at the appropriate point. In general, however, we regard the following works as among the pluralist classics: Robert A. Dahl, *Who Governs?* (New Haven: Yale University Press, 1961); Edward C. Banfield, *Political Influence* (New York: Free Press, 1961); Norton Long, "The Local Community as an Ecology of Games," *American Journal of Sociology*), vol. 64 (November 1958), pp. 251–261; David Truman, *The Governmental Process* (New York: Knopf, 1951); and Aaron Wildavsky, *The Politics of the Budgetary Process* (Boston: Little, Brown, 1964).
11. Two major statements of this view are found in Edward C. Banfield and James Q. Wilson, *City Politics* (Cambridge, Mass.: Harvard University Press and The M.I.T. Press, 1963); and in Wallace S. Sayre and Herbert Kaufman, *Governing New York City* (New York: Russell Sage, 1960).

NOTES FOR CHAPTER 1

1. James Q. Wilson, *Negro Politics* (New York: Free Press, 1960), pp. 63–64.
2. James Q. Wilson, *The Amateur Democrat* (Chicago: University of Chicago Press, 1962). The frustrations of the reformers in Chicago are detailed in Chapter II.
3. J. David Greenstone, *Labor in American Politics* (New York: Knopf, 1969), *passim*, but see in particular Chapter III.
4. Even after the 1968 convention riots, the police killing of two leading members of the Black Panther Party under conditions that were publicly revealed to be scandalous, and manifold instances of corruption and scandal in state and county governments, all Chicago dailies endorsed Mayor Daley for reelection in 1971.
5. Unpublished documents available only from the authors of the study, such as this one, will not be cited in the footnotes.
6. *Chicago Daily News*, April 5, 1965.
7. *Chicago Defender*, February 17, 1965.
8. As Leo Snoiss points out, ". . . the Democratic [Congressional] delegation has obtained much federal help for Chicago . . . Mayor Daley has relied a great deal on his delegation to lobby for the city." Leo Snowiss, "The Metropolitan Congressmen" (unpublished Ph.D. dissertation, Department of Political Science, University of Chicago, 1965), p. 403.
9. Gary Orfield, *The Reconstruction of Southern Education* (New York: Wiley, 1969). Chapter IV relates this story in fascinating detail.
10. The concept "individualistic culture" is developed and applied to Illinois politics in Daniel Elazar, *Cities of the Prairie* (New York: Basic Books, 1970).
11. U.S. Congress, House, Committee on Education and Labor, *Hearings, Examination*

of the War on Poverty Program, 89th Cong., 1st Sess., 1965, Testimony by Deton Brooks, executive director of Chicago Committee on Urban Opportunity, p. 374.

12. A fine sociological analysis of the Philadelphia establishment can be found in Digby Baltzell, *The Philadelphia Gentlemen* (Chicago: Quadrangle, 1971).
13. Among the few comparable cities are Pittsburgh, Saint Louis, and Baltimore. See Robert Crain, *The Politics of Desegregation* (Chicago: Aldine, 1968), Chapter XIII.
14. The best general account of Philadelphia politics during this period is found in James Reichley's *The Art of Government* (New York: Fund for the Republic, 1959).
15. An excellent case study of Philadelphia's juvenile delinquency or "gray areas" program can be found in Peter Marris and Martin Rein, *Dilemmas of Social Reform* (Chicago: Aldine, 1967), Chapter IV.
16. See Chapter 5 in this volume, pp. 137–139.
17. Among the works on Los Angeles and Southern California, which emphasize the significance of political decentralization and fragmentation in the areas, are: James Q. Wilson, *The Amateur Democrat* (Chicago: University of Chicago Press, 1962), pp. 96, 98, 104–105, 203–205; Carey McWilliams, *California the Great Exception* (New York: Wyn, 1949), Chapters I and XIII. See also Carey McWilliams, *Southern California Country* (New York: Duell Sloan and Pearce, 1946), pp. 166, 171, 238–239.
18. McWilliams, *Southern California Country;* Michael P. Rogin and John L. Shover, *Political Change in California* (Westport, Conn.: Greenwood, 1970).
19. Marris and Rein, *Dilemmas of Social Reform,* p. 167.
20. *Ibid.*
21. *Ibid.*
22. See Chapters 6 and 9 in this volume, pp. 140–142, 275–278.
23. Eric Levine, "Research Report on the Los Angeles CAP." Unpublished paper prepared for the Russell Sage Foundation Study of the Community Action Program, Department of Political Science, University of Chicago, Chicago, Illinois, 1967.
24. Greenstone, *Labor in American Politics,* Chapter IV.
25. Stephen M. and Vera H. Sarasohn, *Political Party Patterns in Michigan* (Detroit: Wayne State University Press, 1957).
26. Wilson, *Negro Politics,* pp. 28–32.
27. See Irving Howe and B. J. Widdick, *The UAW and Walter Reuther* (New York: Random House, 1949).
28. John C. Leggett, *Class, Race and Labor in Detroit* (New York: Oxford University Press, 1968).
29. U.S. Congress, Senate Subcommittee on Employment, Manpower, and Poverty of the Committee on Labor and Public Welfare, *Staff and Consultants Reports, Examination of the War on Poverty VI* (September 1967), Jeffrey Goodman, "Report on Detroit," p. 1741. Hereafter this report will be referred to as Goodman.
30. *Ibid.,* pp. 1743–1744.
31. *Ibid.,* pp. 1743–1745.
32. *Ibid.,* pp. 1744–1745.
33. Alan Rosenbaum, "Participation Programs and Politics—the Federal Impact on the Metropolis." Paper presented at the American Political Science Association Convention, Sept. 8–12, 1970, pp. 20–22.
34. David J. Olson, "Racial Violence and City Politics: The Political Response to Civil Disorders in Three American Cities" (unpublished Ph.D. dissertation, Department of Political Science, University of Wisconsin, 1971), p. 248.

35. Arthur F. Bentley, *The Process of Government,* (Evanston, Ill.: Principia Press, 1935); E. Pendleton Herring, *Group Representation Before Congress* (Baltimore: The Johns Hopkins Press, 1929); David Truman, *The Governmental Process* (New York: Knopf, 1953).
36. Giovanni Sartori, "Concept Misformation in Comparative Politics," *American Political Science Review,* vol. 64 (December 1970), pp. 1042–1043.
37. Wallace Sayre and Herbert Kaufman, *Governing New York City* (New York: Russell Sage, 1960).
38. Theodore Lowi, *At the Pleasure of the Mayor* (New York: The Free Press of Glencoe, 1964).
39. David Rogers, *110 Livingston Street* (New York: Random House, 1968).
40. Michael Lipsky, *Protest in City Politics* (Chicago: Rand McNally, 1970).
41. For many insights related to the discussion of welfare politics in New York City we are indebted to Stephen David. For more on New York City welfare politics, see his "A History of the Internal Political Life of the Community Council of Greater New York" (unpublished Ph.D. dissertation, Department of Government, Columbia University, 1967).
42. U.S. Congress, House Committee on Education and Labor, *Hearings, Examination of the War on Poverty Program,* p. 489.
43. J. David Greenstone and Paul E. Peterson, "Reformers, Machines and the War on Poverty." In James Wilson (Ed.): *City Politics and Public Policy* (New York: Wiley, 1968), pp. 278–286.
44. Machine strength was measured quantitatively by calculating the percentage of vote cast for losing candidates in Democratic primaries for the state house of representatives, as presented in Table 8–2 on p. 237. But note carefully the problem discussed in note on pp. 235–236.
45. Chicago's strong political organization inhibits both the formation and effectiveness of group activity; Detroit's impermeable bureaucracy is almost as effective in limiting group activity; groups in Philadelphia have more influence when they promote their interests, but the culture hardly encourages their formation in the first place; groups in Los Angeles can capture pieces of fragmented structure of Los Angeles but they are not as pervasive a part of political life as in New York.
46. The unions in Los Anegeles are few, but comparatively militant. Yet it is the only one of the cities in which the unions did not successfully organize teachers. Philadelphia unions are stronger, but they do not compare with the steelworkers and other large unions in Chicago, a much more important industrial city. Chicago unions, on the other hand, are not as militant, as organized for independent political action as New York's unions, some of which even have been the basis for a significant third-party movement. Even New York unions do not compare in significance to UAW activity in Detroit, however.
47. The justification for this rank ordering is given at the beginning of the Philadelphia case study. See p. 25, this chapter.
48. Fragmentation of governmental structures in New York approaches that of Los Angeles, though its social and political structures give politics in that city more coherence. Philadelphia's governmental structures have been centralized through reform; it has no borough system comparable to New York's. Detroit's active union movement, strong bureaucracies, and responsible business community focuses political activity in that city. But it is Chicago where scholars have found the most coordinated relationships among strong political institutions.
49. Edward C. Banfield and James Q. Wilson, *City Politics* (Cambridge: Harvard Univer-

sity Press and the M.I.T. Press, 1963), *passim*. See also James Q. Wilson and Edward G. Banfield, "Public Regardingness as a Value Premise in Voting Behavior," *American Political Science Review*, vol. 58 (December 1964), pp. 876–887; and their "Political Ethos Revisited," *Ibid.*, vol. 65 (December 1971), pp. 1048–1062.

50. Raymond Wolfinger and John Osgood Field, "Political Ethos and the Structure of City Government," *American Political Science Review* vol. 60 (June 1966), pp. 306–326.
51. Robert L. Lineberry and Edmund P. Fowler, "Reformism and Public Policies in American Cities," *American Political Science Review*, vol. 61 (September 1967), pp. 701–716. See also the exchange between Wilson and Banfield and Wolfinger and Field in "Communications," *Ibid.*, vol. 60 (December 1966), pp. 998–1000.
52. Elazar, *Cities of the Prairie*, pp. 223–230, 312.
53. *Ibid.*, p. 303.
54. *Ibid.*, p. 310.

NOTES FOR CHAPTER 2

1. Richard Flathman, *The Public Interest* (New York: Wiley, 1966), pp. 15–16.
2. *Ibid.*, pp. 16–17.
3. *Ibid.*, p. 17.
4. David Truman, *The Governmental Process*, 2nd ed. (New York: Knopf, 1971), pp. 34–35.
5. See Glendon Schubert, *The Public Interest* (New York: The Free Press of Glencoe, 1960).
6. See Gordon Tullock, *Private Wants, Public Means* (New York: Basic Books, 1970).
7. *Ibid.*, pp. 108–112.
8. See, as just one example, Norman Frohlich, Joe A. Oppenheimer, and Oran R. Young, *Political Leadership and Collective Goods* (Princeton, N.J.: Princeton University Press, 1971), pp. 12–16.
9. Robert A. Dahl, *Who Governs?* (New Haven: Yale University Press, 1961), p. 93.
10. James Q. Wilson, *Negro Politics: The Search for Leadership* (New York: Free Press, 1960), p. 34.
11. Norton E. Long, *The Polity* (Chicago: Rand McNally, 1962) p. 141.
12. Wallace Sayre and Herbert Kaufman, *Governing New York City* (New York: Russell Sage Foundation, 1960), p. 405.
13. The attribution of certain electoral and organizational interests to political actors by these and other scholars is discussed more fully in Chapter 5 of this volume, pp. 125–127.
14. Flathman, *The Public Interest*, p. 22.
15. *Ibid.*
16. Robert Lineberry and Edmund P. Fowler, "Reformism and Public Policies in American Cities," *American Political Science Review*, vol. 61 (September 1967), p. 712.
17. Raymond E. Wolfinger and John Osgood Field, "Communications," *American Political Science Review*, vol. 62 (March 1968), p. 228.
18. We are following Ralf Dahrendorf's usage in his *Class and Class Conflict in Industrial Society* (Stanford, California: Stanford University Press, 1959).
19. See pp. 52–53 of this chapter.
20. Dahrendorf, *Class and Class Conflict*, pp. 173–179.
21. V. Lenin, "What is to be Done?" In J. Fineberg (Ed.): *The Struggle for the Bolshevik Party*, vol. II, *Selected Works* (New York: International, n.d.), p. 52.

22. William H. Grier and Price M. Cobbs, *Black Rage* (New York: Basic Books, 1968).
23. For a critique of this usage, see Paul E. Peterson, "Historical Particularities and Concept Formation: Comments on Burnett and Palmer," *Studies in Philosophy and Education,* vol. 5 (Fall 1967), 407–422.
24. Charles D. Farris, "A Method of Determining Ideological Groupings in the Congress," *The Journal of Politics,* vol. 20 (1968), pp. 308–338. As reprinted in John C. Wahlke and Heinz Eulau (Eds.): *Legislative Behavior* (New York: Free Press, 1959), pp. 399–413.

    Although Philip Converse deliberately steers away from using the concept, ideology, see also his seminal study "The Nature of Belief Systems in Mass Publics." In David Apter (Ed.): *Ideology and Discontent* (New York: Free Press, 1964), pp. 206–261.
25. Robert Agger, Daniel Goldrich, and Bert Swanson, *The Rulers and the Ruled* (New York: Wiley, 1964), pp. 360–376.

NOTES FOR CHAPTER 3

1. Ralf Dahrendorf, *Class and Class Conflict in Industrial Society* (Stanford, Calif.: Stanford University Press, 1959), p. 129.
2. We have adopted the modification of Dahrendorf's formulation of class interest developed in J. David Greenstone, *Labor In American Politics* (New York: Knopf, 1969), pp. 371ff., except that we refer here to the substantive orientation of economic authorities as *economic* rationalization to avoid confusing it with the regime interest in instrumental rationalization. For the further development of this latter concept, see Chapter 4, of this volume, p. 104.
3. Cf. Dahrendorf's analogous but not identical discussion of role deviants, found in *Class and Class Conflict,* especially pp. 190 ff.
4. See Greenstone, *Labor in American Politics,* p. 384, for a further discussion of these points.
5. John Laslett, *Labor and the Left* (New York: Basic Books, 1970), Ch. VIII, especially pp. 302 ff.
6. T. H. Marshall, *Class, Citizenship, and Social Development* (Garden City, N.Y.: Doubleday, 1964), Chapter IV.
7. Reinhard Bendix, *Nation Building and Citizenship* (New York: Wiley, 1964), Chapters 2 and 3.
8. *Ibid.,* p. 41.
9. *Ibid.,* p. 65.
10. See the discussion in Appendix A, p. 320.
11. Greenstone, *Labor in American Politics,* pp. 70–80.
12. V. O. Key, Jr. coined the term "critical election" in his classic article, "A Theory of Critical Elections," *Journal of Politics,* vol. 17 (February 1955), pp. 3–18. For the most comprehensive and illuminating recent analysis, see Walter Dean Burnham, *Critical Elections and the Mainsprings of American Politics* (New York: Norton, 1970).
13. Robert E. Agger, Daniel Goldrich, and Bert E. Swanson, *The Rulers and the Ruled* (New York: Wiley, 1964), pp. 14–32.
14. Barrington Moore, Jr., *Social Origins of Dictatorship and Democracy: Lord and Peasant in the Making of the Modern World* (Boston: Beacon Press, 1966), p. 121, makes this point about slave owners in the pre-Civil War period.
15. See Chapter 5 of this volume, pp. 149–150.
16. Gunnar Myrdal, *An American Dilemma* (New York: McGraw-Hill, 1964), p. 204.

See also Winthrop Jordan, *White Over Black, American Attitudes toward the Negro, 1550–1812* (Chapel Hill: North Carolina Press, 1968).

17. Myrdal, *An American Dilemma,* p. 58.
18. *Ibid.,* pp. 674–675.
19. *Ibid.,* p. 577.
20. *Ibid.,* p. 613.
21. Harold Cruse, *The Crisis of the Negro Intellectual* (New York: Morrow, 1967) offers one of the strongest statements of this position. See, for example, pp. 102 ff.
22. Myrdal, *An American Dilemma,* pp. 576, 679.
23. John Hope Franklin, "The Two Worlds of Race: A Historical View," *Daedalus,* vol. 94 (Fall 1965), p. 901.
24. *Ibid.,* p. 900.
25. *Ibid.,* p. 913.
26. Robert Coles, "It's the Same, but It's Different," *Daedalus,* vol. 94 (Fall 1965), p. 1111.
27. Cf. Perry Miller, *Errand into the Wilderness* (Cambridge, Mass.: Harvard University Press, 1956).
28. Myrdal, *An American Dilemma,* p. 209.
29. *Ibid.,* pp. 53–54.
30. Thomas F. Pettigrew, "Complexity and Change in American Racial Patterns: A Social Psychological View," *Daedalus,* vol. 94 (Fall 1965), p. 975.
31. St. Clair Drake, "The Social and Economic Status of the Negro in the United States," *Daedalus,* vol. 94 (Fall 1965), p. 772.
32. *Ibid.,* p. 771.
33. Stokely Carmichael and Charles V. Hamilton, *Black Power: The Politics of Liberation in America* (New York: Vintage Books, 1967), pp. 19–20.
34. Pettigrew, "Complexity and Change," p. 986.
35. Loren Miller, "The Protest Against Housing Segregation." In Raymond J. Murphy and Howard Elinson (Eds.): *Problems and Prospects of the Negro Movement* (Belmont, Calif.: Wadsworth, 1966), pp. 159–166.
36. Karen Orren, "Life Insurance Politics in Illinois" (unpublished Ph.D. dissertation, The University of Chicago, 1972).
37. Loren Miller, "The Protest Against Housing Segregation," p. 160.
38. William H. Grier and Price M. Cobbs, *Black Rage* (New York: Basic Books, 1968). See also, Joel Kovel, *White Racism: A Psychohistory* (New York: Vintage Books, 1970).
39. Drake, "The Social and Economic Status of the Negro," p. 768.
40. Coles, "It's the Same," pp. 1107 and 1110.
41. Daniel Elazar, *Cities of the Prairie* (New York: Basic Books, 1970), pp. 229–234.
42. Myrdal, *An American Dilemma,* p. 540, Chapter 26; and Pettigrew: "Complexity and Change," p. 979.
43. Drake, "The Social and Economic Status of the Negro," p. 788.
44. Dwaine Marvick, "The Political Socialization of the American Negro." In Harry A. Bailey, Jr. (Ed.): *Negro Politics* (Columbus, Ohio: Merrill, 1967), p. 42.
45. See Maurice Zeitlin, *Revolutionary Politics and the Cuban Working Class* (Princeton, N.J.: Princeton University Press, 1967).
46. Orren, "Life Insurance Politics in Illinois."
47. Edward LaMonte, "Manpower Development and Training Act of 1962" (unpublished M.A. thesis, The University of Chicago, 1968).
48. Drake, "The Social and Economic Status of the Negro," p. 804.

49. Talcott Parsons, "Full Citizenship for the Negro American? A Sociological Problem," *Daedalus,* vol. 94 (Fall 1965), p. 1050. But see p. 90 of this chapter, for Parsons' opposition to the perpetuation of such ascriptive categories as race over the long run.
50. Bendix, *Nation Building and Citizenship,* p. 61 ff.
51. John Stuart Mill, *Principles of Political Economy II* (Boston: Charles C. Little and James Brown, 1848), pp. 322–323. Quoted by Bendix, *Nation Building and Citizenship,* pp. 62–63.
52. *Ibid.*
53. Parsons, "Full Citizenship for the Negro American?" p. 1039.
54. *Ibid.*
55. *Ibid.*
56. *Ibid.,* p. 1022.
57. Carmichael and Hamilton, *Black Power,* p. 10.
58. *Ibid.,* p. 75.
59. Cruse, *The Crisis of the Negro Intellectual,* pp. 120 and 226.
60. *Ibid.,* pp. 98–99.
61. Cf. Parsons, "Full Citizenship for the Negro American?" p. 1023.
62. Cruse, *The Crisis of the Negro Intellectual,* pp. 96–111.
63. *Ibid.,* pp. 202–203.
64. Samuel Huntington, *Political Order in Changing Societies* (New Haven: Yale University Press, 1968).
65. Daniel P. Moynihan, *Maximum Feasible Misunderstanding: Community Action in the War on Poverty* (New York: Free Press, 1969), especially p. 87.

NOTES FOR CHAPTER 4

1. Edward C. Banfield, *Political Influence* (New York: Free Press, 1961), pp. 270–271.
2. Charles E. Lindblom, "The Science of 'Muddling Through'," *Public Administration Review,* vol. 14 (Spring 1959), pp. 79–88.
3. Banfield, *Political Influence,* Chapter 12; Robert Dahl and Charles Lindblom, *Politics, Economics, and Welfare* (New York: Harper & Row, 1953), pp. 82–85. See also, Lindblom's "Review of Richard Flathman's *The Public Interest,*" *The American Political Science Review,* vol. 60 (December 1966), p. 1008.
4. Robert Dahl, *A Preface to Democratic Theory* (Chicago: The University of Chicago Press, 1956), p. 90.
5. Gary Orfield, *The Reconstruction of Southern Education* (New York: Wiley, 1969), relates this story in rich and fascinating detail.
6. Dahl. *A Preface to Democratic Theory,* p. 90.
7. E. Pendleton Herring, *Group Representation Before Congress* (Baltimore: The Johns Hopkins Press, 1929); Herbert Agar, *The Price of Union* (Boston: Houghton Mifflin, 1950).
8. Dahl, *A Preface to Democratic Theory,* p. 14.
9. *Ibid.,* pp. 30–31.
10. Instrumental rationalization is not identical to economic rationalization, since its reference is limited simply to public administration and it may in specific instances actually frustrate the maximization of profit or production. The concept of economic rationalization has been developed and applied in J. David Greenstone's *Labor in American Politics* (New York: Knopf, 1969), Chapter XI.
11. Ralf Dahrendorf, *Class and Class Conflict in Industrial Society* (Stanford, California: Stanford University Press, 1959), *passim,* especially pp. 30–31, 136, 172–173.

12. In particular, we note Clifford Geertz, "Ideology as a Cultural System." In David Apter (Ed.): *Ideology and Discontent* (New York: The Free Press of Glencoe, 1964), pp. 47–76; and Robert E. Lane, *Political Ideology* (New York: The Free Press, 1962).
13. Robert Agger, Daniel Goldrich, and Bert E. Swanson, *The Rulers and the Ruled* (New York: Wiley, 1964), pp. 760–776.
14. Edward C. Banfield and James Q. Wilson, *City Politics* (Cambridge, Mass.: Harvard University Press and The M.I.T. Press, 1963), pp. 125–127, and the material cited therein.
15. Agger, Goldrich, and Swanson, *The Rulers,* seem to realize this at one point themselves (see p. 762).
16. Michael Paul Rogin, in *McCarthy and the Intellectuals: The Radical Specter* (Cambridge, Mass.: The M.I.T. Press, 1967), Ch. II, emphasizes the different mixtures of pragmatic and moralistic elements in most important political perspectives, undermining thereby the distinction between ideologues and pragmatists. Our point here is slightly different. Even the "pure" pragmatism of the machine politicians was principled.
17. See Arthur J. Vidich and Joseph Bensman, *Small Town in Mass Society* (Garden City, N.Y.: Anchor Books, Doubleday, 1958), pp. 111–139, for a discussion of the techniques for minimizing conflicts small-town politicians follow in protecting their personal relationships with one another. Agger, Goldrich, and Swanson, *The Rulers,* in Ch. XI discuss social ostracism as an instrument used for sustaining political power in small towns.
18. Cf. Lester Salamon, "Fear, Apathy, and Discrimination: A Test of Three Explanations of Political Participation Among the Poor," *American Political Science Review,* forthcoming.
19. Seymour J. Mandelbaum, *Boss Tweed's New York* (New York: Wiley, 1965), *passim.*
20. *Ibid.,* p. 168.
21. For a discussion of these practices, see Harold Gosnell, *Machine Politics: Chicago Model* (Chicago: University of Chicago Press, 1968), p. 44; and Leo Snowiss, "The Metropolitan Congressman" (unpublished Ph.D. dissertation, Department of Political Science, University of Chicago, 1965), p. 92.
22. James Bryce, *The American Commonwealth,* vol. II (New York: Macmillan, 1895), p. 97.
23. Banfield and Wilson, *City Politics,* p. 115.
24. Edward J. Flynn, *You're the Boss* (New York: Viking Press, 1947), p. 47.
25. George Washington Plunkitt, "How to Get a Political Following." In Edward C. Banfield, *Urban Government* (New York: The Free Press of Glencoe, 1961), p. 155. Reprinted from "Plunkitt of Tammany Hall," recorded by William L. Riordon (New York: McClure Phillips, 1905).
26. Agger, Goldrich, and Swanson, *The Rulers,* pp. 760–776.
27. Greenstone, *Labor in American Politics,* Chapters II and III.
28. Agger, Goldrich, and Swanson, *The Rulers,* pp. 14 ff.
29. An excellent statement of the views of nineteenth-century theorists on democracy as distinguished from the pluralist viewpoint is given in Jack L. Walker, "A Critique of Elitist Theory of Democracy," *American Political Science Review,* vol. 60 (June, 1966), pp. 285–296.
30. M. Ostrogorski, *Democracy and the Organization of Political Parties* (Garden City, N.Y.: Doubleday, 1964), p. 300.
31. Banfield and Wilson, *City Politics,* p. 345.

32. Banfield, *Political Influence*, pp. 260–262.
33. Zbigniew Brzezinski, "The American Transition" *The New Republic,* vol. 157 (December 23, 1967), p. 19.
34. Wallace Sayre and Herbert Kaufman, *Governing New York City* (New York: Russell Sage, 1960).
35. Agger, Goldrich, and Swanson, *The Rulers,* p. 27.
36. *Ibid.,* p. 25.
37. *Ibid.,* p. 27.
38. *Ibid.,* p. 21.
39. Robert Wiebe, *Businessmen and Reform: A Study of the Progressive Movement* (Cambridge, Mass.: Harvard University Press, 1967), p. 212.
40. Rogin, *McCarthy and the Intellectuals,* p. 198.

NOTES FOR CHAPTER 5

1. Edward C. Banfield, *Political Influence* (New York: Free Press, 1961); Robert A. Dahl, *Who Governs? Democracy and Power in an American City* (New Haven, Conn.: Yale University Press, 1961); and Norton Long, "The Local Community as an Ecology of Games," *American Journal of Sociology,* vol. 66 (November 1958), pp. 251–261.

   Other works that also explicitly and implicitly use one variation or another of the electoral/organizational interest model include Wallace Sayre and Herbert Kaufman, *Governing New York City* (New York: Russell Sage, 1960); James Q. Wilson, *The Amateur Democrat* (Chicago: University of Chicago Press, 1962); Michael Lipsky and David J. Olson, "Riot Commission Politics," *Transaction,* vol. 6 (July–August, 1969). pp. 9–21; David Rogers, *110 Livingston Street* (New York: Random House, 1968); and Aaron Wildavsky, *Leadership in a Small Town* (Totowa, N.J.; Bedminister Press, 1964). While still other works could be cited, the point is that scholars with a wide range of orientations and concerns find themselves comfortably using it.
2. This argument, of course, is not peculiar to the literature in urban politics. In fact it has been developed and applied most successfully in national electoral politics both here and abroad. See, for example, Joseph A. Schumpeter, *Capitalism, Socialism and Democracy* (New York: Holt, Rinehart and Winston, 1960); V. O. Key, Jr., *The Responsible Electorate* (Cambridge, Mass.: Harvard University Press, 1966); E. E. Schattschneider, *Party Government* (New York: Holt, Rinehart and Winston, 1942); and Seymour M. Lipset, *Political Man: The Social Bases of Politics* (Garden City, N.Y.: Doubleday, 1963).
3. Max Weber, "Politics as a Vocation." In H. H. Gerth and C. Wright Mills (Eds.): *From Max Weber* (New York: Oxford University Press, 1958), p. 109.
4. Anthony Downs, *An Economic Theory of Democracy* (New York: Holt, Rinehart and Winston, 1957).
5. William H. Riker, *The Theory of Political Coalitions* (New Haven, Conn.: Yale University Press, 1962).
6. See Banfield, *Political Influence.* In papers later published in *The Polity* (Chicago: Rand McNally, 1962), Norton Long anticipated much of Banfield's argument.
7. See, for example, Banfield, *Political Influence,* Chapter 12, especially p. 328.
8. J. David Greenstone and Paul E. Peterson, "Reformers, Machines and the War on Poverty. In James Q. Wilson (Ed.): *City Politics and Public Policy* (New York: Wiley, 1968), pp. 267–292.

9. Downs, *An Economic Theory*, pp. 100–102.
10. For example, Robert A. Dahl, in "A Critique of the Ruling Elite Model," *American Political Science Review*, vol. 52 (June, 1958), p. 469, objects to attributing interests to groups or individuals unless they themselves recognize them. "One could argue," he says, "that even in a society like ours a ruling elite might be so influential over ideas, attitudes, and opinions that a kind of false consensus will exist—not the phony consensus of a terroristic totalitarian dictatorship, but the manipulated and superficially self-imposed adherence to the norms and goals of the elite by broad sections of a community. A good deal of Professor [C. Wright] Mills' argument can be interpreted in this way, although it is not clear to me whether this is where he means to rest his case. . . .

    "[But] either the consensus is perpetual and unbreakable, in which case there is no conceivable way of determining who is ruler and who is ruled. Or it is not. But if it is not, then there is some point in the process of forming opinions at which the one group will be seen to initiate and veto, while the rest merely respond." Dahl's argument in this passage rejects a latent role-interest analysis, because it depends on overt expressions of opinion as the only mechanism for determining an individual's interests.

    Dahl, in *Who Governs?* p. 93, on the other hand, states that interests can be attributed to politicians in their role as politicians. In an argument that is consistent with the one we present in the text, he writes: "Despite the stereotype, party politicians are not necessarily concerned *only* with winning elections, for the man who is a party politician in one role may in another, be a member of a particular interest group, social stratum, neighborhood, race, ethnic group, occupation, or profession. In this role he may himself help to generate issues. However, simply qua party politician, he not only has a powerful incentive to search for politically profitable issues, but he has an equally strong motive for staying clear of issues he thinks will not produce a net gain in his votes in the next election."
11. Frances Fox Piven, "The Urban Crisis: Who Got What, and Why." In Robert Paul Wolff (Ed.): *1984 Revisited* (New York: Random House, forthcoming).
12. Steven M. Loveday, *Wall Street Journal*, February 18, 1966.
13. The distinction between substantive and symbolic policies is drawn from Murray Edelman, *The Symbolic Uses of Politics* (Urbana, Ill.: University of Illinois Press, 1964).
14. This study was eventually published. See the Institute of Public Administration, *The Administration of Services to Children and Youth in New York City* (New York Institute of Public Administration, 1963).
15. In addition to data from primary sources, this analysis draws upon information reported in the following manuscripts: Donald S. Bradley, "Community Leadership in Two Chicago Inner-City Areas," Research Report No. 4, Center for Social Organization Studies, Department of Sociology, University of Chicago, March, 1967; and Isaac Balbus, "The Evolution of the Community Action Program: A Case Study in American Policy-Making" (unpublished M.A. dissertation, University of Chicago, 1966).
16. In addition to our own interviewing, we are drawing upon data on the Philadelphia juvenile delinquency program reported in Peter Marris and Martin Rein, *Dilemmas of Social Reform* (New York: Atherton Press, 1967), Chapter IV. We are indebted to Professor Rein for his permission to examine this chapter prior to publication.
17. See p. 26 of Chapter 1 for a discussion of these developments.

18. Warren Eisenberg, "Bungle in the Jungle," *Greater Philadelphia Magazine* (December 1964), p. 100.
19. Banfield, *Political Influence,* pp. 27–73.
20. James Ridgeway, "Poor Chicago: Down and Out with Mayor Daley," *New Republic* (May 15, 1965), vol. 152, pp. 17–20.
21. Banfield, *Political Influence,* pp. 264–265.
22. *Philadelphia Bulletin,* January 30, 1965.
23. *Philadelphia Inquirer,* January 24, 1965.
24. *New York Herald Tribune,* May 11, 1965.
25. *The New York Times,* April 17, 1965.
26. *New York Post,* April 18, 1965.
27. *New York Daily News,* April 17, 1965.
28. *New York Journal American,* May 13, 1965.
29. *Chicago Sun-Times,* April 16, 1965.
30. *Chicago Tribune,* April 16, 1965.
31. Because of this tension between low-income whites and blacks, Samuel Lubell argued as early as 1964 that "for some years to come the likely pattern of political conflict promises to be stormier at the local and state levels than at the presidential level." Samuel Lubell, *White and Black: Test of a Nation* (New York: Harper & Row, 1964), p. 160.
32. Walter Dean Burnham, *Critical Elections and the Mainsprings of American Politics* (New York: Norton, 1970), pp. 159–166.
33. David J. Olson, "Racial Violence and City Politics: The Political Response to Civil Disorder in Three American Cities" (unpublished Ph.D. dissertation, Department of Political Science, University of Wisconsin, Madison, 1971).
34. Wilson, *The Amateur Democrat,* pp. 52–58.
35. *Ibid.,* p. 226.
36. U.S. Congress, House Committee on Education and Labor, *Hearings, Examination of the War on Poverty Program,* 89th Congress, 1st Session, 1965, p. 483.
37. *Los Angeles Times,* May 27, 1965.
38. *Ibid.,* May 29, 1965.
39. Emphasis added. *Philadelphia Bulletin,* February 8, 1965.
40. These precautions are elaborated in Chapter 6.
41. Theodore J. Lowi, "Machine Politics: Old and New," *The Public Interest* (Fall 1967), pp. 89–90.

NOTES FOR CHAPTER 6

1. Office of Economic Opportunity, *Community Action Program Guide* (Washington, D.C., 1965), vol. I, p. 18.
2. Hanna Pitkin, *The Concept of Representation* (Berkeley: University of California Press, 1967).
3. *Ibid.,* p. 11.
4. *Ibid.,* p. 43.
5. *Ibid.,* Chapter IV.
6. *Ibid.,* p. 111.
7. *Ibid.,* pp. 209–210.
8. Samuel Huntington, "Political Development and Political Decay," *World Politics* (April 1965), vol. 17, pp. 412–413.
9. See, for example, descriptions of the machine in Richard Hofstadter, *The Age of Reform* (New York: Random House, 1955); and in Martin Meyerson and Edward C.

Banfield, Politics, *Planning and the Public Interest* (New York: Free Press of Glencoe, 1955).

10. CAP officials in Oakland also eliminated middle-class neighborhood leadership seeking to provide universalistic interest representation by requiring that representatives be socially descriptive of their constituency (i.e., having annual incomes of less than $3,000). Nicholas Masters *et al., Politics, Poverty, and Education: An Analysis of Decision-Making Structures,* Report submitted to the Office of Economic Opportunity, Washington, D.C. (February 1968), p. 253.
11. This analysis is based on research in three of Chicago's seven NSCs, including a white and Puerto Rican community on the North Side, a better-organized, more stable Negro community on the South Side, and a disorganized slum providing the first home for southern Negro migrants on the West Side. We wish to thank Isaac Balbus, Marguerite Barnett, and Rennie Davis for granting their permission to use material they have gathered on Chicago's CAP. More supporting evidence for the argument presented here can be found in Paul E. Peterson, "City Politics and Community Action: The Implementation of the Community Action Program in Three American Cities" (unpublished Ph.D. dissertation, University of Chicago, 1967), Chapter III.
12. Mark J. Solomon, "The Los Angeles Neighborhood Adult Participation Project: A Definition of Community Action" (unpublished Masters paper, Department of Political Science, University of Chicago, February, 1970), pp. 66, 84.
13. *Los Angeles Times,* April 4, 1966, as cited in Solomon, "The Los Angeles Neighborhood Adult Participation Project," p. 74.
14. In addition to observation of city-wide developments in Philadelphia, research was conducted in three randomly selected neighborhood council areas. This research is reported in further detail in Peterson, "City Politics," Chapter IV.
15. Arthur B. Shostak, "Containment, Co-option, or Co-determination?" *The American Child,* vol. 47, p. 17.
16. Since the representatives of the poor continued to have some influence over employment of "nonprofessionals," it is an exaggeration to say, as did one close observer of the program, that the "poor were rendered as powerless as ever." Arthur B. Shostak, "Urban Politics and Poverty," Paper presented at the annual meeting of the American Sociological Association, 1966, p. 2. (Mimeographed). Yet the fact that this same observer had earlier reported such a glowing picture of poor people participating in policy-making discloses the declining representation of the poor in Philadelphia. See the article in Note 15 for his earlier, optimistic analysis.
17. See Chapter 1, pp. 37–38.
18. See Chapter 7, pp. 212–214, for a more detailed discussion.
19. Because of the need to examine operating programs in a city where the CAP was slow in being implemented, we selected for investigation the first three neighborhoods in which a CAP was operating. Thus, although data on city-wide developments were collected, this report draws largely upon developments on the Lower West Side and in East Harlem in Manhattan, and in the Bedford-Stuyvesant area of Brooklyn. New York's CAP is discussed in greater detail in Peterson, "City Politics," Chapter V.
20. See Chapter 7, p. 211.
21. A detailed analysis of the attempts by representatives of the poor to change the structure and policies of East Harlem's educational system can be found in Paul E. Peterson, "The Politics of Education Reform." In Frank Lutz (Ed.): *Toward Improved Urban Education* (Columbus, Ohio: Jones, 1970), pp. 209–230.

22. U.S. Congress, Senate Subcommittee on Employment, Manpower and Poverty of the Committee on Labor and Public Welfare, *Staff and Consultants Reports, Examination of the War on Poverty VI* (September 1967), Jeffrey Goodman, "Report on Detroit," p. 1828, hereinafter cited as Goodman, "Report on Detroit."
23. *Ibid.*, p. 1724.
24. Gerald Suttles, *The Social Order of the Slum* (Chicago: University of Chicago Press, 1968), pp. 5–6.
25. *Ibid.*, p. 8.
26. V.O. Key, *Southern Politics* (New York: Knopf, 1950), p. 37.
27. While records were kept on the number of voters for each CAC area as a whole, the number of voters for each voting section within the areas could not be obtained directly. Although the number of votes cast for each candidate within each voting section was available, the sum of these votes could not be accepted as a direct measure of the number of voters because each person was permitted to vote for as many as twelve candidates. Neither was the solution to divide the total number of votes cast in an election by twelve, since many people did not fully utilize all twelve votes. We felt that the best, though far from satisfactory, solution was to assume that at each of the four polling places within a CAC area the voters used equal amounts of their total voting power. Such an assumption enabled us to formulate the following proportion:

$$\frac{S_v}{S_b} = \frac{A_v}{A_b}$$

where S_v equals the total number of voters in the voting section, S_b equals the total number of ballots cast for all candidates in the voting section, A_v equals the number of voters in the CAC area, and A_b equals the total number of ballots cast for all candidates in the CAC area. Since three of the four quantities were known, we were able to solve for the fourth, giving us an estimate of the number of voters in each voting section.

Where more candidates ran for office in a section, it is possible that voters used more amounts of their voting power in order to vote for several of their friends and neighbors on the ballot. If so, this would mean that our assumption that voters used equal amounts of their voting power in estimating the number of voters biases the findings in the direction of estimating more voters in sections that had more candidates. Some of the high correlation between number of candidates and voter turnout, therefore, may be attributable to the exercise of greater voting power by voters in those sections that had more candidates. Even if this were the case, however, it would in no way be contrary to our basic contention that voting behavior was affected by friends-and-neighbors politics.
28. The size and characteristics of the total population in the sample areas were estimated from data made available by Richard H. Uhlig of the Philadelphia Health and Welfare Council. Since voting areas (and sections within areas) did not correspond with census tracts in a number of cases, all calculations based on these data are subject to some error. In addition, our estimate of the population was based on all people eighteen years and older reported in the 1960 census data. Since voting was limited to those twenty-one years and older, our figures underestimate the percentage of those eligible that voted. However, unless the age distribution for the three years, eighteen to twenty-one, varies substantially from one neighborhood to another, it is unlikely that this affects interarea comparisons.
29. Two candidates were excluded from the analysis, because it was impossible to ascertain in which voting section they lived.

30. Of the thirty-five candidates who ran in the Los Angeles elections, we were able to obtain reasonably accurate information on place of residence for thirty-two. Even for some of the thirty-two, we were only able to obtain a general location, such as the City of Pomona. In these cases we counted all the election places within that area as local sections. In addition, as pointed out in the text, for Gutierrez we considered as local sections all those sections where her organization was strong.
31. Although there were only thirty-two candidates for whom a home section could be identified, there were forty-four such sections, because, as pointed out in Note 30, some candidates were regarded as having more than one home section. It should also be noted that three of the 145 sections regarded as having no candidate presumably had living within them one of the three candidates whose place of residence could not be determined.
32. Angus Campbell, Philip E. Converse, Warren E. Miller, and Donald E. Stokes, *The American Voter* (New York: Wiley, 1964).
33. See, for example, Grant McConnell, *Private Power and American Democracy* (New York: Alfred Knopf, 1966).
34. Educational authorities in one community in Great Britain sought to decrease the influence of teachers over policy-making by holding elections as a means of selecting teacher representatives rather than permitting the representatives to be chosen by teacher organizations. Even with this obviously middle-class constituency, the strategy worked to some extent. See Paul E. Peterson, "British Interest Group Theory Re-examined: The Politics of Comprehensive Education in Three British Cities," *Comparative Politics* (April 1971), vol. 3, pp. 393–395.

NOTES FOR CHAPTER 7

1. Wallace Sayre and Herbert Kaufman, *Governing New York City* (New York: Russell Sage Foundation, 1960), Chapter XI.
2. *Ibid.*, pp. 405–407.
3. Cf. Herbert Simon, "Birth of an Organization: the Economic Co-operation Administration," *Public Administration Review*, vol. 13 (1953), pp. 227–236.
4. See Chapter 9, pp. 272–273.
5. See Chapter 1, p. 27; Chapter 5, pp. 137–139.
6. U.S. House of Representatives, Committee on Education and Labor, *Hearings, Examination of the War on Poverty Program*, 89th Cong., 1st Sess., 1965, p. 489.
7. The autonomy of even Chicago's school system is discussed in Paul E. Peterson and Thomas R. Williams, *School Politics: Chicago Model*, in preparation.
8. Sayre and Kaufman, *Governing New York City*, Chapter XI.
9. Theodore Lowi, *At the Pleasure of the Mayor* (New York: Free Press, 1964), Chapters IV and V.
10. The attentive reader will note here an application of the electoral/organizational interest model developed in Chapter 5 of this volume.
11. Daniel Elazar, *Cities of the Prairie* (New York: Basic Books, 1970), pp. 258–262. Inasmuch as Elazar sees a blending of the traditional and individualistic cultures in the contemporary period (p. 266), this does not contradict the argument that Philadelphia had a comparatively "traditional" culture, which was made in Chapter 1 of this volume.
12. See Chapter 1 of this volume, pp. 31–33.
13. See Chapter 1 of this volume, pp. 30–31.
14. *Detroit Free Press*, January 14, 1966.
15. *Infra*, Chapter 7, p. 222.

16. Marver H. Bernstein, *Regulating Business by Independent Commission* (Princeton, N.J.: Princeton University Press, 1955).
17. Philip Selznick, *Leadership in Administration* (New York: Harper & Row, 1957). See also Michael Lipsky and David J. Olson, *Riot Commission Politics: The Processing of Racial Crisis in America* (New York: Dutton, forthcoming).
18. U.S. Congress, *An Act to Mobilize the Human and Financial Resources of the Nation to Combat Poverty in the United States,* Public Law 88–452, 88th Cong., 2nd Sess., 1964, p. 9.
19. Mark J. Solomon, "The Los Angeles Neighborhood Adult Participation Project: A Definition of Community Action" (unpublished Masters paper, Department of Political Science, University of Chicago, February 1970), pp. 4–5.
20. Robert Michels, *Political Parties* (New York: Collier, 1962).
21. Some of the problems of genuinely testing the effectiveness of any CAPs are pointed out in Peter Marris and Martin Rein, *Dilemmas of Social Reform* (New York: Atherton, 1967), Chapter VIII.
22. The exception, Ursula Gutierrez is discussed in Chapter 1 (p. 33) and Chapter 6 (pp. 176, 195) of this volume.
23. See Chapter 1 (p. 38) of this volume.
24. Edward Banfield and James Q. Wilson, *City Politics* (New York: Random House, 1963), p. 345.

NOTES FOR CHAPTER 8

1. See, for example, Robert A. Dahl's discussion of the permeability of the political stratum in *Who Governs?* (New Haven: Yale University Press, 1961), pp. 90–94.
2. Thomas Dye has stated this argument most boldly: "The linkage between socioeconomic inputs and policy outcomes is an unbroken one, and . . . characteristics of political systems do not independently influence policy outcomes. Political systems are, by definition, the structure and processes which function to make public policy, but these systems do not so much mediate between societal requirements and public policy as they reflect social requirements in public policy." Thomas R. Dye, *Politics, Economics and the Public Policy Outcomes in the American States* (Chicago: Rand McNally, 1966), as reprinted in Duane Lockard, *Governing the States and Localities* (London: Macmillan, 1969), p. 146. See also Dye's, "Malapportionment and Public Policy in the States," *Journal of Politics* (August 1965), vol. 27, pp. 586–601, for a similar argument, at least implicitly.

   See also, Raymond E. Wolfinger and John O. Field, "Political Ethos and the Structure of City Government," *American Political Science Review* (June 1966), vol. 60, pp. 306–326. The article is reprinted in Richard Hofferbert and Ira Sharkansky, *State and Urban Politics* (Boston: Little, Brown, 1971), pp. 194–231. Wolfinger and Field are much clearer on the nature of the assumptions underlying this methodologically sophisticated work than are many of the students in this area. Wolfinger and Field explicity state, for example, that "these inferences are based on the assumptions that the strength of the public- and private-regarding ethics is related to the magnitude of the population groupings that supposedly give rise to one ethos or the other, *and* that the two ethics are important causal factors in city politics." (Hofferbert and Sharkansky, p. 204). And the authors quite properly continue with the observation that Banfield and Wilson (whose theory they are testing) seem to have made the same assumption: "Obviously the social and ecological structures of a city largely determine which view as to the proper role of government will prevail in it." (Hofferbert and Sharkansky, p. 204). Lineberry and Fowler's critique of Wolfinger and Field's analysis questions this assumption: "It may also be dubious to assume that the size of an ethnic population is an accurate indicator of influence of ethnic groups." Robert L. Lineberry and Edmund Fowler, "Reformism and Public Policies in American Cities, "*American Political Science Review* (September 1967), vol. 61, pp. 701–716. This citation taken from Hofferbert and Sharkansky's reprint of the work, p. 242.

3. Mancur Olson, Jr., *The Logic of Collective Action* (Cambridge, Mass.: Harvard University Press, 1965).
4. Norman Frolich, Joseph Oppenheimer, and Oran R. Young, *Political Leadership and Collective Goods* (Princeton, N.J.: Princeton University Press, 1971).
5. James Q. Wilson, *Negro Politics* (New York: Free Press of Glencoe, 1960), p. 45. See also V. O. Key, Jr., *American State Politics* (New York: Knopf, 1963), p. 181.
6. The number of candidates aspiring for political office is, to be sure, related to the probability of the party's winning the general election. Where the party has little chance, there may be only one candidate, however weak the organization. But here we are comparing the dominant party organization in each city. Since the Democratic party does well in all three cities in general elections, there are few "safe" Republican seats; thus, this factor should not pose a problem for our intercity comparison.
7. Edward C. Banfield and James Q. Wilson's argument is developed in *City Politics* (New York: Random House, 1963). For further references, see Note 2 of this chapter.
8. Theodore Lowi, *At the Pleasure of the Mayor* (New York: Free Press, 1964).
9. The Democrats had slated both men that year because the Chicago machine had during the preceding two years reached its nadir point by becoming involved in a nasty school scandal that had driven Mayor Kelly from office and because the machine assumed neither would be elected with Harry Truman leading the ticket. James Q. Wilson stresses the importance of Adlai Stevenson's candidacy for the modern reform-club movement. *The Amateur Democrat* (Chicago: University of Chicago Press, 1962), pp. 52–58.
10. Although somewhat dated, a good portrait of the functioning of the Chicago City Council is given in Martin Meyerson and Edward C. Banfield, *Politics, Planning and the Public Interest* (New York: Free Press, 1955), Chapter III.
11. Leo Snowiss, "The Metropolitan Congressman" (unpublished Ph.D. dissertation. Department of Political Science, University of Chicago, 1965), p. 403.
12. Edward J. Flynn, *You're the Boss* (New York: Viking Press, 1947), pp. 53–55.
13. The significance for local politics of national partisan elections, a matter that has been overlooked by most critics of the urban reform movement, is most obvious in British local politics, where the impact of the national trend on localities is overwhelmingly important. The whole problem is examined in some detail in Paul E. Peterson and Paul Kantor, "Citizen Participation, Political Parties, and Democratic Theory: An Analysis of Local Politics in England," Paper presented at the American Political Science Association Convention, Los Angeles, California, September, 1970.
14. Alex Gottfried, *Boss Cermak of Chicago* (Seattle: University of Washington Press, 1962), Chapter XI.
15. *Ibid.*, p. 317.
16. See the more detailed discussion of the conservative character of Philadelphia reformers in Chapter 1 of this volume, pp. 25–27.
17. A good summary of events during this period can be found in Gary Orfield, *The Reconstruction of Southern Education* (New York: Wiley, 1969), Chapter IV. See

also Mary Herrick, *The Chicago Public Schools: A Social and Political History* (Beverly Hills, Calif.: Sage Publications, 1971), Chapters XVI and XVII.

18. Michael Lipsky, *Protest in City Politics* (Chicago: Rand McNally, 1970), p. 3, his emphasis.
19. Isaac Balbus, "Rebellion and Response: A Comparative Study of the Administration of Justice Following Urban Ghetto Revolts in Three American Cities" (unpublished Ph.D. dissertation, Department of Political Science, University of Chicago, 1970), Chapters III and IV. See also Isaac Balbus, *The Dialectics of Legal Repression* (New York: Russell Sage, 1973).
20. J. David Greenstone, *Labor in American Politics* (New York: Alfred Knopf, 1968), Chapter V.
21. Wilson, *The Amateur Democrat,* pp. 377–388.
22. The median year of schooling in Los Angeles in 1960 was 12.2, while in Detroit it was only 9.7. The average 1959 family income for the two cities was more similar: $7,831 for Los Angeles, $7,146 for Detroit.
23. Robert Agger, *et al., The Rulers and the Ruled* (New York: Wiley, 1964), pp. 158–167, 466–471, 600–613.
24. These points are made in Eugene C. Lee. *The Politics of Nonpartisanship* (Berkeley: University of California Press, 1960); Oliver P. Williams and Charles R. Adrian, "The Insulation of Local Politics under the Nonpartisan Ballot," *American Political Science Review* (December, 1959), vol. 53, pp. 1059–1061; and Edward C. Banfield and James Wilson, *City Politics* (Cambridge: Harvard University Press, 1963), Chapter XXI. A skeptical review of these critiques of urban reform can be found in Peterson and Kantor, "Citizen Participation."
25. E. E. Schattschneider, *The Semi-Sovereign People* (New York: Holt, Rinehart & Winston, 1960), p. 71.

NOTES FOR CHAPTER 9

1. Robert Crain, *The Politics of Desegregation* (Chicago: Aldine Press, 1968), pp. 147–148, discusses the tendency of civil rights groups to increase the intensity of conflict, the less responsive governmental officials are.
2. Robert A. Dahl, *Who Governs?* (New Haven: Yale University Press, 1961), p. 305.
3. See Andrew MacFarland, *Power and Leadership in Pluralist Systems* (Stanford, Calif.: Stanford University Press, 1969), Chap. VIII for a discussion of the differences between the structuralist and behavioralist (or what we have called in the text a process) view of political life.
4. James Reichley, *The Art of Government: Reform and Organization Politics in Philadelphia* (New York: Fund for the Republic, 1959.)
5. U.S. Congress, House Committee on Education and Labor, *Hearings, Examination of the War on Poverty Program,* 89th Cong., 1st Sess., 1965, p. 585.
6. Edward C. Banfield, *Political Influence* (New York: Free Press, 1961), pp. 270–276.
7. Dahl, *Who Governs?,* p. 305.
8. U.S. Congress, House Committee on Education and Labor, p. 489.
9. Theodore J. Lowi, "American Business, Public Policy, Case Studies and Political Theory," *World Politics* (July 1964), vol. 16, pp. 690–691.
10. *Ibid.,* p. 690.
11. *Ibid.,* pp. 691, 707 (Note 28).
12. *Ibid.,* see the diagram on p. 713. Some of the points developed in this paragraph are our own extrapolation of Lowi's argument.
13. *Ibid.,* p. 713.

14. *Ibid.*, p. 701.
15. *Ibid.*, p. 703.
16. *Ibid.*, pp. 711–712.
17. *Ibid.*, pp. 703, 705.
18. Walter Dean Burnham, *Critical Elections and the Mainsprings of American Politics* (New York: Norton, 1970), *passim* but see especially Chapter VI.
19. David J. Olson, "Racial Violence and City Politics: The Political Response to Civil Disorders in Three American Cities" (unpublished Ph.D. dissertation, Department of Political Science, University of Wisconsin, 1971).
20. Isaac Balbus, "Rebellion and Response; A Comparative Study of the Administration of Justice Following Urban Ghetto Revolts in Three American Cities" (unpublished Ph.D. dissertation, Department of Political Science, University of Chicago, 1970), Chapter IV.
21. Alan Rosenbaum, "Participation Programs and Politics: The Federal Impact on the Metropolis" (paper presented before the American Political Science Association Convention, September 8–12, 1970).
22. Marilyn Gittell and T. Edward Hollander, *Six Urban School District: A Comparative Study of Institutional Response* (New York: Praeger, 1968).
23. Joel Aberbach and Jack Walker, "Political Trust and Racial Ideology," *American Political Science Review* (December 1970), vol. 64, pp. 1209–1214.
24. For an analysis of the voting in this referendum, see David Abbott, Louis Gold, and Edward T. Rogowsky, *Police, Politics and Race* (New York, American Jewish Committee: Cambridge, Mass.: Joint Center for Urban Studies, 1969).
25. Peggy Cuciti, "A Reply from the New to the Old Reformers: The Development of Neighborhood Government in New York City" (unpublished M.A. paper, Department of Political Science, University of Chicago, 1972).
26. Joel Aberbach and Jack Walker, "Citizen Desires, Policy Outcomes, and Community Control" (paper presented before the American Political Science Association Convention, September 7–11, 1971).
27. Aberbach and Walker, "Political Trust and Racial Ideology," pp. 1209–1214. Note also the analysis of the police review board referendum in New York City found in Abbott, Gold, and Rogowsky, *Police, Politics and Race.*
28. Samuel Huntington, *Political Order in Changing Societies* (New Haven: Yale University Press, 1968), p. 14.
29. *Ibid.*, p. 29.

NOTES FOR CHAPTER 10

1. Daniel P. Moynihan, *Maximum Feasible Misunderstanding: Community Action in the War on Poverty* (New York: Free Press, 1969).
2. *Ibid.*, Chapter I. Of course, Moynihan only sampled a portion of a large body of literature. He might also have mentioned Ortega y Gasset, Arendt, Kornhauser, and many others. José Ortega y Gasset, *The Revolt of the Masses* (New York: Norton, 1932); Hannah Arendt, *Origins of Totalitarianism* (New York: Harcourt, Brace, and World); 1966); William Kornhauser, *The Politics of Mass Society* (Glencoe, Ill.: The Free Press, 1959).
3. See, for example, Moynihan, *Maximum Feasible Misunderstanding*, p. 70.
4. *Ibid.*, p. 193.
5. *Ibid.*, p. 193.
6. *Ibid.*, pp. 178–179. (Emphasis in the original.)
7. *Ibid.*, p. 190.

8. Robert A. Dahl, *Pluralist Democracy in the United States* (Chicago: Rand McNally, 1967), p. 23.
9. *Ibid.*, p. 23.
10. Ralph M. Kramer, *Participation of the Poor: Comparative Case Studies in the War on Poverty* (Englewood Cliffs, N.J.: Prentice-Hall, 1969), p. 269.
11. See Chapter 4 of this volume, pp. 102–104.
12. Edward C. Banfield, *The Unheavenly City* (Boston: Little, Brown, 1970), pp. 128–131.
13. *Ibid.*, p. 130.
14. *Ibid.*, see, in particular, Chapter XI.
15. *Ibid.*, p. 247.
16. *Ibid.*, see, in particular, Chapter IV.
17. Floyd Hunter, *Community Power Structure* (Garden City, N.Y.: Doubleday & Co., 1953); C. Wright Mills, *The Power Elite* (New York: Oxford University Press, 1956).
18. For example, see Robert Agger, Daniel Goldrich, and Bert Swanson, *The Rulers and the Ruled* (New York: Wiley, 1964).
19. Peter Marris and Martin Rein, *Dilemmas of Social Reform* (New York: Atherton, 1967), p. 45.
20. Kenneth Clark and Jeannette Hopkins, *A Relevant War Against Poverty* (New York: Harper & Row, 1970), pp. 245–246.
21. *Ibid.*, p. 249.
22. Frances Fox Piven and Richard Cloward, *Regulating the Poor* (New York: Pantheon, 1971).
23. *Ibid.*, Chapters IV and V.
24. *Ibid.*, Chapters II, IX, and X.
25. *Ibid.*, pp. 256–282.
26. *Ibid.*, pp. 275–276.
27. *Ibid.*, pp. 276–282.
28. Grant McConnell, *Private Power and American Democracy* (New York: Knopf, 1966).
29. *Ibid.*, pp. 335–340.
30. Theodore Lowi, *The End of Liberalism* (New York: Norton, 1969).
31. *Ibid.*, p. 245.
32. *Ibid.*
33. *Ibid.*
34. *Ibid.*
35. Louis Hartz, *The Liberal Tradition in America* (New York: Harcourt, Brace and World, 1955).
36. The power of Newark blacks just shortly before CAPS began in that city is discussed in Michael Parenti, "Power and Pluralism: A View from the Bottom," *Journal of Politics* (August, 1970), vol. XXXII, pp. 501–530. The role of poverty agencies in expressing black demands during the Newark riots is discussed briefly in Tom Hayden, "The Occupation of Newark," *New York Review of Books* (August 24, 1967), pp. 14–24.
37. Consider, for example, McConnell, *Private Power and American Democracy*, pp. 120 ff.
38. Anthony Downs, *An Economic Theory of Democracy* (New York: Harper & Row, 1957), Chapter XIV.
39. Cf. Leonard J. Fein, "Community Schools and Social Theory: The Limits of Uni-

versalism." In Henry M. Levin, *Community Control of Schools* (Washington, D.C.: The Brookings Institution, 1970).

40. Bayard Rustin, "The Failure of Black Separatism," *Harpers* (January 1970), vol. 240, pp. 25–32 ff.
41. *Ibid.*, p. 25.
42. *Ibid.*, p. 31.
43. *Ibid.*, p. 31.
44. *Ibid.*, p. 26.
45. *Ibid.*, p. 34.
46. *Ibid.*, p. 25.
47. *Ibid.*, p. 32 (emphasis supplied).
48. *Ibid.*, p. 28.
49. *Ibid.*, p. 32.
50. *Ibid.*, p. 29.
51. *Ibid.*, p. 26.
52. Mildred Schwartz, "Trends in White Attitudes Toward Negroes," National Opinion Research Center Report No. #119. (Chicago: University of Chicago, 1967).

NOTES FOR APPENDIX A

1. Ralf Dahrendorf, *Class and Class Conflict in Industrial Society* (Stanford, Calif.: Stanford University Press, 1959).
2. This tendency is pointed out in William C. Mitchell's *Sociological Analysis and Politics: The Theories of Talcott Parsons* (Englewood Cliffs, N.J.: Prentice-Hall, 1967).
3. Dahrendorf, p. 160.
4. See Shlomo Avieneri, *The Social and Political Thought of Karl Marx* (Cambridge, Mass.: Cambridge University Press, 1968).
5. Dahrendorf, p. 160.
6. David Easton, *The Political System* (New York: Knopf, 1953), Chapter 11.
7. J. David Greenstone, "Stability, Transformation and Regime Interests," *World Politics*, volume 22 (April 1970), pp. 448–473.
8. Max Weber, *The Protestant Ethic and the Spirit of Capitalism* (New York: Scribners, 1958).
9. Dahrendorf, pp. 260 ff.
10. Dahrendorf, p. 190.
11. Robert A. Dahl, *A Preface to Democratic Theory* (Chicago· The University of Chicago Press), pp. 75 ff.
12. Robert A. Dahl, *Who Governs?* (New Haven: Yale University Press, 1961), p. 318.
13. *Ibid.*, pp. 319 and 321.
14. *Ibid.*, pp. 322 ff.
15. *Ibid.*, p. 324.
16. Barrington Moore, *Social Origins of Dictatorship and Democracy* (Boston: Beacon Press, 1966), Chapter III.
17. Stanley Rothman has written an important critique of Moore's argument to which Moore briefly rejoined. "Barrington Moore and the Dialectics of Revolution: An Essay Review," *American Political Science Review*, vol. 64 (March 1970), pp. 61–82, 182–183.
18. Philip Converse, "The Nature of Belief Systems in Mass Publics." In David Apter, *Ideology and Discontent* (New York: The Free Press of Glencoe, 1964), pp. 249–252.

19. Kenneth M. Stampp, *And the War Came* (Baton Rouge: Louisiana State University Press, 1950).
20. Moore, p. 121.
21. A parallel argument, stressing at least the contributory role of regime interests, can be made about the South. The apparent safety of slavery in the fifteen slave states makes it difficult to trace their militancy to a direct economic interest. Much of their concern, then, reflected the North's disregard of pluralist bargaining and, thus, the threat to their fundamental expectations about the use of political authority.

NOTES FOR APPENDIX B

1. Duncan MacRae provided considerable assistance in the development of the index of localism.
2. The index of overrepresentation has been used widely by political scientists and sociologists. See, for example, Donald R. Matthews, *U.S. Senators and Their World* (Chapel Hill: University of North Carolina Press, 1960), pp. 273–274.

INDEX